Bernice S. Elger • Catherine Ritter • Heino Stöver
Editors

Emerging Issues in Prison Health

 Springer

Editors
Bernice S. Elger
Institute for Biomedical Ethics
University of Basel
Basel, Switzerland

Catherine Ritter
Federal Office of Public Health
Bern, Switzerland

Heino Stöver
Faculty 'Health and Social Work'
Frankfurt University of Applied Sciences
Frankfurt, Germany

ISBN 978-94-017-7556-4   ISBN 978-94-017-7558-8   (eBook)
DOI 10.1007/978-94-017-7558-8

Library of Congress Control Number: 2016940965

Printed on acid-free paper

This Springer imprint is published by Springer Nature
The registered company is Springer Science+Business Media B.V. Dordrecht

Foreword

There is now a growing comparative academic literature which describes conditions in prisons around the world. This research complements the exhaustive reports which are produced on a regular basis by international bodies such as the United Nations and the International Committee of the Red Cross, by regional bodies such as the European Committee for the Prevention of Torture, and by many national inspecting and monitoring bodies. In addition, regional courts, such as the European Court of Human Rights and the Inter-American Court of Human Rights, frequently produce important judgements on prison conditions.

All of these documents paint a remarkably consistent picture of the general situation in many prisons around the world: prisons in developed and developing countries, in the northern and the southern hemispheres, and in the east and the west. Features such as overcrowding, lack of resources, poor conditions, violence, and lack of control are present in all prison systems. Only the degree of each of them varies. In some countries, for example, overcrowding may imply that two or three prisoners are required to live in a cell which was designed to hold one person. In other countries, it may mean that over one hundred prisoners are crammed into a room which has space for no more than twenty or so, sometimes required to sleep on the floor in shifts. In some the lack of resources may mean that prisoners have unbalanced diets and are left in small cells for much of the day and the night with little or nothing to do. In others it may mean that the prison administration cannot afford to buy fuel for transport to take accused persons to the courthouse. In some prisons, violence may involve low-level harassment and bullying from other prisoners or from staff. In others it may mean that prisoners go daily in fear of their lives with a possibility that they will not survive till the end of their sentence.

The prisoners themselves will not be a cross section of civil society. Rather, they will come from the marginalised and most disadvantaged sections of the community: the mentally ill, drug or alcohol abusers, ethnic minorities, and, increasingly, foreign nationals. Many of them will have very poor health profiles when they enter prison and will have acute or chronic health problems, often because of their previous lifestyle. In addition, many of them may become ill in the course of their time in prison as a consequence of the conditions of their detention. In many prisons there will be a real danger of contracting an infectious illness of one form or another.

Those of us who are active in prison reform have long been aware that real improvement will never be achieved unless close attention is paid to the health needs of prisoners. Our first challenge was to convince prison administrators of the fact that proper health-care provision was not a luxury but rather an essential feature of good prison management. Our second challenge was to convince health professionals of this same fact. In too many countries there is a reluctance on the part of those responsible for national health-care systems to involve themselves with the health needs of prisoners. They regard that as a matter which is beyond their obligation, particularly when resources are scarce.

There are two reasons why health-care professionals need to be concerned with the health of people who are in prison. The first is because they are human beings and are entitled, in the same way as all others, to what the International Convention on Economic, Social and Cultural Rights describes as 'the highest attainable standards of physical and mental health'. The second reason is a pragmatic one. The walls of the prison are not impermeable. Many people move in and out of the prison on a regular basis, and the vast majority of prisoners will return to the community from which they originally came. Infectious and other diseases do not respect the prison boundaries.

The contributors to this volume include health professionals, experts in legal medicine and in ethics; others are involved in inter-governmental and non-governmental health bodies; others have practical knowledge in delivering health-related programmes in prison or are involved in the administration of health care in prisons. The wide spectrum of professional backgrounds from which the authors are drawn is a model of the multi-professional approach which is required if the health problems of persons who are in prison are to be dealt with in a proactive manner. It epitomises the need for collaboration between policy, academia, and practice.

The topics dealt with in each chapter cover a wide range of themes. They include key issues such as mental health, drug and alcohol, infectious disease, and deaths in custody. They also deal with issues which have emerged in more recent years, including problems presented by the increasing cohort of older prisoners, of immigrants, and of foreign national prisoners. They also look to the wider environment and examine the needs of families and children of women and men who are in prison, as well as the need to be aware of the stress experienced by staff who can spend a lifetime working in unhealthy environments.

For all of these and other reasons, this volume is to be very much welcomed. Its publication at this juncture is timely. There is an increasing awareness that 'prison health' is a public health matter and a new willingness on the part of some to become involved in this field which is of crucial importance. This publication is an important contribution to a very topical debate.

International Centre for Prison Studies   Andrew Coyle
University of Essex
11 Belgrave Road
London SW1V 1RB, UK

Preface

Prisons worldwide tend to be overcrowded, stressful, hostile, and regularly violent places. Ethnic and social minorities and members of the most disadvantaged groups in society are over-represented in the prison population. Communicable diseases, licit and illicit drug abuse, mental health problems, and other health risks are more prevalent in prisons than in the general community. Most prisoners remain in prison for short periods and diseases are spread through the 'revolving prison doors' both within the prison and also within the communities to which prisoners return after imprisonment. Against this background, health problems become a major threat not only for the prison administration but also for public health in general. These health problems are not confined to certain states or regions, but are found globally. Global efforts are therefore necessary to recognise and address the health-care issues of prisoners, to establish best practice, and to learn about approaches to these challenges from around the world.

The authors of this book share their international practical experience in important matters related to the health of prisoners. In this context, health is considered not only in the sense of general physical and mental well-being (even if this seems an almost unachievable aim, given the conditions that characterise most prisons), but also in the sense of having the necessary ability and opportunities to fulfil one's personal aims in life.

Health in prison has raised concerns that extend beyond the groups of health professionals working in correctional institutions. Indeed, the immense consequences that inadequate medical treatment and insufficient prevention in detention faculties have for societies have been recognised by public health professionals, prison administrations, and stakeholders from the judicial system and politics for some time. Although some progress has been made, the academic world is not yet sufficiently involved to permit the best possible evidence-based decision making. This book fills an important gap because it will present new evidence on several emerging and classical prison health issues that remain so far under- or unaddressed.

Its aims are threefold. The first goal is to address emerging issues related to health in prison. Second, the book presents the most recent research-based evidence and translates it to the practice. The third aim is to allow for sufficient diversity while also incorporating updates of some important already recognised prison health topics and collecting different point of views on the health of diverse groups of prisoners. The authors of the various chapters represent a broad range of specialties, and they consider a variety of important aspects of prisoners' health.

Prison health is a far more complex issue than it might appear at first glance when one simply combines the two words 'prison' and 'health'. It is increasingly recognised as an important field among professionals, particularly from a public health point of view, and is mentioned among most international declarations regarding the rights of prisoners. Prison health needs to be examined through diverse lenses, and general knowledge of recognised and emerging issues in this field has become essential for a large number of stakeholders. Readers of this book will be informed regarding various aspects of prison health. The variety of material provides high-quality and practically useful information about emerging or thus far-neglected health issues in prison while at the same time giving a much needed update on the most typical questions related to highly prevalent health problems such as psychiatric disease and hepatitis C. Diversity of views is important because the way of looking at prison health-related issues is necessarily different depending on the background of various professionals. A medical doctor, a psychologist, a spiritual advisor, a researcher, a lawyer, an ethicist, or a nurse contribute important knowledge and experiences about the reality they encounter and the people and problems they take care of. The collection of texts within this book is therefore a much needed interdisciplinary and interprofessional collection that bridges the gap between evidence-based academics and practical application of existing knowledge.

The realities reported here are a mosaic of experiences and knowledge from different regions. The chapters combine global experience, e.g. in the chapter on the new guidelines from the International Committee of the Red Cross (ICRC) guidelines on Death in Custody, the chapters on diet, and the use of guidelines in prison. Other chapters start more closely in the specific work that the authors are familiar with in their geographical context and provide the opportunity to test and transplant those experiences to other areas. This double approach, combining global experience with concrete ideas that always start within a specific individual context, is necessary to appropriately and efficiently address the extreme diversity of prison health practice across the world. While many recommendations apply globally, other new ideas start locally in one or only a few closed institutions. This book helps not only to inform about global evidence-based prison medicine, but also to spread promising ideas and much-needed new approaches from one area and to a worldwide audience.

The title *Emerging Issues in Prison Health* implies that there is no given identical reality regarding prisons across the world, even if there are global issues and common aspects throughout closed settings. Subjects that can be considered as emerging in one part of the world might either be completely absent in other countries or already part of normal practice. Drug use among incarcerated people illustrates well that discrepancy, depending on the countries and on access to the substances, issues related to drug use are only emerging: in some countries, they might not be considered at all as a true reality that should be addressed and that needs specific responses. In many Western countries, drug use by prisoners is a conventional issue. But although it is a field for which numerous 'good practices' and international recommendations exist, even in many Western countries access to methadone replacement therapy and access to clean needles is still widely lacking and has only emerged in a minority of institutions.

Several of the authors in this book address important and persistent problems that have been known for some time, but that have not been addressed at all or only in a very marginal way in the current literature, such as the questions of how to deal with deaths in custody, the role of interim measures, and the role of guidelines to prevent human rights violations; how to ensure a balanced diet in prison, the role of spiritual advisors, art therapy, or the role of sports for self-esteem, identity, and masculinity; and, finally, how to address family members detainees, in particular the most vulnerable affected 'others': the children of prisoners. Other issues have already been explored and discussed by practitioners and field experts. Although they are not 'new' subjects as such, the particular views and presented evidence emerges from a unique context and presents details and ideas that are important for many other professionals worldwide. The title and with it the scope of this book 'emerged' from the multiple experiences of all three editors who have worked and carried out prison-focused research on several continents.

Traditionally, the first way to look at a patient's reality is usually medical. In other words, the initial approach to find an answer to a given health problem is mostly influenced by how doctors and nurses are trained: collect symptoms and signs from a personal history, make a diagnosis, and prescribe a treatment, with or without medicines. Experienced health personnel know that this approach is insufficient. It is of crucial importance to include other elements in order to efficiently solve many complex health problems. This is particularly true in the prison context: a medical doctor's impact is highly limited by the environment, the conditions of imprisonment, access to appropriate hygiene, nutrition, healthy psychological stimuli, and, finally, medical care. While many health problems in prison originate outside prison walls and are influenced by many factors in prison that are not under the control of health personnel, a high number of health-related issues cannot be resolved without the specific input of doctors. 'Emerging issues' related to health in prison should also be understood to mean the following: when trying to provide medically indicated care to a certain person or when facing a given health-related situation, other issues (including spiritual, social, and human rights related issues), other partners (spiritual advisors, human rights experts), or specialties (art therapy) that were not considered at the first 'purely medical' stage have to be included, too. Finally, demographic changes have affected patient populations in all parts and sectors of the world, including prisons. Health care for ageing prisoners is one emerging issue that is unfolding at an ever-accelerating speed.

Topics we have chosen not to include were those 'classical' issues that have been largely addressed in other publications from specific fields, such as health care for female prisoners and juvenile detainees, treatment for specific subgroups, such as sex offenders, or for well-known diseases such as HIV infection or tuberculosis.

Prisons are isolated places that are usually kept separate from areas where general society lives. This means not only that prisoners are largely isolated from the community during the time they are incarcerated, but that some type of isolation is also present for prison staff, including health personnel. Many of those professionals are isolated from their usual professional networks not only geographically, but also concerning training opportunities and access to professional literature, in particular costly full text medical databases. Working in prisons is still often considered as less prestigious than working in a first-class university hospital, or in cutting-edge medical services in highly esteemed 'modern' specialties like cardiology and neurosurgery, which require access to specialised technical platforms. This book has provided the opportunity to authors from different professional backgrounds to make their experience available to the numerous colleagues that are otherwise easily cut off from new information. All authors have a long-lasting significant experience in their field. They have been committed to solving different and numerous problems regarding the health of prisoners for many years. Important examples of such valuable experience and the emerging new approaches are provided in the chapters regarding spiritual help and the support of prisoners' families. Their unique and very promising new approaches complement other chapters written by professionals who have succeeded at remaining in or establishing close contact with academic environments. Overall, the diversity of professionals and their backgrounds is illustrated by the content of their corresponding chapters, but also by the way the authors look at, focus on, or report their experience. The true novelty of this book is that it provides space not only to academic disciplines but initiated important collaborations between practitioners, generating new ideas and academic fields that are likely to help spread new ideas in the future. Indeed, only if those who can show directly what kind of problems they are facing on a daily basis and how they tend to resolve it are listened to will awareness be raised and new practically applicable solutions be found. Our aim has been to combine and disseminate different types of evidence based on traditional academic research and resulting from qualitative and intervention-based approaches.

All authors who contributed to this book are strongly committed to international human rights and humanitarian law which stipulate the fundamental principles that should govern health care in prisons. These international law and 'soft law' texts require that health-care practice takes into account a prisoners' or patient's needs and that authorities grant prisoners access to appropriate treatments and preventive measures that are in line with the famous principle of equivalence of care. Imprisonment limits the right to freedom, but should not entail limitations to access to health care. All prisoners should be able to access health-care measures that are available in the communities around prisons, and the quality of health care in detention facilities should be in line with that prevailing for society at large.

A particularly difficult challenge concerning health in prison concerns the question of how global best practice guidelines can be successfully implemented at a local level. In the first place, local stakeholders need to be made aware of such global best practice guidelines. Second, global guidelines might not always be adapted to all types of prison environments. It is therefore not an easy task for field professionals to adapt global guidelines to the characteristics of a particular environment without losing the essential content of the recommendations. Indeed, local lack of resources is too often an easy excuse for not fully implementing needed and justified health strategies. We have therefore included chapters where authors show in detail how specific work is done in a given country, as shown, for example, in the chapter on psychiatric problems. Other chapters offer a more global picture of the current state in a given field across the world, as, for example, in the chapter on confidentiality in prison health care. Both types of chapters are important in order to provide help to multidisciplinary professionals and to enable them to learn how to implement particular health-care strategies and solutions in a specific context. Both general best practice recommendations and unique, locally based, experiences and solutions help to develop the most adapted response at a given time and place. We have developed this twofold approach based on our experience during conferences on prison health: while general best practice approaches are important, conference participants are always particularly interested in how a colleague has developed his own solution to a comparable problem in the field. A presentation of specific examples is crucial to make the relevance of local contexts understandable and is fundamentally complementary to more general presentations regarding good practice.

The scope of this book is at the same type specific and diverse enough to cover the interests of a large audience that includes many types of practitioners involved in health-related issues in the field of prison health care, such as psychologists, nurses and prison administration officers responsible for health care, legal professionals, and social workers. The many chapters considering so far under- or unaddressed medical and social issues (e.g. ageing prisoners) or specific legal and ethical aspects (international human rights aspects and confidentiality of care for example) are particularly important for all professional groups involved in prisons, including administrators and politicians, and will in the long run raise awareness and strengthen the prevention of human rights abuses.

For many of the professions concerned by the interdisciplinary issues presented in this book, in particular nursing and paramedical personnel as well as administrative prison staff, books can be more accessible than journal articles. Prison training centre libraries and local training initiatives can make them easily available. Readers will find it useful to discover the comprehensive collection of issues treated in this book and to be up to date on academic evidence and practically useful implementation of new ideas and evidence. The material provided in this book is useful not only to established practitioners, but also to those involved in various types of training, preparing an academic dissertation or those otherwise interested in prison health.

Finally, the most difficult task is not so much to reach prison health staff and to encourage them to consider the many aspects treated in this book, but to reach prison administrators. In general, they are facing highly difficult and challenging situations, without being provided with specific resources that open their views to interdisciplinary aspects. Our own experience within local prisons, but also with the International Corrections & Prisons Association (ICPA), has shown that many administrators and members of prison staff are highly interested in knowing more about prison health issues so as to understand details that they have not studied directly, but that they are confronted with every day, be it related to mental health, various types of medico-social disabilities of detainees, infectious diseases, or the legal and ethical framework of health care in prison. A book regarding health that contains chapters also addressed to this audience and written in a form that is easily understandable (e.g. avoiding too many specialised and medical vocabulary) will be of significant interest to them with regard to particular topics such as masculinity or immigration detention.

Confident that this book is filling a significant gap and will be helpful for a multitude of academics and practitioners, we would like to express our gratitude to all the authors who shared their experience and views in areas regarding prison health that are less commonly addressed in publications regarding prisons, but are nevertheless extremely important for detained people.

We also thank Daniela Vavrecka-Sidler, Marianne Weber, and David Shaw for their important support in editing the manuscripts for submission and correcting the English.

Basel, Switzerland   Bernice S. Elger
Bern, Switzerland   Catherine Ritter
Frankfurt, Germany   Heino Stöver

Contents

1 Aging Inside: Older Adults in Prison 1
Adrian J. Hayes

**2 Supporting Families and Children Living in the Shadow
of Prisoners** 13
Viviane Schekter, Marcello Ienca, and Bernice S. Elger

**3 Death in Custody: Towards an International Framework
for Investigation and Prevention** 35
Gloria Gaggioli and Bernice S. Elger

**4 Sudden Deaths in Police Custody (and Other Detention
Facilities) – Analysis of Causes and the Need for Prevention** 55
Christoph G. Birngruber, Reinhard B. Dettmeyer,
Sönke Janzen, and Bernice S. Elger

5 The Continuing Emergence of Art Therapy in Prisons 67
David E. Gussak

**6 Spiritual Help During Detention: Specific Responses
to Different Stages and Types of Imprisonment** 85
Frank Stüfen, Marcello Ienca, and Bernice S. Elger

7 A Balanced Diet – From Facts to Solutions 107
Bernice S. Elger

8 Doing Gender in Prisons: Sport as a Way of Creating Masculinity .. 123
Heino Stöver

**9 Psychiatric Problems in Prisoners: Screening, Diagnosis,
Treatment, and Prevention** 133
Annette Opitz-Welke

10 **Drug Services and Harm Reduction Practice in Prisons** 143
    Heino Stöver

11 **Hepatitis C Viral Infection in Prisons** 169
    Geert Robaeys, Amber Arain, and Heino Stöver

12 **Confidentiality in Prison Health
    Care – A Practical Guide** 183
    Bernice S. Elger and David M. Shaw

13 **Preventing Human Rights Violations in Prison – The Role
    of Guidelines** 201
    Bernice S. Elger and David M. Shaw

14 **Immigration Detention and Health in Europe** 217
    Barbara Rijks, Caroline Schultz, Roumyana Petrova-Benedict,
    and Mariya Samuilova

15 **Detained Migrants in Conditions of Extreme Danger:
    How Does the European Human Rights System Protect them?** 237
    Clara Burbano-Herrera

16 **Prison Staff Under Stress: Causes, Consequences
    and Health Promotion Strategies** 253
    Heino Stöver

Contributors

Amber Arain has worked since January 2011 on a clinical PhD project supported by Uhasselt (University of Hasselt), Limburg Clinical Research Program and Ziekenhuis Oost-Limburg, Genk. Her research focuses on improving hepatitis C management in drug users. She did her Masters in Clinical Molecular Science and her Bachelor of Biomedical Sciences degrees at Hasselt University, Diepenbeek, Belgium.

Limburg Clinical Research Program, Faculty of Medicine and Life Sciences, Hasselt University, Hasselt, Belgium

Christoph G. Birngruber specialises in legal medicine and works as a doctor at the Institute of Legal Medicine in Giessen. He was born in Rothenburg ob der Tauber, Middle-Franconia, in 1982 and studied medicine in Giessen, Germany. His studies included stays in Togo and South Africa. His doctoral thesis won an award from the German Society of Legal Medicine in 2010. Besides publishing in national and international journals, he has contributed to several book projects and regularly attends symposia.

Department of Legal Medicine, University of Giessen, Giessen, Germany

Clara Burbano-Herrera has a PhD in Law, an LLM in Fundamental Rights, a Postgraduate Degree in Constitutional Law, and a Law Degree. She is currently a lecturer and postdoctoral research fellow at the Human Rights Centre at Ghent University and at the Flanders Research Foundation in Belgium. With her research, she won the Prince Bernhard Price for Innovative Research (The Netherlands, 2008) and has twice been awarded the Prize for Academic Merit of the Lucía Patiño Osorio Foundation (Colombia, 2000–2001). Her current research interests are the European, Inter-American, and African systems of human rights and interim measures in international human rights law, specifically the three regional human rights systems.

FXB Center for Health and Human Rights, Harvard University, Cambridge, MA, USA

Max Planck Institute for Comparative Public Law and International Law, Heidelberg, Germany

Human Rights Centre, Ghent University, Ghent, Belgium

Reinhard B. Dettmeyer is a general and forensic pathologist and doctor of law, and has been head of the Institute of Legal Medicine at Justus-Liebig-University, Giessen, Germany, since October 2007. He has authored and co-authored several books concerning questions of medicine and law, medical maltreatment, child abuse, and forensic histopathology. He was born in 1957 and studied medicine and jurisprudence.

Department of Legal Medicine, University of Giessen, Giessen, Germany

Bernice S. Elger is Director of the Institute for Biomedical Ethics, University of Basel, Switzerland, and Associate Professor at the Center for Legal Medicine of the University of Geneva. She holds degrees in medicine and Protestant theology and has been working in prison medicine for more than 15 years. In 2005, she obtained an advanced researcher grant from the Swiss National Science Foundation, as well as various other distinctions: the Arditi Award in Ethics 1997; the Award of the Medical Faculty, University of Geneva (best doctoral thesis in clinical medicine) 1999; the Bizot Award in 2005; and the Swiss Research Award in Primary Care 2010. She has published widely on ethical issues related to prison medicine.

Institute for Biomedical Ethics, University of Basel, Basel, Switzerland

Gloria Gaggioli is a postdoctoral fellow at the Faculty of Law, University of Geneva. She wrote her doctoral thesis on the right to life and was a member of the research project "Death in Custody" carried out at the University of Geneva between 2008 and 2011. Before joining the University of Geneva as a postdoctoral fellow, she worked several years in the law department of the International Committee of the Red Cross in Geneva.

Faculty of Law, University of Geneva, Genève, Switzerland

David E. Gussak is Chair of the Department of Art Education and Clinical Coordinator of the Graduate Art Therapy Program for the Florida State University in Tallahassee, FL. He has a PhD and is a certified art therapist (ATR-BC). He has published and presented extensively on art therapy in correctional settings and with violent and aggressive clients. His latest book, *Art on Trial: Art Therapy in Capital Murder Cases*, will be published in spring 2013.

Department of Art Education, Florida State University, Tallahassee, FL, USA

Adrian J. Hayes is currently a foundation year doctor at South Warwickshire Foundation NHS Trust, UK. He studied medicine (MBChB) and has a Masters in Research (MRes). He was previously a researcher at the Offender Health Research

Network, University of Manchester, UK. His current research interests are offender health, suicide and self-injury, forensic psychiatry, and patient safety.

Department of Psychiatry, University of Oxford, Oxford, UK

Marcello Ienca (M.Sc., M.A.) is a PhD student and research assistant at the University of Basel, Institute for Biomedical Ethics. His research focuses on the ethical implications of neuroscience, neurotechnology and clinical psychiatry. In 2015 he was awarded the Prize A. Pato de Carvalho for Social Responsibility in Neuroscience. He serves as chair of the student/postdoc committee of the International Neuroethics Society.

Institute for Biomedical Ethics, University of Basel, Basel, Switzerland

Sönke Janzen is a medical research assistant at the Department of Legal Medicine at Justus-Liebig University, Giessen, Germany.

Department of Legal Medicine, University of Giessen, Giessen, Germany

Michael Levy is the Director of Justice Health Services in the Australian Capital Territory (ACT). He is a Public Health Physician with international experience in prisoner health and has worked with the World Health Organization and the European Committee for the Prevention of Torture (CPT). He is an international leader in the field of application of harm minimisation to the prison environment and has been an observer and presenter to the WHO Health in Prisons Program (European Regional Office). He has resumed active clinical practice since 2007, developing the primary care model for adult and juvenile persons in detention.

Mental Health, Justice Health and Alcohol & Drug Services Hume, Alexander Maconachie Centre, Hume, Australia

Annette Opitz-Welke is a psychiatrist and has been Deputy Head of the Department of Forensic Psychiatry in Berlin since 2006. She studied medicine at the universities of Marburg and Berlin, Germany. She graduated as a specialist in psychiatry. Her current research interest is the epidemiology of forensic psychiatry.

Department of Psychiatry, Justizvollzugskrankenhaus Berlin, Berlin, Germany

Roumyana Petrova-Benedict is Senior Regional Migration Health Advisor for Europe and Central Asia for the Migration Health Division (MHD) of the International Organization for Migration, Regional Office in Brussels. She has over twenty years' experience in global public health, development and research from within academic, civil society, and intergovernmental institutions in several continents. Her main interests are migration and health, primary health care, human resources, community development and care, health information systems, TB, HIV, and other STIs. Currently continuing work related to immigration detention, *inter alia*, within the framework of a direct grant agreement with the EU, DG Health and Consumers:

Fostering health provision to migrants, the Roma and other vulnerable groups – EQUIHEALTH.

Migration Health Division, International Organization for Migration, Brussels, Belgium

Barbara Rijks works at the Migration Health Division of the International Organization for Migration, Geneva, Switzerland. She has a Masters degree in Political Science from the University of Amsterdam. Her previous work was with Amnesty International's Department of Refugees, the UN Population Fund (UNFPA), and the UN High Commission for Refugees (UNHCR) with a focus on migration, refugees, and health/HIV in the southern African region. Her current research interests are migration, health, and development.

Migration Health Division, International Organization for Migration, Geneva, Switzerland

Catherine Ritter trained as a medical doctor. She worked as an independent expert in prison health. Her areas of interest are addiction, transmittable diseases, and health promotion among prisoners and migrants. She recently joined the Federal Office of Public Health.

Federal Office of Public Health, Bern, Switzerland

Geert Robaeys is a medical doctor and hepatologist – gastroenterologist with a PhD in Internal Medicine. He works at the Department of Gastroenterology and Hepatology at Genk hospital in Belgium. He is also member of the research group at the Limburg Clinical Research Program at Hasselt University, Belgium. He works as a consultant at the Department of Hepatology of the University Hospitals in Leuven, Belgium; is a professor in Medicine and Life Sciences at Hasselt University, Belgium; and is Vice-President of the International Network on Hepatitis in Substance Users and a member of the Ethics Committee at Hasselt University. His current research interest is Hepatitis C viral infection in at-risk groups.

Department of Gastroenterology and Hepatology, Ziekenhuis Oost Limburg, Genk, Belgium

Department of Hepatology UZ Leuven, Leuven University, Leuven, Belgium

Limburg Clinical Research Program, Faculty of Medicine and Life Sciences, Hasselt University, Hasselt, Belgium

Mariya Samuilova is Migration Health Officer for Europe and Central Asia and works at the Migration Health Division (MHD) of the International Organization for Migration's Regional Office in Brussels. Under the direct supervision of the Senior Regional Migration Health Advisor for Europe and Central Asia & Liaison to the EU, she is responsible for the development, coordination, and implementation of projects and liaison to the EU institutions on migration health. She is educated in and has practical experience in social research and social policy analysis. Currently continuing work related to immigration detention, *inter alia,* within the framework of a direct grant agreement with the EU, DG Health and Consumers: *Fostering health provision to migrants, the Roma and other vulnerable group*s – EQUIHEALTH.

Migration Health Division, International Organization for Migration, Brussels, Belgium

Viviane Schekter is a forensic psychologist (SSPL), Director of Relais Enfants Parents Suisse and a teacher at the Swiss Prison Staff Training Centre. She has a Masters degree in psychology, education, and cognitive and systemic psychotherapy.

Relais Enfants Parents Romands (REPR), Anciennement Carrefour Prison, Lausanne, Switzerland

Caroline Schultz works at the Migration Health Division of the International Organization for Migration, Geneva, Switzerland. She has degrees in Philosophy and Economics (B.A.) from the University of Bayreuth, Germany, and in Migration Studies (M.Sc.) from the University of Oxford, UK. Her current research interests are migration policy and health, development, international relations, and labour migration.

Expert Council of German Foundations on Integration and Migration, Berlin, Germany

David M. Shaw is Senior Researcher at the Institute for Biomedical Ethics at the University of Basel. From 2007 to 2012, he was Lecturer in Ethics in the School of Medicine at the University of Glasgow and an Associate of the Centre for Applied Ethics and Legal Philosophy. His previous post was Research Fellow in Ethics, Philosophy, and Public Affairs at the University of St. Andrews, and he completed his doctorate in Moral Philosophy and Bioethics at the University of Lausanne in Switzerland. He is interested in all areas of bioethics, with a particular interest in research ethics, end-of-life issues, and emerging technologies.

Institute for Biomedical Ethics, University of Basel, Basel, Switzerland

Heino Stöver is Director of the Institute of Addiction Research, Frankfurt am main, Germany. He is President of the German Harm Reduction Umbrella Network (www.akzept.org). He graduated in social sciences, and his current research interests are health promotion among vulnerable groups, drug services, and health issues in closed settings (HIV/AIDS, Hepatitis C and drug dependence, health of prison staff).

Faculty 'Health and Social Work', Frankfurt University of Applied Sciences, Frankfurt, Germany

Frank Stüfen is a reverend and prison chaplain, and Head of the Prison Chaplaincy Department of the Swiss Reformed Church in Zurich, Switzerland. He has a degree in theology and prison chaplaincy and is a member of the Steering Committee of the Swiss Prison Chaplaincy Association. His current research interest is to develop a new concept of prison chaplaincy from the perspective of theological, philosophical, and psychoanalytical freedom.

Seelsorger JVA Pöschwies, Regensdorf, Switzerland

Introduction

Prisoner health has made great advances since the very early descriptions of rudimentary health services for prisoners in the mid-1970s. However, it is necessary to acknowledge some difficult truths.

The actual number of prisoners in the world remains unknown; is it eight million or ten million? Identifying the exact number is difficult because countries define prisoners in different ways – China is notable for sequestering hundreds of thousands of people into institutions that are not called prisons, but whose residents are by any measure 'prisoners'.

For prison health practitioners, perhaps the hardest truth is that most prisoners do not even have access to rudimentary health services, when the international standard should be 'equivalent' health services to those in the community. Equity should be the standard for commissioning prisoner health services – where the needs are greater, funding needs to match those needs so that the desired equivalent outcomes are achieved. This is the task that faces future generations of human rights advocates, health funders, and professional associations. One day, the World Health Organization will perhaps give substance to the principle that 'Prisoner Health is Public Health'.

This publication brings together a mixture of various standard prisoner health concerns and a number of state-of-the-art specialist concerns. Drug and alcohol abuse, mental illness, and disability (in all its manifestations) are all highly prevalent in prisoner populations. Transmission of a number of infectious conditions of public health concern (HIV, hepatitis C, and tuberculosis) will continue to present challenges to civil society as long as prisoners are not fully integrated into community responses. New and even existing treatments will not deliver benefits unless prisoners are targeted – this was the lesson from HIV and tuberculosis and will be even more true of hepatitis B and hepatitis C treatments. Prisoners frequently cannot access standard pharmacotherapies, and safe injecting equipment and barrier contraception are even harder to obtain.

The challenge for prison authorities and civil society is clearly presented in this important publication. Both groups should learn about the health issues that affect prisoners, learn how better to deliver health services to prisoners, and accept that prisons can be the site for some truly innovative and visionary work. If human rights can be protected, health outcomes can be improved and civil society can be enhanced.

The authors and editors are to be congratulated for this important collection of work.

Mental Health   Michael Levy
Justice Health and Alcohol & Drug Services Hume Health
Alexander Maconachie Centre
Hume, ACT 2620
Australia

Chapter 1
Aging Inside: Older Adults in Prison

Adrian J. Hayes

Abstract The number of older prisoners is rising rapidly throughout the world and this trend is expected to continue. In this chapter, the characteristics and needs of older adults in prison will be discussed, including their differences in comparison to younger prisoners. I will present the main challenges that elderly prisoners are raising, and my personal experience of conducting research among elderly detainees. Currently there is little in the way of age-specific service provision for elderly offenders despite their high degree of chronic physical and mental health need. In contrast to other offenders, this group is more likely to have mobility needs as well as a different pattern of social and custodial problems. Research into this area is limited, though growing, particularly in the US and UK, with some interesting developments being made. A strong evidence-base is needed to inform national and international policy about how best to care for and manage older offenders.

1.1 The Aging Prison Population

Until recent years, elderly people in prison have been a forgotten group. They were present in most establishments but for the most part seen as a small group who, whilst not representing the typical prisoner, got on with their sentence quietly and without much disturbance. Sporadic research papers detailed their characteristics, but they did not command a large degree of attention. In contrast, today many countries have seen a dramatic increase in the number of older prisoners, and there is an enhanced interest in their health and custodial needs. A combination of the aging population, increased prison population, and legislation mean that this group is expected to continue rising, and it seems researchers, if not yet policy-makers have woken up to this fact.

A.J. Hayes (✉)
Department of Psychiatry, University of Oxford, Warneford Lane, Oxford OX3 7JX, UK
e-mail: adrian.hayes@nhs.net

© Springer Science+Business Media Dordrecht 2017
B.S. Elger et al. (eds.), *Emerging Issues in Prison Health*,
DOI 10.1007/978-94-017-7558-8_1

June 2012 saw publication of the American Civil Liberties Union report 'At America's Expense: The Mass Incarceration of the Elderly'. This report is striking for its inclusion of photographs illustrating the daily lives of older people in custody, one annotated with the legend 'An elderly prisoner spends the final stages of his life in prison hospice care. The man died later that afternoon and was buried in the prison cemetery' (ACLU 2012 pG). At America's Expense suggests that the US population of prisoners aged 50 and over has grown by 1300 % since the 1980s. While the prison population as a whole has vastly increased (by 400 %) in this time, this is still clearly a disproportionate increase. The US may have the largest rise, but many other countries have reported increasing numbers of older prisoners. In England and Wales, prisoners over 60 years of age are now the fastest-growing group in the prison estate with numbers more than doubling between 1999 and 2009 (Ministry of Justice 2010). In Australia, the proportion of those over 50 rose by 180 % from 1987 to 1997 with the absolute number trebling (Grant 1999), and in Canada by 46 % in 5 years between 1993 and 1998 (Uzoaba 1998). Gautier (2011) also describes the difficulties in managing rising numbers of older prisoners in France.

As demonstrated by the US figures, this phenomenon cannot be explained solely by the rise in the number of prisoners. In Japan, data show the number of older adults newly received into custody has risen by seven times between 1973 and 2003 (Ministry of Justice 2004), suggesting a new influx of elderly offenders. In contrast, the UK data show that, although new admissions of older prisoners have risen, the rate is not in keeping with the high number of elderly people in prison (Ministry of Justice 2007). Hence older people appear to stay in prison for longer than their younger counterparts. Whilst the data suggest harsher sentencing for older offenders, this does not seem likely and certainly there is some evidence from the US that older offenders receive more leniency in sentencing than for younger people (Steffensmeier and Motivans 2000). Alternatively there could be an artefact due to those older people convicted of less serious offences receiving non-custodial sentences, thus those actually sent to prison representing the most serious offences and given proportionately longer sentences than the average.

At first glance, the rises are astonishing and appear to suggest that prisons are now bursting with elderly people. However, the reality is that their absolute numbers are small and still do not form a noticeably large group on any general prison wing. In England and Wales, 5–6 % of prisoners are aged 60 and over, and their relatively inconspicuous nature has been highlighted by Her Majesty's Inspectorate of Prisons (HMIP 2004). HMIP named their thematic review of this population 'No Problems: Old and Quiet' after an entry found in one elderly prisoner's record. In comparison with prisoners who have acute mental health problems, drug withdrawal and suicidal behaviours, older prisoners can appear as having fewer needs and may be less likely to come to the attention of staff. The research evidence tells a different story; their needs are complex and chronic, and require considerable resources. Specific policy for the care and management of older prisoners is as yet rare around the world but the recent interest and acknowledgement of their presence will hopefully make this more likely.

1.2 Personal Aside

The majority of my own experience of working with older prisoners was in the completion of a PhD into their health, social and custodial needs in the North West of England. The results are described in more detail below, but as a personal note I found them to be rather different to the general prison population in a number of ways. In previous research, I had only come across a few older prisoners and had thought it unusual that they existed, being unaware at that time of the rise in population. Most strikingly, the proportion of those convicted of sexual offences was much higher amongst the older group. Many prisoners were suspicious of my motives as a university researcher, but most warmed up to the interviews and appeared to answer my questions truthfully and comprehensively. There was a noticeable 'despair' amongst many interviewees who felt unequipped to deal with prison in terms of the physical environment, being located with younger prisoners, and a general loss of control. Most of those participating in my research were in prison for the first time in their older age and did seem to have more difficulty adjusting to prison life than younger prisoners. Others had a new lease of life in prison, finding themselves respected by others for helping them with paperwork and legal matters. There were also a few who had been sent to prison more than 20 years ago and who had lived out most of their adult life in custody. One I remember in particular had come to prison before decimalisation in the UK and appeared to me to be so institutionalised, I had no confidence he could survive in the outside world. Overall it was interesting to gather information on the group spread as they were between a large number of prisons. Whilst they are a quiet group, my interviews revealed a complex set of needs different to those faced by younger prisoners.

1.3 Quantitative Evidence

In (1961), Adams and Vedder wrote:

> 'Except for a greater amount of malingering, more resentment of authority, and the extremely unnatural environment of custody, the medical problems of the aged prisoner are not vastly different from those of the aged person in the free world' (p178).

We now have a growing literature which disputes this. Quite a number of studies have described the prevalence of physical and mental health disorder amongst older prisoners in various populations. Most have been carried out in the US where this group appears to have been identified earlier than in other countries. Across seven American studies, between 29 and 64 % of older male prisoners rated themselves as having some health problems (Colsher et al. 1992; Aday 2003; Marquart et al. 2000; Loeb and Steffensmeier 2006). Others have examined specific health issues (Douglass 1991; Baillargeon et al. 2000; Aday 2003), finding that the most common were hypertension (13–50 %), arthritis (2–56 %) and chronic back pain (6–63 %), with other conditions including COPD (15–27 %), ischaemic heart disease (7–48 %), diabetes (5–17 %), asthma (5–12 %) and liver disease (3–7 %). Data from the UK suggest that 83–95 % of older prisoners had a chronic illness or disability (Fazel et al. 2001a, b; Hayes et al. 2012), most commonly in the musculoskeletal (43–57 %) or cardiovascular (36–54 %) systems.

For mental health, 11–16 % of older prisoners in the US have been found to have a psychiatric diagnosis recorded in case notes (Baillargeon et al. 2000; Brown and Brozowski 2003; Caverley 2006; Regan et al. 2002). Depressive disorder was the most common conditions at 3–16 %. In comparison, UK data shows a prevalence for mental illness of 46 % by case note review (Taylor and Parrott 1988), and 32–50 % by structured clinical assessment (Fazel et al. 2001a, b; Hayes et al. 2012; Kingston et al. 2011). Again, depressive disorder was the most common condition (26–42 %), with only 3–5 % showing symptoms of psychosis. Personality disorder was found in 15–31 % of older prisoners, and dementia in 2 %.

There are few data on substance misuse amongst elderly prisoners. Fazel et al. (2001a, b) found 4.5 % of prisoners from England and Wales had current misuse/dependence at the time of interview. This is much lower than in the general prison population: Farrell et al. (2002) found a rate of drug dependence of 43 % in a sample of 503 prisoners also from England and Wales. My own study showed a lifetime drug misuse disorder of 9 %. This may represent a cohort effect whereby younger people are more likely to take drugs, and substance misuse problems may be a greater problem in the older sample as the current drug-users age (Tarbuck 2001). On the other hand, alcohol misuse may be more common in this group. Whilst most studies do not separate substance use disorders, I found a rate of 31 % for alcohol use disorders, compared with only 9 % for drug (Hayes 2010).

Two further UK studies have assessed the extent to which health needs of older prisoners are met. Fazel et al. (2004) found that medication was inappropriately targeted between 15 and 82 % of the time, with the higher value representing psychiatric medication. My own PhD research (Hayes 2010) found that 33 % of older men had unmet needs in physical health, and 17 % for psychological distress.

The figures quoted above may appear to suggest that UK prisoners have higher rates of mental health disorder than those in the US. This is almost certainly an artefact of differing methodologies whereby studies involving only case-note review are likely to under-report the true rates of disorder as undiagnosed conditions are not represented, as demonstrated in Kingston et al. (2011). Several of the studies listed above have also compared their findings with local or national prevalence data and concluded that the prevalence of both physical and mental disorder is greater than that seen in older adults in the community, and also greater than the general prison population (e.g. Fazel et al. 2001a, b).

There is some difficulty in comparing these figures directly due to the difference in types of prison (and prisoner) studied and measures for assessing health, including design (case-note review vs. interview) as well as the assessment tools themselves. However, another problem in this area of research is the lack of consensus on an age definition for the older prisoner. The literature contains studies which have used 40, 45, 50, 55, 60, and 65 as a cut-off (Cormier et al. 1971; Curtice et al. 2003; Fazel et al. 2001a, b; Gallagher 1990; Goetting 1992; Paanila et al. 2000 respectively). This inconsistency is probably partly driven by the need to ensure large enough numbers to complete a study (Kakoullis et al. 2010), but also because there is no recognised age designation for older offenders. Flynn (2002) describes how the US National Institute of Correction suggested that 50 should be used as an appropriate age designation, but that adherence to this has been variable. In US research, 50 and 55 are the most commonly used age definitions in the research (Human Rights Watch 2012), but in the UK it is 60 (Wahadin and Aday 2005). In my own research, I compared subgroups of older prisoners and found little difference between those aged 50–59 and those aged over 60 in terms of physical health. The younger group were more likely to have mental health problems and poorer quality of life, but in a different pattern to younger prisoners. Hence, I suggested that 50 should be used to identify older prisoners. There is some indication in the literature that prisoners aged 50 are similar in terms of their health to those in the community aged 60 (Falter 2003; Smith 1982), but more recent analysis suggests this to be an oversimplification (Spaulding et al. 2011) and this has yet to be explored thoroughly.

1.4   Qualitative Evidence

The quantitative evidence presented above is fairly difficult to assimilate due to differences in settings and methodologies, though the overall message is that older prisoners have a high level of physical and mental health need, particular for chronic disorders, and pose a different challenge to health service provision than the average prisoner. A flavour for the specific experiences and challenges faced by older prisoners can be found in the qualitative literature. For example, Crawley (2005) described a phenomenon of 'institutional thoughtlessness' relating to prison services not meeting the specific needs of older prisoners, and often being unaware that they have different needs to the general prison population. Staff appeared to be making an effort to provide consistency for all prisoners in their expectations of behaviour. Since older prisoners are not officially designated as a special group, they are often not given what may be seen as special privileges if not earned, and may be allocated to top bunk beds and have to climb many flights of stairs to get around the prison at the same speed as others. This was thought to lead to 'hidden injuries' (Crawley and Sparks 2005) which occurred incidentally (and without malice) during the prison regime which were unnoticed by staff and unacknowledged by prisoners. Raised awareness for the different needs of older prisoners may alleviate these problems, primarily for staff but also for other prisoners.

In the US, Ronald Aday has written extensively on the experiences of older male prisoners, often touching on aspects of health. He found that many prisoners felt their health had deteriorated in prison and that their health was worse than those living in the community (Wahadin and Aday 2005). Many worried about dying in prison, and felt there was a stigma to not dying 'a free man'. Thoughts of suicide on entry to prison appeared to be common with feelings of depression due to perceptions of shame and letting their families down.

Azrini Wahadin has written a great deal on the experiences of older female prisoners in the UK. A common theme from her in-depth interviews is fear of becoming ill and having to rely on fellow prisoners to help them in their daily activities (Wahadin 2004). Several described themselves as being 'at war' with the prison system in addressing their health needs, with some officers reportedly not taking prisoners seriously resulting in medical emergencies such as missed stroke. They often found health services to be disorganised with records and prescriptions frequently misplaced, and medications changed or withdrawn without warning. The author described some of these practices, as well as high rates of sedation prescription, as an exertion of control which adversely affected rehabilitation. Specific concerns were gaps of age-specific service provision such as for mammograms, cervical cytology and those taking hormone replacement therapy. Wahidin's work is enlightening as to the everyday lives and concerns of older women in prison, and particularly as there is little empirical work conducted with this group. This is probably due to small numbers of older women in individual prison, but is an area which should be the focus of future systematic research.

1.5   Social and Custodial Need

Older people in prison have greater health needs than younger inmates. However, they have additional social and custodial needs specific to their age group. While disability can affect people of any age, older people are more likely to have problems with mobility and day-to-day functioning. The prison environment is not designed with older people in mind with, as described above, many sets of stairs often separating areas such as cells, dining rooms and workshops. There is recognised difficulty in meeting functional needs within prison; Frazer (2003) interviewed a number of staff groups working in prisons in the UK and found that neither health care staff not officers felt that such 'social care' was part of their everyday role. My own research found 11 % of prisoners over 60 had needs related to person care, less than half of which was met (Hayes et al. 2012). While this represent be a small number of individuals, the lack of assistance in this area is a key concern in the management of older offenders.

A variety of additional social needs have also been reported for this age group. Availability of activities and rehabilitation for older prisoners has been criticised. HMIP (2004) noted that prisoners over retirement age did not have to work but were often confined to their cells and earned less than working prisoners for essentials such as toiletries. In both the UK and the US, activities specific to older people are documented in some establishments, but these have been set up on an ad hoc basis rather than resulting from any informed policy or national directive (Frazer 2003; Kratcoski and Babb 1990). Contact with friends and family is often reduced. Bond et al. (2005) found that older prisoners had smaller social networks than the younger, while my PhD research showed that 45 % were far from their home area and 40 % had no visitors while in prison (Hayes 2010). Older prisoners are more likely to have an elderly spouse who may find it difficult to travel to prisons, which are often located in remote areas. Psychological abuse was a common finding in Kerbs and Jolley's (2007) study of victimisation as well as some physical abuse. HMIP (2004) too noted bullying experienced by older prisoners, while Hayes and Fazel (2008) argued that poor identification and management of needs may amount to institutional neglect. Finally, resettlement can be another difficult area and locating suitable community-based placements for older prisoners on release is challenging (HMIP 2004).

While the England and Wales prison inspectors increasingly comment on provision for older prisoners, criticising its lack and praising where addressed (Hayes and Shaw 2011), their recommendations such as dedicated health clinics, gym sessions and daytime activities are not compulsory and are unlikely to be fully implemented without government mandate.

1.6 Ethical and Legal Issues

The detention in custody of elderly people raises a number of ethical and legal challenges. One regards the treatment of those who develop cognitive impairment during imprisonment. While in the UK there is established protocol for those suffering from severe mental illness (i.e. transfer to a secure psychiatric facility), there is no equivalency for those meeting criteria for dementia. Both Fazel et al. (2001a, b) and Kingston et al. (2011) identified two such prisoners in the course of their studies, while Hayes et al. (2012) found that 15 % of prisoners over 60 screened positive on the Mini Mental State Assessment (Folstein et al. 1975), suggesting further assessment for cognitive impairment was necessary. Fazel et al. (2002) later described these cases in more detail, using them to discuss the rationale for imprisonment in general, i.e. whether it is deterrence to others, prevention of further crime, rehabilitation, symbolic 'disapproval' of crime by society, or restorative justice. For these prisoners, who were neither aware they were in prison nor of what actions had let them there, many of these factors are debatable. Continued thought will need to be given to provision for these people as the number of older offenders continues to rise.

A further ethical point raised by this population is the utility of imprisoning elderly people at all; whether age and/or health status should be taken into account in sentencing and disposal. In the US prison hospices are relatively established, where long sentences and variable availability of procedures for early release leads to a life sentence often meaning whole life imprisonment (Linder and Meyers 2007). In the UK, the Home Secretary has the power to grant compassionate discharge, and parole boards can take health status into account for making decisions on continued detention. HMIP (2004) documented that release can be granted if a prisoner has fewer than 3 months to live, is bedridden or severely incapacitated, or where imprisonment is likely to endanger health. Steiner (2003) reported that despite this, there is no formal system for early release and that prisoners with a significant media profile may be denied release because a precise enough prognosis could not be determined, resulting in distressing and undignified deaths in prison. Steiner also described the system in France where 'medical parole' is applicable to those 'whose life expectancy is threatened or whose state of health is incompatible with continued detention'. No nature or severity of illness is required to meet the criteria, which allows for decisions being made without a definite prognosis, for example in prisoners with a terminal illness.

International differences in this area are symbolised by the case of 'Lockerbie bomber' Abdelbaset al-Megrahi who was released by the Scottish government on compassionate grounds (a move criticised by the US government), and who died from prostate cancer almost 3 years after he was assessed to have 3 months to live (BBC 2009, 2012). In my own research, I was informed of the deaths of three interviewees, all in prison and of natural causes, though unexpected. The decision whether to provide in-prison facilities for end-of-life care or to have procedures for compassionate discharge is an interesting area for further discussion.

1.7 The Future

Since the number of older prisoners is growing, and no evidence currently exists on best practice for how they should be managed, there is scope for some exploratory suggestion. Perhaps the elderly should be separated from the general prison population and housed together in dedicated units? This would mean that the environment could be designed around those with a high degree of mobility and personal care need, run by staff trained in age-specific awareness, with input from services such as old age psychiatry and older adult volunteer agencies. The security level of such a facility may not need to be as high as other prisons. However, the small number of prisoners involved, even in the US, would mean that units like this would be spread much further apart than existing prisons. The result would be many more offenders being held far from their home areas and families. Furthermore, the general prison population would lost the positive influence that older prisoners are perceived to bring (Frazer 2003), and those who enjoyed the company of younger prisoners would be moved away. Finally, current disability legislation tends to favour adapting current provision to be suitable for all levels of ability rather than segregating on the basis of age alone. This idea of a complete separation in dedicated units, then, seems unworkable.

A compromise may be the development of 'elderly wings', where prisoners have (or earn) the choice to be house in an area of the prison inhabited only by older people. Thus, those who preferred to be mixed with the general prison population could continue to do so, while others could be partially separated. A small number of prisons have this configuration, three of which I visited during my PhD. There, the 'elderly wing' was popular, and my research showed that prisoners located on these wings had improved quality of life and greater engagement with activities than those on the common wings (Hayes 2010). In one site, there was a waiting list for older prisoners wanting to move to this dedicated wing.

1.8 Current Work

My research group in Manchester, UK, has recently completed a programme of research looking at transitions of care for elderly prisoners. Funded by the NHS Service Delivery and Organisation Programme and soon to report, the research focused on entry to and exit from custody as key points where health and social needs should be identified and addressed. Based on the hypothesis developed from my PhD research that these prisoners experienced most problems when first coming to prison, we conducted a needs assessment within the first 2 weeks of imprisonment. We also set up an action learning group with input from staff and prisoners to devise a measure for identifying needs on reception to custody, with a subsequent care plan constructed and reviewed at appropriate intervals. The OHSCAP (Older Prisoner Health and Social Care Assessment and Plan) was piloted at one prison and enhanced over the course of several months. We hope to use this initial data to inform a large-scale trial examining its effectiveness for older prisoners more widely in England and Wales.

Our other area of enquiry was the period around release, as again I had identified specific concerns from this group of prisoners getting ready to leave prison. We carried out qualitative interviews with older prisoners before leaving, and then conducted follow-up interviews in the community. This approach provided an interesting opportunity to compare prisoners' fears about release with the reality, and to accurately describe the important challenges to meeting health and social need during this time.

1.9 Recommendations

The current interest in research around older prisoners is helpful in raising awareness that this group exists, is growing, and has different needs to other prisoners. However, there is now a need to amass data on what services would effectively meet these needs. Many researchers have called for national strategies for the management of older prisoners, and there are now several studies showing high-quality evidence as to their characteristics. This should continue to be developed, with the addition of interventional studies targeting the most common and important needs. Some recent projects have been doing just this, with recent novel interventions such as Sumner's (2012) assessment tool for physical, social and mental health need, Wheldon and Williams' (2012) prison outreach service led by geriatricians, and Phillips et al.'s (2011) work on preferences of prisoners about end-of-life care. While research, and particularly the conduct of controlled trials, is difficult in prison, it is not impossible and should be encouraged.

This field is not new but is under-represented in the offender health literature. While the vast majority of work in this area has been conducted in the US, national projects in other countries would be very welcome, initially in documented prevalence of health status and quantifying need. Practical and financial difficulties may exist to conduct such large-scale research, but collecting the data would be worthwhile and much valued. There is no sign of the numbers of older prisoners reducing, and service provision will need to rely on a solid evidence base.

References

Adams, M., & Vedder, C. (1961). Age and crime: Medical and sociological characteristics of prisoners over 50. *Geriatrics, 16*, 177–181.

Aday, R. H. (2003). *Aging prisoners: Crisis in American corrections*. Westport: Praeger Publishers.

American Civil Liberties Union. (2012). *At America's expense: The mass incarceration of the elderly*. https://www.aclu.org/files/assets/elderlyprisonreport_20120613_1.pdf. Accessed 27 Aug 2012.

Baillargeon, J., Black, S. A., Pulvino, J., & Dunn, K. (2000). The disease profile of Texas prison inmates. *Annals of Epidemiology, 10*(2), 74–80.

Bond, G. D., Thompson, L. A., & Malloy, D. M. (2005). Lifespan differences in the social networks of prison inmates. *International Journal of Aging and Human Development, 61*(3), 161–178.

British Broadcasting Corporation. (2009). *Lockerbie bomber freed from jail*. http://news.bbc.co.uk/1/hi/scotland/south_of_scotland/8197370.stm. Accessed 3 Oct 2012.

British Broadcasting Corporation. (2012). *Lockerbie bomber Abdelbaset al-Megrahi dies in Tripoli*. http://www.bbc.co.uk/news/world-africa-18137896. Accessed 3 Oct 2012.

Brown, G. P., & Brozowski, K. (2003). Golden years: The incarceration of the older offender. *Geriatrics Today, 6*, 32–35.

Caverley, S. J. (2006). Older mentally ill inmates: A descriptive study. *Journal of Correctional Health Care, 12*(4), 262–268.

Colsher, P., Wallace, R., Loeffelholc, P., & Sales, M. (1992). Health status of older male prisoners: A comprehensive survey. *American Journal of Public Health, 82*(6), 881–884.

Cormier, B. M., Boyer, R., Morf, G., Kennedy, M., Boulanger, P., Barriga, C., et al. (1971). Behaviour and ageing: Offenders aged 40 and over. *Laval Médical, 42*, 15–21.

Crawley, E. (2005). Institutional thoughtlessness in prisons and its impacts on the day-to-day lives of elderly men. *Journal of Contemporary Justice, 21*(4), 350–363.

Crawley, E., & Sparks, R. (2005). Hidden injuries? Researching the experiences of older men in English prisons. *Howard Journal of Criminal Justice, 44*(4), 345–356.

Curtice, M., Parker, J., Wismayer, F. S., & Tomison, A. (2003). The elderly offender: An 11 year survey of referrals to a regional forensic psychiatric service. *Journal of Forensic Psychiatry and Psychology, 14*(2), 253–265.

Douglass, R.L. (1991). Old-timers: Michigan's Elderly Prisoners. Lansing, MI: Michigan Department of Corrections.

Falter, R. G. (2003). Elderly inmates: An emerging correctional population. In J. Moore (Ed.), *Management and administration of correctional health*. Kingston: Civic Research Institute.

Farrell, M., Boys, A., Bebbington, P., Brugha, T., Coid, J., Jenkins, R., Lewis, G., Meltzer, H., Marsden, J., Singleton, N., & Taylor, C. (2002). Psychosis and drug dependence: Results from a national survey of prisoners. *British Journal of Psychiatry, 181*, 393–398.

Fazel, S., Hope, T., O'Donnell, I., & Jacoby, R. (2001a). Hidden psychiatric morbidity in elderly prisoners. *British Journal of Psychiatry, 179*, 535–539.

Fazel, S., Hope, T., O'Donnell, I., Piper, M., & Jacoby, R. (2001b). Health of elderly male prisoners: Worse than the general population, worse than younger prisoners. *Age and Ageing, 30*(5), 403–407.

Fazel, S., McMillan, J., & O'Donnell, I. (2002). Dementia in prison: Ethical and legal implications. *Journal of Medical Ethics, 28*, 156–159.

Fazel, S., Hope, T., O'Donnell, I., & Jacoby, R. (2004). Unmet treatment needs of older prisoners: A primary care survey. *Age and Ageing, 33*, 396–398.

Flynn, E. E. (2002). Life at the margins: Older women living in poverty. In R. Sarri & J. Figueira-McDonough (Eds.), *Women at the margins neglect, punishment, and resistance*. London: Taylor & Francis.

Folstein, M. F., Folstein, S. E., & McHugh, P. R. (1975). "Mini-mental state": A practical guide for grading the cognitive state of patients for the clinician. *Journal of Psychiatric Research, 12*, 189–198.

Frazer, L. (2003). *Ageing inside: School for policy studies working paper series; paper number 1*. Bristol: School for Policy Studies.

Gallagher, E. (1990). Emotional, social and physical health characteristics of older men in prisoner. *International Journal of Aging and Human Development, 30*(4), 251–265.

Gautier, S. (2011). Viellir et mourir en prison. *Soins Gerontologie, 88*, 22–24.

Goetting, A. (1992). Patterns of homicide among the elderly. *Violence and Victims, 7*(3), 203–215.

Grant, A. (1999). *Elderly inmates: Issues for Australia. Trends & issues in crime and criminal justice*. Canberra: Australian Institute of Criminology.

Hayes, A. J. (2010). *The health, social and custodial needs of older men in prison*. PhD Thesis, Division of Psychiatry, University of Manchester, UK.

Hayes, A. J., & Fazel, S. (2008). Older adults in prison: Vulnerability, abuse and neglect. In J. Pritchard (Ed.), *Good practice in safeguarding adults: Working effectively in adult protection* (pp. 138–150). London: Jessica Kingsley Publishers.

Hayes, A. J., & Shaw, J. (2011). Practice into policy: The needs of elderly prisoners in England and Wales. *Prison Service Journal, 143*, 38–45.

Hayes, A. J., Burns, A., Turnbull, P., & Shaw, J. (2012). The health and social needs of elderly male prisoners. *International Journal of Geriatric Psychiatry, 27(11)*, 1155–1162.

Her Majesty's Inspectorate of Prisons. (2004). *'No problems – old and quiet': Older prisoners in England and Wales*. London: HMIP.

Human Rights Watch. (2012). *Old behind bars. The aging prison population in the United States*. New York: Human Rights Watch.

Kakoullis, A., LeMesurier, N., & Kingston, P. (2010). The mental health of older prisoners. *International Psychogeriatrics, 22*(5), 693–701.

Kerbs, J. J., & Jolley, J. M. (2007). Inmate-on-inmate victimization among older male prisoners. *Crime and Delinquency, 53*(2), 187–218.

Kingston, P., LeMesurier, N., Yorston, G., Wardle, S., & Heath, L. (2011). Psychiatric morbidity in older prisoners: Unrecognized and undertreated. *International Psychogeriatrics, 23*(8), 1254–1260.

Kratcoski, P. C., & Babb, S. (1990). Adjustment of older inmates: An analysis by institutional structure and gender. *Journal of Contemporary Criminal Justice, 6*, 264–281.

Linder, J. F., & Meyers, F. J. (2007). Palliative care for prison inmates: 'Don't let me die in prison'. *Journal of the American Medication Association, 298*(8), 894–901.

Loeb, S. J., & Steffensmeier, D. (2006). Older male prisoners: Health status, self-efficacy beliefs, and health-promoting behaviours. *Journal of Correctional Health Care, 12*, 269–278.

Marquart, J. W., Merianos, D. E., & Doucet, G. (2000). The health-related concerns of older prisoners: Implications for policy. *Ageing and Society, 20*, 79–96.

Ministry of Justice. (2004). *White paper on crime 2004: Treatment of offenders.*http://hakusyo1.moj.go.jp/en/50/nfm/mokuji.html. Accessed 27 Aug 2012.

Ministry of Justice. (2007). *Statistical bulletin: Offender management caseload statistics 2006.* London: Ministry of Justice.

Ministry of Justice. (2010). *Statistical bulletin: Offender management caseload statistics 2009.* London: Ministry of Justice.

Paanila, J., Eronen, M., Hakola, P., & Tiihonen, J. (2000). Aging and homicide rates. *Journal of Forensic Science, 45*(2), 390–391.

Phillips, L. L., Allen, R. S., Harris, G. M., Presnell, A. H., DeCoster, J., & Cavanaugh, R. (2011). Aging prisoners' treatment selection: Does prospect theory enhance understanding of end-of-life medical decisions? *Gerontologist, 51*(5), 663–674.

Regan, J. J., Alderson, A., & Regan, W. M. (2002). Psychiatric disorders in aging prisoners. *Clinical Gerontologist, 26*(1/2), 117–124.

Smith, B. C. (1982). The use of health hazard appraisal in a prison population. *Journal of Prison and Jail Health, 2*, 58–66.

Spaulding, A. C., Seals, R. M., McCallum, V. A., Perez, S. D., Brzozowski, A. K., & Steenland, N. K. (2011). Prisoner survival inside and outside of the institution: implications for health-care planning. *American Journal of Epidemiology, 173*, 479–487.

Steffensmeier, D., & Motivans, M. (2000). Older men and older women in the arms of criminal law: Offending patterns and sentencing outcomes. *Journal of Gerontology: Social Science, 55B*(3), 141–151.

Steiner, E. (2003). Early release for seriously ill and elderly prisoners: Should French practice be followed? *Probation Journal, 50*, 267–276.

Sumner, A. (2012). Assessment and management of older prisoners. *Nursing Older People, 24*(3), 16–21.

Tarbuck, A. (2001). Health of elderly prisoners. *Age and Ageing, 30*, 369–370.

Taylor, P. J., & Parrott, J. M. (1988). Elderly offenders: A study of age-related factors among custodially remanded offenders. *British Journal of Psychiatry, 152*, 340–346.

Uzoaba, J. H. E. (1998). *Managing older offenders: Where do we stand?* (Report No. R-70). Ottowa: Research Brance, Corporate Development, Correctional Service of Canada.

Wahadin, A. (2004). *Older women in the criminal justice system: Running out of time.* London: Jessica Kingsley Publishers.

Wahadin, A., & Aday, R. H. (2005). The needs of older men and women in the criminal justice system: An international perspective. *Prison Service Journal, 160*, 13–22.

Wheldon, A., & Williams, R. (2012). Development of a geriatrician led outreach service for older prisoners. *Age and Ageing, 41*(S2), 14.

Chapter 2
Supporting Families and Children Living in the Shadow of Prisoners

Viviane Schekter, Marcello Ienca, and Bernice S. Elger

Abstract The potential adverse effects of imprisonment on prisoners' relatives and family still remain largely unexplored. This chapter provides a detailed analysis of the psychosocial impact of imprisonment on the families of detained persons. Starting from the direct experience in a correctional facility in Switzerland, the authors describe how the lives of families tend to change over the time of imprisonment and how this change is influenced by a number of factors. A special focus is attributed to the children of imprisoned parents, as they are often the most vulnerable persons collaterally affected by the experience of imprisonment. After providing a detailed analysis of these problems, the authors identify some important forms of support, including innovative strategies enabled by new information technology, which could be implemented by professionals and NGOs.

2.1 Introduction

Lucy[1] is 5 years old. She looks at the ground in front of the large prison door and picks up a couple of flowers. 'They're for daddy', she says. But she knows that no flowers are allowed in the visiting area. She looks at me and asks: 'Do you think that if I hide them just here in the corner, daddy will find them when he comes out?' (Figs. 2.1 and 2.2).

---

[1] All names of quoted persons in this chapter are fictive pseudonyms.

V. Schekter (✉)
Relais Enfants Parents Romands (REPR), Anciennement Carrefour Prison, Rue du Tunnel 1, 1005 Lausanne, Switzerland
e-mail: schekter@repr.ch

M. Ienca • B.S. Elger
Institute for Biomedical Ethics, University of Basel, Bernoullistrasse 28, 4056 Basel, Switzerland

© Springer Science+Business Media Dordrecht 2017
B.S. Elger et al. (eds.), *Emerging Issues in Prison Health*,
DOI 10.1007/978-94-017-7558-8_2

13

Fig. 2.1 Prison du Bois-Mermet, Switzerland: REPR was able to arrange for a young father to take care of his three-week-old son

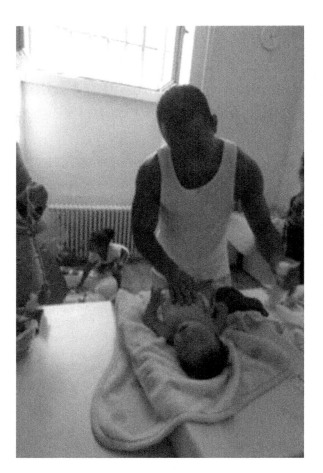

Fig. 2.2 Prison du Bois-Mermet, Switzerland: playing with a ball and running around the place is possible in the special visits with REPR

Lucy is one of the 800,000 European children that, as estimated by the *Children of Prisoners Europe* (COPE), are living in the shadow of prisoners.[2] While the number of children experiencing parental imprisonment is increasing in Western industrialized countries (Murray and Farrington 2008; Sharratt 2014), little information is available regarding the consequences on a child and on the whole family resulting from this phenomenon. As extensive research has pointed out, the families of prisoners tend to alter their patterns during the prisoner's absence in a manner that may determine a complete restructuring of their lives (Crépin 2000; Ghetti 2000). The aim of this chapter is to explore the phenomenon of parental imprisonment from the perspective of children and other family members. The goal is not only to provide a descriptive analysis of the phenomenon but to also develop a normative framework in order to address the question of how to better support the families and children of imprisoned persons while respecting their needs and rights.

Particular attention will be devoted to the role of families as crucial factors of re-socialization for former prisoners. Evidence shows that constant family support mechanisms play a key role in favouring a successful re-entry and re-socialization of former prisoners in to communities (Martinez 2006). For example, pioneering interview-based research at the Vera Institute of Justice involving prisoners during the first 35 days after their release concluded that families are a decisive factor as to how successfully a former prisoner re-enters society within 1 month of release (Nelson et al. 1999). However, it is not always clear how family ties can be maintained throughout the period of imprisonment in a manner that can favour the achievement of a successful re-socialization. In this chapter, the impact of incarceration on the families of prisoners and their role in favouring the re-socialization of former prisoners will be evaluated. The evidence is taken from the literature where available. Because of the scarceness of studies in the field, we will also refer to typical cases, that the privately funded support organisation *Relais Enfants Parents Romands* has observed during their work with children and families of prisoners.

2.2 What Is It Like to Be a Family of a Prisoner?

2.2.1 Family Support

Globally, the percentage of male prisoners is significantly higher than that of female prisoners (Carson and Golinelli 2013). In the US, the male-female ratio is 9–1 (Guerino et al. 2011). According to the Swiss Federal Statistical Office, more than 93 % of detainees in Swiss jails are men (Office 2010). In Australia the gender imbalance is even bigger: 96 % of prisoners are male (Ross and Skondreas 2000). This means that there is a high number of spouses and female partners being

---

[2]Children of Prisoners Europe, www.childrenofprisoners.eu.

confronted with the experience of their partner's absence. Most of these women never imagined being confronted with this crucial role. While families can be one of the most powerful support mechanisms for prisoners, they can at the same time increase prisoners' stress if imprisonment leads to conflict and abandonment. Although some couples tend to be strengthened by the difficulties resulting from the imprisonment of a partner, others may be weakened, to a point where the relationship is no longer a point of reference for the prisoner once outside. In many cases, the supportive role of families is better understood in the light of the entire judicial and social process in which they are directly or indirectly involved. Often, family members report that they feel useful – and sometimes even used – during the trial, but they also claim that they felt like having lost their role once the trial is over. Usually, after the trial follows a period – the prison sentence – during which families may feel 'excluded' by the judicial authorities. That relative 'exclusion' lasts until they are contacted by the prison authorities and asked to play the role of guarantor for their partner's first day on leave. This can occur after several months or even years of detention.

From this follows that in order to maintain the central role of families in the re-socialization process their continuing involvement in the entire social and judicial process should be favoured and they should be offered constant support. Such an active approach towards the families would contribute to reduce the perceptions of difficulty and isolation which many spouses or other family members experience during the imprisonment of their significant others.

2.2.2 Arrest

> When the police came to our home and arrested John, I thought this was a mistake and then I felt as if I was in a bad movie [. . .] I have discovered so many things about my husband since then . . . I think I still love him, but I am not always sure about it [. . .]. (Giulia, wife of a prisoner in Geneva).

Often, the most stressful moment for family members in the entire imprisonment process of a relative is the arrest. Seeing police officers entering one's home early in the morning, searching through the whole house, handcuffing one's husband or brother is usually perceived as a traumatic experience. The sudden removal of a central figure in their lives is for many people very distressful. Particularly for children, witnessing the arrest of one of their parents can cause very harmful consequences on their psychological development (J. Murray and Farrington 2005, 2008). King (2002) reminds the authorities of the legal and ethical obligations towards children in such situations:

> The arrest of a parent in the presence of a child must respect the child's right to privacy, family life, and their right to be heard. Police officers should be trained specifically in handling situations where an arrest is made in the presence of a child (King 2002).

At the time of arrest, the priority for authorities is of course the detention of the person under suspicion. As a consequence, and in spite of existing legal and ethical obligations, the needs and experience of children, spouses and other significant others are too rarely taken into account during this process. However, a few countries, including Denmark and Poland, show that exceptions are possible. Those countries provide specific training for officers to prepare them about how to deal with family members during these stressful situations. King shows how families can be severely affected, if measures to spare them humiliation and fear are only put into place partially:

> The officer said that we had to leave the room so he could check it for drugs. When we were on the way out of the room, he opened my drawers and began throwing out my underwear etc. all over the place. It was so insulting I felt as if I was a criminal (King 2002).

From the moment of the arrest families are confronted with the discovery of new realities and so far to them unimaginable practices related to the world of jail. They are frequently required to readjust their everyday life to the new events. The impact of imprisonment on families is therefore large and comprises several levels: economic, psychological and social.

2.2.3 Economic, Psychological and Social Impact on the Family

On the economic side, the major consequence is the abrupt interruption of the main salary, which, under many circumstances, obligates family members to search for a new, more affordable, accommodation or to look for a new job (DeFina and Hannon 2010). These activities tend to result in a significant life change.

On the psychological side, increased levels of stress, sleep disturbances, as well as psychological disorders such as depression and anxiety are frequently observed (Murray and Farrington 2008). This is particularly the case during pretrial detention, due to the incapacity for prisoners and their families to project into future scenarios (e.g. 'when will he or she be released?', 'What will happen then?').

One further factor of stress is that families usually tend to seclude information about their imprisoned relative from their friends, acquaintances or even from more distant relatives. For example, at Relais Enfants Parents Romands (REPR) we experienced the case of a woman who would visit her imprisoned husband every Thursday afternoon. In order to seclude information about her imprisoned spouse from her acquaintances, she would justify her absences from work to her colleagues and boss by saying that she was attending several sessions of physiotherapy due to a pain in her shoulder. However, this protective attitude tended to initiate a vicious circle that led to increased negative emotions and sense of isolation as she could not share her overwhelming emotions, questions and anxiety with other people after returning from visiting her husband. It is realistic to think that similar elusive behaviour is adopted by many other spouses of prisoners as a strategy to prevent social stigmatization. Family members describe the fear being cast aside by others, as if committing a crime is somehow similar to a contagious disease.

Psychologists working for REPR have repeatedly witnessed the social impact of imprisonment on families: fear, shame, and anxiety are emotions that have a social impact. Frequently they act as isolation factors for the families of imprisoned persons. Often family members prefer to stay away from people in order to avoid answering questions. A relatively young mother of a prisoner confided to a psychologist during a private consultation: 'I feel imprisoned outside, in a glass prison that nobody sees.' Many families discover the world of prison. The knowledge about the specific language and rules of the prison world isolate them from their previous social contacts that have only vague and often wrong perceptions of prisons and prisoners.

Over a decade ago, a French study has shown that conflict, stigma and isolation are the three main consequences for families when a member is imprisoned (Dubéchot et al. 2000). In that study, it was found that 80 % of families believed that the incarceration of their relative affected their lives on at least one major level, whether financial, professional, relational, or with regard to their home (the need to move to another house, for example). These results show that the impact of imprisonment on families is massive and complex.

2.2.4 Mothers and Fathers

From the perspective of the mothers and fathers of prisoners, many questions surround their own parental responsibility. The typical questions that burden parents of imprisoned children are: 'How can I live with the idea that my son took the life of someone else's son? What did I miss? What did I do wrong?' The complex psychological challenges for families in this context are visible in the following exchange that took place between an REPR psychologist and the mother of a young man who had stabbed to death another man in a fight. Entering the court, she saw the family and friends of the victim. The mother stated:

> I thought I should go and talk to them, tell them that I understood their pain [...] and I thought I should apologize [...] but apologize for what? And then I saw the way they looked at me [...] unbearable [...] and finally I said nothing and tried to disappear in the crowd.

This example shows the transformative process that mothers may experience as a consequence of their children's incarceration. During this process the mother does not any longer perceive herself as her child's mother but rather as the mother of a murderer. Would one expect that the unconditional love of a mother implies or at least should imply unconditional maternal support even after a severe crime? The answer to that question is difficult and presumably very subjective. However, it seems clear that the feeling of helplessness perceived by members of those families is huge and requires special support. In addition, the level of emotional and affective support showed by the mother towards the imprisoned child seems to have a direct link with the feeling of social inclusion and appreciation of the child him- or herself.

In fact, if the child does not feel loved by the person that is supposed to love him or her more than any other, than those children will have the feeling that they are not loved by nor capable of being loved by anyone for anyone (Brodsky 1975; Crépin 2000).

2.2.5 Siblings

A major problem faced by the brothers and sisters of inmates is related to loyalty. The imprisonment of a child takes up a lot of time and space in the family, and sometimes siblings develop feelings of jealousy and guilt. This can be better grasped through the following report from a 14-years-old sister of a young prisoner, provided to psychologists of REPR:

> When I see my mom being worried one week before the visit to my brother in prison and sad for one week after this meeting I want to tell her, I am here, I need you too and I didn't do anything wrong. At that time, I want to say rude things to my brother and hit him . . . but I can only cry alone.

Indeed, given their young age and direct emotional involvement, the psychological distress of siblings is often tainted by contradictory feelings.

2.2.6 Couples/Partners

For couples, incarceration is a major challenge. Sitting in a room face to face with one's partner, on opposite sides of a table with nothing to do but talk for 1 h (not a second longer), as it is frequently the routine in prisons during visiting hours, is experienced as a puzzling and unusual situation by many couples. Usually, couples share various moments and activities such as eating together, reading, watching TV, or walking around. The effects of having regular meetings over months or years without sharing any activity other than talking for 1 hour sharp under the watchful eye of a guard are devastating for a couple (Comfort et al. 2005). Fortunately, some modern prisons organize special visits in which partners of prisoners have the possibility of spending more time with their significant others and engaging in activities such as eating together and sharing in some intimacy. These opportunities contribute to preserve semi-normal couple relationships. However, at present they are not yet organized routinely in all detention facilities.

The experience of romantic love among the partners is also challenged by incarceration. Reports collected from personal experience show that spouses of inmates often talk about their partners as if they were ill. Typical questions that arise in these situations are: When is the right moment to ask for separation and leave him/her? How to tell him/her? After the trial, or after the first day's leave? And if the partner decides to leave, will he/she have some visits? Who will bring the children? Who will be guarantor when the spouse is released from jail?

Their answers to these questions are frequently influenced by multiple factors.

In some particular circumstances, however, the experience of partner imprisonment may have an unexpectedly positive impact on romantic conjugal love. Some couples report that they rediscover their love through the experience of missing each other. The physical absence of their significant other forces them to engage in activities, such as writing letters, of which they got out of the habit or even to develop new forms of communication. From a psychological point of view, this occurs in general because the difficulties experienced by those couples cause a reinforcement of their feelings.

2.3 Being a Parent and Imprisoned

2.3.1 Paradoxical Positions

Particular attention should be devoted to the condition of being a parent in prison. The reason for that stems from the fact that it is very difficult to maintain one's parental role within prison. The prison system usually treats detainees in a similar manner as if they were in the position of children: they have diminished autonomy; they have to obey and follow predetermined rules, and have diminished capacity for decision-making. In this context, the parenting role of prisoners is confined to 1 h every 7 or 15 days, the usual time and frequency attributed to a detainee for family visits. During this short interval of time parents are supposed to exert their parental role in all its forms: setting rules for the children, training them, providing advice etc. This paradoxical condition is well captured by Scharff-Smith and Gampell (2011):

> This means that detained persons have to have good skills and clear ideas about roles. A significant problem is that much of the behaviour and many of the strategies which prisoners often acquire in an attempt to handle prison life better can be directly counter-productive in relation to life outside of the walls (Scharff-Smith and Gampell 2011).

2.3.2 Keeping in Contact or Not

While most parents in prison want to be part of their children's lives outside, they are completely dependent on the support of others in maintaining any kind of parental role. Examples of people supporting imprisoned parents in their parental role include the carers of children, the families and friends of prisoners, external professionals, and the professionals in the prison. The attitudes of professionals with regard to parenting in prison have a major influence on maintaining links between parents and children and developing special programs for them. Policymakers, sentencing authorities and professionals working with children need to be trained to deal with the special needs of children. A major problem, in fact, is that many professionals base their evaluations on general rules without any specific competence or training. For example, several authorities and professionals tend to limit the visits of children based on the personal assumptions that 'prisons are not a place for children' and that 'children must never come to visit because it can cause trauma'. These assumptions are usually based neither on scientific evidence from the psychological and behavioural sciences nor on direct reports from children but rather on their personal intuitions. These types of attitudes risk oversimplifying the complex and unique situation experienced by children of imprisoned parents and eventually have a negative impact on their development. As Ayre et al. (2006) state:

> Although they may never meet a prisoner's child, these professionals need to know their decisions impact on these children (Ayre et al. 2006)

Given these limitations, some prisoners find it so difficult to maintain their parental function during their imprisonment that they may decide to take care again of their children only once released. But also this choice seems to be very problematic as the lack of contacts usually generates additional issues. Some detained persons live with the daydream that when will be released, the situation will be identical to that prior to their arrest. However, this is often far from truth since during that interval of time several families readjust to the new situation in a manner that significantly reshapes the familiar environment (Murray and Farrington 2008). A detained male adult who had been in prison for 2 years reported at REPR that when he got home right after his release, he discovered that many little but significant things had changed; for example, the room he used to sleep in with his wife was now the room of his teenage daughter and his 11-year-old son was now sitting at the family table. These are examples of readjustments in daily family life that also affect the role of each family member. These adjustments may cause disorientation in newly released prisoners as they may fail to grasp their new role and position within the family. The problem of returning home also raises questions concerning the high expectations about release experienced both by imprisoned parents and their children. In Denmark, members of the NGO *SAVN* have observed that once the parent is released from prison the family often passes through a huge disappointment:

> Perhaps the prisoner feels that he is the same, but the family has changed. The children are older, the girlfriend or boyfriend has become more independent and used to managing everything alone. On the other hand, the children have an idea that the family will have a nice time and do fun things all day long (Scharff-Smith and Gampell 2011)

Preparing parents and children to cope with their new life after prison is a crucial process in the support of prisoners and their families. Ideally, this process should begin as early as possible, in order to prevent the post-release disorientation and communication difficulty between prisoners and their families. This preparation should actively support the successful post-release restoration of family life.

2.3.3 Support for Parents

Since changes and adjustments occur in virtually all families, it is necessary to support detained parents and help them maintain these important family ties.

Organizing groups of parents in prison, providing information about child-centred visits, and preparing parenting courses are all necessary tools to achieve this goal. However, these tools are not available in all prisons.

In Europe, the variety of support and educational programs for imprisoned parents is large. In the Lombardy region (Italy), for example, the association *Bambini Senza Sbarre*[3] offers crafts workshops for imprisoned parents and parenting support schemes focusing on parenting support and conflict resolution (Carmignani 2012). In Milan Opera, a support project offers a physical space organized as a private home as well as psychological support from experts in family dynamics and child psychology (Scharff-Smith and Gampell 2011).

In several countries, sessions for prisoners are organized by NGOs to raise awareness and enable parents in prison to discuss their parental role (Scharff-Smith and Gampell 2011).

2.4   Being the Child of a Detained Person

2.4.1   Invisible Children

It is estimated that over 800,000 children in Europe have a parent in prison.[4] In the USA-the country with the highest rate of incarceration in the world- this number is believed to be between two and three millions (Eddy and Poehlmann 2010). In the UK, the number of children with imprisoned parents (160,000) is double than the number of children in care and over six times higher than the number of children on the child protection register' (Robertson 2012). It is worth to notice, however, that the exact number of children separated from a parent by prison is hard to determine. Children of prisoners are usually perceived as nobody's concern, hence are almost invisible. Nevertheless, they exist and experience specific issues and need specific support. As Robertson (2012) points out:

> The children of prisoners are the invisible victims of crime and the penal system. They have done no wrong, yet they suffer the stigma of criminality. Their rights to nurture are affected both by the criminal action of their parent and by the state's response to it in the name of justice (Robertson 2012: 2).

These children may be 'invisible', but they are not alone. Over the years, a growing number of NGOs have developed working programs on this specific issue. Among the objectives achieved by these programs these are particularly worth mentioning: improving prison visits, helping families and persuading policymakers to consider the rights of prisoners' children. A proof of these achievements is that in September 2011, this topic has been discussed in detail for the first time by the UN during the Day of General Discussion.

---

[3]or more information see http://www.bambinisenzasbarre.org. Accessed 11 March 2013.

[4]See Children of Prisoners Europe: http://tinyurl.com/oevyznn. Accessed 03 December 2014.

2.4.2   Specific Risks

During the aforementioned UN Day of General Discussion,[5] several individuals, groups and country representatives provided examples of good practice regarding the children of prisoners. However, it was also highlighted that children living in the shadow of prisons are too easily ignored in criminal justice. One reason for that stems from the fact that authorities often reduce the situation of these children to a security assessment. In other words, they mostly care about minimizing potential risks for the prison associated with the possibility for the children to see their parents. Globally, as we have seen, numerous prisoners have children. Although their experiences may be very heterogeneous, it seems reasonable to assume that the removal and detention of a parent is a negative experience for most of the children. As Robertson (2012: 2) states, there are five main areas of risk associated with parental incarceration:

1. Deprivation of basic necessities and opportunities
2. Danger of secondary victimization and depersonalization
3. Deterioration of the overall situation of a child
4. Distance from the incarcerated parent
5. Descent into antisocial behaviour

Each child deals with the incarceration of his or her parent differently, even within the same family. For some children, the relationship with their incarcerated fathers or mothers may become even stronger than before. For others, imprisonment is synonymous with loss and absence of contacts of any kind. Many families try to protect children from this situation by secluding relevant information about the abrupt disappearance of their parent.

From the perspective of children of imprisoned parents, the separation from the father or mother could bring several different, potentially conflicting emotions. At the psychological level, many children show a reaction of shock, ranging from physical pain to numbness. These feelings are externalized differently depending on various factors (e.g. closeness with the parent before incarceration and age of the child). At the pragmatic level, children often experience important practical changes in their everyday life.

2.4.3   Rights of the Child with Imprisoned Parents

There is a general agreement that the best interests of the child must be a priority when dealing with children with imprisoned parents. Worldwide, numerous guidelines have been produced with the aim of ensuring and protecting the best

---

[5] See: http://tinyurl.com/mgqzmzc. Accessed 03 December 2014.

interest of the child. An example of such guidelines is provided by the NGO *San Francisco Partnership for Incarcerated Parents*, which has produced a document named 'Bill of Rights' in which the following rights inherent to children with imprisoned parents are proclaimed:

- To be kept safe and informed at the time of my parent's arrest.
- To be heard when decisions are made about me.
- To be considered when decisions are made about my parent.
- To be well-cared for in my parent's absence.
- To speak with, see and touch my parent.
- To support as I face my parent's incarceration.
- Not to be judged, blamed or labelled because my parent is incarcerated.
- To a lifelong relationship with my parent.[6]

2.4.4 Telling the Truth to Children

One major issue in caring for children with imprisoned parents is telling them the truth. Many children are not informed about their mother's or father's incarceration. The abrupt absence of the family member is often explained by appealing to well-intentioned lies such as saying that their parent is away on a work-trip or has been hospitalized. Some other children are taken to visit their imprisoned parent in prison having been told they are visiting their mum's or dad's workplace. These facts help us grasp two core problems faced by families who care for children with imprisoned parents:

> For imprisoned parents with families who can care for children, two of their primary concerns are organizing the first visit with the children; and what to say to the children (Scharff-Smith and Gampell 2011: 171).

Most of the time, these well-intentioned lies are aimed at protecting the child, but they frequently cause more difficulties for the child's development. In a survey conducted in 2002 at Mountjoy Prison in Dublin, almost two thirds of the parents in prison said that their children did not know that they were incarcerated (King 2002).

As psychoanalyst Françoise Dolto[7] has repeatedly argued, it is advisable that children transparently informed about their parents' detention (Dolto 2012). The reason for that stems from the fact that extensive psychological evidence on the effect of secrets on children with imprisoned parents shows that it is virtually

---

[6]San Francisco Partnership for Incarcerated Parents (SFPIP) is a coalition of social service providers, representatives of government bodies, advocates and others, who work with or are concerned about children of incarcerated parents and their families. Formed in 2000, this NGO works to improve the lives of children of incarcerated parents and to increase awareness of these children, and of their needs and their strengths.

[7]Françoise Dolto is a French doctor and psychoanalyst, famous for her research on babies and childhood, and for her psychotherapeutic work with the mother-baby dyad.

impossible to predict the impact of each secret on the psychological and psychosocial development of the child. In addition, it also shows and that children will likely perceive the unusual, incomprehensible and often inconsistent character of those visits and their related explanations.

This impact will vary depending on several factors including the age of the child, the quality of parental ties before the arrest, the length of detention, the general family make-up and many other factors. However, it seems to be a quite generalizable consequence that the child will search for an explanation, interpret the loss of contact with the parent as her own fault. This sense of guilt can be very harmful for the psychological development of the child and may harm her self-esteem. Finally, children who are not informed are likely to imagine what has happened and make hypothesis and conjectures that are often worse than reality. This can easily cause anxiety. For this reason, it is important that children are persuaded that they are not responsible for the situation faced by their mother or father.

To summarize, although parents in prison often think that informing their children about their imprisonment may have negative and traumatizing consequences on their psychological health, it seems that even worse consequences may be caused by secluding that information. The advisability of informing children about their parents' imprisonment is clearly reported by the guide for teachers and education professionals, where it is stated:

> Agencies working with children and families affected by imprisonment recommend that adults tell children what is happening at the earliest possible stage. In the end, however, when, how and whether to tell a child is always up to each individual family (Ormiston Children Family and Trust 2007: 19).

To understand this, most parents will need time and support. Helpful books for both children and parents are available.[8]

Another aspect worth of reflection is that the information children receive should be adapted to their age and stage of psychological development.

2.5 Support for Children

2.5.1 Maintaining Relations with Parents Benefits Children

As psychologist Alain Bouregba stated at the 2012 General Assembly of the European Network for Children of Incarcerated Parents, the imprisonment of a parent does not in itself indicate a psychopathological difficulty for the child. However, incarceration, separation and the disappearance of the parent can expose

---

[8]The Children of Prisoners Europe website has some examples of the books and videos available: http://www.childrenofprisonerseurope.eu/recommended-reading/books-for-children. Accessed 11 March 2013.

the child to some increased risks. A rigorous analysis of these risks indicates that helping to support and maintain the relationship between the child and his parent would benefit both children development and public health (Rosenberg 2009). At present, public health measures along these lines have not yet been recognized, considered or promoted by the relevant EU or national legislatures and policy makers. Therefore, we call for raising awareness on this topic at the regulatory level and for promoting a discussion aimed at producing specific measures for the support of children of imprisoned parents and their families.

In this context, the fundamental question to be addressed by professionals is not *whether* the link between child and parent must be maintained, but *what* contact can be maintained between child and parent with the help of professionals and NGOs. In fact, it is not reasonable to ask *whether* the link between child and parent must be maintained as those ties, once established, will endure whatever happens in life. Separation can reinforce those ties in a rigid way, but will not destroy them.

2.5.2 Questions Children Ask About Prison

Most children have many questions about the conditions in which their parents are living in prison. Typical questions are: 'Do they have a real mattress or do they sleep on the floor?'; 'Do they have a hot meal every day?'; 'Is it cold inside prison?' etc.

They often imagine conditions that are worse than reality. For this reason, providing them with concrete and simple information, such as photographs or drawings of the cell of their parents, is very important to diminish their anxiety. In some prisons in Switzerland the director and his staff authorize direct visits in the cell for children. This is a very powerful means of reducing children's anxiety. As 7-year-old Sarah reported to us after visiting her imprisoned father:

> I even saw pictures of me and my last drawing in daddy's room, and it was nice and clean.

Today, several booklets that explain prison to children are available. These booklets can be very useful in preparing children before visits, and can also help parents in prison to imagine what kind of questions they will have to answer.

Another important factor to take into account is the potential stress and anxiety caused by guards: for many children uniforms can be intimidating. To avoid this intimidation, prison staff must be trained to ensure child-friendly behaviour towards visitors. A step in this direction has been taken by the Swiss Prison Staff Centre in Switzerland, which has decided to include this issue in the obligatory staff training (3 years), thus indicating the importance of this topic.

2.5.3 Play Areas in Prisons

The way children may visit their imprisoned parents is very diverse. For example, visits may be either public or private, may last from 30 min to several hours or even days, and may occur at different frequencies. In addition, some prisons provide specific spaces for children's visits whereas others do not. However, the general goal of these visits is to strengthen the child-parent relationship. In this section, we offer some examples of good practice for children visits. The Askham Grange prison in North Yorkshire, England, has a special house where children up to the age of 18 can stay overnight, unsupervised, with their incarcerated mothers. While most children reported to find ordinary visits 'fake' or inadequate because they felt unable to raise important issues due to the public space and limited time for visits, the overnight visits were highly valued and could have a strong positive effect on the mental health of the children involved, including those with mothers serving long sentences (Robertson 2012).

Another example is the Jyderup State 'open prison' in Denmark. In the facilities of this prison weekend visiting times extend from 9:30 am to 7:30 pm, which gives families greater flexibility. Visits inside the prison typically take place in the prisoner's own room, and facilities are provided so that families can cook meals and eat together, have time to play and watch TV, and so on. Additionally, the prison has accessible outdoor areas where parents can play with their children (Scharff-Smith and Gampell 2011).

In Switzerland, the practice of children visiting prisons is growing, but much remains to be done. Some prisons still use visiting areas without any physical contact, where the parent is forced to stay behind a glass window. Some prisons accept children visits, but without enabling any possibility of engaging in interactive and relational activity.

In the context of this urgent need for a modernization of the Swiss prison facilities and social policies, the Relais Enfants Parents Romands (REPR) team works within several prisons in Switzerland with the scope of creating new settings and spaces for interaction and support. With regard to children visits, these settings may include: special visits with plays and music, visits with the possibility of sharing a meal and visits for special events like Christmas and Father's day. In several prisons, the REPR's team accompanies children every month to attend the so-called 'Ateliers Créatifs': special visits where children and parents (mothers or fathers) have the possibility of playing together. The *ateliers créatifs* involve activities that are tailored to the age of the child. Due to limitations in the existing facilities, the rooms where these activities take place are often small. However, these spatial limitations are compensated by the creativity of our team members. Different areas are set up. These include an area for creative activities, such as painting, playing cards and writing; an area for more physical games such as games involving running and jumping; and finally, a cocooning corner, in which parents and children can sit down together on comfortable cushions and enjoy reading or cuddling.

This 'triple play areas' model is largely inspired by the important experience of the Belgian 'Relais Enfants Parents asbl' team.[9] In designing these settings a

---

[9] For more information see http://www.relaisenfantsparents.be. Accessed 11 March 2013.

fundamental assumption is made: giving birth is not enough to become a parent. Interactions with children are also crucial in making people become parents. These interactions are thought to be essential to the development of proper parental role. Therefore, making these interactions possible is thought to be essential to maintaining and preserving the parental role of imprisoned mothers and fathers. The specific goal of supporting these types of children visits is to try to maintain the quality of contacts so that children and parents can come to know themselves and discover and improve their roles.

2.5.4 Collaboration with Prison Staff

Cooperation with prison staff and shared activities with them are paramount in the development of appropriate settings for children visits. A successful example of this cooperation with prison staff favoured by REPR is the visit of Louis, a 6-year-old boy, who was enabled to bake a cake with his imprisoned father. The cake was then shared between all visitors, the REPR social worker and the guard. When Louis came out of prison, he referred to the guard as 'the nice man who takes care of my Daddy'. This visit has contributed to significantly reshape Louis' ideas about his father's imprisonment and favour the persuasion that his father is in a safe place and supportive environment.

As Scharff-Smith and Gampell report, 'prison staff are frequently not aware how small changes in their behaviour and attitude can impact on children' (Scharff-Smith and Gampell 2011). In Switzerland, an internal questionnaire built up by the Relais Enfants Parents Romand team revealed that the majority of surveyed prison officers believed that they had no specific skills to cope with children and that they would benefit from a wider educational program.[10] A similar situation is reported to apply to several European countries. For instance, Scharff-Smith and Gampell – who conducted interviews with prison staff in Poland – report that also in the Polish context 'there are no specific procedures for dealing with children who visit their parents, but that prison officers use their skills and judgment when facilitating such visits' (Scharff-Smith and Gampell 2011).

Therefore, it is important that all staff working on visits, including security staff, should be trained in understanding the needs and perspectives of children visiting their parents in prison. As Ayre et al. (2006) writes: 'Prison officers have a difficult dual role based on interpersonal work combining two extremes: security and respect for human dignity. Training needs to reflect both roles' (Ayre et al. 2006: 86).

---

[10]Questionnaire conducted by Michele Poretti (Institut Universitaire Kurt Bösch) in December 2013. Work unpublished.

2.5.5 *Indirect Contact*

Indirect contacts are contacts other than *face to face* encounters. These types of contacts should also be favoured and supported. Indirect contacts, however, should supplement but not replace in-person visits. Usually, exchanging letters is an effective and well-established way of communication between imprisoned people and their families. However, this way of communication is becoming increasingly outdated and unusual nowadays. People talk preferably on the phone or write SMS, MMS and e-mails from their smartphones. Phone calls are usually possible in most prisons, but only mono-directionally, i.e. only when the prisoner calls to the family. Therefore, it would be very useful to improve communication between detainees and their families to enable, under controlled conditions, phone-calls from the outside. In this way children of imprisoned parents could be in control of the decision about when to talk to their parents and prepare themselves for that contact. Some prisons are working on providing prisoners with more-up-to-date means of communication such as Skype calls. As Scharff-Smith and Gampell report, the current scenario of communication technology in European prisons is rapidly changing:

> Very few prisons allow children to phone in to the prison to talk to their parents, although some prison staff in Poland reported that they will facilitate such contact in an emergency. Since April 2010, medium security prisoners in Italy have been able to use mobile phones, thereby facilitating two-way contact between parents and children and, in Denmark, the Prison and Probation Service is currently conducting a trial project installing mobile phones in cells in an open-prison (Scharff-Smith and Gampell 2011).

This update in communication technologies within prisons should be aimed at enabling children with imprisoned parents to communicate with their parents in ways that resemble usual forms of communication.

2.5.6 *'Dangerous' Parents*

In some situations it is necessary to protect children from their parents. For example, this is the case when the parent suffers from significant mental health problems and/or when the child has been a direct victim of parental abuse, violence or negligence. In these situations, the question on how much contact should be maintained is very complex. At the 4th Conference on Parenthood and Detention (Geneva, May 2012)[11] Alain Bouregba, president of Eurochips, suggested to stop asking the question on whether we should or should not support the relationship, depending on the quality of the parent.

The risk of asking this question is that it may cause severe negligence in the social support services. The relational ties upon which the child's development is

---

[11] Conference organized by Carrefour Prison (Relais Enfants Parents Romands).

based are laid down forever. Therefore, what is relevant is not to establish whether the parent is 'good enough' or too 'bad' to be allowed to see his or her children, but to ensure that the child can construct his or her own internal connections with the parent and determine how to support their relationship regardless of external moral evaluation of the parent (Bouregba 2013). Physical support and accompaniment for children during their visits is, in addition to psychological support regarding their internal deliberations, highly needed. These needs, however, should not be based on the 'moral quality' of the parent, but on the internal images that the child is able to build about his or her parents.

2.6 Support for Families

Families can be a source of special support for detainees and a real link with the outside world but they can also be a source of abandonment and breakdown. Although some relationships solidify during incarceration, many relationships weaken to the point that they are no longer important once the detained person is released. This creates a real social problem. Assuming that the main goal of imprisonment is re-socialization, and families are a crucial factor in this re-socialization process, then families are a crucial factor in the achievement of the goals of imprisonment. In this sense, supporting families also means offering a chance to maintain family ties and ensure that rehabilitation is possible.

In contrast, silence and shame have the consequence of creating a sort of additional prison around the families themselves. In many families, the fear of social stigma leads family members to avoid important questions regarding their administrative, financial and social condition, letting their administrative, financial and social problems grow (Ghetti 2000; Rosenberg 2009). For this reason, information and support should be provided. Members of the prison staff report that when detainees perceive that their families have a good understanding of the system they feel reassured because they think that their beloved family is being provided with support and specific help.

2.6.1 Prison Visitor Centres

Worldwide, many NGOs have the aim of supporting families of prisoners. Some of these NGOs, such as *Families Outside* in Scotland, have created helplines for families. Others, such as *SAVN* in Denmark, have organized recreational weekends for the families of prisoners. In France, the association 'Fédération des Relais Enfants Parents' has been active for more than 20 years in this field, organizing activities aimed at improving support.

In the french speaking part of Switzerland, seven visitors centers have been developed, copying the model of the typical Chalet that has been built directly in front of the biggest pre-trial prison in Geneva. The philosophy of this establishment is to inform families who are coming to visit an imprisoned relative and to offer them a warm, welcoming and cosy environment. This service is completely free of charge and allows guests to stay for up to 4 hrs.

Usually, the most urgent need of visitors is the provision of practical information about the prison and the judicial system in force at that institution. This practical information may include how to book a visit, what baggage items are restricted or prohibited in the prison during the visit, how to find a lawyer, and so on. More private and relational questions are also a major concern. Typical questions with this regard include: 'How can I stay with my husband after what he has done? What do I say to my children, to the neighbours, to my colleagues?' Many issues surround the topics of trust, loyalty and guilt. For example, parents of imprisoned children tend to feel a strong sense of guilt and ask themselves what they have done wrong. Similarly, partners of detainees frequently appear to experience regrets or feel they could have prevented the incarceration of their significant other. To these pressing questions, there are no simple answers. However, several strategies can be developed to offer support. Volunteers at REPR are trained to listen carefully and without prejudice to those families. This volunteering activity configures itself as citizens taking charge of other citizens. As shame and guilt are very present feelings among families of imprisoned parents, volunteers at the REPR's Chalet in Geneva, offer them counselling and support on those topics. As a visitor reported:

'Every Friday I come to visit my man in prison, but outside, I said nothing [. . .] I said to everybody, even my own family that my husband is on a trip in a foreign country for his work [. . .] but when I come back from those visits, I am always sad and sometimes angry and I feel so lonely [. . .] In the chalet, I can talk about my feelings, and share my ideas with someone,' said Elise, who's been visiting the Chalet every week for more than a year.

Another good practice example is the program Kids VIP, run by the NGO Pact (Prison Advice & Care Trust), which is a specialist national agency working to improve contacts between children (up to the age of 18) and their imprisoned relatives in the UK. Kids VIP produced a special guide on good practice in order to help organizations to build up prison visitor centres. They also provide training for prison staff and volunteers working directly with children and families of prisoners in the UK.[12]

2.6.2 Helplines and Internet

Some NGOs have created helplines and use online communication systems such as Facebook and other social media to support families of detained persons. In Scotland, *Families Outside* is the only national charity that works solely to support the families of people involved in the criminal justice system. This organisation

---

[12]See http://www.prisonadvice.org.uk. Accessed 17 February 2015.

has a helpline that offers support and practical or general information to families experiencing the imprisonment of one of their members.[13]

When receiving councelling and contacting REPR via helpline or website, it is possible for families to remain anonymous. On Facebook and other social media specific support can be offered to younger people confronted with the incarceration of their parents or partners. These services represent one of the very few channels through which families can share their doubts, angers, and anxiety with other people, and hopefully relieve their feelings. The goal of all these helplines and forums is to help families find their own way of coping with situations that are always unique.

2.7   Conclusion

As Robertson (2012) writes: 'It's hard to find a sense of value if everybody tells you you're not worth anything' said a child of a prisoner (Robertson 2012: 4). Not all children of prisoners will suffer from psychological difficulties, but the mental health risk they present is a public health concern.

2.7.1   Collateral Victims

Families and children of detainees are collateral victims of our penal system, and ignoring them will increase their difficulties. In contrast, offering help and support would help them to better cope with the situation and overcome those difficulties. The provision of help and support is also to be seen as a form of relapse prevention: a prisoner who maintains important bonds with his family and who has been able to maintain his or her parental role is less likely to re-offend. A break-down in family relations is a major cause of difficulties in the rehabilitation process. In his pioneering work, Brodsky (1975) underscored how prisoners who maintained family ties were less recidivist and encountered fewer disciplinary problems within the prison setting (Brodsky 1975). Yet it is up to the childcare professionals, psychologists, paediatricians and educational specialists to evaluate to what extent and in which situations, the relationship between a child and his or her imprisoned parent should be supervised. In a previous study, Holt and Miller (1972), had shown that offenders who had regular, on-going visits were six times less likely to re-enter prison during their first year following release than those who had no visits (Holt and Miller 1972).

At present, further research on the situation of families, the impact of parental detention on children and the impact of the various programs on society is needed.

---

[13] See http://www.familiesoutside.org.uk. Accessed 3 December 2013.

Nonetheless, some promising research is already being carried out. An example of that is, at the European level, the so-called COPING project.[14] In Switzerland, a 3-year project has been recently launched with the aim of defining the needs of prisoners' children and evaluating the quality of the programs organized so far.

The complex situation faced by children of imprisoned parents, in which they experience social and psychological difficulties and distress without being responsible for that situation, is concisely captured by the slogan 'Not my crime, still my sentence', which was the slogan of the European campaign for the rights prisoners' children in 2012.

The children's right to family life is recognized by the UN Convention in the Declaration on the Rights of the Child, the EU Charter of Fundamental Rights, and other international treaties.[15] However, the implementation and execution of these rights are still difficult to obtain. Without support, many affected children risk experiencing significant psychological difficulties. Yet few countries impose a statutory obligation on prison authorities or other relevant bodies to provide special services for the children of prisoners, and the effects of parental incarceration on children are often not taken into account. Sometimes very simple changes in prison policy could make a parent's sentence less traumatic and punitive for a child.

As Gwénola Ricordeau writes: 'Families want to hold the prisoner in their arms but are afraid to be burdened by him' (Ricordeau 2008).[16] Supporting families of prisoners and bringing them out of the shadows would allow them and the prisoner themselves to better function as full members of our society, even during detention.

References[17]

Ayre, L., Philbrick, K., & Reiss, M. (2006). *Children of imprisoned parents: European perspectives on good practice*. Montrouge: Eurochips.

Bouregba, A. (2013). *Les troubles de la parentalité: approche clinique et socio-éducative*. Paris: Dunod.

Brodsky, S. L. (1975). *Families and friends of men in prison: The uncertain relationship*. Boston: DC Heath.

Carmignani, S. (2012). Carcere e formazione. Analisi critica dei progetti di formazione per detenuti in Italia. EL. LE Educazione linguistica. *Language and Education, 1*(2), 379–401.

Carson, E. A., & Golinelli, D. (2013, December 1). Prisoners in 2012. Washington, DC: Bureau of Justice Statistics.

---

[14]For more information about the COPING project please see: http://www.coping-project.eu/.

[15]See the European Network of Ombudsmen for Children, ENOC, www.crin.org/enoc. Accessed 11 March 2013.

[16]In the original French: 'Les familles ont envie de serrer le détenu dans leur bras mais ont peur de l'avoir sur les bras.'

[17]*Find out more through specific websites linked to the topic of this chapter.*

Comfort, M., Grinstead, O., McCartney, K., Bourgois, P., & Knight, K. (2005). "You can't do nothing in this damn place": Sex and intimacy among couples with an incarcerated male partner. *Journal of Sex Research, 42*(1), 3–12.

Crépin, C. (2000). Les détenus et leur famille: les effets de l'incarcération. *Recherches et prévisions, 61*, 92–94.

DeFina, R. H., & Hannon, L. (2010). The impact of adult incarceration on child poverty: A county-level analysis, 1995–2007. *The Prison Journal, 90*, 377–396.

Dolto, F. (2012). *La cause des adolescents*. Paris: Robert Laffont.

Dubéchot, P., Fronteau, A., & Le Quéau, P. (2000). La prison bouleverse la vie des familles de détenus. *CRÉDOC–Consommation et Modes de Vie, 143*.

Eddy, J. M., & Poehlmann, J. (2010). *Children of incarcerated parents: A handbook for researchers and practitioners*. Washington, DC: ERIC.

Ghetti, C. (2000). *Carcere e famiglia: gli aspetti del disagio*. Milano: Caritas Italia-na-Fondazione Zancan, La rete spezzata, Feltrinelli.

Guerino, P., Harrison, P. M., & Sabol, W. J. (2011). *Prisoners in 2010*. Washington, DC: Bureau of Justice Statistics.

Holt, N., & Miller, D. (1972). *Explorations in inmate-family relationships*. Sacramento: California Department of Corrections.

King, D. (2002). *Parents, children and prison: Effects of parental imprisonment on children*. New York: New York University Press.

Martinez, D. J. (2006). Informal helping mechanisms: Conceptual issues in family support of reentry of former prisoners. *Journal of Offender Rehabilitation, 44*, 23–37.

Murray, J., & Farrington, D. P. (2005). Parental imprisonment: Effects on boys' antisocial behaviour and delinquency through the life-course. *Journal of Child Psychology and Psychiatry, 46*(12), 1269–1278.

Murray, J., & Farrington, D. P. (2008). The effects of parental imprisonment on children. *Crime and Justice, 37*, 133–206.

Nelson, M., Dees, P., & Allen, C. (1999). The first month out. *Post-37*.

Office, S. F. S. (2010). *Prisons, pre-trial detention: Data, indicators*. QUNO Office, Geneva.

Ricordeau, G. (2008). *Les détenus et leurs proches: solidarités et sentiments à l'ombre des murs*. Paris: Autrement.

Robertson, O. (2012). *Collateral convicts: Children of incarcerated parents*. Recommendations and good practice from the UN committee on the rights of the child day of general discussion.

Rosenberg, J. (2009). *Children need dads too: Children with fathers in prison*. Human Rights and Refugees Publications, Geneva.

Ross, S., & Skondreas, N. (2000). *Female prisoners: Using imprisonment statistics to understand the place of women in the criminal justice system*. Paper presented at the women in corrections: Staff and clients conference' convened by the Australian Institute of Criminology in conjunction with the Department for Correctional Services South Australia, Adelaide.

Scharff-Smith, P., & Gampell, L. (2011). *Children of imprisoned parents*. University of Ulster and Bambinisenzasbarre, The Danish Institute for Human Rights, Denmark, European Network for Children of Imprisoned Parents. http://childrenofprisoners.eu/wp-content/uploads/2014/01/Full-report-Children-of-Imprisoned-parents.pdf

Sharratt, K. (2014). Children's experiences of contact with imprisoned parents: A comparison between four European countries. *European Journal of Criminology, 11*, 760–775.

Chapter 3
Death in Custody: Towards an International Framework for Investigation and Prevention

Gloria Gaggioli and Bernice S. Elger

Abstract Deaths in custody warrant scrutiny, not only because they might be due to torture, abuse and inadequate medical care, but also because they pose challenges for detaining authorities. It is a widely overlooked problem that in many prisons deaths are frequent and most of them are considered 'normal' or 'natural' and not necessarily investigated while some of them were preventable. The lack of guidance to health care workers or international personnel in the field as to how to proceed in cases of deaths in custody is one of the reasons why investigations into deaths in custody are not conducted or are ineffective. In light of this real and persistent problem, a multidisciplinary research project on the legal, medical and forensic aspects of investigating deaths in custody has been carried out between 2008 and 2013 by the University Centre for Legal Medicine of Geneva and Lausanne, the Geneva Academy of International Humanitarian Law and Human Rights, the University of Bern, the International Centre for Prison Studies (King's College London) and the ICRC. As a result of this collaborative effort, the *Guidelines for investigating deaths in custody* have been published by the ICRC in 2013. The latter Guidelines fill an important gap by offering practical guidance to detaining authorities, investigating authorities, humanitarian agencies and others on the standards and procedures to be followed when a death occurs in custody. This chapter presents the background, content and usefulness of the Guidelines after having discussed some of the key medical and legal issues related to death in custody such as: how to define deaths in custody? What are the most prevalent causes of deaths in custody? What is the legal framework pertaining to the prevention and investigation of deaths in custody? How to investigate and prevent deaths in custody?

G. Gaggioli (✉)
Faculty of Law, University of Geneva, Boulevard du Pont-d'Arve 40, 1205 Genève, Switzerland
e-mail: gloria.gaggioli@unige.ch

B.S. Elger
Institute for Biomedical Ethics, University of Basel, Bernoullistrasse 28, 4056 Basel, Switzerland
e-mail: b.elger@unibas.ch

© Springer Science+Business Media Dordrecht 2017
B.S. Elger et al. (eds.), *Emerging Issues in Prison Health*,
DOI 10.1007/978-94-017-7558-8_3

3.1 Death in Custody: Various Definitions

Existing soft law and guidelines define 'death in custody' in various ways. Differences exist, first, with respect to the places that are considered as 'custody'. According to the definition used 'custody' might narrowly refer to police custody (Aasebo et al. 2003; Atanasijevic et al. 2007; Best et al. 2006; Bhana 2003) or more widely include other forms of detention (Okoye et al. 1999). More rarely, death in custody studies include not only deaths in certain places, but also deaths that occur 'during an interaction between a law enforcement officer (on or off duty) and a suspect' (Koehler et al. 2003). In international soft law instruments, only the United Nations Rules for the Protection of Juveniles Deprived of their Liberty provide a definition: 'The deprivation of liberty means any form of detention or imprisonment or the placement of a person in a public or private custodial setting, from which this person is not permitted to leave at will, by order of any judicial, administrative or other public authority' (United Nations 1990).

Second, some jurisdictions and researchers include only deaths, which occur before release (Fazel and Benning 2006; Fruehwald et al. 2004; O'Driscoll et al. 2007), others include also the timeframe after release during which deaths are still considered as 'deaths in custody' (Schmidt et al. 1999). In addition, mortality studies have been carried out among the population of those imprisoned during a defined period of several years. Mortality data were analyzed for this group independently from the fact whether prisoner remained in prison or were released (Kariminia et al. 2007b). Others have investigated deaths occurring during the first weeks or months after release from prison (Binswanger et al. 2007; Bird and Hutchinson 2003; Harding-Pink 1990; Kariminia et al. 2007c; Pratt et al. 2006). A third way of analyzing the subject could be to include the presence or absence of a cause related to custody as part of the definition. This means that deaths that are not influenced by the fact that a person is in custody are excluded, such as natural or 'expected' deaths that occur in custody. This definition is problematic because natural deaths, i.e. deaths caused by a natural disease during imprisonment, could still be caused by the incarceration if the disease could have been cured outside the prison and deaths have been caused by the lack of adequate treatment in the detention facility. In spite of the difficulties to define the influence of imprisonment and which deaths may be reasonably to be expected and which not, a similar definition based on what seems 'natural' or 'expected' is used by studies that examine in particular unexpected deaths in custody (Tiainen and Penttila 1986).

In the case of a death that occurs a long time after imprisonment, the cause might still be related to the prison stay, such as in a case where a detainee has contracted a resistant tuberculosis strain during incarceration. Of course, the longer the timeframe, the more difficult it becomes to establish and prove a causal relationship. Therefore it is not surprising that the longest period in international soft law for the timeframe to be included in the definition of deaths in custody is 6 months following release from prison. This is the case in Rule 57 of the United Nations Rules for the Protection of Juveniles Deprived of their Liberty (United Nations 1990).

It is obvious that the distinct definitions of death in custody in different studies make a comparison of data stemming from different prisons or countries very difficult.

In the present chapter, the definition adopted includes all deaths that occur during any form of detention where a person is not permitted to leave at will. More precisely,

> Custody is considered to begin from the moment a person is apprehended, arrested or otherwise deprived of his or her liberty by agents of the State, or by agents of any other public or private entity or organization, including in particular correctional or medical institutions or security companies, operating within the jurisdiction of that State. It includes, notably, detention or imprisonment, or any other placement of a person in a public or private custodial setting that he or she is not permitted to leave at will. It ends when a person is free to leave and is no longer under the effective control of State agents, or of agents of a public or private entity or organization, including in particular correctional or medical institutions, or security companies, operating within the jurisdiction of that State. (International Committee of the Red Cross (ICRC) Guidelines on Deaths in Custody, 2013, p.8).

Deaths occurring after this period may still be in a causal relationship with detention. They are called deaths related to custody.

3.2 Prevalence and Causes of Deaths in Custody[1]

Causes of death in custody vary significantly according to the regions where prisons are situated. A very important factor is the availability of resources for water, food, hygiene and health care in a country globally and the relative amount of resources dedicated to prisons. In several regions of the sub-Saharan Africa, prisoners still die today of starvation (Alexander 2009) and of diseases caused by the lack of vitamins (Ahoua et al. 2007; de Montmollin et al. 2002). Lack of health care, in particular for the numerous HIV infected prisoners, is also an important cause for deaths in African prisons and represents a 'double sentence'. The lack of health care transforms the prison stay into a 'death sentence' for many AIDS patients (Alderman 1991; Simooya and Sanjobo 2006).

Lack of ventilation and of efficient treatment strategies is a cause for deaths in custody in Eastern Europe, especially in countries of the former Soviet Union, where multi-resistant strains of tuberculosis are highly prevalent (Nechaeva et al. 2005; Shukshin 2006). In Eastern Europe, a significant number of deaths could be avoided that are presently due to high levels of mental illness and infectious diseases for which treatment exists, but is, for various reasons, not sufficiently made available in prisons (Bobrik et al. 2005; Yerokhin et al. 2001).

---

[1] In the ICRC Guidelines for Investigating Deaths in Custody, the definition adopted is relatively restrictive, see ICRC Guidelines on Deaths in Custody, 2013, p.8.

Lack of health care is also a cause of avoidable deaths in the United States (US). This concerns somatic as well as psychiatric diseases. Insufficient diagnosis and treatment of hypertension in young offenders (Wang et al. 2009), untreated heart attacks (Thomas 2005), unavailable defibrillators (Roessler et al. 2007), as well as under-treatment of substance abuse disorders and their related health care problems (Fiscella et al. 2004) have been reported to contribute to an (over)mortality in detention facilities in the US. Indeed, although the benefit, including prevention of deaths, of methadone treatment for heroin addicts has been shown (Brugal et al. 2005; Kimber et al. 2010) and that cost-benefit analysis speaks in favor of methadone treatments in prison (Warren et al. 2006), in many states in the US, but also in many prisons in Europe, methadone is not part of routine treatment, in part because knowledge about this treatment is not sufficient (Springer and Bruce 2008).

Numerous studies in the US and many other countries have shown that insufficient prevention and treatment for drug addicts causes not only avoidable deaths from overdose in prison, but in particular a significant increase of deaths during the first 2 weeks after release from prison (Binswanger et al. 2007; Bird and Hutchinson 2003; Farrell and Marsden 2008; Harding-Pink 1990; Krinsky et al. 2009; Seaman et al. 1998).

Insufficient risk reduction strategies as well as unavailable treatment for hepatitis C is also a concern in the US and causes a significant amount of avoidable deaths (Harzke et al. 2009). Since about 40 % of prisoners in US detention facilities are infected it is not surprising that hepatitis C infection contributed to the cause of death in 15 % of chronic liver disease and/or cirrhosis deaths, 33 % of liver cancer deaths, 81 % of hepatitis B deaths, and 7 % of HIV deaths (Baillargeon et al. 2004, 2009b; Hunt and Saab 2009).

Moreover, unavailability of HIV treatment in prisons is causing deaths among US prisoners (Baillargeon et al. 1999, 2000). Access to clinical trials with new HIV medication in prison is one of the factors that has motivated an Institute of Medicine (IOM) commission to propose a revision of federal law in the US concerning the regulation of research ethics (Elger and Spaulding 2006; Gostin 2007; Gostin et al. 2006).

Finally, studies in the US have shown that 'contracting out', i.e. the transfer of the responsibility of prison health care to private companies increases mortality (Bedard and Frech 2009).

Although in many European countries and in Australia concerns exist also about the quality of somatic health care (Freckelton 2009), the majority of avoidable deaths in these countries are due to inadequately treated psychiatric disease (Sailas et al. 2006), especially resulting in suicide (Bell 1999; Blaauw et al. 1997a; Bourgoin 1993; Cox and Skegg 1993; Fazel et al. 2005; Fruehwald et al. 2000, 2003; O'Driscoll et al. 2007). Suicide is also a frequent cause for deaths among US prisoners (Baillargeon et al. 2009a, Hayes 1999, 2005).

Prevention of suicide in prison does not follow international standards (ECHR 2008; Smith et al. 2008). Apart from relative lack of psychiatric care in prison, separation policies (the isolation of detainees) are clearly an important contributing factor to the high suicide rate in prison (Camilleri and McArthur 2008; Champion

2009; Martire and Larney 2010). Suicide rates are also increased in recently released prisoners compared to the general population (James 2006; Stewart et al. 2004; Verger et al. 2003).

Finally, causes of death due to torture or violence caused by third persons are less well documented in the medical literature. As far as (possibly proportional) violence during arrest is concerned, more and more recent studies show that a sizable percentage of deaths are linked to particular arrest measures, such as tasers (Ho et al. 2009; Jauchem 2010; Lee et al. 2009; Vilke et al. 2009) and restraints (Dickson and Pollanen 2009; Hollins 2010). Restraints are an important contributing factor to a disease entity called 'excited delirium'. This syndrome may result in death, which is probably among other things caused by positional asphyxia (Das et al. 2009; Grant et al. 2009) and restraints (Otahbachi et al. 2010).

Disproportional violence is more difficult to prove in scientific studies. Homicide has been identified as the cause for 5 % of deaths in US detention recently (Kim et al. 2007). In Iraq, the cause of death in prison was not clear in 44 % of analysed cases; in the remaining cases, the majority of deaths in prisons were due to untreated or insufficiently treated infectious diseases (Khaji 2009). Deaths in prisons related to disproportional violence and to lack of health care have also been reported from Afghanistan (Allen et al. 2006).

3.3 Deaths in Custody as Violations of Human Rights and/or Humanitarian Law

International human rights and humanitarian law stipulate that prisoners have the right to be treated humanely and not to be arbitrarily deprived of their life. These fundamental obligations, applicable both in peacetime and wartime situations, implies negative and positive obligations for detaining authorities (Gaggioli and Kolb 2007a, b; Gaggioli 2013).

As regards negative obligations, it is self-evident that summary executions of detainees are absolutely prohibited.[2] The same can be said concerning torture or any other form of cruel, inhuman, or degrading treatment.[3] In brief, any form of coercion against detainees is prohibited even for interrogation purposes (Gaeta 2004). Not only States will be considered as responsible on the international level for this kind

---

[2]See, art. 6 of the International Covenant on Civil and Political Rights (ICCPR); art. 2 of the European Convention on Human Rights (ECHR); art. 4 of the American Convention on Human Rights (ACHR), art. 4 of the African Charter on Human and Peoples' Rights (AfCHPR); art. 3 common to the four Geneva Conventions (GC); art. 12 GCI, 12 GCII, 13GCIII, 32 GCIV; art. 75§2 Additional Protocol I to the Geneva Conventions (API); art. 4§2a Additional Protocol II to the Geneva Conventions (APII).

[3]See, art. 7 ICCPR; art. 3 ECHR; art. 5§2 ACHR; art. 5 AfCHPR; art. 3 common to the four GC; art. 12 GCI, 12 GCII, 17GCIII, 32 GCIV; art. 75§2 API; art. 4§2a APII.

of violations but the perpetrators may be held criminally responsible at the national and international level (see International Criminal Court (ICC) Statute, arts. 6–8).

State responsibility can also be incurred if detaining authorities failed to take positive steps, which may have prevented the death of a detainee. There are numerous decisions and recommendations from universal and regional human rights bodies like the European Court of Human Rights (ECtHR) as well as a growing body of soft law (Elger 2008c), which indicate that inadequate health care, lack of hygiene and insufficient nutrition can lead to a violation of the prohibition of inhumane and degrading treatment.[4]

Inadequate health care, lack of hygiene and insufficient nutrition can be the cause of increased mortality and so called 'natural' deaths in custody, although they are clearly related to inadequate conditions of custody (Elger 2008a, b). If death is the consequence of inadequate detention conditions, the right to life can be considered as violated as well.[5] International humanitarian law (IHL) also provides many detailed rules regarding the treatment of persons deprived of their liberty in connection with an armed conflict, including the obligation to provide adequate food and water, medical attention etc.[6]

Detaining authorities are indeed vested with a particular role of guarantor and must take all measures, which can be reasonably expected from them to protect the life of the persons they guard. These measures must also include those to ensure the security of detainees from 'external' threats, which comprise the obligation to protect detainees against other inmates' violence, against suicides, against external attacks/threats (fire, bombings etc.), and against violence by third actors in the context of extraditions or other removals for instance.[7] In rare cases, the lack of positive measures to protect the life of detainees may even lead to the commission of an international crime and thus lead to the individual criminal responsibility of the persons in charge of the detainees. The act of intentionally and 'deliberately inflicting on [a national, ethnical, racial or religious] group conditions of life calculated to bring about its physical destruction in whole or in part' is an act of genocide' (see ICC Statute, art. 6c).

---

[4]See among many others: Mukong vs. Cameroon, Human Rights Committee, comm. 458/1991; Kalashnikov vs. Russia, ECtHR, 15.7.2002; Juvenile Reeducation Institute vs. Paraguay, Inter-American Court of Human Rights (IACtHR), 2.9.2004.

[5]See among many others: Titiahongo vs. Cameroon, Human Rights Committee, 26.10.2007; Ahmet Özkan vs. Turkey, ECtHR, 6.4.2004; Ximenes-Lopes vs. Brazil, IACtHR, 04.07.2006.

[6]See, Third Geneva Convention, arts 21–81; Fourth Geneva Convention, arts 79–135; Additional Protocol I, art. 75 API; Additional Protocol II, arts. 4 and 5.

[7]E.g. Paul and Audrey Edwards vs. United Kingdom, ECtHR, 14.3.2002 (violence among detainees); Barbato et al. vs. Uruguay, Human Rights Committee, 21.10.1982 (suicide); Juvenile Reeducation Institute vs. Paraguay, IACtHR, 2.9.04 (fire); Haitian interdiction vs. United States of America, Inter-American Commission on Human Rights, 13.3.1997 (repatriation).

States have moreover also post-mortem obligations. Whenever a person dies in custody, an investigation must be conducted.[8] This is an immediate (*ex officio*) obligation of the State and it does not depend on an action from the relatives of the detainee who died. The investigation has not always to be a criminal one. In case of apparently natural death, an administrative investigation may be enough.[9] In any case, the investigation must be conducted by an impartial and independent body. It must be initiated and conducted thoroughly and diligently. It must also be conducted with the participation of the next of kin of the deceased person and include some element of public scrutiny. In cases of suspicious deaths possibly involving a violation of the right to life, an investigation should include notably a thorough collection and analysis of all relevant physical and documentary evidence, statements from witnesses and a proper autopsy (see 'Minnesota Protocol').

The international legal basis of the obligation to investigate can be found in human rights treaties as part of judicial guarantees (right to an effective remedy essentially). Regarding deaths in custody, the obligation to investigate is also intrinsically linked with the right to life. Human rights bodies have consistently underlined that in order to effectively guarantee the right to life it is necessary to comply with the obligation to investigate suspicious deaths.[10] Therefore the absence, or inadequacy, of an investigation into the death of a detainee may amount to a violation of the right to life under its procedural aspect.

In times of armed conflict, international humanitarian law treaties, like the 1949 Geneva Conventions and its additional Protocol I from 1977, do also provide for the obligation to investigate suspicious deaths, or deaths the cause of which is unknown, of prisoners of war and of civilian internees (GCIV, art. 121 GCIII and art. 131). The obligation to investigate is also implicit in the obligation to prosecute grave breaches.[11] It would indeed be impossible to prosecute war criminals without conducting a proper investigation first. It should be recalled that the willful killing of detainees, like prisoners of war or civilian internees, is a war crime. The obligation to investigate war crimes is also considered as part of customary law for international and non-international armed conflicts (e.g. Henckaerts and Doswald-Beck 2009).

As a final remark, it may be noted that at the universal level, in parallel to the International Covenant on Civil and Political Rights (ICCPR) and the UN Convention against Torture, the adoption of the International Convention for the Protection of All Persons from Enforced Disappearance (United Nations 2006),

---

[8]E.g. Concluding Observations: United States of America, Human Rights Committee, 15.9.2006, §14; Salman vs. Turkey, ECtHR, 27.6.2000; 'Juvenile Reeducation Institute' vs. Paraguay, IACtHR, 2.9.2004.

[9]E.g. Balci vs. Turkey, ECtHR, 17.2.2009, §34.

[10]See, General Comment n°6: Right to Life (article 6); Human Rights Committee, 1982, §3 (implicit in the obligation to prosecute); McCann v. United Kingdom, ECtHR, 27.09.1995; Myrna Mack Chang v. Guatemala, IACtHR, 25.11.2003.

[11]See, GCIV, Arts. 49, 50/50, 51/129, 130/146 and 147; API. arts. 11, 85 and 86.

which entered into force in December 2010, is a major landmark for the purpose of establishing a comprehensive framework for preventing and investigating death in custody.

3.4   How to Investigate Deaths in Custody? The Need for Clear and Realistic Guidance

Deaths in custody warrant scrutiny (Allen et al. 2006), not only because they might be due to torture, abuse and inadequate medical care, but also because they pose challenges for detaining authorities (Gaeta 2004, 2008). Any death in custody can lead to accusations stemming from family members and human rights organizations. In several countries, especially from the Northern hemisphere, guidelines on death in custody exist that range from advice to nurses about resuscitation (South Worcestershire Primary Care Trust NHS 2005) to guidelines about the investigation and prevention of deaths in incarcerated aborigines populations (Biles 1988; Spencer 1989) to general guidelines from Amnesty International on the documentation of situations where deaths are suspected to have resulted from torture (Amnesty International and Council for the Development of Social Science Research in Africa 2000). In some cases – where events take place in highly mediatized places and torture is suspected – deaths in custody are getting particular attention (Okie 2005). It is instead a widely overlooked problem that in many prisons deaths are frequent (Fazel and Benning 2006) and most of them are considered 'normal' or 'natural' (Grant et al. 2007) because (1) there are no external signs of violence, (2) there are other health related reasons that seem obvious and (3) time, guidelines and material is lacking to advise health care workers or international personnel on the spot how to proceed in such cases.

In light of this real and persistent problem, the ICRC launched an initiative in 2008 to develop a set of concise guidelines for its field staff, other humanitarian workers, detaining authorities and other stakeholders to clarify the basic considerations in cases of deaths in custody, from the management of the scene to disposal of remains and prevention (Gaggioli and Elger 2010). These guidelines were adopted in 2013 and aim at filling an important gap since there is so far no other international document offering practical guidance on the standards and procedures to be followed when a death occurs in custody. Existing guidelines such as the Minnesota and the Istanbul Protocols cover the subjects of suspected extra-judicial executions, arbitrary or illegal killings, and the documentation of torture. This is insufficient for the vast majority of deaths in custody worldwide. These deaths are attributed to natural causes such as illnesses or suicide related to psychiatric disease (Kariminia et al. 2005, 2007a, b, c). However, as explained above, death in this context could still be classified as inhuman and degrading treatment if it is due to inadequate medical treatment (Kariminia et al. 2007a; O'Driscoll et al. 2007) and lack of hygiene or nutrition. Indeed, decisions of the European Court of Human Rights and reports from the European Committee for the Prevention of Torture (CPT) have considered adverse events from these conditions a violation of article 3 (inhuman and degrading treatment) of the European Convention of Human Rights or, depending on the outcome, a violation of article 2 (right to life, Gaggioli and Kolb 2007a, b; Gaggioli 2013). Appropriate investigation is the prerequisite for adequate preventive measures and is required by international law. Unfortunately, these deaths occur often in places where there is no forensic capacity to carry out a thorough investigation.

In addition, experience from forensic specialists who have been later solicited by families to investigate death that was declared as 'due to natural causes' by authorities, shows not only that it is often trying if not impossible to conclude from second autopsies (Rainio et al. 2001), but also that in the absence of scientifically valid standards for death investigation it will be difficult to convince family members that no evidence for unnatural causes has been detected (Brandt-Casadevall et al. 2003). This underlines the immense importance of immediate, independent and scientifically sound investigation of so called natural deaths in custody and calls for further reflections about impartiality (Lorin de la Grandmaison et al. 2006) and a reinforced role of organizations such as the ICRC or the CPT.

The efficiency of humanitarian workers in this field relies on a detailed knowledge of, first, existing local, national and international policies and legal provisions defining the framework of investigation and prevention. Second, it is clear that it is not always easy for humanitarian workers to tackle at present the investigation of deaths in custody, as shown by the subsequent qualitative interview study. The results show the difficulties expressed by experts and stakeholders involved in the investigation of deaths in custody (Ruiz et al. 2014; Wangmo et al. 2014). Empirical research has been an indispensable basis for consecutive reflection on appropriate procedures and guidelines. While it is important to develop minimum standards not only for developed countries (Aghayev et al. 2008; Hiss and Kahana 1996; Thali et al. 2003; United Nations 1991), but also in other settings, studies from developing countries on deaths in custody are scarce. Indeed, in humanitarian settings (Stöver et al. 2003) death inquiry and forensic evaluations will often need to be done by ordinary health care workers and other non-specialists (Brandt-Casadevall et al. 2003). The latter need to have access to appropriate guidelines where basic tasks of the interaction with authorities as well as of the investigation are described. They need to know in particular the simple but efficient technical means that have been determined by forensic specialists, together with practical strategies and their legal enforcement in order to obtain access to the death scene without delay and the best possible assistance by forensic expert. Details for such assistance need to be developed and could for example consist in a form of 'tele-autopsies' or 'tele-death-investigation' (a forensic expert could comment on the scene through telecommunication systems, analogue to 'telemedicine' where medical information is transferred via telephone, the Internet or other networks for the purpose of consulting, and sometimes remote medical procedures or examinations).

3.5 An International Research Project About Death in Custody

The drafting of the guidelines was preceded by several steps that took place between 2008 and 2013 and were part of a larger research project carried out by the University Centre for Legal Medicine of Geneva and Lausanne, the Geneva Academy of International Humanitarian Law and Human Rights, the University of Bern, the International Centre for Prison Studies (King's College London) and the ICRC.

First, a comprehensive review of the scientific literature and of other documents on the investigation of deaths in custody in the fields of forensic medicine, medical ethics and health law has been conducted. The aim of this analytical part was to gather and summarize the existing knowledge on how extensively deaths in custody have been examined in the past. It was shown that reports exist predominantly from countries from North America, Australia and certain countries in Europe (Blaauw et al. 1997a, b; Frost and Hanzlick 1988; Fruehwald et al. 2000; Thomson and McDonald 1993; Wobeser et al. 2002). The existing literature was examined with respect to the following questions: what were the causes for the deaths in different regions (Steffee et al. 1995; Steinhauser 1997), what were the problems encountered during death investigations, how adequate and extensive were the forensic death investigations carried out, and what was the role of medical and/or forensic intervention (Blaauw et al. 1997b; Cordner 1991; Franklin 2000; Segest 1987) as well as strategies of prevention and their outcome.

Second, questionnaires were developed and transmitted to prison administrators and other experts to be used in order to collect information from local authorities about their official or usual practice to investigate deaths in custody. Questionnaires were distributed at conferences organized for prison administrators and other personnel working in places of detention. They were instructed to contact their hierarchy of relevant local authorities in the field and ask them whether they could provide any written official local guidance or whether they could describe any instructions they have received on how to approach deaths in custody. These questions did not interfere with confidentiality policies because the answers did not consider identifiable institutions or persons, but only existing official policy and past anonymized cases. Anonymity of results was granted on the individual level (expert or prison administrator involved) as well as on the country or regional level if required by the statutes of the institution. Before carrying out the empirical parts of the project, the protocol was submitted to the president competent Ethics Committee of the core team in Geneva and obtained permission to realize the questionnaire[12] and interview study.

---

[12] The results of the mixed questionnaires (quantitative and qualitative parts) were published as part of the Master thesis at the faculty of medicine at the University of Geneva,. Jehan, M. (2011). Death in custody: how is it investigated? A semi-qualitative study on the challenges and best practices experienced by prison administrators following the death of an inmate.

Third, based on the results from the first two steps, semi-directive interview guides and a semi-structured questionnaire have been developed. Interviews were held over the phone or in person with more than 2 dozens of experts, including CPT members, ICRC delegates, prison administrators, forensic experts and NGO members working in the field. The objective was to identify and to compare existing strategies for investigation of deaths in custody and to evaluate knowledge of interviewees about legal frameworks for deaths investigation, as well as about adequate forensic techniques, including basic forensic techniques feasible in countries where local forensic specialists are not available (Ruiz et al. 2014; Wangmo et al. 2014).

Fourth, information obtained from the previous steps were analyzed and summarized in short presentations. A conference funded by the European Science Foundation took place in Linköping, Sweden, in May 2010, where the existing preliminary results as well as propositions for international guidelines about the investigation and prevention of deaths in custody have been presented to several types of specialists who work in the fields of deaths in custody worldwide.

The experts, who gathered in Linköping, were from the fields of criminology, law and human rights with experience in prisons. They have been identified through a selection method known as purposive sampling. Purposive sampling is often used in qualitative studies to identify groups of people with specific characteristics or circumstances (Dornan and Bundy 2004; Patton 2002). In purposive sampling, researchers choose study participants based on identified variables under consideration. In the present case, experts were selected based on previous ICRC and CPT experience, networks from the International Centre for Prison Studies (King's College London), publications and a snow-ball system, in order to reflect a wide range of professional backgrounds and regions. During the conference, experts discussed among others the appropriate and most efficient ways to obtain independent death investigations in custody.

Another group of experts came from the field of forensic science. Experts were chosen based on their experience in humanitarian work and death investigations in prison. They were selected according to purposive sampling as described above with particular support from the International Academy of Legal Medicine and included forensic scientists from several Eastern European countries, as well as Asia and North America. The experts were confronted with the collected information and draft guidelines and discussed minimal techniques permitting efficient death investigation, with a special focus on countries with limited forensic infrastructure.

Those various steps and expert consultations provided the background for the final guidelines work.[13]

---

[13] See, Bollmann, M., Coyle, A., Gaggioli, G., Hight, I., Khamis, S., Mutzenberg, P., . . . Elger B. (2013). Guidelines for investigating deaths in custody. International Committee of the Red Cross. http://www.icrc.org/eng/resources/documents/publication/p4126.htm.

3.6   The ICRC Guidelines for Investigating Deaths in Custody

On the basis of the aforementioned background research on the legal, medical and forensic aspects of investigating deaths in custody and collaborative efforts of the various institutions listed above, guidelines for investigating deaths in custody have been published by the ICRC in 2013.[14]

The objective of the guidelines is to provide guidance to detaining authorities, investigating authorities, practitioners and others as to the standards to be followed when a death occurs in custody. The guidelines are based not only on international binding rules but also on best practices and domestic policies. They can be used for drafting or updating domestic legislations, for providing training and building capacity as well as for ascertaining whether authorities have respected minimum standards and procedures following a death in custody. Although non-state actors – and in particular organized non-state armed groups in the context of a non-international armed conflict – also have an obligation to investigate suspicious deaths occurring in custody, the guidelines deal exclusively with the obligations of States to investigate deaths in custody.

The guidelines are the result of a truly interdisciplinary endeavor as they develop both legal aspects pertaining to the investigation of deaths in custody and medical/forensic aspects.

As per the legal aspects, the guidelines recall that there is, first, a strong obligation to respect and protect the life of persons deprived of their liberty that is derived from both the fundamental human right to life and from international humanitarian law; and, second, that these bodies of law provide for a specific obligation to investigate deaths in custody. The guidelines then elaborate on the basic standards for investigating deaths in custody that can be derived from soft law instruments, such as the 'Minnesota Protocol', and international jurisprudence. These standards are essential to determine the criteria that should be fulfilled to consider an investigation as effective. In particular, and as highlighted above, any investigation should be thorough, undertaken *ex officio*, independent and impartial and should include some degree of public scrutiny as well as involve the next of kin. Moreover, in suspected cases of arbitrary deprivation of life, the investigation should include all relevant physical and documentary evidence, statements from witnesses and a proper autopsy. The legal section is complemented by two annexes. A first one provides eight key elements flowing from the duty to conduct effective investigations into deaths in custody and a second one summarizes the main international legal sources of the obligation to investigate.

As regards the medical and forensic section, the guidelines include precise and concrete guidance based on international standards and good practice as to how the death scene and dead body should be managed. This guidance makes clear

---

[14] See, http://www.icrc.org/eng/resources/documents/publication/p4126.htm.

that a precise contingency plan and proper training of the detaining authorities are essential to ensure that deaths in custody are investigated properly. The nature, scope and basic principles that should govern post-mortem examination are developed. A section also clarifies how investigators should involve and inform the next of kin of the deceased in accordance with the principle of humanity. The medical and forensic section is also complemented by two annexes. A first one provides a simplified checklist for the management of the death scene and a second one elaborates a detailed checklist for conducting autopsies.

Lastly, an entire section is dedicated to the prevention of deaths in custody. Investigations play not only a role in elucidating the death of a person but also in preventing further similar deaths by providing the necessary information to address possible direct or indirect root causes. The guidelines provide an overview of factors that increase the likelihood of deaths in custody (i.e. inadequate conditions of detention; insufficient access to health care; insufficient contact with the family; inadequate safeguards against suicide and arbitrary deprivation of life, torture and other forms of ill-treatment) and recommend some measures for preventing deaths in custody.

3.7 Conclusions

Deaths in custody need to be studied more systematically, according to similar definitions and methods in different countries in the world in order to be able to compare efficiently mortality causes and rates between various countries and to describe adequately trends and changes within the same region over time. The ability to prove unlawful violence as cause of death as well as inadequate health care, nutrition and hygiene depends on the quality and timeliness of forensic. The impartiality, effectiveness and timeliness of a judicial investigation have not only a significant influence on truth finding, but also on the prevention of deaths in custody. The persistence of avoidable deaths in police custody in Germany (Heide et al. 2009a, 2010) has been attributed among other things to the lack of efficient prosecution due to the high standard of proof required in the German justice system. According to Heide et al. (2009a, b, 2010) therefore no incentives exist for policemen in Germany to use available adequate preventive measures, such as conducting arrested persons more often to the hospital when in doubt about their health (Heide et al. 2009b).

It is to be hoped that the ICRC Guidelines for investigating deaths in custody will also be helpful to forensic practitioners, prison administrators and the justice system and will constitute an incentive to adapt or even develop appropriate domestic standards and procedures. However, domestic standards and procedures are only a first step, and they need to be accompanied by clear messages enshrined in public policy. As Frater has recently put it: 'Deaths in custody. The risk factors are known, but public policy is lagging behind (Frater 2008, p. 845f).'

References

Aasebo, W., Erikssen, J., & Jonsbu, J. (2003). Deaths in police custody. *Tidsskrift for den Norske Lægeforening, 123*(8), 1066–1067.

Aghayev, E., Christe, A., Sonnenschein, M., Yen, K., Jackowski, C., Thali, M. J., Dirnhofer, R., & Vock, P. (2008). Postmortem imaging of blunt chest trauma using CT and MRI: Comparison with autopsy. *Journal of Thoracic Imaging, 23*(1), 20–27.

Ahoua, L., Etienne, W., Fermon, F., Godain, G., Brown, V., Kadjo, K., Bouaffou, K., Legros, D., & Guerin, P. J. (2007). Outbreak of beriberi in a prison in Cote d'Ivoire. *Food and Nutrition Bulletin, 28*(3), 283–290.

Alderman, C. (1991). HIV in prison: A double life sentence? *Nursing Standard, 5*(39), 18–19.

Alexander, J. (2009). Death and disease in Zimbabwe's prisons. *Lancet, 373*(9668), 995–996.

Allen, S. A., Rich, J. D., Bux, R. C., Farbenblum, B., Berns, M., & Rubenstein, L. (2006). Deaths of detainees in the custody of US forces in Iraq and Afghanistan from 2002 to 2005. *Medscape General Medicine, 8*(4), 46.

Amnesty International, & Council for the Development of Social Science Research in Africa. (2000). *Monitoring and investigating death in custody.* http://www.codesria.org/IMG/pdf/custody.pdf?888/d9d00caa8d1bcad28137c3e6b20a0ed9cec8a3a1. Accessed 29 April 2015.

Atanasijevic, T., Nikolic, S., & Popovic, V. (2007). Death during police interrogation – Case report. *Srpski Arhiv za Celokupno Lekarstvo, 135*(5–6), 342–345.

Baillargeon, J., Borucki, M., Williamson, J., & Dunn, K. (1999). Determinants of HIV-related survival among Texas prison inmates. *AIDS Patient Care and STDs, 13*(6), 355–361.

Baillargeon, J., Grady, J., & Borucki, M. J. (2000). Immunologic predictors of HIV-related survival among Texas prison inmates. *AIDS Patient Care and STDs, 14*(4), 183–187.

Baillargeon, J., Black, S. A., Leach, C. T., Jenson, H., Pulvino, J., Bradshaw, P., & Murray, O. (2004). The infectious disease profile of Texas prison inmates. *Preventive Medicine, 38*(5), 607–612.

Baillargeon, J., Penn, J. V., Thomas, C. R., Temple, J. R., Baillargeon, G., & Murray, O. J. (2009a). Psychiatric disorders and suicide in the nation's largest state prison system. *Journal of the American Academy of Psychiatry and the Law, 37*(2), 188–193.

Baillargeon, J., Snyder, N., Soloway, R. D., Paar, D., Baillargeon, G., Spaulding, A. C., Pollock, B. H., Arcari, C. M., Williams, B. A., & Raimer, B. G. (2009b). Hepatocellular carcinoma prevalence and mortality in a male state prison population. *Public Health Report, 124*(1), 120–126.

Bedard, K., & Frech, H. E., 3rd. (2009). Prison health care: Is contracting out healthy? *Health Economies, 18*(11), 1248–1260.

Bell, D. (1999). Ethical issues in the prevention of suicide in prison. *Australian and New Zealand Journal of Psychiatry, 33*(5), 723–728.

Best, D., Havis, S., Payne-James, J. J., & Stark, M. M. (2006). Near miss incidents in police custody suites in London in 2003: A feasibility study. *Journal of Clinical Forensic Medicine, 13*(2), 60–64.

Bhana, B. D. (2003). Custody-related deaths in Durban, South Africa 1998–2000. *American Journal of Forensic Medicine and Pathology, 24*(2), 202–207.

Biles, D. (1988). *Draft guidelines for the prevention of aboriginal deaths in custody.* http://www.aic.gov.au/publications/other/dic1992/2.html. Accessed Mar 2008.

Binswanger, I. A., Stern, M. F., Deyo, R. A., Heagerty, P. J., Cheadle, A., Elmore, J. G., & Koepsell, T. D. (2007). Release from prison – A high risk of death for former inmates. *New England Journal of Medicine, 356*(2), 157–165.

Bird, S. M., & Hutchinson, S. J. (2003). Male drugs-related deaths in the fortnight after release from prison: Scotland, 1996–99. *Addiction, 98*(2), 185–190.

Blaauw, E., Kerkhof, A. D., & Vermunt, R. (1997a). Suicides and other deaths in police custody. *Suicide Life Threat Behaviour, 27*(2), 153–163.

Blaauw, E., Vermunt, R., & Kerkhof, A. D. (1997b). Deaths and medical attention in police custody. *Medical Law Review, 16*(3), 593–606.

Bobrik, A., Danishevski, K., Eroshina, K., & McKee, M. (2005). Prison health in Russia: The larger picture. *Journal of Public Health Policy, 26*(1), 30–59.

Bollmann, M., Coyle, A., Gaggioli, G., Hight, I., Khamis, S., Mutzenberg, P., Tidball-Binz, M., Gaeta, P., & Elger B. (2013). *Guidelines for investigating deaths in custody. International committee of the red cross.* http://www.icrc.org/eng/resources/documents/publication/p4126. htm. Accessed 29 Apr 2015.

Bourgoin, N. (1993). Mortality due to suicide in prison. *Revue d'Épidémiologie et de Santé Publique, 41*(2), 146–154.

Brandt-Casadevall, C., Krompecher, T., Giroud, C., & Mangin, P. (2003). A case of suicide disguised as natural death. *Science and Justice, 43*(1), 41–43.

Brugal, M. T., Domingo-Salvany, A., Puig, R., Barrio, G., Garcia de Olalla, P., & de la Fuente, L. (2005). Evaluating the impact of methadone maintenance programmes on mortality due to overdose and aids in a cohort of heroin users in Spain. *Addiction, 100*(7), 981–989.

Camilleri, P., & McArthur, M. (2008). Suicidal behaviour in prisons: Learning from Australian and international experiences. *International Journal of Law and Psychiatry, 31*(4), 297–307.

Champion, M. K. (2009). Commentary: Doing time in maximum security – The pains of separation. *Journal of the American Academy of Psychiatry and the Law, 37*(2), 194–200.

Chetail, V. (2006). Le Comité des Nations Unies contre la torture et l'expulsion des étrangers: dix ans de jurisprudence. *Revue Suisse de Droit International et Européen, 26*(1), 63–104.

Chetail, V. (2007). Le Conseil des droits de l'homme des Nations Unies: l'An I de la réforme. *Refugee Survey Quarterly, 26*(4), 104–130.

Cordner, S. (1991). The royal commission into aboriginal deaths in custody. Aspects of medical interest. *Medical Journal of Australia, 155*(11–12), 812–818.

Cox, B., & Skegg, K. (1993). Contagious suicide in prisons and police cells. *Journal of Epidemiolgy and Community Health, 47*(1), 69–72.

Das, C. K., Ceelen, M., Dorn, T., & de Jong, J. T. (2009). Cocaine use and sudden death: Excited delirium syndrome. *Nederlands Tijdschrift voor Geneeskunde, 153*, B299.

De Montmollin, D., MacPhail, J., McMahon, J., & Coninx, R. (2002). Outbreak of beri-beri in a prison in West Africa. *Tropical Doctor, 32*(4), 234–236.

Dickson, B. C., & Pollanen, M. S. (2009). Fatal thromboembolic disease: A risk in physically restrained psychiatric patients. *Journal of Forensic and Legal Medicine, 16*(5), 284–286.

Dornan, T., & Bundy, C. (2004). What can experience add to early medical education? Consensus survey. *British Medical Journal, 329*, 834.

ECHR. (2008). *European Court of Human Rights.* Renolde vs. France; Decision 16.10.2008: http://www.menschenrechte.ac.at/docs/08_5/08_5_14. Accessed Aprl 2009.

Elger, B. S. (2008a). Medical ethics in correctional healthcare: An international comparison of guidelines. *Journal of Clinical Ethics, 19*(3), 234–248.

Elger, B. S. (2008b). Research involving prisoners: Consensus and controversies in international and European regulations. *Bioethics, 22*(4), 224–238.

Elger, B. S. (2008c). Towards equivalent health care of prisoners: European soft law and public health policy in Geneva. *Journal of Public Health Policy, 29*(2), 192–206.

Elger, B. S., & Spaulding, A. (2006). Research on prisoners – A comparison between the IOM Committee recommendations and European regulations. *Bioethics, 24*(1), 1–13.

Farrell, M., & Marsden, J. (2008). Acute risk of drug-related death among newly released prisoners in England and Wales. *Addiction, 103*(2), 251–255.

Fazel, S., & Benning, R. (2006). Natural deaths in male prisoners: A 20-year mortality study. *European Journal of Public Health, 16*(4), 441–444.

Fazel, S., Benning, R., & Danesh, J. (2005). Suicides in male prisoners in England and Wales, 1978–2003. *Lancet, 366*(9493), 1301–1302.

Fiscella, K., Pless, N., Meldrum, S., & Fiscella, P. (2004). Benign neglect or neglected abuse: Drug and alcohol withdrawal in U.S. jails. *Journal of Law, Medicine and Ethics, 32*(1), 129–136.

Franklin, P. (2000). The medical management in police custody of alcohol dependent detained persons. *Journal of Clinical Forensic Medicine, 7*(4), 201–203.

Frater, A. (2008). Deaths in custody. *British Medical Journal, 336*(7649), 845–846.

Freckelton, I. (2009). Safeguarding the vulnerable in custody. *Journal of Law and Medicine, 17*(2), 157–164.

Frost, R., & Hanzlick, R. (1988). Deaths in custody. Atlanta City Jail and Fulton County Jail, 1974–1985. *American Journal of Forensic Medicine and Pathology, 9*(3), 207–211.

Fruehwald, S., Frottier, P., Eher, R., Gutierrez, K., & Ritter, K. (2000). Prison suicides in Austria, 1975–1997. *Suicide Life Threat Behaviour, 30*(4), 360–369.

Fruehwald, S., Frottier, P., Matschnig, T., & Eher, R. (2003). The relevance of suicidal behaviour in jail and prison suicides. *European Psychiatry, 18*(4), 161–165.

Fruehwald, S., Frottier, P., Matschnig, T., Koenig, F., Lehr, S., & Eher, R. (2004). Do monthly or seasonal variations exist in suicides in a high-risk setting? *Psychiatry Research, 121*(3), 263–269.

Gaeta, P. (1995). Cancellazione dal ruolo e trattamenti disumani e degradanti: il caso Hurtado davanti alla Corte europea dei diritti dell'uomo (Striking a case off the list and inhumane and degrading treatment: The Hurtado case before the European Court of Human Rights). *Rivista di diritto internazionale*, 149–167.

Gaeta, P. (2004). May necessity be available as a defence for torture in the interrogation of suspected terrorists? *Journal of International Criminal Justice, 2*(3), 785–794.

Gaeta, P. (2007). Tortura (Torture). In M. Flores (Ed.), *Dizionario dei diritti umani*. Torino, I: Utet.

Gaeta, P. (2008). On what conditions can a state be held responsible for genocide? *European Journal of International Law, 18*(4), 631–648.

Gaggioli, G. (2013). *L'influence mutuelle entre les droits de l'homme et le droit international humanitaire à la lumière du droit à la vie*. Paris: Pedone.

Gaggioli, G., & Elger, B. (2010, April). Investigating deaths in custody: The need for guidelines. *The Correctional Psychologist, 42*(2), 17–18.

Gaggioli, G., & Kolb, R. (2007a). A right to life in armed conflicts? The contribution of the European Court of Human Rights. *Israel Yearbook on Human Rights, 37*, 115–163.

Gaggioli, G., & Kolb, R. (2007b). L'apport de la Cour Européenne des Droits de l'Homme au droit international humanitaire en matière de droit à la vie. *Revue Suisse de Droit International et Européen, 1*, 3–11.

Gostin, L. O. (2007). Biomedical research involving prisoners: Ethical values and legal regulation. *Journal of the American Medical Association, 297*(7), 737–740.

Gostin, L. O., Vanchieri, C., Pope, A., & IOM Committee on Ethical Considerations for Revisions to DHHS Regulations for Protection of Prisoners Involved in Research. (2006). *Ethical considerations for research involving prisoners*. Washington, DC: The National Academies Press.

Grant, J. R., Southall, P. E., Fowler, D. R., Mealey, J., Thomas, E. J., & Kinlock, T. W. (2007). Death in custody: A historical analysis. *Journal of Forensic Science, 52*(5), 1177–1181.

Grant, J. R., Southall, P. E., Mealey, J., Scott, S. R., & Fowler, D. R. (2009). Excited delirium deaths in custody: Past and present. *American Journal of Forensic Medicine and Pathology, 30*(1), 1–5.

Harding-Pink, D. (1990). Mortality following release from prison. *Medicine, Science, and the Law, 30*(1), 12–16.

Harzke, A. J., Baillargeon, J. G., Goodman, K. J., & Pruitt, S. L. (2009). Liver cancer mortality among male prison inmates in Texas, 1992–2003. *Preventive Medicine, 48*(6), 588–592.

Hayes, L. M. (1999). Suicide in adult correctional facilities: Key ingredients to prevention and overcoming the obstacles. *Journal of Law, Medicine and Ethics, 27*(3), 260–268.

Hayes, L. M. (2005). Juvenile suicide in confinement in the United States results from a national survey. *Crisis, 26*(3), 146–148.

Heide, S., Kleiber, M., Hanke, S., & Stiller, D. (2009a). Deaths in German police custody. *European Journal of Public Health, 19*(6), 597–601.

Heide, S., Kleiber, M., & Stiller, D. (2009b). Legal consequences in cases of deaths in police custody. *Gesundheitswesen, 71*(4), 226–231.

Heide, S., Henn, V., Kleiber, M., & Dressler, J. (2010). An avoidable death in police custody? *American Journal of Forensic Medicine and Pathology, 31*(3), 261–263.

Henckaerts, J. M., & Doswald-Beck, L. (2009). *Customary international humanitarian law, vol. I: Rules*. Cambridge: Cambridge University Press.

Hiss, J., & Kahana, T. (1996). Medicolegal investigation of death in custody: A postmortem procedure for detection of blunt force injuries. *American Journal of Forensic Medicine and Pathology, 17*(4), 312–314.

Ho, J. D., Dawes, D. M., Heegaard, W. G., Calkins, H. G., Moscati, R. M., & Miner, J. R. (2009). Absence of electrocardiographic change after prolonged application of a conducted electrical weapon in physically exhausted adults. *Journal Emergency Medicine, 41*(5), 466–472.

Hollins, L. (2010). Managing the risks of physical intervention: Developing a more inclusive approach. *Journal of Psychiatric and Mental Health Nursing, 17*(4), 369–376.

Hunt, D. R., & Saab, S. (2009). Viral hepatitis in incarcerated adults: A medical and public health concern. *American Journal of Gastroenterology, 104*(4), 1024–1031.

James, J. S. (2006). Prisoner death rate very high immediately after release. *AIDS Treatment News, 421*, 5–6.

Jauchem, J. R. (2010). Deaths in custody: Are some due to electronic control devices (including TASER devices) or excited delirium. *Journal of Forensic and Legal Medicine, 17*(1), 1–7.

Kariminia, A., Butler, T. G., Corben, S. P., Kaldor, J. M., Levy, M. H., & Law, M. (2005). Mortality among prisoners: How accurate is the Australian National Death Index? *Australian and New Zealand Journal of Public Health, 29*(6), 572–575.

Kariminia, A., Butler, T. G., Corben, S. P., Levy, M. H., Grant, L., Kaldor, J. M., & Law, M. G. (2007a). Extreme cause-specific mortality in a cohort of adult prisoners – 1988 to 2002: A data-linkage study. *International Journal of Epidemiology, 36*(2), 310–316.

Kariminia, A., Law, M. G., Butler, T. G., Corben, S. P., Levy, M. H., Kaldor, J. M., & Grant, L. (2007b). Factors associated with mortality in a cohort of Australian prisoners. *European Journal of Epidemiology, 22*(7), 417–428.

Kariminia, A., Law, M. G., Butler, T. G., Levy, M. H., Corben, S. P., Kaldor, J. M., & Grant, L. (2007c). Suicide risk among recently released prisoners in New South Wales, Australia. *Medical Journal of Australia, 187*(7), 387–390.

Khaji, A. (2009). Mortality of the Iranian ex-prisoners of war in Iraqi detention camps (1980–1990). *Archives of Iranian Medicine, 12*(2), 140–144.

Kim, S., Ting, A., Puisis, M., Rodriguez, S., Benson, R., Mennella, C., & Davis, F. (2007). Deaths in the Cook County jail: 10-year report, 1995–2004. *Journal of Urban Health, 84*(1), 70–84.

Kimber, J., Copeland, L., Hickman, M., Macleod, J., McKenzie, J., De Angelis, D., & Robertson, J. R. (2010). Survival and cessation in injecting drug users: Prospective observational study of outcomes and effect of opiate substitution treatment. *British Medical Journal, 341*, c3172.

Koehler, S. A., Weiss, H., Songer, T. J., Rozin, L., Shakir, A., Ladham, S., Omalu, B., Dominick, J., & Wecht, C. H. (2003). Deaths among criminal suspects, law enforcement officers, civilians, and prison inmates: A coroner-based study. *American Journal of Forensic Medicine and Pathology, 24*(4), 334–338.

Krinsky, C. S., Lathrop, S. L., Brown, P., & Nolte, K. B. (2009). Drugs, detention, and death: A study of the mortality of recently released prisoners. *American Journal of Forensic Medicine and Pathology, 30*(1), 6–9.

Lee, B. K., Vittinghoff, E., Whiteman, D., Park, M., Lau, L. L., & Tseng, Z. H. (2009). Relation of Taser (electrical stun gun) deployment to increase in in-custody sudden deaths. *American Journal of Cardiology, 103*(6), 877–880.

Lorin de la Grandmaison, G., Durigon, M., Moutel, G., & Herve, C. (2006). The international criminal tribunal for the former Yugoslavia (ICTY) and the forensic pathologist: Ethical considerations. *Medicine, Science, and the Law, 46*(3), 208–212.

Martire, K. A., & Larney, S. (2010). An estimate of the number of inmate separations from Australian prisons 2000/01 and 2005/06. *Australian and New Zealand Journal of Public Health, 34*(3), 255–257.

Nechaeva, O. B., Skachkova, E. I., & Podymova, A. S. (2005). Tuberculosis in the prisons of the Sverdlovsk Region. *Problemy Tuberkuleza i Bolezneĭ Legkikh, 5,* 16–18.

O'Driscoll, C., Samuels, A., & Zacka, M. (2007). Suicide in New South Wales Prisons, 1995–2005: Towards a better understanding. *Australian and New Zealand Journal of Psychiatry, 41*(6), 519–524.

Okie, S. (2005). Glimpses of Guantanamo – Medical ethics and the war on terror. *New England Journal of Medicine, 353*(24), 2529–2534.

Okoye, M., Kimmerle, E. H., & Reinhard, K. (1999). An analysis and report of custodial deaths in Nebraska, USA. *Journal of Clinical Forensic Medicine, 6*(2), 77–84.

Otahbachi, M., Cevik, C., Bagdure, S., & Nugent, K. (2010). Excited delirium, restraints, and unexpected death: A review of pathogenesis. *American Journal of Forensic Medicine and Pathology, 31*(2), 107–112.

Patton, M. Q. (2002). *Qualitative research and evaluation methods* (3rd ed.). Newbury Park: Sage Publications.

Pratt, D., Piper, M., Appleby, L., Webb, R., & Shaw, J. (2006). Suicide in recently released prisoners: A population-based cohort study. *Lancet, 368*(9530), 119–123.

Rainio, J., Lalu, K., & Penttila, A. (2001). Independent forensic autopsies in an armed conflict: Investigation of the victims from Racak, Kosovo. *Forensic Science International, 116*(2–3), 171–185.

Roessler, B., Fleischhackl, R., Fleischhackl, S., Singer, F., Mittlboeck, M., Fachberger, J., Malzer, R., Koller, A., Lang, G., Foitik, G., & Hoerauf, K. (2007). Death in correctional facilities: Opportunities for automated external defibrillation. *Resuscitation, 73*(3), 389–393.

Ruiz, G., Wangmo, T., Mutzenberg, P., Sinclair, J., & Elger, B. S. (2014). Understanding death in custody: A case for a comprehensive definition. *Journal of Bioethical Inquiry, 11*(3), 387–398.

Sailas, E. S., Feodoroff, B., Lindberg, N. C., Virkkunen, M. E., Sund, R., & Wahlbeck, K. (2006). The mortality of young offenders sentenced to prison and its association with psychiatric disorders: A register study. *European Journal of Public Health, 16*(2), 193–197.

Schmidt, P., Dettmeyer, R., Musshoff, F., & Madea, B. (1999). Sudden death after release from police detention. *Archiv für Kriminologie, 203*(5–6), 138–146.

Seaman, S. R., Brettle, R. P., & Gore, S. M. (1998). Mortality from overdose among injecting drug users recently released from prison: Database linkage study. *British Medical Journal, 316*(7129), 426–428.

Segest, E. (1987). Police custody: Deaths and medical attention. *Journal of Forensic Science, 32*(6), 1694–1703.

Shukshin, A. (2006). Tough measures in Russian prisons slow spread of TB. *Bulletin of the World Health Organization, 84*(4), 265–266.

Simooya, O. O., & Sanjobo, N. (2006). HIV/AIDS is still a double sentence in prisons. *British Medical Journal, 332*(7533), 119–120.

Smith, A. R., Witte, T. K., Teale, N. E., King, S. L., Bender, T. W., & Joiner, T. E. (2008). Revisiting impulsivity in suicide: Implications for civil liability of third parties. *Behaviour, Science and Law, 26*(6), 779–797.

South Worcestershire Primary Care Trust NHS. (2005). *Death in custody guidelines*. http://www.hacw.nhs.uk/EasySiteWeb/GatewayLink.aspx?alId=8860. Accessed May 2015.

Spencer, J. (1989). Aboriginal deaths in custody. *Australian and New Zealand Journal Psychiatry, 23*(2), 164–165.

Springer, S. A., & Bruce, R. D. (2008). A pilot survey of attitudes and knowledge about opioid substitution therapy for HIV-infected prisoners. *Journal of Opioid Management, 4*(2), 81–86.

Steffee, C. H., Lantz, P. E., Flannagan, L. M., Thompson, R. L., & Jason, D. R. (1995). Oleoresin capsicum (pepper) spray and in-custody deaths. *American Journal of Forensic Medicine and Pathology, 16*(3), 185–192.

Steinhauser, A. (1997). Analysis of cause of death in Central Rhine prisons and in police detention centers 1949 to 1990. *Archiv für Kriminologie, 199*(3–4), 88–96.

Stewart, L. M., Henderson, C. J., Hobbs, M. S., Ridout, S. C., & Knuiman, M. W. (2004). Risk of death in prisoners after release from jail. *Australian and New Zealand Journal of Public Health, 28*(1), 32–36.

Stöver, E., Haglund, W. D., & Samuels, M. (2003). Exhumation of mass graves in Iraq: Considerations for forensic investigations, humanitarian needs, and the demands of justice. *Journal of the American Medical Association, 290*(5), 663–666.

Thali, M. J., Braun, M., Wirth, J., Vock, P., & Dirnhofer, R. (2003). 3D surface and body documentation in forensic medicine: 3-D/CAD Photogrammetry merged with 3D radiological scanning. *Journal of Forensic Science, 48*(6), 1356–1365.

Thomas, S. P. (2005). From the editor – Harrowing deaths in prison. *Issues of Mental Health Nursing, 26*(6), 559–560.

Thomson, N. J., & McDonald, D. (1993). Australian deaths in custody, 1980–1989. 1. Relative risks of aborigines and non-aborigines. *Medical Journal of Australia, 159*(9), 577–581.

United Nations. (1990). *United Nations rules for the protection of juveniles deprived of their liberty.* Adopted by General Assembly resolution 45/113 of 14 December 1990. http://www.un.org/documents/ga/res/45/a45r113.htm. Accessed 29 Aprl 2015.

United Nations. (1991). *United Nations manual on the effective prevention and investigation of extra-legal, arbitrary and summary executions ('Minnesota Protocol'),* U.N. Doc. E/ST/CSDHA/.12 (1991). http://www1.umn.edu/humanrts/instree/executioninvestigation-91. html. Accessed 29 Aprl 2015.

United Nations. (2006). *International convention for the protection of all persons from enforced disappearance* (Adopted December 2006 and opened for signature February 2007). http://www.ohchr.org/EN/HRBodies/CED/Pages/ConventionCED.aspx. Accessed Mar 2015.

Verger, P., Rotily, M., Prudhomme, J., & Bird, S. (2003). High mortality rates among inmates during the year following their discharge from a French prison. *Journal Forensic Science, 48*(3), 614–616.

Vilke, G. M., Johnson, W. D., Castillo, E. M., Sloane, C., & Chan, T. C. (2009). Tactical and subject considerations of in-custody deaths proximal to use of conductive energy devices. *American Journal of Forensic Medicine and Pathology, 30*(1), 23–25.

Wang, E. A., Pletcher, M., Lin, F., Vittinghoff, E., Kertesz, S. G., Kiefe, C. I., & Bibbins-Domingo, K. (2009). Incarceration, incident hypertension, and access to health care: Findings from the coronary artery risk development in young adults (CARDIA) study. *Archives of Internal Medicine, 169*(7), 687–693.

Wangmo, T., Ruiz, G., Sinclair, J., & Elger, B. S. (2014). The investigation of deaths in custody: An analysis of problems and prospects. *Journal of Forensic and Legal Medicine, 25*, 30–37.

Warren, E., Viney, R., Shearer, J., Shanahan, M., Wodak, A., & Dolan, K. (2006). Value for money in drug treatment: Economic evaluation of prison methadone. *Drug and Alcohol Dependence, 84*(2), 160–166.

Wobeser, W. L., Datema, J., Bechard, B., & Ford, P. (2002). Causes of death among people in custody in Ontario, 1990–1999. *Canadian Medical Association Journal, 167*(10), 1109–1113.

Yerokhin, V. V., Punga, V. V., & Rybka, L. N. (2001). Tuberculosis in Russia and the problem of multiple drug resistance. *Annals of the New York Academy of Sciences, 953*, 133–137.

Chapter 4
Sudden Deaths in Police Custody (and Other Detention Facilities) – Analysis of Causes and the Need for Prevention

Christoph G. Birngruber, Reinhard B. Dettmeyer, Sönke Janzen, and Bernice S. Elger

Abstract When a suspect or delinquent is taken into custody, the custodian (state authority) has to ensure, that custody is safe for the detainee and fulfills human rights standards. Nevertheless, (sudden) deaths in custody occur, that provoke questions and/or allegations towards the custodian. In these cases, independent (medico-legal) investigations are essential to clarify the circumstances of death and to identify risk-factors that can be considered in prevention campaigns.

'Custody' derives from the Latin word 'custodia', meaning 'guarding' and refers to any type of deprivation of liberty, including police custody and detention in prisons or closed mental institutions. Even if the reasons for taking a person into custody differ in the cases of a suspect, a sentenced delinquent or a person suffering from a severe mental disorder, these types of case all have one thing in common: a 'custodian' who is in charge of the execution of the custody. This person has the obligation to ensure a form of detention that is safe for society in the sense of being 'escape-proof' but is also safe for the detainee.

For the latter reason, cases of death in custody often provoke questions and, if it comes to the worst, allegations towards those who are in charge of the custody. In these cases, it is important to clarify the circumstances and the causes of death in order to identify unnatural deaths and where applicable, work on strategies to prevent situations or change operational procedures that may cause risks to the life of a detained person.

C.G. Birngruber (✉) • R.B. Dettmeyer • S. Janzen
Department of Legal Medicine, University of Giessen, Frankfurter Str. 58,
35392 Giessen, Germany
e-mail: christoph.birngruber@forens.med.uni-giessen.de

B.S. Elger
Institute for Biomedical Ethics, University of Basel, Bernoullistrasse 28, 4056 Basel, Switzerland
e-mail: b.elger@unibas.ch

© Springer Science+Business Media Dordrecht 2017
B.S. Elger et al. (eds.), *Emerging Issues in Prison Health*,
DOI 10.1007/978-94-017-7558-8_4

55

This chapter will examine the situation of deaths in custody with a particular focus on sudden deaths in police custody, where the risk of positional asphyxia in agitated detainees is high. Findings are relevant also for psychiatric settings, where restraint-related fatalities can contribute to avoidable deaths. After a more general introduction, we will review and present data on cases of deaths in police custody and prisons[1] in Germany and other countries, including the US and Canada. We will critically review the data and discuss the emerging lessons for professionals in contact with detainees.

4.1 Introduction

In many countries, forensic pathologists are involved to clarify the cause of suspect deaths. Diligent forensic investigation includes autopsy and, if necessary, further investigations such as toxicological analysis and microscopic examination of samples from all internal organs are undertaken. This approach enables investigators to distinguish between natural deaths, for example due to myocardial infarctions, and non-natural deaths, including suicides, homicides and drug-induced deaths. At the end of the forensic investigation process, the provision of a written expert opinion, which is requested by the prosecuting attorney, is mandatory.

It is important that a state involves independent forensic pathologists for all cases of death in custody in order to clarify the cause of death. Indeed, in the context of custody, any death should be considered suspect, first because of the high risk of non-natural deaths in this setting, but also because the context of detention imposes an obligation to investigate on the 'custodian'. In addition, public authorities have an obligation to implement prevention strategies, which include maintaining the quality of training for policemen and the provision of adequate medical care for detainees.

The reasons why someone is taken into custody can be very diverse and different kinds of custody can be applied depending on the circumstances that lead to a person's arrest. In the majority of detention cases, a person is first taken into police custody e.g. to allow identification or further immediate investigation after a criminal offence. If an individual's behaviour suggests that he/she is an acute danger to him-/ herself or others, temporary custody can be indicated to prevent any harm. When dealing with injured persons, individuals that show symptoms of excited delirium or arrestees who might be under the influence of alcohol or other drugs, the executing forces (i.e. the police) need to ensure, that the detainee can be monitored during custody to prevent a critical state of health. If physical or mental fitness is unclear, medical advice has to be sought. Depending on the circumstances,

---

[1] The term 'prison' is used to refer to any kind of detention facility including remand prisons or jails and penitentiaries. The terms 'prisoner' and 'detainee' are used interchangeably, indicating any person detained in a prison.

temporary custody in a medical institution is indicated. This is the case if a person is suicidal or suffers from any other serious mental disorder that causes increased risk of self-harm or unpredictably aggressive behaviour. Typically acute psychotic disease or any other severe emotional disturbance pose a risk to the detainee him- or herself and/or to third parties and such symptoms are therefore a reason to transfer the detainee to an appropriate mental health facility. In the psychiatric hospital, mental-health professionals are in charge of assessing the arrestee's state of mind and advising executive authorities whether acute therapy could lead to reconstitution or whether a long-term therapy in custody is required. When found guilty, the punishment may consist in a fine or a prison sentence, depending on the offence. In the latter case, the question arises of whether the detainee is physically and/or mentally fit to undergo detention and a doctor needs to certify fitness after proper examination if there is any doubt.

No matter what kind of detention is applied, the detaining authorities have the obligation to ensure that it is safe. Detention has to be safe for society in the sense of being 'escape-proof' but at the same time must be safe for the detainee, i.e. it should not cause any serious health impairment. Nevertheless, cases of death in custody occur. At a basic level, this is not surprising as deaths also occur outside custody and death in custody would be expected to occur statistically at a predictable rate, depending on the life expectancy and pre-incarceration morbidity of the detained population.

However, in many countries the death rate in prison exceeds the number predicted using population statistics (Frater 2008; Rabe 2012; Wobeser et al. 2002).

As the custodian is in charge of the safety of custody, cases of death in custody will provoke questions and, if it comes to the worst, allegations about law enforcement authorities and possibly about involved health care personnel. Severe diseases that could explain the death are often not known particularly in cases, where the detainee's medical history is not available. In all cases of death in custody, further investigation is required. This is obvious if death occurs unexpectedly within a short period of time. However, thorough forensic investigation is also important in cases where natural death is the most likely explanation. Indeed, even a detainee who has pre-existing health problems might die due to non-natural causes which may represent human rights violations. Some examples of frequent violations are various kinds of violence, inadequate conditions of detention and inadequate medical treatment in prison. It is important to clarify the circumstances and the causes of death with utmost diligence in order to identify natural and unnatural deaths and, where applicable, work on strategies to prevent situations or change operational procedures that may pose risks to the life and health of a detained person.

In the following section, the situation of sudden deaths will be explored based on the available literature. Particularly revealing data from Germany and other countries such as the US and Canada on deaths (1) in police custody and (2) in prisons will be reviewed and additional new data from Germany will be presented. A particular focus will be on the risk of positional asphyxia in detainees suffering from excited delirium. The underlying theme is that the analysis of relevant data from Germany and selected other countries provides important and valuable insights for prison authorities, the police, health care personnel and forensic pathologists worldwide regarding the causes of deaths in custody.

4.2 Sudden Deaths in Police Custody

Most deaths that occur in police custody can be classified as sudden. When a person needs to be taken into custody, police officers (or law enforcement personnel in general) often have to deal with resistance on behalf of the detainee. In these cases, acts of de-escalation, including 'talking down' the person and the use of a conciliatory body language would be the preferred method to facilitate the immobilization and arrest of the delinquent. However, people cannot always be reached by verbal communication, particularly if they are highly agitated and/or under the influence of alcohol and drugs. Under these circumstances, the use of physical force to permit arrest of the respective person may be justified.

In the context of sudden deaths that occur during or shortly after the act of taking highly agitated individuals into custody, the phenomenon of 'positional asphyxia' (physical restraint, restraint asphyxia) must be mentioned (Chan et al. 1998; Dettmeyer et al. 2009; O'Halloran and Lewman 1993; Otahbachi et al. 2010; Reay and Howard 1999; Stratton et al. 2001). Although its pathogenesis still needs further research and the phenomenon itself is not free of controversy, various cases of sudden deaths related to 'positional asphyxia', which in the past were mainly reported from the US, show similarities that justify the description of a typical pattern or distinct pathology (O'Halloran and Frank 2000).

Almost all individuals who later died from physical restraint showed highly agitated and sometimes extremely aggressive behaviour and did not reply to any attempts at verbal communication. This state of mind – so-called 'excited delirium' – was either caused by drugs like amphetamine and cocaine or high doses of alcohol, or is due to pre-existing mental illnesses such as schizophrenia with an acute psychotic episode. The assistance of several police officers using physical force is necessary to get the agitated person under control. The restraint often takes place in a prone position and requires considerable time because of the individual's fierce resistance and endurance. In addition to handcuffs (which are used to attach the individual's wrists together behind his back), 'hobble' restraint (binding together the individual's ankles) and 'hogtie' restraint (connecting the hobbled ankles to the bound wrists) are often used for fixation. At this point, the individual is exhausted from the previous fight with the policemen and his or her body is still in a state of alert, both of which are associated with high blood-concentrations of adrenalin and lactate and a fast heartbeat and breathing rate. At the same time, the prone position and restraint impair the individual's breathing activity and prevent recovery. This maximal amount of stress to the body can lead to circulatory arrest and, if not detected fast enough, to irreversible brain damage or to the death of the restrained person.

O'Halloran and Stratton examined cases of sudden death related to restraint and were able to determine several risk factors including excited delirium, hobble restraint and the use of stimulant drugs. Furthermore, autopsies revealed chronic diseases (including obesity) in more than 50 % of deceased persons. In addition, almost 50 % of the deceased had a history of chronic cocaine use (Stratton et al. 2001). Common elements or risk factors related to the syndrome of restraint asphyxia include: prone restraint with pressure on the upper torso; handcuffing, leg restraint or hogtying; acute psychosis and agitation, which are often induced by stimulant drugs; physical exertion and struggle, and obesity (O'Halloran and Frank 2000).

The mentioned elements were partly present in the majority of case reports from Germany. In one case, the autopsy revealed pre-existing heart damage as an additional risk factor (Ehrlich et al. 1999; Zack et al. 2009).

To prevent cases of sudden death due to restraint-related asphyxia, law enforcement personnel must know the risk factors and try to achieve a reduction of stress for the person who is to be detained (Otahbachi et al. 2010). The practices of hobble or hogtie restraint should be obsolete, as they both constitute risk factors that can be controlled by law enforcement staff. In general, the use of physical force should be reduced to a minimum, and the detainee should be under continuous surveillance to ensure that any loss of consciousness, or pulmonary or cardiac arrest is instantly detected so resuscitation can be attempted.

As an alternative to physical force, the use of so-called non-lethal or less-than-lethal weapons is becoming more and more popular. From the perspective of police officers, the responsible application of these weapons leads to a considerable reduction in injuries during police use-of-force events (MacDonald et al. 2009). However, the safety of these weapons is still discussed as electrical guns such as Tasers can cause life-threatening events. Unpredictable cardiac and mental alterations in people who were Tasered have been reported, as have perforating injuries due to the darts that are employed by the device (Cao et al. 2007; Feeney et al. 2010; Han et al. 2009; Mangus et al. 2008; Multerer et al. 2009). The use of Tasers was considered a potential or contributory cause of death in 27 % of cases of restraint-related sudden death involving persons with excited delirium (Strote and Range-Hutson 2006).

Another situation where policemen are involved and sudden deaths are likely to occur is law enforcement-forced-assisted suicide. The term law enforcement-forced-assisted suicide or 'suicide by cop' describes an incident, in which a suicidal individual provokes police officers to shoot the individual in self-defence or to protect civilians. The individual therefore engages in life-threatening and criminal behaviour with a lethal weapon or what appears to be a lethal weapon toward law enforcement officers or civilians to specifically provoke officers to shoot (Hutson et al. 1998). Strote and Range-Hutson (2006) reviewed files of officer-involved shootings (437 cases) investigated by the Los Angeles County Sheriff's Department from 1987 to 1997. Suicide by cop accounted for 11 % of all officer-involved shootings (46 cases). Ninety-eight percent of the suicidal individuals were male and the median time from arrival of the officers at scene to the time of shooting was 15 min. The weapons displayed consisted of firearms (22 cases), followed by knives, replica firearms and blunt objects. All deaths were classified as homicides by the coroner. The authors conclude that 'suicide by cop' is an actual form of suicide and a phenomenon that law enforcement officers need to be aware of. But even if the situation is recognized by police officers as being an attempt at suicide by cop, the circumstances remain life-threatening for the officers as the firearms used by the suicidal individuals are operative and loaded in most cases. Where attempted, efforts of verbal dissuasion or the use of less lethal weapons was unsuccessful.

To examine more closely the situation of people who have been arrested and find themselves in police custody, Heide and colleagues reviewed all cases of death in German police custody between 1993 and 2003 (Heide et al. 2009). Cases where death was directly related to the process of arrest (e.g. violent arrest), and cases where acutely ill persons had been brought to a hospital prior to their demise were excluded. A total of 128 cases involving persons who died in German police custody remained of which 60 had records that accessible for detailed research. The deceased were male in all but one case and the average age was 41.1 years with age showing a huge variation from under 20 up to 60 years and older. The most frequent cause of death was acute alcoholic intoxication (15 cases), followed by fatal poisoning with medical or illegal drugs and cerebral trauma (11 cases of each) and hanging (8 cases). Furthermore, pneumonia, acute myocardial infarction and myocarditis all caused death more than once. Overall, the manner of death was determined as unnatural in 80 % and natural in 20 % of cases.

A total of 33 of the 60 cases revealed some kind of failure by police officers, including failure to seek medical attention (14 cases), deficiencies in monitoring detainees (12 cases) and insufficient body searches, e.g. with the consequence that one person was able to self-administer a lethal overdose of methadone while in custody. In 23 cases, the detainees had been seen by a physician in order to determine their fitness for detention. In 15 of these cases the analysis detected deficiencies in the physicians' approach, including failure to diagnose a significant pathology and failure to admit a person to an inpatient medical facility.

Retrospective assessment showed that death would very probably have been unavoidable in 16 of the 60 cases including cases of natural death, where the detainees had not been under medical treatment before and did not present with detectable symptoms while in custody. Furthermore, not all of the persons who hung themselves exhibited suspicious behaviour prior to their suicide.

Nevertheless, a remarkable number of cases remain in which death would probably have been avoided by transferring detainees to a hospital or by more frequent monitoring. Deficiencies in monitoring and failure to demand a medical examination carried out by a physician in order to determine the detainee's fitness could be in part attributed to the federal system in Germany where legal regulations differ from state to state and are very diverse.

Another fact that must be mentioned is that only 75 of the 128 persons who died in German police custody underwent an autopsy. Although data are not available for all cases because three forensic university institutes did not provide any information, this does not fully explain the huge discrepancy. Considering legal practice in

Germany, one would expect a post mortem in every single case to identify the exact cause of death, especially given the allegations frequently made about policemen or physicians after such deaths.

To compare the number of deaths in police custody in Germany with that in other countries, Heide et al. (2009) calculated a 'death coefficient' by dividing the number of deaths in police custody by the average population in the respective country. Of course it would have been more accurate to correlate the number of deaths with the number of people who were taken into custody during that period, but as the total number of people, who had been taken into custody could not be assessed, the average population was used to achieve an approximate comparison. The 'death coefficient' ranged from 0.14 deaths in custody per one million citizens per year in Germany (period 1993–2003) to 2.02 in Finland (period 1975–1984).

Following the study investigating sudden deaths in custody, Heide et al. (2012) took a close look at medical examination of fitness for police custody in Germany. A total of 3674 medical records from two large German towns were reviewed to evaluate the circumstances, quantity and quality of the medical examinations that had been performed on detainees in police custody. Due to considerable differences in state law and provisions regulating the medical aspects of police custody, there are large differences in practice between federal states in Germany, for instance in respect to surveillance modalities (e.g. monitoring of the detained person) or the reasons for medical consultation. The variation range of the frequency of such examinations in states where statistics are available ranged from 5.5 % in Lower Saxony to 48.3 % in Schleswig-Holstein (not all federal states provide official statistics). According to the reviewed medical records, 90.5 % of the examined persons were male and three-quarters were between 14 and 40 years old. The most frequent indications for assessment of fitness for custody were acute alcoholic intoxication (32.2 %) and substance withdrawal symptoms (20.6 %). Assessment was requested due to trauma in 10.3 % and due to internal diseases in 8.5 % of all cases. In 5.2 % of cases, mental disorders were present and in the remaining cases a physician was called because of other specific or unspecific indications. Overall, only 1462 persons (39.8 %) were found to be unconditionally fit for custody, and in 1855 cases (50.5 %) fitness for custody was declared dependent on certain conditions. These conditions mainly consisted of 'frequent monitoring' (79.8 %) and the advice that the detainee would require reassessment if his/her actual condition deteriorated (52.1 %). A total of 357 detainees (9.7 %) were declared unfit after medical examination, mostly because of mental disorders (25 %), drug withdrawal syndrome (16.2 %), inebriation (14.7 %), alcoholic intoxication (10.3 %) or alcohol withdrawal syndrome (8.8 %).

The authors point out the importance of legal regulation of the medical aspects of police custody in order to clarify the conditions that have to be met in order to mandate medical assessment. Furthermore, on the one hand, the physical assessment must be properly documented and medical advices have to be articulated in a way that is intelligible to police officers, i.e. medical laymen. On the other hand, custody facilities and monitoring measures need to be adequate to guarantee good examination and regular monitoring conditions.

As the results of Heide et al. (2009, 2012) show, the frequency and causes of deaths in police custody vary due to differences in existing regulation and in the availability and quality of medical evaluation and health care for detainees during custody. This is clearly the case for sudden deaths, many of which may be prevented by appropriate procedures for arrest, monitoring and evaluation.

There are also significant regional variations in the number of non-sudden deaths in police custody and prisons, many of which are related to the general availability of medical care in different countries. In developed countries suicide is one of the leading causes of deaths in custody, while in developing countries deaths due to undertreated medical diseases such as AIDS and tuberculosis or lack of adequate nutrition are more frequent (Alexander 2009; Dogra et al. 2008; Frater 2008; de Montmollin et al. 2002).

4.3 Comparing Deaths in Prisons with Deaths in Police Custody

Various studies have found significant differences between the causes and manners of deaths that occurred in police custody and those of deaths that took place in prison.

Wobeser and colleagues reviewed 308 cases of death in custody in Ontario, Canada, between 1990 and 1999 (Wobeser et al. 2002). Data were available for 291 of the 308 cases, and concerned 283 male and 8 female deceased detainees. The review included cases from federal penitentiaries, provincial prisons and police cells. Further data were available that enabled the researchers to evaluate age and circumstances and causes of death.

Of 283 deaths involving men, 59 % (168 cases) were non-natural or violent: suicide by strangulation (90 cases), poisoning (including accidental and intentional overdose, 48 cases) and homicide (16 cases). Natural causes accounted for 41 % (115 cases) of deaths among male prisoners, with cardiovascular disease being the most common (62 cases) and cancer the second most common causes (18 cases). Most of the deaths among male prisoners (48 %) occurred in federal institutions, with 31 % and 21 % respectively occurring in provincial institutions and police cells. Overall, the causes of death differed between institutions. In police cells (which hold people for short stays after their arrest) the cause of death was classified as natural in only 6 cases (compared with 52 violent deaths). In provincial prisons (housing people sentenced to less than 2 years) a total of 42 natural and 46 violent deaths occurred, and in federal penitentiaries (housing people sentenced to 2 or more years) natural deaths (67 cases) were almost as common as those characterized as non-natural (70 cases).

Compared to the non-incarcerated male Canadian population, the risk for male inmates of dying from an unnatural death (suicide, poisoning, homicide) as well as the rate of death from cardiovascular diseases was significantly higher. Among prison inmates, death due to drug overdose was up to 50 times, and suicide by strangulation up to 10 times more common than among Canadian men of a similar age.

In a US study, all cases of death between 1995 and 2004 in a large urban jail in Chicago were reviewed (Kim et al. 2007). During this period, a total of 178 prisoners died. A total mortality rate of 180 per 100.000 inmates was calculated using the average daily census (the average number of detainees registered in prison per day). According to forensic records, the cause of death was infectious or inflammatory illness in 19.7 % and other types of illness in 53.4 % of cases, with heart and cerebrovascular diseases being the main causes of death (28.7 % of all cases). Other causes of death, including suicide, drug overdose and withdrawal, homicide, unintentional injuries, etc. were identified in 27 % of the cases. Assuming, that the manner of death could be classified as natural in cases where death occurred as a consequence of any kind of illness, more than 70 % of all cases would be natural deaths. However, the high rate of deaths due to infectious disease is surprising given the treatment options available today. When the authors of this study examined medical records they found discrepancies between the cause of death as reported by the forensic pathologist and the medical history, pointing towards possible misclassifications. For example, although the final cause of death in one case was reported by the forensic pathologist as being due to heart failure, the medical record showed a history of insufficiently treated bladder infection; the authors suspected that the patient died from sepsis. If deaths due to disease are related to inadequate medical diagnosis and treatment, they may appear 'natural' but still represent a human rights violation, i.e. in the present cases a violation of the prisoner's right to receive health care equivalent to that available to non-incarcerated prisoners (Elger 2008, 2011).

We searched among post mortem records archived between 1975 and 2010 at the Institute of Legal Medicine in Giessen, Germany who died in local prisons and underwent autopsy. We report yet unpublished data (Table 4.1). In total, 60 post-mortem exams were performed; the identified cases concerned only male detainees. It was not possible to identify the exact place of detention from the records. The deceased persons' age ranged between 18 and 69 years (average age: 40 years). In 56.7 % of cases, the inmates died from unnatural causes. In 28 cases, the prisoners committed suicide (hanging: 24 cases, cutting of wrists or of the common carotid artery: 3 cases, intended intoxication: 1 case). Hence, suicide represented 46.7 % of all deaths and 82.4 % of all unnatural deaths. Other unnatural causes of death were drug overdoses and accidents. In 26 cases (43.3 % of all cases) the manner of death was classified as natural with heart and cerebrovascular diseases being the main cause of death in 21 cases (equivalent to 35 % of all cases, and 80.8 % of all natural deaths).

A comparison of the data with three other German studies concerning deaths in custody revealed no significant differences in the leading manner and cause of death. A literature review revealed studies from Bavaria (investigation period: 1945–1974) (Spann et al. 1979), North Rhine-Westphalia (1949–1990) (Steinhäuser 1997) and

Table 4.1 Autopsies of people who died in custody, performed at the department of Legal Medicine in Giessen between 1975 and 2010: 60 cases, all deceased were male

Cause of death	Total	Total (%)
Cardiovascular diseases	17	28.3
Cerebrovascular diseases	4	6.7
Infectious/inflammatory diseases	2	3.3
Other diseases	3	5.0
Natural causes	*26*	*43.3*
Suicide by hanging	24	40.0
Intoxication	5	8.3
Suicidal self-cutting	3	5.0
CO-intoxication	1	1.7
Burns	1	1.7
Non-natural causes	*34*	*56.7*
Total	*60*	*100.0*

a more recent study from Hamburg, investigating the period from 1990 to 2001 (Anders et al. 2003).

The manner of death was non-natural in 62 % (Hamburg) and 63 % (North Rhine-Westphalia) of cases. Suicides, and hanging in particular, accounted for most of the non-natural deaths. In Hamburg, 96 % of all suicides were committed by hanging, and in North Rhine-Westphalia the figure was 98 %. The Bavarian study took into account only suicides in prisons and revealed a total of 86 % cases of hanging among all analysed suicides. The second most frequent non-natural causes of death were drug-related deaths, most of which were cases of acute lethal intoxications. Among the natural causes of death, cardiovascular diseases were most frequent.

4.4   Lessons for Professionals in Contact with Detainees

The reported data are of significant importance for a variety of professionals, including health care personnel, prison administrators, the police, legal professionals, and forensic pathologists. Although the causes and frequencies of deaths are known to vary between countries (Space I and II 2008) the underlying mechanisms relevant for preventive measures are comparable. A significant number of deaths would be avoidable if the involved professionals were able to solve certain types of problems, of which a few will be summarized here. Sudden deaths in police custody or in psychiatric hospitals due to exited delirium can be prevented through adequate training of the detaining agents, who should know how to deal with and decrease agitation in arrestees. Appropriate training and regulation should also be available to educate detaining authorities about the circumstances in which medical examination and transfer to a hospital are indicated.

Many deaths including suicides could be avoided if the conditions of detention were improved to create a healthy environment, and if appropriate resources were made available to screen and treat mentally and physically ill detainees adequately, i.e. to a degree that is equivalent to that provided by the health care available outside prisons, as required by human rights law and conventions ratified by a majority of countries worldwide. Health care personnel, prison guards, the police and legal professionals should be thoroughly educated about international recommendations and states should enact detailed provisions to ensure compliance. This implies that necessary resources be directed to surveillance in police custody, health care for detainees in prison and transfer to hospitals where appropriate (Fazel and Benning 2006).

Another lesson to be learned from the available data is that adequate investigation is in the interest of all stakeholders, including detaining authorities and health professionals. Investigations can help to avoid different kinds of harm, including prisoners becoming ill and dying, but also harm from accusations against professionals. In rich countries, including Germany, Canada and the US, autopsies must be performed after any type of death in custody and appropriate resources must be available for independent forensic examination. This extends to an obligation to examine systematically the medical records of persons who die during detention, as inadequate medical treatment in prison can cause apparently natural deaths.

Professionals working in the context of detention are obligated to provide maximum transparency, to do their best to prevent deaths in custody, and to diligently investigate any deaths that do occur. Fulfilling these obligations is also in their own interests.

References

Alexander, J. (2009). Death and disease in Zimbabwe's prisons. *Lancet, 373*(9668), 995–996.

Anders, S., Tsokos, M., & Püschel, K. (2003). Todesfälle im Gewahrsam. *Rechtsmedizin, 13*(2), 77–81.

Cao, M., Shinbane, J. S., Gillberg, J. M., Saxon, L. A., & Swerdlow, C. D. (2007). Taser-induced rapid ventricular myocardial capture demonstrated by pacemaker intracardiac electrograms. *Journal of Cardiovascular Electrophysiology, 18*(8), 876–879.

Chan, T. C., Vilke, G. M., & Neuman, T. (1998). Reexamination of custody restraint position and positional asphyxia. *The American Journal of Forensic Medicine and Pathology, 19*(3), 201–205.

de Montmollin, D., MacPhail, J., McMahon, J., & Coninx, R. (2002). International Committee of the Red Cross, Geneva, Switzerland. Outbreak of beriberi in a prison in West Africa. *Tropical Doctor, 32*(4), 234–236.

Dettmeyer, R., Preuss, J., & Madea, B. (2009). Lagebedingter Erstickungstod - Positionale Asphyxie - bei polizeilichen Massnahmen. *Kriminalistik, 63*, 161–167.

Dogra, T. D., Bhardwaj, D. N., Sharma, G. A., & Lalwani, S. (2008). Postmortem examination in cases of custodial death in India. *Journal of the Indian Medical Association, 106*(2), 101–106.

Ehrlich, E., Maxeiner, H., & Klug, E. (1999). Plötzlicher Tod bei der polizeilichen Festnahme unter Cocainintoxikation. *Rechtsmedizin, 9*, 73–76.

Elger, B. S. (2008). Towards equivalent health care of prisoners: European soft law and public health policy in Geneva. *Journal of Public Health Policy, 29*(2), 192–206.

Elger, B. S. (2011). Prison medicine, public health policy and ethics: The Geneva experience. *Swiss Medical Weekly, IF 1.8.*

Fazel, S., & Benning, R. (2006). Natural deaths in male prisoners: A 20-year mortality study. *European Journal of Public Health, 16*(4), 441–444.

Feeney, C., Vu, J., & Ani, C. (2010). Acute agitated delirious state associated with Taser exposure. *Journal of the National Medical Association, 102*(12), 1254–1257.

Frater, A. (2008). Deaths in custody. *British Medical Journal, 336*(7649), 845–846.

Han, J. S., Chopra, A., & Carr, D. (2009). Ophthalmic injuries from a TASER. *Canadian Journal of Emergency Medical Care, 11*(1), 90–93.

Heide, S., Kleiber, M., Hanke, S., & Stiller, D. (2009). Deaths in German police custody. *European Journal of Public Health, 19*(6), 597–601.

Heide, S., Stiller, D., Lessig, R., Lautenschlager, C., Birkholz, M., & Fruchtnicht, W. (2012). Medical examination of fitness for police custody in two large German towns. *International Journal of Legal Medicine, 126*(1), 27–35.

Hutson, H. R., Anglin, D., Yarbrough, J., Hardaway, K., Russell, M., Strote, J., Canter, M., & Blum, B. (1998). Suicide by Cop. *Annals of Emergency Medicine, 32*(6), 665–669.

Kim, S., Ting, A., Puisis, M., Rodriguez, S., Benson, R., Mennella, C., & Davis, F. (2007). Deaths in the Cook County jail: 10-year report, 1995–2004. *Journal of Urban Health: Bulletin of the New York Academy of Medicine, 84*(1), 70–84.

MacDonald, J. M., Kaminski, R. J., & Smith, M. R. (2009). The effect of less-lethal weapons on injuries in police use-of-force events. *American Journal of Public Health, 99*(12), 2268–2274.

Mangus, B. E., Shen, L. Y., Helmer, S. D., Maher, J., & Smith, R. S. (2008). Taser and Taser associated injuries: A case series. *The American Surgeon, 74*(9), 862–865.

Multerer, S., Berkenbosch, J. W., Das, B., & Johnsrude, C. (2009). Atrial fibrillation after taser exposure in a previously healthy adolescent. *Pediatric Emergency Care, 25*(12), 851–853.

O'Halloran, R. L., & Frank, J. G. (2000). Asphyxial death during prone restraint revisited: A report of 21 cases. *The American Journal of Forensic Medicine and Pathology, 21*(1), 39–52.

O'Halloran, R. L., & Lewman, L. V. (1993). Restraint asphyxiation in excited delirium. *The American Journal of Forensic Medicine and Pathology, 14*(4), 289–295.

Otahbachi, M., Cevik, C., Bagdure, S., & Nugent, K. (2010). Excited delirium, restraints, and unexpected death: A review of pathogenesis. *The American Journal of Forensic Medicine and Pathology, 31*(2), 107–112.

Rabe, K. (2012). Prison structure, inmate mortality and suicide risk in Europe. *International Journal of Law and Psychiatry, 35*(3), 222–230. doi:10.1016/j.ijlp.2012.02.012.

Reay, D. T., & Howard, J. D. (1999). Restraint position and positional asphyxia. Letter to the Editor. *The American Journal of Forensic Medicine and Pathology, 20*(3), 300–301.

Space I and II (2008). *1 Annual penal statistics of the Council of Europe—2006 enquiry.* www.coe.int/legalcooperation. Accessed 5 Aprl 2013.

Spann, W., Liebhardt, E., & Seifert, S. (1979). Suizide in bayerischen Vollzugsanstalten. *Münchener Medizinische Wochenschrift, 121*(9), 315–316.

Steinhäuser, A. (1997). Analyse der Todesursachen in mittelrheinischen Haftanstalten und im Polizeigewahrsam von 1949 bis 1990. *Archiv für Kriminal-Anthropologie und Kriminalistik, 199*, 88–96.

Stratton, S. J., Rogers, C., Brickett, K., & Gruzinski, G. (2001). Factors associated with sudden death of individuals requiring restraint for excited delirium. *The American Journal of Emergency Medicine, 19*(3), 187–191.

Strote, J., & Range-Hutson, H. (2006). Taser use in restraint-related deaths. *Prehospital Emergency Care, 10*(4), 447–450.

Wobeser, W. L., Datema, J., Bechard, B., & Ford, P. (2002). Causes of death among people in custody in Ontario, 1990–1999. *Canadian Medical Association Journal = Journal de l'Association medicale canadienne, 167*(10), 1109–1113.

Zack, F., Rummel, J., Wegener, R., & Büttner, A. (2009). Plötzlicher Tod nach der Festnahme eines exzitierten Mannes. *Rechtsmedizin, 19*(5), 341–344.

Chapter 5
The Continuing Emergence of Art Therapy in Prisons

David E. Gussak

Abstract While it is clear that prison populations require mental health attention, there are some fundamental difficulties with providing care to those that cannot or should not admit to weaknesses and vulnerabilities or may even lie for their own benefits and gains. However, research has revealed that art therapy may be an effective approach for addressing mental health issues in correctional settings. This chapter presents the difficulties of providing mental health care to inmates, a short overview of tarts in American prison, and recent theories on the advantages of art therapy in prison. It will also provide recent empirical research that has determined that indeed art therapy is effective in addressing issues pervasive with the prison population, particularly depression, locus of control and problem-solving skills. Such results have naturally led to various art- programs as introduced at the end of this chapter.

5.1 Mentally Ill in Prisons in the US

People with mental illnesses have a tendency to become criminalized (Gibbs 1987) as they are often imprisoned for even negligible crimes brought about by their symptoms. Simultaneously, prisons aggravate and intensify already existing underlying psychiatric problems (Aufderheide and Brown 2005; Fox 1997) co-creating a situation that results in a pervasive mentally ill population in correctional settings. It was estimated that 'at midyear 2005 more than half of all prison and jail inmates had a mental health problem' (James and Glaze 2006: 2). Thus, prison administrators find themselves addressing mental health needs while simultaneously concerned with security.

The cause of this massive incarceration of the mentally ill are many, but corrections and mental health professionals in the United States point primarily to inadequate community mental health services and the country's punitive criminal justice police. Mental health hospitals across the country were shut down over the

D.E. Gussak (✉)
Department of Art Education, Florida State University, Tallahassee, FL, USA
e-mail: dgussak@fsu.edu

© Springer Science+Business Media Dordrecht 2017
B.S. Elger et al. (eds.), *Emerging Issues in Prison Health*,
DOI 10.1007/978-94-017-7558-8_5

67

last couple of decades. As a consequence, many of the mentally ill, particularly those who are poor and homeless, are unable to obtain the treatment they need . . . large numbers commit crimes and find themselves swept up into the burgeoning criminal justice system. Jails and prisons have become, in effect the country's front line mental health providers (Human Rights Watch 2003).

Thus, there is a constant need for mental health treatment in prisons. Consequently, most correctional institutions provide mental health services.

The types of therapy offered, however, may not be the most appropriate. Inmates who need mental health treatment may be seen as weak and vulnerable by their peers, and to be labelled as such can be dangerous (Gussak 1997b) as they in turn may become 'victimized by predatory inmates [. . .]' (Warner n.d.). Consequently, there are major challenges that therapists face working in forensic settings. Inmates may be appropriately reticent in talking about their difficulties, as they fear others may take advantage of these voiced vulnerabilities; thus rigid defences are established to achieve basic survival. Some of these defences may entail silence, lying or transforming the perceived reality, or even manipulation and fighting. Therefore, art therapy has been seen as an apt alternative to verbal therapy, providing needed expression in such an environment.

5.2   Art in Prison

While it is difficult for some to envision that something creative can emerge from such a repressive environment, art creation is prolific in prisons (Kornfeld 1997; Ursprung 1997). This is evident in prison craft shops, prison wall murals, envelopes decorated and then bartered by talented inmates to send letters home, and of course intricate designed tattoos proudly worn (Gussak and Ploumis-Devick 2004). The inmates who can create 'good' art earn respect and friendship from others (Kornfeld 1997).

In a culture where prison inmates are social outcasts, the art they produce is significantly appreciated by the 'outside' culture for its decorative and illustrative quality. However, the art form provides advantages other than for merely aesthetic reasons. While the correctional environment dehumanizes their wards (Fox 1997), the art making can re-humanize the creators through the eyes of those outside the system as well as amongst themselves (Gussak 1997a, 2004a, 2007a). As a natural form of expression for prison inmates, art can foster frustration tolerance, alleviate depression and increase problem solving and socialization.

As well, creating art has been directly linked to aggression. 'The impulses that drive some people to create are perhaps alike [to aggression] primarily in the fact that both can be considered expressions and agents of feelings' (Dissanayake 1992: 140) and may result from the sublimation of aggressive impulses (Kramer 1993; Rank 1932; Rubin 1984). While aggression has been seen as detrimental and destructive, making art may redirect aggressive impulses in a safer, more productive manner. Art making also allows the inmate to 'escape' from their dismal surroundings (Gussak 1997b; Hall 1997). 'The making of art in prison provides a [...] space for the prisoner overwhelmed by the clatter and disruption of prison life ... and it opens the possibility of a more creative life for many after release' (Liebmann 1994, forward). Additionally, art is an acceptable form of expression by the inmates; it can earn respect for the artist from his or her peers (Cheney 1997; Kornfeld 1997), which can in turn, build self-respect, and decrease a need to act out within the prison.

In 1983 fewer disciplinary reports were recorded on inmates who participated in the California Arts-in-corrections program (Brewster 1983); in one institution, the reduction was as high as 80 %. The California Department of Corrections revealed in (1987) that recidivism decreased for those who participated in the Arts In Corrections program. Unfortunately, there have been no recent studies since that have demonstrated the benefits of the arts in correctional environments. However, many programs recognize the benefits of the arts in prison settings (Alexander 2003; Bruna 2007; Florida Department of State 2005; Tannenbaum 2000; Williams 2003). The art therapist naturally takes advantage of these benefits, and there have been some recent studies that specifically explore the efficacy of art therapy in correctional institutions.

5.3 Art Therapy in Prisons

Art therapy is:

> [...] the therapeutic use of art making, within a professional relationship, by people who experience illness, trauma, or challenges in living, and by people who seek personal development. Through creating art and reflecting on the art products and processes, people can increase awareness of self and others, cope with symptoms, stress, and traumatic experiences; enhance cognitive abilities; and enjoy the life-affirming pleasures of making art (American Art Therapy Association).

Art therapists understand the characteristics of art materials and the degree of structure within an art directive; they use the art making process to facilitate expression, problem-solving, self-awareness and change in mood. As well, the final product may be used to facilitate communication and improve the sense of self. The finished products may also provide a permanent record of the sessions for reflection and progress evaluation. Ultimately, it can provide therapeutic change with little verbal interaction.

Gussak outlined eight specific advantages of art therapy in the correctional arena (Gussak 1997a, 2012; Gussak and Cohen-Liebman 2001). Art therapy:

- Utilizes tasks whose simplicity may result in the expression of '[..-]complex material which would not be available for communication in any other form [...]' (Kramer 1993).
- Has the advantage of bypassing unconscious and conscious defenses, including pervasive dishonesty.

- Promotes disclosure, even while the inmate/client is not compelled to discuss feelings and ideas that might leave him vulnerable.
- Supports creative activity in prison and provides necessary diversion and emotional escape.
- Does not require that the inmate/client know, admit, or discuss what he has disclosed. The environment is dangerous, and any unintended disclosure can be threatening.
- Permits the inmate/client to express himself in a manner acceptable to both the prison and outside culture.
- Can diminish pathological symptoms without verbal interpretation.
- Is helpful in the prison environment, given the disabilities extant in this population, contributed to by organic brain disorders such as drug induced deterioration, a low educational level, illiteracy, and other obstacles to verbal communication and cognitive development.

As already stressed, in the prison environ, weakness is exploited and survival of the fittest is the rule. The art therapist is able to get past the defenses inmates build for survival in order to help develop a healthier ego, improve anger management and problem-solving skills, while decreasing depression and psychiatric symptoms. They are able to do so without forcing this population to give voice to such vulnerabilities.

To best provide services that would not run contrary to the correctional institution's norms while still meeting the mental health needs of his or her clients, it behooves an art therapist to learn the conventions of the prison sub-culture and adapt to these limitations. For example, Merriam (1998) used art therapy with female inmates, allowing them 'to reach a more complete understanding of themselves without feeling that they had been utterly exposed. Their artwork became a container for powerful, potentially destructive emotions . . . ' (p.169).

More recently, Breiner et al. (2011) demonstrated that art therapy could be combined with a cognitive-behavioural model to develop an anger management program. They demonstrated that the art process, when combined with traditional methods, could increase socialization and improve anger control. The understanding of the value of prison art therapy programs continues to expand. Recent requests for information on art therapy in correctional settings have been frequent and varied, from such places as Korea, Macedonia, and Latvia, publications have been reprinted in Russia (Gussak 2007c) and Slovakia (Gussak 2004b). Art therapists, as a general rule, work for prisons in Great Britain (Liebmann 1994; Wylie 2007). However, while art therapy continues to permeate prison health care programs, there is still a need for robust empirical support. It has only been recently that such studies have been conducted.

5.4   Overview of Recent Art Therapy Prison Studies

Gussak, recognizing the need for empirical support for this work, began establishing quantifiable examinations on the benefits of art therapy within correctional institutions. Beginning the summer of 2003 with the assistance of a number of art therapy practicum students and graduate assistants, several studies were conducted in various North Florida prisons, within a partnership between the Florida State University Graduate Art Therapy Program and the Department of Corrections. These first studies were conducted in a men's moderate-maximum security prison, which housed a large mental health population. Eventually, the studies expanded to include another men's minimum to moderate security prison and a woman's minimum to moderate security prison. The three prisons ranged in number of total detainees from 1280 to 1544 inmates. The following section will provide a brief summation of the art therapy directives and the studies conducted to date in those three settings.

5.4.1   Description of the Directives Used in Those Art Therapy Studies

To maintain consistency and standardization throughout, the studies followed a similar series of interventions with clear and focused goals. The length of treatment administered for each of these three studies ranged from 4 to 15 weeks, depending on the particular study. The directives began simply and became increasingly more complicated; early sessions focused on the individual, but became progressively more group-focused. For example, an early art therapy directive asked participants to complete a name embellishment by writing their name on a piece of paper and then adorn the name in such a way that would tell the other members of the group something new about themselves, i.e. a hobby or occupation (see Fig. 5.1). In an environment where the inmates are generally known as numbers, this emphasized individuality and self-identity.

A later directive focused on addressing frustration tolerance and problem solving. For example, the participants were asked to construct three-dimensional forms, such as a white paper sculpture, with few supplies (paper, glue, and safety scissors) (Fig. 5.2).

The participants were able to relate to such a directive, as clearly, within the prison system, most of the inmates need to learn to adapt with very little resources. The project emphasized this shortcoming and provided an applicable metaphor for the participants; in an environment where identity is suppressed and conformity is expected, each person can create something unique using exactly the same materials. This stressed the concept of the individual.

Later on, as the sessions progressed towards group interaction, the inmates participated in the draw and pass directive; each participant drew an image within

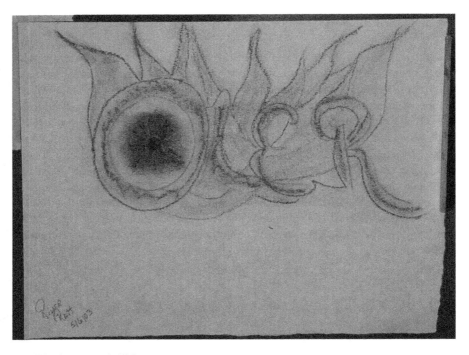

Fig. 5.1 A name embellishment

a few minutes. Once the time was up, they passed the drawing to the person sitting next to them and worked on the drawing in front of them for a few more minutes. This continued until all of the participants added something to each drawing (Fig. 5.3). Such a task can address frustration tolerance and group communication.

The sessions often culminated in a large, more complicated group task. For example, the participants may be asked to design and construct as a group a large three-dimensional form, such as their ideal or dream environment or a bridge construction. This project often took several sessions to complete (Fig. 5.4).

Although several of the participants may work on individual components, as the project evolved they worked together to construct the final piece. By this time, it was expected that all of the participants would communicate well and their problem-solving skills improved dramatically. This series of directives was expected to improve the participants' problem-solving and socialization skills.

5.4.1.1   Setting 1: Pilot Study

Using this curriculum, a pilot study was established to examine the effects of art therapy on male prison inmates in a male moderate-maximum security prison. A quasi-experimental, single-group pre/post-test design was used to test the hypothesis that inmates receiving art therapy services would demonstrate marked change

Fig. 5.2 White paper sculpture

Fig. 5.3 Draw and pass

Fig. 5.4 Group dream environment

(Gussak 2004a). Art therapy group sessions were conducted in the prison's mental health unit by the researcher and four art therapy practicum interns. Forty-four participants attended eight 1 h group art therapy sessions that were chosen by the facility's mental health counsellor; there were no more than eight inmates assigned to a single group These men had varied demographics (age, race, marital status, education, socio-economic status and crimes).

Two measurement tools were applied: a survey developed by the prison's mental health staff and an established, standardized art therapy assessment, the Formal Elements Art Therapy Scale (FEATS). The surveys addressed such issues as compliance with medication, compliance with unit rules, and improved social interaction. The art-based assessment relied on standardized drawing materials on 12 in. × 18 in. white paper; the participants were asked to complete a picture of a person picking an apple from a tree (PPAT). These drawings were evaluated using the FEATS[1] (Gantt and Tabone 1998). This assessment is composed of 14 scales each with a possible score of 0 through 5 that focus on individual formal drawing elements such as space, implied energy, colour, integration, logic, realism, problem solving, line quality, developmental level, rotation and perseveration. A combination of these formal elements assesses for diagnostic criteria such as depression,

---

[1]For a comprehensive description of this assessment, please refer to the FEATS rating manual (Gantt and Tabone 1998).

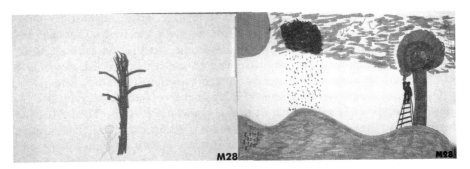

Fig. 5.5 (**a** and **b**) Pre and post person picking an apple from a tree drawings

schizophrenia, bipolar tendencies and organicity. [For example, Fig. 5.5a, b indicate two PPAT drawings completed prior to and after the sessions]

These procedures were administered as pre and posttests to evaluate outcome measures, and the changes between these assessments were measured to see if any change occurred. It should be noted that the correctional and mental health counselling staff completed surveys about the participants whereas the drawings were administered and evaluated by the art therapy personnel.

The comments from the correctional staff and the inmates indicated the program was well received. Overall, the statistical and qualitative results indicated a decrease in depression and an increase in problem solving and socialization. The inmates who participated in the program followed directions better, were more compliant with the prison rules and were less impulsive (for complete study statistical results, please refer to Gussak 2004a, 2007b). The scores of the FEATS drawings also indicated an elevation of mood and an increase of energy and problem solving. Hence these results supported the hypothesis—that those inmates who participated in art therapy sessions demonstrated a measureable change.

5.4.1.2   A Follow-up Study: A Randomized, Controlled Trial

The following year a follow-up study was conducted at this same moderate-maximum security correctional facility. A pre/post-test design was used to determine if art therapy would help reduce depression in prison populations compared to a control group (Gussak 2006). This study again used the FEATS and the Beck Depression Inventor-Short Form (BDI-II) as a pre and posttest evaluation for change in mood. The BDI-II is a standardized psychological assessment (Beck et al. 1974; Beck and Steer 1993) that has been used effectively to assess depression with correctional inmates (Boothby and Durham 1999). The results of the experimental group were compared to the control group to determine if it was the art therapy intervention that effected change with all confounding variables being controlled.

The volunteers were randomly assigned to the control group or the experimental group. A similar schedule of the art therapy directives outlined above (simple to complex, individual to group focused) were once again provided for those in the experimental group. Those in the control group received no sessions but still completed the pre and post assessments in the same period as those in the experimental group; however, they were assured that if they wished, they would receive art therapy sessions at a later date after completion of the study period.

Overall, the sample sizes were considerably smaller (experimental group N = 16, control group N = 13) as only one art therapist provided sessions. The BDI-II and the qualitative evaluations indicated that, overall, the art therapy elicited positive and statistically significant change in the inmates' mood, problem-solving and socialization abilities; the results of the FEATS, however, were mixed (for complete study statistics, please refer to Gussak 2006, 2007b).

5.4.1.3 Setting 2 and 3: Studies Comparing Male and Female Inmates

The study was expanded over several years, from 2006 to 2008, to include a men's minimum to moderate security correctional institution and a woman's minimum to moderate correctional institution (Gussak 2009a). Research was conducted consistently with various subtle changes. The length of time for sessions was increased to 15-weeks and another assessment tool was introduced, the Adult Nowicki-Strickland Locus of Control Scale (ANS) (Nowicki and Duke 1974) often used by the Department of Corrections. The ANS had, in the past, specifically been used to ascertain whether or not the participants had primarily internal or external locus of control (LOC). Over 2 years, there were one to two art therapy graduate interns placed in each facility. The session formats as described above were closely adhered to (directives that are simple to complex, with format moving from individually focused to group focused). Control groups were implemented and, as before, received the assessments during the same designated period as the experimental group members. One unintended outcome was the opportunity to assess not only the benefits of art therapy in these correctional environments but also any differences between male and female inmates.

These studies used a pretest—posttest control group design to test two hypotheses: If male inmates receive art therapy services, then they will exhibit marked improvement in mood, socialization, problem-solving abilities and locus of control within the correctional environment; and If female male inmates receive art therapy services, then they will exhibit marked improvement in mood, socialization, problem-solving abilities and locus of control within the correctional environment. When these two hypotheses were supported, a third one was established: Although both male and female inmates will exhibit marked improvement, the male inmates will exhibit different responses to the art therapy services in mood and locus of control than female inmates within their respective correctional environments. This final hypothesis was supported: the female inmate population demonstrating more marked change in LOC and Mood than the male inmate population. Ultimately, the study concluded that, while both the men's and women's group ended the sessions with similar scores on the measurement tools, the women exhibited scores that reflected greater depression and external locus of control than their male counterparts prior to receiving treatment (Gussak 2009b). The success of these studies provided an opportunity for more expanded arts programs.

5.4.2   The Inmate Mural Arts program (IMAP)

In 2007, the Deputy Secretary of the Florida Department of Corrections (DOC) formed the Florida Arts in Corrections Program. This group was comprised of members of the Department of Corrections, representatives from the Florida community, one former inmate and one art therapy intern and chaired by the author. Ultimately, the purpose of the 'Arts in Corrections program is to enhance offenders' personal, educational and workforce development while supporting successful community re-entry and institutional safety' (cite). The Deputy Secretary recognized the benefits the arts provided in creating a safe and effective means of expression while building a bridge to the community. This group was implemented to expand and organize the arts throughout Florida into a single, centralized organization. Although it was soon disbanded due to bureaucratic and legislative reorganization, the Inmate Mural Arts Program emerged.

Relying on a great deal of backstage negotiations (Gussak 2001), the murals that were developed from this program relied on cooperation between the correctional institutions, its administrators, correctional officers and the inmates, members of the community and the Florida State University Graduate Art Therapy program. The actual projects were completed by graduate students who elected to take part in these projects to fulfil their masters' project requirement, with the faculty member's supervision. The institution's and the community's focus was on creating a large art piece that reflected the talent of the inmates. The goals of the art therapists included team building, socialization and problem solving. The project worked because all of these goals were addressed simultaneously.

5.4.2.1   Mural 1: Wakulla Correctional Institution (WCI)

The first mural, entitled 'Transformation through Unity,' was completed in a men's prison, the Wakulla Correctional Institution (WCI), a minimum to moderate security facility (Argue et al. 2009). As an example of successful formal and informal negotiations, this mural could not have succeeded without 'institutional buy-in.' Although the Deputy Secretary of DOC wanted this mural to happen, meetings were held with the warden, assistant warden, the heads of Maintenance, Classification, Security and Psychology departments and the chaplain of the institution, along with the Director of DOC Program development and the art therapy students and faculty who would be coordinating the project. This was to ensure that all parties were invested. Once the institution was assured that safety and institutional security –i.e., that the inmates will not fight, steal or run off—was a priority, the administrators became enthusiastic about the mural project. They offered the prison's chapel wall on which to paint it. This wall, (22 ft × 47 ft) was highly visible to all visitors and prisoners, and could be clearly seen from the parking lot.

The two graduate students who coordinated this project began working with the fourteen volunteers selected by the institution's classification officer and chief psychologist based on their history, ability to stay on programmatic tasks and psychological needs. Initially, four 1-h weekly meetings were conducted to develop ideas, sketches and ultimately the final image that would be placed on the wall. To get them started, the inmates were asked to think about 'who you are and what you have to say.' Although many of the participants were initially overwhelmed with the scale of the project, with the guidance and support by the art therapy students, they were able to complete an image they were all were excited about. With a final colour image available, all negotiations and planning with administration and security complete and supplies obtained, the mural was ready to be applied.

Preliminary steps were taken to facilitate the process. Color copies of the sketch were laminated and distributed as a map, the paint obtained through donations were pre-mixed and stored in containers for a consistent palette, the wall was cleared of all impediments (including an air conditioning unit that was moved to another side of the building) and scaffolding was acquired. Of course, as scaffolding could be deemed a security risk, erected so close to the barbed fences of the compound, maintenance staff had to set up, dismantle and store the scaffolding each day.

After transferring the image onto the wall with a data projector one night, the inmates began the painting. Over the next 6 weeks, in the sweltering Florida sun and unpredictable storming weather (as long as there was no lightning, the inmates opted to work on the painting), with all of the inmates—and at times the two students—on the scaffolding at one time, the painting took shape. In August of 2008, the mural was completed and presented in a formal unveiling ceremony (see Fig. 5.6).

The responses from the inmates who participated in the project were gratifying and validated efforts towards the project. They all indicated a sense of pride and belonging and felt rewarded by the experience. All seemed to gain a sense of empowerment and accomplishment and were well invested in the process. As Argue, Bennett and Gussak (2009) reflected:

> The art therapists were able to monitor closely the dynamics that occurred around the art making—between the participants and within each participant, encourage reflective distancing when necessary, understand and encourage discussions on the latent and manifest content of the artwork, and facilitate the group process that went into planning and executing the finished piece. Significantly, the art therapists maintained the vision of the therapeutic goals—improving socialization, problem-solving skills and appropriate expression of artistic endeavours—that resulted in greater insight, interaction and self-esteem than may have otherwise been achieved. […] The necessary formal and informal negotiations that were conducted on a daily basis ultimately succeeded in producing a major product that demonstrated the value and benefits of art for this population.

Shortly after its completion, an exhibit of the development of this project was displayed at Florida's Department of State Division of Cultural Affairs Gallery. The success of this project led to the development of two more murals.

Fig. 5.6 Transformation through unity – mural done with male prison inmates on the prison's chapel wall at the Wakulla Correctional Institution (WCI)

5.4.2.2 Mural 2: Downtown City of Colquitt

The following year, the City of Colquitt's Miller Arts Council in Georgia contracted with the Florida State University Art Therapy Program and its Inmate Mural Arts Program to complete a similar project on a wall in the downtown Colquitt area. With a focus on all forms of art, this city has become known as 'Georgia's First Mural City,' and boasts more than a dozen murals painted along its downtown structures. After hearing of the IMAP project completed at the Wakulla Correctional Institution, the Miller Arts Council provided a grant to the IMAP team to work with the male inmates of the Miller County Jail– a detainment facility used to house lawbreakers prior to court or sentencing– to create the mural.

The IMAP team, which consisted of a faculty member from the art therapy program and two recent graduates who had worked on the WCI mural, used a process similar to that used for the previous project to develop the idea and image. This project also relied on cooperation and negotiation with the city, the administration and security of the jail and the art therapists.

The goals for the city and of the art therapists remained similar to those mentioned in the previous project. Ultimately, the theme that emerged was based on the Anglin Brothers, two depression-era men from Colquitt and surrounding areas with a history of small-time bank robberies and subsequent jail breaks. John and Clarence Anglin were sent to Alcatraz, believed to be inescapable at the time. On June 11, 1962, John and Clarence Anglin attempted to escape with Frank Morris, another Alcatraz inmate; they were never found. The common legend is that their escape was successful (DeNevi 1991). This escape was featured in the film, Escape from Alcatraz, with Clint Eastwood as Frank Morris.

Using a much smaller group of jail inmates than the WCI mural—six instead of eleven—the 35 × 51 ft mural was painted over 6 weeks in the autumn of 2008. The sheriff who ran the jail selected these inmates, based on interest, low security risk and good behaviour. The process of painting the mural drew crowds and words of encouragement from passersby. The final image consisted of a collage of symbols and figures that told the story of the two infamous Anglin brothers (Fig. 5.7), portrayed as old men looking over the detritus of their life, each piece signifying a different part of the folklore. This painting became known as 'Gospel of the Rock' and has since been featured in the city's downtown mural tours and exhibitions.

5.4.2.3 Mural 3: Women's Prison, Gadsden Correctional Institution

The third and most recent mural, which remains untitled, was completed in a women's prison, Gadsden Correctional Institution. More similar to the Wakulla project than Colquitt, this mural was completed at a facility with a strong commitment to the arts and already had several outdoor and indoor murals completed. This painting proved to be the most ambitious thus far. It too was painted on the

Fig. 5.7 Gospel of the Rock – mural done with male jail inmates of Miller County completed on a building in downtown Colquitt, GA

chapel wall, which faced the main area of the prison at the end of a long walkway; it was 22 × 70 ft. This mural was the first to receive public donations.

The process in developing and completing the mural was almost identical to the one undertaken at Wakulla Correctional Institution. The major difference was, because of the number of volunteers committed to work on the painting, around 16 inmates, the women had to be divided into two groups of 8—one that worked in the morning and one in the evening. Coordinated by two graduate art therapy students and supported by the administration and security of the facility, this painting took 5 weeks to finish during the hot summer of 2009. The mural, which reflects the vision of all those that contributed, had one unique feature—the squares of the filmstrip that outlined the bottom portion of the painting were deliberately left unpainted. After the rest of the painting was finished, each participant was assigned a square to paint anything they wanted, thus providing the artists an opportunity for their own individual identity within this group project (see Fig. 5.8).

The response to this project was overwhelming, and it seemed clear that the therapeutic goals focused on for this project were addressed. The women gained a mastery over the process, developed group cohesion and problem-solving skills and all voiced a tremendous sense of accomplishment. Together, these three projects underscored the importance of applying the benefits of art therapy in the correctional milieu into a community-based and focused art product. Not only can the art therapist address the mental health needs of prison inmates through individually prescribed treatment plans, but through dynamically oriented group art endeavours as well.

Fig. 5.8 Beacon of Hope: mural completed by female prison inmates on a building at the Gadsden Correctional Institution (GCI)

5.5 Looking Towards the Future and Recommendations

While most of the literature on art therapy in prisons presents traditional therapeutic applications, the future may encompass a need to expand social action and community-enhanced art therapy. In this manner, the art therapist may become a mediator between the clients and society (Potash 2011). Still addressing the mental health needs of the client as discussed in the beginning of this chapter, art therapists who help an inmate reconnect to the community from whence he or she came may in fact encourage and facilitate wellness. The very act of creating art and having it seen by members of the community may re-humanize the inmate and facilitate reintegration. What is more, such nonverbal tools enable expression and honest communication by those that may otherwise be reluctant to do so. Therefore, it is recommended that art therapists continue to negotiate with governmental policy makers and prison administrators to expand the use of art and art therapy programs within the correctional milieu. It is also important, however, for the artists and art therapist to negotiate with those who work directly with the inmates. As presented within this chapter, the literature underscores the importance of working within the confines of the institution, that artists and art therapists present themselves almost as an ambassador within a new cultural environment, and that they learn to develop the ability to communicate in a fashion that representatives of the correctional setting can understand. Artists and art therapists, at least in the United States, may expect some resistance to such programming. However, the artists and art therapists wishing to begin such programs need to emphasize how the arts: assist in decreasing aggression; increase safety and security within the institution; improve socialization and problem-solving; and that it is a cost-effective means of decreasing depression and increasing productivity. Using the art already completed by the inmate population as an illustration on what they can accomplish would help.

While art therapy programs need to continue in prisons and correctional settings, those providing services also need to learn how to conduct research to measure its effectiveness. Unfortunately, the bulk of the current empirical research on the benefits of art therapy in the correctional setting has been limited to a single geographical and geopolitical area in the U.S.; it behoves professionals in other parts of the country to demonstrate its generalizable worth through hard data. Recording not only the changes that occur in those that take part in such activities, but the finished products through photographs and video is important to furthering the impact that such research can make. Such research would continue to demonstrate to those making the decisions that the arts and art therapy would benefit this population and the institutions themselves.

This chapter presented a number of different approaches on how art therapy is applicable to the correctional milieu. Regardless of the approach art therapists take or the foci they adopt, the benefits of the arts for prison inmates continue to emerge.

References

Alexander, B. (2003). Smitty, prayer, astronomy, 'Y2K and the wicked stepmother', and Asia Romero: Dimensions in the work of the prison creative arts project. In R. M. C. Williams (Ed.), *Teaching the art behind bars* (pp. 125–137). Boston: Northeastern University Press.

American Art Therapy Association. http://www.arttherapy.org. Accessed 8 Mar 2013.

Argue, J., Bennett, J., & Gussak, D. (2009). Transformation through negotiation: Initiating the Inmate Mural Arts Program. *Arts in Psychotherapy, 36*, 313–319.

Aufderheide, D. H., & Brown, P. H. (2005). Crisis in corrections: The mentally ill in America's prisons. *Corrections Today, 67*, 30–33.

Beck, A. T., & Steer, R. A. (1993). *Beck Depression Inventory manual*. New York: Harcourt Brace.

Beck, A. T., Rial, W. Y., & Rickets, K. (1974). Short form of depression inventory: Cross-validation. *Psychological-Reports, 34*(3), 1184–1186.

Boothby, J. L., & Durham, T. W. (1999). Screening for depression in prisoners using the Beck Depression Inventory. *Criminal Justice and Behavior, 26*(1), 107–124.

Breiner, M., Tuomisto, L., Beuyea, E., Gussak, D., & Aufderheide, D. (2011). Creating an art therapy anger management (ATAM) protocol for male inmates through a collaborative relationship. *International Journal of Offender Therapy and Comparative Criminology, 56*(7), 1124–1143.

Brewster, L. G. (1983). *An evaluation of the arts-in-corrections program of the California Department of Corrections*. San Jose: San Jose State University.

Bruna, K. (2007). *Creating behind the razor wire: An overview of arts in corrections in the U.S.* http://www.communityarts.net/readingroom/archivefiles/2007/01/creating_behind.php#_ftnref4. Accessed 8 Mar 2013.

California Department of Corrections. (1987). *Research synopsis on parole outcomes for arts-in-corrections participants paroled December, 1980-February 1987*. Sacramento: CDC.

Cheney, J. (1997). Suspending normal prison taboos through the arts. In D. Gussak & E. Virshup (Eds.), *Drawing time: Art therapy in prisons and other correctional settings* (pp. 87–98). Chicago: Magnolia Street Publishers.

DeNevi, D. (1991). *Riddle of the rock*. Amherst: Prometheus Books.

Dissanayake, E. (1992). *Homoaestheticus: Where art comes from and why*. New York: The Free Press.

Florida Department of State. (2005). *Culture builds Florida's future strategic plan*. Tallahassee: Florida Department of State.

Fox, W. M. (1997). The hidden weapon: Psychodynamics of forensic institutions. In D. Gussak & E. Virshup (Eds.), *Drawing time: Art therapy in prisons and other correctional settings* (pp. 43–55). Chicago: Magnolia Street Publishers.

Gantt, L., & Tabone, C. (1998). *The formal elements art therapy scale: The rating manual*. Morgantown: Gargoyle Press.

Gibbs, J. J. (1987). Symptoms of psychopathology among jail prisoners: The effects of exposure in the jail environment. *Criminal Justice and Behavior, 14*(3), 288–310.

Gussak, D. (1997a). The ultimate hidden weapon: Art therapy and the compromise option. In D. Gussak & E. Virshup (Eds.), *Drawing time: Art therapy in prisons and other correctional settings* (pp. 59–74). Chicago: Magnolia Street Publishers.

Gussak, D. (1997b). Breaking through barriers: Advantages of art therapy in prison. In D. Gussak & E. Virshup (Eds.), *Drawing time: Art therapy in prisons and other correctional settings* (pp. 1–12). Chicago: Magnolia Street Publishers.

Gussak, D. (2001). *The work of the art therapist: A social interactionist perspective*. Unpublished dissertation. Emporia KS: Emporia State University.

Gussak, D. (2004a). A pilot research study on the efficacy of art therapy with prison inmates. *The Arts in Psychotherapy, 31*(4), 245–259.

Gussak, D. (2004b). Čas kreslit': Arteterapia vo väzení [Drawing time: Art therapy in prison]. *Arteterapeutické Listy [Art Therapy Letters], 3*(4), 7–11.

Gussak, D. (2006). The effects of art therapy with prison inmates: A follow-up study. *Arts in Psychotherapy, 33*, 188–198.

Gussak, D. (2007a). Raising the bars: Art therapy in the American prison system. In D. Spring (Ed.), *Art in treatment: A transatlantic dialogue*. Springfield: Charles, C. Thomas, Publishers.

Gussak, D. (2007b). The effectiveness of art therapy in reducing depression in prison populations. *International Journal of Offender Therapy and Comparative Criminology, 5*(4), 444–460.

Gussak, D. (2007c). Арт-терапия В системе американскйх тюрем [Art therapy in the American prison system]. Исчепяюжее Искусство: Международный журнал арт-терапий [The healing arts]. *International Journal-Russian Art Therapy Association, 10*(2), 39–59.

Gussak, D. (2009a). The effects of art therapy on male and female inmates: Advancing the research base. *The Arts in Psychotherapy, 36*(1), 5–12.

Gussak, D. (2009b). Comparing the effectiveness of art therapy on depression and locus of control of male and female inmates. *The Arts in Psychotherapy, 36*(4), 202–207.

Gussak, D. (2012). Comparing art therapy in prisons to arts in corrections: Process to product and back again. In L. Cheliotis (Ed.), *The arts of imprisonment: Essays on control, resistance and empowerment* (pp. 243–253). Surrey: Ashgate Publishers.

Gussak, D., & Cohen-Liebman, M. S. (2001). Investigation vs. intervention: Forensic art therapy and art therapy in forensic settings. *The American Journal of Art Therapy, 40*(2), 123–135.

Gussak, D., & Ploumis-Devick, E. (2004). Creating wellness in forensic populations through the arts: A proposed interdisciplinary model. *Visual Arts Research, 29*(1), 35–43.

Hall, N. (1997). Creativity and incarceration: The purpose of art in a prison culture. In D. Gussak & E. Virshup (Eds.), *Drawing time: Art therapy in prisons and other correctional settings* (pp. 25–41). Chicago: Magnolia Street Publishers.

Human Rights Watch. (2003). *Rates of incarceration of the mentally ill. Ill-Equipped: U.S.* Prisons and Offenders with Mental Illness. http://www.hrw.org/reports/2003/usa1003/1.htm. Accessed 15 208 Aprl 2013.

James, D. J., & Glaze, L. E. (2006). *Mental health problems of prison and jail inmates* (Bureau of Justice Statistics—Special report, pp. 1–12). Washington, DC: U.S. Deptartment of Justice, Office of Justice Programs, Bureau of Justice Statistics.

Kornfeld, P. (1997). *Cellblock visions: Prison art in America*. Princeton: Princeton University Press.

Kramer, E. (1993). *Art as therapy with children* (2nd ed.). Chicago: Magnolia Street Publishers.

Liebmann, M. (1994). *Art therapy with offenders*. London: Jessica Kingsley Publishers.

Merriam, B. (1998). To find a voice. *Women & Therapy, 21*(1), 157–171.

Nowicki, S., & Duke, M. (1974). A locus of control scale for non-college as well as college adults. *Journal of Personality Assessment, 38*, 136–137.

Potash, J. (2011). Art therapists as intermediaries for social change. *Journal of Art for Life, 2*(1), 48–58.

Rank, O. (1932). *Art and artist*. New York: W.W. Norton.

Rubin, J. A. (1984). *The art of art therapy*. New York: Brunner/Mazel Publishing.

Tannenbaum, J. (2000). *Disguised as a poem: My years teaching poetry at San Quentin*. Boston: Northeastern University Press.

Ursprung, W. (1997). Insider art: The creative ingenuity of the incarcerated artist. In D. Gussak & E. Virshup (Eds.), *Drawing time: Art therapy in prisons and other correctional settings* (pp. 13–24). Chicago: Magnolia Street Publishers.

Warner, G. (n.d.) *NAMI-NYC Metro: Affiliates of the national Alliance for the Mentally Ill*. http://www.naminycmetro.org/inmatehealthcare.htm. Accessed 9 Mar 2005.

Williams, R. M. C. (2003). Introduction. In R. M. C. Williams (Ed.), *Teaching the art behind bars* (pp. 3–13). Boston: Northeastern University Press.

Wylie, B. (2007). Self and social function: Art therapy in a therapeutic community prison. *Journal of Brand Management, 14*, 324–334.

Chapter 6
Spiritual Help During Detention: Specific Responses to Different Stages and Types of Imprisonment

Frank Stüfen, Marcello Ienca, and Bernice S. Elger

Abstract The provision of spiritual advice in prisons must be adapted to a number of factors and, hence, cannot be reduced to a one-fits-all strategy for prisoners in various settings. This chapter describes the major topics and issues arising when providing spiritual advice. Two variables are of particular importance and must be taken into account by spiritual advisors: the type of facility in which the person is imprisoned and the duration of the imprisonment. After presenting an overview of the main issues encountered by those who provide spiritual advice in modern correctional institutions, the authors discuss possible solutions to existing problems. They argue that spiritual help in the correctional context should be understood within a wide context that cannot be reduced exclusively to religious ritualism but must also take into account other cultural and psychological considerations. An interdisciplinary approach for spiritual advice is proposed that combines more specifically spiritual or religious communication strategies and care solutions with those from other humanistic and care-providing disciplines.

The goal of this chapter is to show that the issues faced by those providing spiritual advice in prisons are not generally the same concerning all prisoners[1] and are not influenced only by individual needs. Nevertheless, for we can specify topics and issues that arise during encounters with imprisoned people when two dominant factors are taken into account: the type of facility in which someone is imprisoned and the duration of his or her imprisonment. In this paper we describe the issues with

---

[1]In this chapter the terms prisoner and prison will be used synonymously with detainee and detention facility, including both pre-trial and sentenced prisoners and the related detention centers.

F. Stüfen (✉)
Seelsorger JVA Pöschwies, Roosstrasse 49, 8105 Regensdorf, Switzerland
e-mail: frank.stuefen@ji.zh.ch

M. Ienca • B.S. Elger
Institute for Biomedical Ethics, University of Basel, Bernoullistrasse 28, 4056 Basel, Switzerland
e-mail: b.elger@unibas.ch

© Springer Science+Business Media Dordrecht 2017
B.S. Elger et al. (eds.), *Emerging Issues in Prison Health*,
DOI 10.1007/978-94-017-7558-8_6

which those who provide spiritual advice are confronted in modern correctional
services named and solutions for the encountered problems and discuss. Spiritual
help in this context has to be understood within a wide context, including work with
religious symbols as well as work with methods from other humanistic and care
providing disciplines.

6.1 Introduction

Spiritual advice in prisons is a form of counselling offered to every prisoner
irrespective of religious affiliation (or absence of any). It is provided free-of-charge
and the involved personnel are completely independent of the prison itself and of
the justice system. The encounter with the spiritual advisors is non-judgemental
during all phases during and after the judicial procedures. Prison spiritual advisors
are sworn to secrecy: confidentiality is of very high importance for the credibility
of any spiritual advisor and of the most precious value to prisoners. Knowing this
allows prisoners to feel at ease and to discuss their concerns within a protected
relationship. The problems reported by prisoners are mostly personal, prison or
family related, autobiographical or of a religious nature. Personal guilt is the main
reason for spiritual advice requests among prisoners. The fact that the spiritual
advisor doesn't write reports of any sort for the authorities, for the prosecutors or
for law enforcement, reduces mistrust.

Two factors affect the main challenges of spiritual advice in prisons: the type of
facility in which someone is imprisoned and the duration of his or her imprisonment.
In this chapter, we will outline questions and problems emerging with time, stage
and type of imprisonment (e.g. remand, pre-trial and prior to deportation) and suggest ways in which spiritual advice for prisoners should react and take into account
those factors. The second main part of this chapter will examine cases of convicted
prisoners sentenced under Swiss Criminal Law (SCL) to undergo psychotherapy in
a maximum security facility (Art. 59.3) or preventive detention (Art. 64). We will
explore the challenges posed by these legal measures to spiritual advice in prisons
with regard to the country of origin and religious affiliation of the convicted person.

Spiritual advice for prisoners requires different and expanded competencies in its
work for promoting what we will call here the 'inner freedom' or 'spiritual balance'
of imprisoned persons. This chapter focuses on the specific issues of spiritual advice
in the context of Swiss detention facilities. Nevertheless, a significant degree of gen-
eralizability is recognizable as detainees in Switzerland come from many countries
and religions. Our experiences in the Swiss context are similar to those described by
colleagues from Germany, whose preventive detention mechanisms are comparable
to those in Switzerland, and also consistent in some ways with lifetime convictions
in other countries such as Canada (with the Dangerous Offender Designation).[2]

---

[2] See Public Safety Canada. http://www.publicsafety.gc.ca/cnt/cntrng-crm/crrctns/protctn-gnst-
hgh-rsk-ffndrs/dngrs-ffndr-dsgntn-eng.aspx.

6.2 The Role of Spiritual Advice for Prison Health

Spiritual care in prisons is part of the care system in facilities containing accused and/or convicted prisoners. Spiritual advice for prisoners is often considered part of the task of social workers or of the care provided by psychologists. While it is true that both professional groups will be confronted with questions related to spiritual well-being, advice provided by personnel with specific religious training should be defined within a broader perspective. Those who provide spiritual advice work at the nexus of prison and society. They provide beneficial services not only to prisoners, but to the wider system. Similar to health care workers in general, they also have to acknowledge dual loyalties to the correction systems and to their religious entities such as for example the church that employs them. Such dual loyalties create particular work conditions, especially within a prison, a place that has been described as 'Total Institution' (Goffman 1968).

Spiritual advice in prisons cares as much about the development of just and efficient correctional systems as about its 'clients,' including their concerns about the criminal procedures, their prison experiences and their personal needs. The scope of advice is not limited to the spiritual dimension, but considers everything that threatens or restricts the 'inner freedom' of the accused or convicted client at a socio-cultural, economical, religious, ideological or personal level. The spiritual help provided addresses all these levels. Spiritual advisors have to be aware of the reality of a prison (its system and its life) as well as the objective and subjective reality of the prisoner in order to react in an adequate manner that offers personal attention to the individual detainee. The purposes of spiritual advice are defined within the context of imprisonment and of the personal distress of the clients. Sworn to secrecy, the chaplain cares about his or her clients in a healing, comforting, encouraging, liberating way and offers comfort, carefully regarding the client's autobiography and addressing the burdensome weight of guilt (Green 2013; Mitchell and Latchford 2010; Todd and Tipton 2011). All this should be done in a non-judgemental manner based on the resources of the advisor's background, faith and culture. Given this, we defend the approach that spiritual advice in prisons undertakes the major task to facilitate 'inner freedom' which can be reached through a form of (spiritual) healing that affects both the body and the soul.

6.3 The Main Problems in Prison Chaplaincy – Reasons for Today's Issues

In 1993 a prisoner committed a murder while on an unescorted leave of absence.[3] This incident, which is known in Switzerland as the 'murder of Zollikerberg,' has deeply affected the public and those working in the correctional system

---

[3]Firstly reported in: Neue Zürcher Zeitung, 1. November 1993, S. 22.

(Röthlisberger 2005). The reaction of the prison system had significant consequences for prisoners. Since the early 1980s, i.e. before this crime, spiritual care for prisoners had already begun to change into a more professionally-equipped and specially trained profession. In the 1990s, Patrice Demestral and Dr. Willy Nafzger, both prison chaplains and pastors, introduced their educational programs for prison spiritual advice, raising it to a professional level. Since then, a post-graduate degree 'Pastoral Care in Swiss Correctional Systems' of a high academic standard is still offered today at the University of Berne. As a result of this innovative educative program and of the new ideas that emerged from it, the work of prison spiritual advisors was separated from that of parish ministries. Whoever wants to work in this field in Switzerland today, even as a part-time chaplain, is required to take this course and obtain certification (Advanced Studies of Prison Chaplaincy).

After the 'murder of Zollikerberg' in 1993, public safety and the need to prevent new victims became the top priority in the correctional system of Zurich and Switzerland in general. As a consequence, the staff in the psychological and psychiatric services of the canton of Zurich increased in number from 5 to more than 65 professionals at the present time. The professionals working in this service, jointly with other similar services offered in different cantons, have also developed a program focusing upon the psychological factors of dangerous criminal behaviour. The objective of this program is to reduce the inmates' probability of re-offending upon release. The pursuit of this aim is based upon a risk assessment and a prognosis of the probability for re-offending at present and within the subsequent 10 years.

Risk assessment has also become the main focus in social work. To this purpose, for example, a 'Dangerous Offender Commission' has been created in the canton of Zurich to make decisions concerning detainees who are assessed as dangerous to society. The purpose of the commission is to advise on the threats posed by these detainees and to assess the possibilities of success of their potential release trajectory (e.g. if they can be considered for moving a further step towards release in their trajectory). Its recommendation is based solely on existing files, without direct contact with the detainee.

These important developments greatly affect the practice of spiritual advice in prisons and required chaplains and other spiritual advisors to change and adapt to them. In this perspective, a 'spiritual only' line of work (i.e. working strictly with religious symbols like prayers and blessings) is too limited of a definition of the chaplaincy practice in prisons; hence it no longer represents a valid option. In contrast to that traditional and limited approach, appropriate spiritual advice, nowadays, must address real-life topics such as guilt and forgiveness, grace and reconciliation without fear of using methods from other disciplines. Prison chaplaincy has been enriched by competencies from various fields including psychology, psychotherapy, social work and community chaplaincy.[4] In addition, basic knowledge in the field

---

[4]For more information visit the website of the Swiss churches for advanced training. www.weiterbildungkirche.ch.

of law enforcement and immigration policies has also become a required element in a prison chaplain's curriculum.

6.3.1 Spiritual Advice and the Type, Nature and Timeframe of Imprisonment

In the canton of Zurich facilities for pre-trial and sentenced prisoners are separate. The journey of a pre-trial detainee leads from the arrest – during the first 3–7 days in police custody – to investigative custody. The length of each phase depends on how quickly law enforcement makes the decision to pronounce criminal charges. The accused person remains in investigative custody until the trial date or until a decision is made regarding the possibility of transferring the person into a remand prison or a (forensic) psychiatry facility prior to the trial date.[5] The next step is sentencing. The sequential transfer into long term prison or a security facility depends on the outcome of the sentence: in case of sentences of up to 24 months, the person will be transferred into a standard security prison; those sentenced to indeterminate security measures will be transferred into a medium or maximum-security facility based on the detainee's perceived dangerousness. From the perspective of prison chaplaincy, there are specific differences between people serving custodial sentences and those for whom a court ordered indeterminate security measures, in most cases in the form of therapy in a closed facility. These clients are under the jurisdiction of SCL Art. 63. 59 or 64 (für Statistik 2007). Another specific case are individuals who are under immigration law and unwilling to leave the country; they are held in a deportation centre. Furthermore some people could also remain imprisoned because they are unable to pay a fine.

We will start with examining the main issues that arise during pre-trial detention. During the first days of imprisonment two different types of prisoners are prevalent. First, there are prisoners who were involved in drug-related crimes. These clients often live on the margins of society and know the procedure of imprisonment well. Their crimes are mostly small in legal terms: theft, drug abuse or drug dealing to finance their own drug addiction. More detailed information about this group will be provided in the paragraph on alternative custody.

The second type of pre-trial detainees prevalent in the first days of imprisonment is represented by the neophytes, i.e. detainees who are in prison for the first time. These prisoners usually lack experience regarding their current situation and often experience high levels of distress. Frequently, they are under shock due to the imprisonment and appear disoriented; many of them are in denial, show incredulity about the entire situation, or feel ashamed and desperate. If there is a

---

[5]Those remarks are related to the group of accused who are actually imprisoned. There is a significantly larger group of accused people who are not imprisoned while waiting for their court date.

risk of collusion or the possibility that an accused prisoner might interfere with the investigation, the investigating administration can order restrictions. Examples of restrictions include: ban on reading newspapers, watching TV, having visitors or making phone calls. Only a few people are allowed to visit the detainee during this period; among those few is the spiritual advisor. Often, prison staff will call the chaplain or another spiritual advisor if they realize that prisoners are in need of human contact. Visits of spiritual advisors often interrupt the immense isolation of such prisoners and prevent them from deep brooding over their situation and from obsessive behaviour (e.g. the unceasing walking around in circles). During these visits the atmosphere is so tense that the task for the chaplain can be twofold: providing relief through techniques of crisis intervention and reassuring prisoners that they are not left alone. It is usually at this stage that praying provides strong relief. At this stage prisoners are relieved by the experience of not being judged by the chaplain but being seen as a human being, and not being defined by the accusation of having committed a crime regardless of whatever burden of guilt detainees may carry. The visit, which is in most cases offered spontaneously by the chaplain, shows to prisoners the existence of a world in which they are not exclusively seen as rejected and forgotten but as human beings in a crisis who still need and are worthy of affection and attention. Knowledge of the new Swiss federal criminal procedure law of 2011 allows the chaplain to provide some orientation help by pointing out existing possibilities for action, in addition to the crisis intervention and prayers. This means that a chaplain needs to acquire some knowledge about legal procedures, not in the sense of counselling in a strong legal sense, but in the sense of being a voice of reason in a time of great insecurity. This task of chaplaincy remains important throughout the entire first phase of imprisonment, especially because about 80 % of men in investigative custody are foreigners, hence accustomed to often very different justice systems and jurisdictions (Achermann 2009).

6.3.1.1 Concepts of Spiritual Advice During Investigative Custody: Dealing with Distress

From the perspective of spiritual help, investigative custody presents a situation of escalation and consolidation. In Switzerland, investigative custody may be prolonged for as much as 3 months at a time, depending on considerations of risk of flight or collusion.

An important procedural opportunity in many encounters of spiritual advisors with the pre-trial detainee is the fact that, in Switzerland, the Bureau for Counsel for the Defence appointed by the court is part of the prosecutor's office. Seeing through the eyes of pre-trial detainees from a foreign culture who may not be accustomed to the same legal standards or procedures to which they are now subject, it is easy to perceive that detainees lack trust in this form of defence that seems too close to the prosecution authorities. Therefore, a recurrent task for the chaplain is to explain the justice system as well as the criminal procedural law to the detainees in order to minimize the psychological effects of suspiciousness and insecurity.

Of course this task should primarily be the duty of the legal counsel, but the frequency of contacts with the defence attorney varies based on the ability of a detainee to pay for those services. For detainees who depend on the obligatory and free defence attorneys, such contacts are often reduced to only once a month. In contrast, chaplains are usually able to visit a detainee once a week. As a consequence, it is easy to understand why these questions emerge repeatedly in spiritual advice. One pressing challenge for chaplains is to maintain and build helpful contacts with various actors of the legal system.[6]

In the process of investigative custody there are two main elements of interest: the first follows from the challenges caused by frequent interrogations that often lead to special emotional distress. Many detainees experience an urgent need to talk about their stressful experiences. It is important to recognise that prisoners can talk to spiritual advisors in a very different way than they may with prison guards, social workers and other prisoners (whom they may encounter during their daily hour's walk). Co-prisoners are part of a forced community that follows its own unspoken code. A major rule of this code is that prisoners have to conceal any weaknesses. In addition, the forced community has developed its own system of values concerning sexual offences; accordingly, prisoners accused or convicted of sexual offences rarely tell anyone about their past, as that would trigger violence from other prisoners. Detainees often think that guards are part of the criminal investigation and suspect them of being informers. Conversations about current events during the encounter with a spiritual advisor are highly important during this phase and may be accompanied and supported by religious acts such as prayers or blessings.

In general, the longer the period of imprisonment lasts, the more the shock of imprisonment decreases. This phenomenon can be better grasped through the following anecdotal evidence from one of the authors (FS) regarding the spiritual advice of a man imprisoned in a small Swiss remand prison for an attempted sexual offence. The man went through different and typical phases during his encounters with the spiritual advisor during pre-trial detention. When starting the spiritual advice sessions, this detainee offered the chaplain (FS) a cup of coffee. This act gave some kind of normalcy to the situation, evoking the freedom of an encounter outside a context of incarceration. In that situation, the detainee was able to view himself not exclusively as a person in need, but also as host. Conversations in this first phase may appear superficial, but serve to establish a basic relationship and trust. Only in the second phase of the encounters the detainee became able to talk about the crimes he was accused of. Because of the shameful and sexually violent connotations of the criminal charges he started to tell his story only when he came to realise that the chaplain's response was free of negative judgements and moral accusation. The description of the crime provided by the detainee at this stage, however, was still significantly different from reality. Only in the last part of this

---

[6]See Street Level.

phase, when the prisoner was experiencing the relationship with the chaplain as stable, he was able to tell the facts and events in a transparent and reliable way.

In this phase of pre-trial detention it is useful for the spiritual advisor to be knowledgeable about the procedures and speed of a criminal inquiry, the frequency of contact with the officially appointed legal counsel, therapeutic measures according to SCL (Art. 63 and 59) and the advisability and possibility for the detainee to obtain a private defence attorney.

After that, there is in general a longer phase after the final interrogation when – in a legal sense – the detainee is mostly waiting for the next event, the court appearance. During this time the focus of prisoners tends to shift to their social, professional, private and family-related environment. For example, the prisoner mentioned above happened to have very little opportunity for contacts with the outside world, partly because of the criminal inquiry, and partly due to his family situation. Indeed, many families react in a hostile way to accused sexual offenders and family members and friends may refuse to stay in contact with the detainee.

Experiences in this last phase can be very depressing for detainees. In the case just described, the prisoner's ex-employer let the work place of the detainee stand empty for a while before firing him; in addition, his girlfriend abandoned him shortly after learning about his accusations. The only person who maintained a connection with him was his mother. She occasionally came to see him, but communicating through the glass caused difficulties for both of them. The father remained absent. The prisoner had to give up his apartment due to lack of income; friends from a club emptied it for him. Social pressure upon the whole family became enormous when the media made the case public and the isolation of the detainee increased further.

The events experienced by this detainee illustrate two main typical problems: first, the accused experiences what Goffman (1968) calls 'social death.' Second, the question is raised what should and can be the role of social work in remand prisons. If a pre-trial detainee lacks any intact familial or social structure – which experience shows is often the case – the individual is in danger of losing his or her social standing and self-definition or even their previous identity or position in life altogether. In addition, it is important to remember that the presumption of innocence must apply at this stage: the accusation could be false or perhaps cannot be proven sufficiently. Spiritual advisors have a duty that they will barely be able to fulfil: to offer or coordinate assistance with a high range of social problems emerging from imprisonment. To address them, their communication skills are highly needed in prison cells, partly to complement the lack of sufficient time of social workers, partly because they offer specific advice that goes further than the professional advice provided by social workers. From the point of view of prison chaplaincy it would be desirable to make available a community chaplaincy *outreach* project. Such a project would be mandated to establish and coordinate much needed links between prisons and the world outside, in cooperation with the prison chaplain.

During this phase of imprisonment pre-trial detainees may free themselves from the fixation on criminal inquiry and court procedures and begin to question the reasons and motivation which brought them into that situation. Usually, these questions focus on the material causes of imprisonment, with little (moral) evaluation in terms of guilt or innocence. This reflection deals first of all with the reality of a detainee's life. Detainees start to examine factors, decisions, attitudes and ideas, which have contributed to their current situation.

During investigative custody, psychological care is mostly delegated to psychiatric emergency services. The reason for that seems to be related to the (not necessarily justified) perception in the canton of Zurich that therapy can rarely begin in a serious way before a detainee is sentenced, except in the special case of court orders to start therapeutic measures before the end of the trial. Other cantons in Switzerland have established psychiatric services that provide regular supportive care also to pre-trial detainees (Elger 2008). Pastoral and therapeutic competence of the spiritual advisor is challenged by the lack of therapy. If the relationship between the detainee and the chaplain is solid in this last phase of investigative custody and profound life-concerning topics arise, some form of minimal therapeutic competence is needed. However, spiritual advice does not systematically raise therapeutic issues nor avoids them in case they are raised by the detainee. It should be added here that minimal competence means that a spiritual advisor should be able to recognize severe psychological dysfunction of a detainee and advise or obtain directly professional help, e.g. in the case of acute suicidal intentions or a psychotic decompensation of a detainee.

As time in investigative custody is limited, pastoral and therapeutic skills should be used in a well-defined setting. Solution-oriented methods offer important competencies and skills for questioning and defining a contract between client and chaplain.[7]

6.3.1.2 Possible Solutions

The main problem with clients in investigative custody is the incredible stress level that this type of imprisonment causes: at this point of the encounter between the spiritual advisor and the detainee the future of the latter is unclear. This causes a very high distress for detainees, even if they are aware and admit the crime they committed. The question remains for them: what will happen to me and will there ever be a possibility of returning to my life, my family or my job? In investigative custody there are few options for dealing with the problems usually faced by detainees. To solve the issues of insecurity and existential questions with clients, it would be ideal to engage in interdisciplinary councils bringing together several professional groups including prison medical doctors, social workers, psychological staff, lawyers and chaplains in a manner that is respectful of the boundaries between those disciplines and the legal obligations of confidentiality for the different professions. The presumption of innocence is a prerequisite for this type of case management.

---

[7]For more information see www.weiterbildungkirche.ch.

Such form of case management would contribute to a broader assessment of the needs of detainees. For example, the need for sleep medication could be mitigated if the social worker had knowledge of private information such as familiar pressures or job-related matters and could alleviate insomnia of detainees by providing help with the causes for it. At the same time, detainees would need fewer psychiatric interventions if anxiety can be avoided because the attorney helps a detainee to know the next steps and to have a realistic picture of time frames. For chaplains and other spiritual advisors, participation in this process would lead to a necessary widening of their skill-sets. In addition to their pastoral skills, chaplains need to gain competencies in various fields of expertise. For example, a cursory knowledge of foreign languages is becoming a fundamental requirement. The translation of legal documents and the promotion of the client's understanding of those documents are also crucial.[8]

Opportunities for psychotherapy during investigative custody are sadly lacking at the present time in many detention facilities. Therefore, spiritual advisors must have competencies and experience in crisis intervention as well as deeper therapeutic knowledge of a relevant psycho-therapeutic system (e.g. systemic, client centred, solution oriented or others) and be sensitive to time and frequency of visits in this setting.

The bond between social workers and spiritual advisors should be strengthened. For example, one frequent challenge for clients is that there are very few people willing to give a hand with the task of cleaning out the detainee's flat while he or she is imprisoned. Local parishes are often able to support social workers with volunteers who are happy to help.

6.3.2 Being Sentenced and Beginning a Prison Term

During trial and sentencing, spiritual advice has to face new and varied situations and to choose among different approaches. There are many issues to tackle for spiritual advisors that become exacerbated in closed prisons and forensic psychiatric facilities.

In this paper, the discussion will be limited to a few distinct types of detention, each of which raises specific questions to be addressed by spiritual advisors: halfway houses, semi-detention,[9] and other (alternative) types of custody including minimum security.

---

[8]In some countries, there is a council of three men: inmate-selected, nominated and elected by other inmates and approved by wardens. This council could provide the basic help others need with translation etc. inside prisons.

[9]This term refers to semidetentiom ('Halbgefangenschaft'), describing a sentence serving 12 month or less. The prisoners are free during the day to do their work for a maximum of 13 h. At weekends and evenings they are imprisoned.

6.3.2.1 Halfway Houses and the Experience of Shame

With halfway houses we refer here to a form of open custody where sentenced detainees have the obligation to follow different types of treatment for addiction disorders or a program of resocialisation. In general, a certain time often elapses between sentencing and the beginning of the detention in a halfway house. Everyday life runs its course – and all of a sudden the start of the sentence is due. Experience in chaplaincy shows that details of the client's offence as well as the treatment requirements during the stay at the halfway house are kept secret as much as possible among detainees and the people with which they are in contact. Many detainees refuse to acknowledge their feelings of shame. For spiritual advisors this implies that any work on the reasons and the mode of delinquency, or any dialogue about the disturbing situation of imprisonment with the detainee is difficult. Spiritual advisors have to carefully and sensitively search for openings that permit to start a conversation in order to begin the process of working through the problems of the clients. Experiments with electronic monitoring in Basel and (soon) in Zurich with the aim to permit detainees to live in their own homes suggest that these problems will become more pronounced in the future, but will be thereby removed from the responsibilities of institutional spiritual advisors. Committal of the sentenced detainees to halfway houses will probably occur less frequently, because detainees are rather 'detained' to stay within a defined distance of their homes thanks to electronic monitoring. These offenders will be invisible to chaplaincy, and the challenge for spiritual advisors in those cases will be to find a way to know about those cases and to get permission to contact them at home in order to continue offering pastoral care in this special situation.[10] As reported in the literature, the issues of shame (Wurmser 1994) and secrecy are preoccupying detainees and can have harmful effects on mental health if they go untreated and unnoticed.

We report on the case of a man in a halfway house who was found guilty of having committed fraud and was sentenced to stay in this type of institution for 6 months. The fraud had been committed almost 2 years prior to the conviction. During the 2 years between the offence and the conviction, the man had been able to return to his normal life in an unconscious attempt to deny the sentence. He had more or less managed to live a life without contact with the justice system, found a new girlfriend and a new job and appeared very proud of what he had achieved so far. But then, suddenly, he had to start his halfway house detention. This event challenged his ability to handle the situation. The man felt overwhelmed by questions and doubts: What should he tell his girlfriend? How much should he tell his employer? As it is often the case, the first question to rise was: 'is there any person with whom I could talk?' Shame is an extremely powerful emotion and is known to discourage sharing this experience with others. Spiritual advisors have to

---

[10]Canadian community chaplain Patricia Wilson in Halifax /NS, speaking in a private interview about her work in this field with electronic monitoring and people under house arrest, reported that both types of punishment often lead to shame.

be sensitive to these difficulties and find ways to subtly inquire about the detainees' well-being. Shame can make detainees take far-reaching decisions, for example, to leave a partner, the girlfriend in this case, in order to avoid disclosing information about the committed crime. The risk, in this context, is that such a decision of secrecy about someone's present situation can lead to loneliness in a time when the comfort and encouragement of other people is strongly needed.

6.3.2.2   Resolution of the Issue

Halfway houses are not necessarily offering the service of spiritual advice, due to the prevailing opinion that such form of detention is *easier to support* than detention in a closed prison. However, even in a halfway house, detainees have to face a high level of distress because of social and family-related issues, possible upcoming financial problems, shame about what has happened and unresolved autobiographical issues.

In this context, two points must be clarified. First of all, the service of spiritual advice should be accessible for everyone. The thought that, in open forms of detention, whoever is in need of support could speak to a spiritual advisor in his or her religious community overlooks the reality that shame often prevents otherwise instinctive and rational help-seeking behaviour. Therefore, the initiative has to be on the side of the help-offering person: spiritual advisors should come and offer counsel and advice on pressing matters and should actively explore feelings of shame concerning past crimes. They should help their clients to accept and not to suppress their feelings of shame and to understand that emotions have a meaning and can be overcome with time.

Second, spiritual advisors need specific competencies in dealing with shame. They need to learn how to encourage detainees to be mindful and to acknowledge their emotion and to take responsibility for their own lives. Studies have shown that this type of psychological approach in which spiritual advisors could take part, has an effect to facilitate reintegration and to prevent further offences (Kesten et al. 2011).[11]

6.3.3   Other Types of (Alternative) Custody

In order to analyse the challenges for spiritual advice in other types of (alternative) custody, including semi-detention where a detainee only spends the night in prison, we will have to consider again the difficulties faced by detainees in the beginning of any prison or alternative custody sentence. Many detainees are from vulnerable populations, they come from the margins of society and have never found – or have

---

[11] See also the program 'start now' under the direction of RL Trestman: http://cmhc.uchc.edu/programs_services/startnow.aspx.

lost – access to the so-called *civil world* due to risky behaviour such as (poly)drug-abuse or alcoholism. These detainees tend to serve short sentences. Therefore, spiritual advice should mainly concentrate on helping offenders to reflect on and initiate discussion of possible further and imminent steps. Here, spiritual advisors must take the initiative in reaching out to and collaborating with other services for the good of their clients. They should aim at working collaboratively with social services, as well as with federal and non-governmental providers of housing and care after prison discharge. From the point of view of prison chaplaincy, it is an obvious step to put into place an outreach office that works on the threshold between prisons and the community in order to develop solutions for and with the client who is willing to risk an (other) attempt to restart his life. The concept of this service is well-known in the Anglo-Saxon correctional and church services under the label of 'community chaplaincy' (Bunniss et al. 2013).

6.3.3.1 Solutions

Since the prison sentence is usually relatively short (from a few days to 6 months), time is usually a crucial factor in alternative custody. The time spent in prison may be seen by some marginalised clients as a period for rest and renewal of mental and physical strength. During this time, it is important to work together with social workers and medical personnel. The main task of spiritual advisors is to help everyone to think about the situation together and to discern possible next steps in the collaborative process. As spiritual advice compared to other professionals has specific means and a specific explanatory context – spirituality – to address and interpret the situation, it is recommended that a qualified community chaplain or other type of spiritual advisor is available and ready to accompany the client through these steps if the detainee agrees.

In collaboration with social workers and institutional chaplains, community chaplains could address the need for a bridge between the world within the facilities and the outside world, with the task of providing outreach programs or discussing opportunities with the client. In other words, a major goal is to work towards a new and less self-destructive life for the client.

6.3.4 Custody for Deportation and the Issues of Rage and Grief

This kind of imprisonment, in Switzerland, is a purely administrative measure within immigration law and not, strictly speaking, based upon the violation of criminal law. Therefore, it should be clearly distinguished from investigative or prison custody. The time frame of custody for deportation is limited, and since the agreements between the EU and Switzerland have been in place, the duration of stay for people detained under immigration law has shortened considerably. New regions of crisis emerge continually worldwide, with changing socio-cultural and geographic or religious conditions. Nonetheless two key issues remain constant: personal fate and the question of justice in the world. These two issues repeatedly produce tears and rage in the men and women with whom spiritual advisors come into contact. Fear arising from the uncertainty of the trip to the country of origin is common. Reasons for such fears may be related to complex family contexts, as well as the experience of failure, or the question of whether or not suppression of of threats to the life and integrity of the persons themselves or their ethnic group will continue. Questions surrounding economic realities may also be at stake. With regard to this kind of custody, the question of justice is important at several levels: personal, social and economic. It is the task of the spiritual advisor to bear and to support this reflection, the rage and helplessness of the detained persons. But it is also necessary for spiritual advisors to be able to explain some of the realities of the global world and its disparate systems of society and economy in a realistic and knowledgeable way. Moreover, these answers need to be framed in a theological or multi-religious context. Justice in a secular belief-system can reflect different contents than in a Christian, Muslim, Buddhist or Hindu system.

Men and women in this type of custody usually show emotional responses such as rage and frustration (Graf et al. 2013). Typical claims heard in custody for deportation according to the first author's own experience include: 'I've done nothing!'; 'I didn't steal!'; 'I didn't kill!'; 'I've just tried to build myself a new life in this part of the world!'; 'Now I'm imprisoned for nothing and I don't know when I am allowed to go!'; 'Do you think this is right?'

It is a great challenge for spiritual care in a multi-cultural society to gain fundamental knowledge of unfamiliar systems of thought, while remaining open to personal encounters that reflect broad and diverse perspectives.

6.3.4.1 Solution

The key problems related to injustice in the context of custody for deportation obviously cannot be entirely and exclusively solved by the spiritual advisor. However, in this kind of custody, the chaplain must actively mobilize and expand his own knowledge and empathy resources. With many clients coming from foreign countries, there is a way to ease their pain by connecting with them: namely, by remembering that the chaplain is a pastor and responding spiritually. Even when those in custody are believers in a non-Christian religion, the chaplain can establish a connection with them by relating moments of grief and pain to the blessings of a 'Supreme Entity' that are pertinent to the clients and their situation. In this way, clients can usually find a common ground for joining in prayers and intercessions. In such moments in life, it is not the differences between religions that matter, but rather the encounter with another human being and the shared connection to the spiritual world. Prayers, blessings, rosaries, crosses and representations of other faiths are extremely important as is the reassurance that the 'God,' or 'divine presence' in the client's worldview is present in time of need.

Yet, even this may not be sufficient. In addition, it is important to be very *serious* about the issues of justice. Discussing the lack of justice in this world is a way to bring reality back into the situation of the imprisoned client. Since lack of justice occurs at almost every level of human experience, it is important to be able to relate to it in a multilevel way, including the personal, the economic, the socio-cultural and several other levels. These are the competencies which a spiritual advisor should acquire in order to be truly helpful in the context of custody for deportation.

6.4 Challenges in Closed Facilities and Forensic Psychiatric Therapeutic Facilities

6.4.1 Conditions for Chaplaincy: Cultural and Religious Factors

In Switzerland, up to 80 % of pre-trial detainees and 70 % of sentenced prisoners come from foreign cultures (für Statistik 2010). While the multiplicity of languages is a relevant topic in investigative custody and requires multi-lingual abilities of the spiritual advisor, this problem vanishes almost completely in closed facilities. The average duration of a stay in those high security prisons is 3 years (not including the time detainees have already served in investigative custody) – long enough to learn the national language sufficiently for conversations with the chaplain.

In this multi-cultural setting the primacy of a Christian chaplaincy service has been questioned. The answer provided is partial and refers to the understanding that the chaplaincy mandate in Switzerland is aimed at the care of the whole of society and that it is an agreed fundament of the Swiss constitution that in many situations the confederation and church share a task (Widmer et al. 2008).[12] Within the mandate of spiritual advice for society, all ethnic, cultural, and religious diversities are included as a matter of course.

In contrast, among prisoners sentenced to a therapeutic measure under SCL Art.59.3 or Art.64 – Swiss people are predominant (around 70 %); this group is around 70 % Christian (für Statistik 2010).

6.4.2 Persons Sentenced to Indeterminate Security measures

Persons sentenced to indeterminate security measures are in general under the obligation to undergo mandatory psychiatric and other types of treatment.

In Switzerland, criminal law distinguishes two types of indeterminate security measures. Clients belonging to the group of people under Art 59.3 of the Swiss

---

[12] See also See Nationale Forschungsprogramme Schweiz (2011).

criminal law code are sentenced to an in-house therapeutic measure that is to be re-evaluated after 5 years. Courts may produce a request of release from prison, or decide that the security measures should continue in an appropriate form (für Statistik 2007). The experience of the last author during 20 years of prison medicine has shown that reluctance is often considerable to release prisoners who have been considered dangerous in the past, even if the risk of a re-offence is low. Indeed, those who have to decide about release are often held responsible if a released prisoner commits another crime and media attention is very high. In this context, detainees may feel under extensive psychological pressure which can be intensified by the fact that annual therapeutic reports will be established to inform the annual re-examination of the sentence by the office responsible for the security measures.

We need to distinguished are the cases of clients in indefinite detention under Art 64 of the Swiss criminal law code that became part of the revision of the code in 2006 in the context of an increased focus on protection of society over the last 10 years.

The statistics summarizing sentences under Art 59.3 during the past years show that the number of prisoners under security measures is steadily growing.[13] That means clients needing intense care from chaplaincy will increase further in the future.

6.4.2.1 Challenges for Spiritual Advice

Any comfort that comes from the certainty of a definite time frame of incarceration lacks completely during indefinite imprisonment. In his book 'Ärztliche Seelsorge' (1946), the Austrian psychiatrist Viktor Frankl reflected upon a personal observation he made while being a prisoner in a concentration camp: the pressure of indefinite imprisonment can induce a feeling of no future (Frankl 1946). It becomes almost impossible to set goals, existence is reduced to the present moment, and life threatens to lose its content and meaning. This feeling that there is 'no future' can lead to dramatic consequences including total neglect and suicidal tendencies (Frankl 1946). The absent or unknown date of release is a common factor between indefinite detention under SCL and Frankl's observation.

Indefinite sentences lead to more persistent and pressing existential issues for spiritual advisors and the health care team, in particular issues of ageing and death. In this context, one of the most urgent questions for spiritual advice in prison is if and how age, sickness or dementia will affect risk assessments concerning re-offence. It is often recognised by experts that age is a soft factor in re-offending prognosis tools (Lösel 2010; Tinik and Hudak 2014). Yet, even if it is possible to weigh age as an important factor in prognosis, such an analysis tends to neglect

---

[13]See Bundesamt für Statistik: Kriminalität, Strafvollzug – Daten, Indikatoren, Sanktionen und Untersuchungshaft: Erwachsene (http://www.bfs.admin.ch/bfs/portal/de/index/themen/19/03/03/key/ueberblick/03.html).

that there are many unknown factors, especially in the context of mental and physical illness. From direct observations made by the first author in the context of imprisonment, it can be inferred that acute phases of disease cannot be predicted accurately, since actual physical and mental changes in the course of disease and the slow machinery of administrative evaluation are almost never in mutual accordance. The low chances of being released once a security measure is decided lead to many cases of virtually indeterminate imprisonment and this has significant effects on the personal dignity of ill prisoners. The first author has observed several cases where dignity was negatively affected, especially from a chaplain's perspective. Imagine, for instance, a person transferred to the outside hospital 2 days prior to death; since the person is judged as extremely dangerous because of his or her status of indefinite detention, the routine security procedure is applied. That means that two police officers are appointed to keep watch at the door of a dying human being, a situation that would appear paradoxical and morally problematic.

Nowadays, there is a consensus between correctional services and spiritual advisors that such a scenario is morally not acceptable because it is not in line with respect for human dignity. From the perspective of the dying prisoner, a new inner existential process has begun – and the violation of human dignity resulting from the application of the standard procedure is seen as endangering this process in an unjustified way. In addition, from the perspective of the divine (however conceived) the existential condition of a dying human being demands the same respect for all persons, independently of the legal definition of 'dangerous person.'

In light of what has been said so far, the following normative claim is advanced which unites spiritual advisors from various backgrounds: Human dignity shall be inviolable. This claim must hold true for every single person, including the most violent criminal.[14] Human dignity is an intrinsic value. It is violated when a certain group is denied the opportunity to die with dignity. The protection of human dignity must be one of the greatest duties for society.

Being a constitutive component of the life cycle, the process of dying must be allowed to unfold in the most dignifying state possible for as long as the dying person is under the custody of the government. Indeed, true respect for human dignity would mean that human beings should die outside of detention facilities. However, the fear that a detainee could still be dangerous even at the end of life has led to increased reluctance of authorities to pronounce an interruption of the sentence upon medical advice at the end of life. This has significant implications for the education of prison staff given the enormous amount and quality of care required by vulnerable persons such as people affected by dementia, critical illnesses or displaying peculiar needs during the dying process.

---

[14]See German constitution Art 1(1): 'Human dignity shall be inviolable. To respect and protect it shall be the duty of all state authority.'

From a prison chaplain's perspective, it is recommended that the following merciful procedure should be acknowledged as minimum standard of care: a shortened risk assessment for at least the three following categories of people:

(a) Detainees suffering from acute or chronically-acute conditions
(b) Detainees diagnosed with dementia or presenting severe age-related cognitive decline
(c) Dying prisoners

The main question to address is how such decisions can be made responsibly in prisons where security issues have to be balanced with respect for the dignity of dying prisoners. The first step would be to request a medical evaluation of the prognosis and of the remaining physical abilities of the detainees. Problematic in this respect is the lengthiness of administrative procedures. It is crucial to be able to make decisions timely based on the changing conditions of an ill prisoner. A place where prisoners can die with dignity should be found in advance and proportionate security measures should be decided in advance. Spiritual advisors in prison can help to engage in the dialog with authorities to find humane solutions that are possible within the legal context.

The following case observed by the first author can serve to illustrate the difficulties spiritual advisors encounter when taking care of detainees sentenced to indeterminate security measures. A man who had been imprisoned for over 20 years and was suffering from the conditions of his imprisonment advanced a request to share with the spiritual advisor his feeling about indefinite detention. From the resulting conversation it emerged that his suffering was primarily of social and psychological nature because he blamed a lack of contact with the world. Because of his social isolation he increasingly experienced prison as a hostile environment. This individual experience is not rare. As human beings' well-being depends on the benevolent 'you' of the other it is understandable that prisoners suffer from the fact that their 'you' is restricted to other prisoners and guards who are rarely in a position to represent a benevolent 'other.' Despite the varying conditions throughout Swiss prisons it is a common experience that restrictions and prohibitions (e.g. diminished possibilities to be visited or to make phone calls, prohibition of cell phones, censoring of mail, impossibility of writing and receiving e-mails etc.) are for many prisoners very hard to bear. Indefinite detention is a security measure imposed in the interest of public safety to prevent the inmate from re-offending. However, the concept of punishment applies to crimes that have been already committed, not for those one might commit in the future. Knowing this, the situation of a prisoner with a limited sentence is clearly different from that of a prisoner who has served his time but remains detained not because he deserves further punishment, but in order to prevent a risk to society. This risk may be statistically small but since the consequences can be severe, i.e. sexual abuse or physical harm to others, those who have to make these decisions often tend to be risk averse and to decide in favour of prolonged detention in doubtful cases.

For the detainees this often results in feelings of helplessness and the impression of having lost control over their lives. The situation of being imprisoned for over

20 years with only four hours of visiting time per month, with only 120 min per month for phone calls, the knowledge that every written word will be read by the prison staff, and the impossibility of using modern communication tools (such as cell phones, text messaging or e-mails) is very likely to generate a partial or even total loss of social contact. As time passes, it becomes hard to find anyone who is willing to visit or who wants to be called. Imprisonment can lead to the social death of a person (Liebling and Maruna 2013). Prolonging this situation for an indefinite amount of time is, in itself, a very strong interference with human rights and has the detrimental consequences on physical and mental health and spiritual wellbeing. From the perspective of spiritual advice, this situation is perceived as endangering the spiritual health of a person as the social and communitarian context is a key element of the spiritual dimension. Having committed a crime and being incarcerated leads to being reallocated to a facility (i.e. the prison) and a community (i.e. prisoners and guards) which have not been freely chosen by the detainee. Nonetheless, it is possible and even desirable to provide prisoners with the opportunity to celebrate and live their personal spiritual life within and despite of these constraints. This function can be primarily implemented by the spiritual advisor. Spiritual care, indeed, can introduce a new element of sense even in the context of indefinite incarceration. Since indefinite detention also implies the difficulty to determine where punishment ends and security measures begin, detainees may be facing indeterminate feelings of shame. Sometimes the experience of prolonged punishment is only relieved by death. Some form of perceived inner freedom, i.e. the feeling to remain the 'captain of [one's] soul,'[15] to have maintained control over their own spiritual life, is for inmates one of the most important issues that spiritual advisors in prison must address, not only with regard to the clients themselves but also to the community at large.

To appreciate what it means to address freedom as a spiritual help issue, the following case of a sentenced paedophile may be paradigmatic. This person had undergone many years of therapy in the prison system and experienced over 20 years of various psychological approaches. After a first, more favourable evaluation, he faced the threat of being re-assigned and falling back into indefinite detention during his next re-evaluation. At that stage, true spiritual help appeared crucial to maintain contact with the client and to be aware of the client's fear and desperation without minimizing or worsening it. This goal was accomplished by more frequent visits of the chaplain. In that specific situation, it was fundamental to help the prisoner discover the range of (inner) freedom, albeit limited, to which he could have access.

---

[15] See in this context the famous poem 'Invictus' by Arthur Quiller-Couch that helped Nelson Mandela to keep his inner freedom during his long imprisonment. Its last part was cited by B. Obama: 'It matters not how strait the gate/How charged with punishments the scroll/I am the master of my fate/I am the captain of my soul' (Memorial 2014).

6.5 Conclusion: Spiritual Help and Freedom

The search for spiritual healing calls upon the role of the spiritual advisor to support and favour contacts of detainees with people outside prison. This role is crucial for facilitating connections with the world outside prison and for supporting the families of prisoners. Authentic spiritual help would also include working in multiple ways to address the issue of (inner) freedom. This issue should be addressed in several ways: philosophically, psychologically, theologically or in whichever way it presents itself in the client-advisor encounters. The purpose of this freedom-creating work is to assist and support prisoners in the process of understanding how the meaning of life can be preserved within prison walls and how life after imprisonment is still worth living. Freedom, in this definition, is primarily conceived as *inner freedom*, that is the possibility to understand who you are, what your life really is about, the act of trying to live in the current situation without fear and the perception to remain 'captain of one's soul.' Creativity is the key to this kind of spiritual work. This is illustrated by an emblematic case that occurred during a spiritual care project in which the first author was personally involved and which used rap as a means of self-expression. A young man was enrolled in the project with the goal to help him to increase his inner freedom. At the beginning, however, he was only capable to rap about drugs and violence in a way that was not helping him to perceive the deeper meaning of his life. But after discussing his rap lyrics with a group of fellow inmates, he was able to move forward and to find the confidence and inner freedom to address the deeper issues that were underlying those lyrics. The group discussion motivated him to accept being confronted with values and meanings related to his experience of imprisonment, his future and the people he loved, such as his mother. This generated in him the desire to make his mother proud of him again.

> 'I find myself standing at the prison gates feeling so helpless. Where should I go now? What's happening to me next? Freedom so endless – but there will be no help. Who needs a prisoner from the compound? Thank God I have mother in my life. Still one more chance to make her proud.' (by Level Zero)[16]

Connected with the issue of indefinite detention and its place within the correctional system is the issue regarding the anthropological stance of spiritual care (Geist 2010). This issue represents a constant challenge for chaplaincy and spiritual care in general. For example, the Christian anthropological stance in prison chaplaincy finds its starting point in the biblical notion of *Imago Dei* (Gen 1, 26ff).[17] According to Christian anthropology what could be said about God can also be said about men. From this perspective it is believed that, although it may be hard

---

[16] Song 'for my moma' by Level Zero from the CD 'Through the walls' edited by prison hope, release planned for spring 2013.

[17] See the Bible Gen 1.26ff: 'And God said, Let us make man in our image, after our likeness. So God created man in his own image, in the image of God created he him; male and female created he them' (Jacob et al. 2007).

sometimes to see a man as an image of God, it is the task of the spiritual advisor to emphasize the potential that every human being has, even if it is unseen for the time being. In this anthropological stance, no man can be viewed as forever defined the same, unchangeable and therefore untreatable. Part of the fundamental work of every spiritual advisor in prison must be to proclaim this anthropological approach of creative freedom that each single human is to be conceived as *imago Dei* and to help and support prisoners independently of their crime. Failing to accomplish this goal would have profound consequences for society.

References

Achermann, C. (2009). Multi-perspective research on foreigners in prisons in Switzerland. In V. Bilger & I. Van Liempt (Eds.), *The ethics of migration research methodology: Processes, policy, and legislation in dealing with vulnerable immigrants* (pp. 49–79). Sussex Academic Press.

Bundesamt für Statistik. (2007). Verwahrungen: Verurteilungen und Vollzug. *Neuchâtel: Bundesamt für Statistik.* http://www.bfs.admin.ch

Bundesamt für Statistik. (2010). Freiheitsentzug, Strafvollzug – Daten, Indikatoren.

Bunniss, S., Mowat, H., & Snowden, A. (2013). Community chaplaincy listening: Practical theology in action. *The Scottish Journal of Healthcare Chaplaincy, 16*, 42–51.

Elger, B. S. (2008). Towards equivalent health care of prisoners: European soft law and public health policy in Geneva. *Journal of Public Health Policy, 29*(2), 192–206.

Frankl, V. E. (1946). *Ärztliche Seelsorge.* Wien: Deuticke.

Geist, M. (2010). *Das Menschenbild im Strafrecht. Internationale Tagung in Wien vom 21. bis 24. September 2009 im Bundesministerium für Justiz.* Wien: Neuer Wissenschatlicher Verlag.

Goffman, E. (1968). *Asylums: Essays on the social situation of mental patients and other inmates.* New Brunswick: AldineTransaction.

Graf, M., Wermuth, P., Häfeli, D., Weisert, A., Reagu, S., Pflüger, M., & Jones, R. (2013). Prevalence of mental disorders among detained asylum seekers in deportation arrest in Switzerland and validation of the Brief Jail Mental Health Screen BJMHS. *International Journal of Law and Psychiatry, 36*(3), 201–206.

Green, H. F. (2013). *Prison stories: Living the life of a prison Chaplain.* Bloomington: Author House.

Jacob, B., Jacob, E., & Jacob, W. (2007). *The first book of the Bible, Genesis.* Jersey City: KTAV Publishing House.

Kesten, K. L., Leavitt-Smith, E., Rau, D. R., Shelton, D., Zhang, W., Wagner, J., & Trestman, R. L. (2011). Recidivism rates among mentally ill inmates: Impact of the connecticut offender reentry program. *Journal of Correctional Health Care, 18*(1), 20–28.

Liebling, A., & Maruna, S. (2013). *The effects of imprisonment.* London: Routledge.

Lösel, F. (2010). *What works in reducing reoffending: A global perspective.* Paper presented at the First European Seminar of the STARR project. Cambridge, UK.

Memorial, N. M. S. (2014). Transcript of Barack Obama's speech at Nelson Mandela's memorial. In *Francophone African poetry and drama: A cultural history since the 1960s.* Jefferson: McFarland & Company, Inc. 173.

Mitchell, J., & Latchford, G. (2010). Prisoner perspectives on mental health problems and help-seeking. *The Journal of Forensic Psychiatry & Psychology, 21*(5), 773–788.

Röthlisberger, P. (2005). *Skandale: Was die Schweiz in den letzten zwanzig Jahren bewegte.* Zürich: Orell Füssli.

Tinik, N., & Hudak, D. (2014). *Examining the factors associated with recidivism.* Retrieved from https://dspace.rmu.edu/xmlui/bitstream/handle/11347/25/Tinik.pdf?sequence= 1&isAllowed=y

Todd, A., & Tipton, L. (2011). *The role and contribution of a multi-faith prison chaplaincy to the contemporary prison service.* Retrieved from http://orca.cf.ac.uk/29120/1/Chaplaincy %20Report%20Final%20Draft%20%283%29.pdf

Widmer, T., Strebel, F., Landert, C., Brägger, M., Rüesch, P., Burla, L., & Laubacher, A. (2008). *Studie zur Stellung der muslimischen Bevölkerung im Kanton Zürich. Bericht zuhanden der Direktion der Justiz und des Inneren.* Zürich: IPZ.

Wurmser, L. (1994). *The mask of shame.* Northvale: Jason Aronson.

Chapter 7
A Balanced Diet – From Facts to Solutions

Bernice S. Elger

Abstract It is well known that health is in large part dependent on diet. Inadequate nutrition causes health issues and fatalities among prisoners; food-related contagions are a regular occurrence in prisons; and prisoners are often overweight or obese due to their poor diet and infrequent physical activity. The issue of prisoners' diets is now being recognized as an important aspect of public health, particularly given that access to food is a human right. In this chapter the barriers to good diets for prisoners and the role of healthcare professionals in maintaining prisoner nutrition are described.

A balanced diet is an important determinant of health. Vitamin deficiency in prison has led to many deaths among inmates in the past and continues to cause health problems and death in a substantial number of prisons worldwide. In Western prisons, outbreaks of foodborne diseases are regularly reported. Prisoners often gain weight in prison due to an unhealthy diet and lack of exercise. Experts have started to address a balanced diet in prison as being an important public health topic, especially in countries with rising populations of ageing prisoners. Access to adequate food is a basic human right and international soft law requires prison physicians to advise prison administrations on prisoner nutrition. The chapter presents barriers to a balanced diet in prison and discusses in more detail the role of health care professionals.

7.1 Introduction

In most detention facilities, prisoners' access to food depends to a large extent or even exclusively on the incarcerating authorities. In many Western countries, prisoners who have their own funds may buy food from the prison shop. Relatives

B.S. Elger (✉)
Institute for Biomedical Ethics, University of Basel, Bernoullistrasse 28, 4056 Basel, Switzerland
e-mail: b.elger@unibas.ch

© Springer Science+Business Media Dordrecht 2017
B.S. Elger et al. (eds.), *Emerging Issues in Prison Health*,
DOI 10.1007/978-94-017-7558-8_7

may send food which is in general strictly controlled by prison security personnel to avoid the entering of illegal substances or weapons.

Access to adequate nutrition is a human right (Robinson 1999). 'Every prisoner shall be provided by the administration at the usual hours with food of nutritional value adequate for health and strength, of quality and well prepared and served' (United Nations 1977).

Food is an important determinant of health. Consequences of insufficient nutrition comprise different diseases and death for example through starvation, vitamin deficiency, diet-influenced heart disease, and foodborne diseases such as cholera or botulism. Food is culturally and religiously regulated and lack of access to authorized food provokes conflicts. In a number of diseases, medical treatment involves particular diets, the most prevalent case being diabetes. Anaphylactic shock is a life-threatening event if prisoners with food allergies are exposed to allergens. Several double blind intervention studies have established a decrease in violence in prisoners who received vitamin and lipid supplements (Bohannon 2009; Gesch et al. 2002). In the following parts, the significance of a balanced diet in prison will be discussed and solutions to overcome barriers will be presented.

7.2   Malnutrition

Malnutrition and contaminated food have caused many deaths of prisoners in the past, particularly during wars. In prisons and concentration camps, scurvy (vitamin C deficiency) and diarrheic diseases were well known (Carpenter 2006; Heraut 2008; McRorie Higgins 2006; Tharakan 2010).

Malnutrition still remains an important problem in many prisons worldwide, although vitamin treatment (e.g. vitamins A, B, C) is easy and cheap. Scurvy, uncommon in modern times, is a problem in prisons in Africa. Prison health personnel need to know about its presence and its presentations to avoid misdiagnoses. The International Committee of the Red Cross (ICRC) observed swollen and hard legs in prisoners that proved to be caused by insufficient blood levels of vitamin C (Bennett and Coninx 2005).

Beri-beri, which is caused by vitamin B deficiency killed a significant number of prisoners in several African prisons and has been underreported (Ahoua et al. 2007; Ake-Tano et al. 2011; de Montmollin et al. 2002). The typical triad that led the International Committee of the Red Cross to diagnose beri-beri was a positive squatting test, oedema and a diet consisting exclusively of white rice. 'The disease is more common than generally assumed, also in Africa and especially in prisons' (de Montmollin et al. 2002: 234). Thiamin treatment provoked an immediate decline of the symptoms.

Vitamin A deficiency has been described as a significant public health problem among prisoners in Kenya and may cause blindness (Mathenge et al. 2007). A cross-sectional observation study of 148 male inmates in a provincial prison in Papua New Guinea showed a 10.4 % sample prevalence of clinical optic neuropathy that was associated with folate deficiency (Tousignant et al. 2013). Malnutrition of prisoners has also been incriminated as a factor causing increased disease susceptibility because lack of proteins in known to affect immune defence (Mataev et al. 2004). A study among prisoners in Nigeria found decreased serum proteins within an average of 7 months confinement (Olubodun et al. 1996). Permanent neurological damage to malnourished prisoners has also been described (Olubodun et al. 1991) and food deprivation has been suspected to have caused mental disorders in Russia (Marilov 1998).

A study in the US found 'elevated rates of cancer among HIV-infected individuals' in prison and the authors discussed poor diet as the likely cause (Baillargeon et al. 2004).

In prisons that provide a sufficiently balanced diet, vitamin deficiencies may be caused by politically motivated hunger strikers (Kalk et al. 1993) or food refusal due to psychiatric disease. Larkin found a high prevalence of mental disorders amongst remand prisoners refusing food (Larkin 1991).

7.3 Foodborne Infectious Diseases

Foodborne infectious diseases are preventable if food production in correctional facilities meets 'minimum safety standards, including sufficient refrigeration facilities, training of food handlers, and exemption of ill food handlers from work' (Cieslak et al. 1996: 1883). Foodborne enteric disease is not limited to prisons in a few non-Western countries (Ranjbar et al. 2010). In the United States foodborne gastrointestinal outbreaks occur regularly in correctional facilities. From 1974 to 1991, 88 foodborne outbreaks involving 14307 cases of illness were reported from 31 states and territories. Among those were the cause was identifiable, Salmonella species, Clostridium perfringens, and Staphylococcus aureus were the leading pathogens. Researchers voiced concern about increasing outbreaks caused by Salmonella species because they are dangerous for prisoners suffering from HIV infection (Cieslak et al. 1996).

More recent studies confirm the notoriety of foodborne outbreaks. In an outbreak due to Clostridium perfringens at a county jail in Wisconsin, an environmental investigation determined the cause to be a casserole that was composed of improperly prepared and stored food (CDC 2009).

Greig and colleagues (2011) carried out a literature review over a 10 year period to analyse documented enteric outbreaks worldwide and to identify effective infection control interventions. Where available they examined outbreak investigation reports. A total of 76 % and 21 % of the outbreaks were found to be associated with bacterial agents and viral agents, respectively. The most frequent identified pathogens were Salmonella, Clostridium perfringens, norovirus, pathogenic Escherichia coli and Campylobacter species. Recommendations about prevention of outbreaks list as a priority measure the monitoring of food temperatures and effective infection control procedures. The authors advise prison facilities to train inmates working in the kitchen in safe food handling (Greig et al. 2011).

A study from the UK also confirmed foodborne enteric disease to be caused by inappropriate food preparation. An outbreak of Salmonella enterica serovar Enteritidis caused symptoms in 327 of 1419 inmates at a London prison. The study showed that food distribution and individual food history complemented by microbiological investigation permitted identification of the food item that had caused the outbreak: prisoners who had eaten egg cress rolls were 26 times more likely to be affected (Davies et al. 2012).

In the US, an environmental investigation carried out after an outbreak of Shiga toxin-producing Escherichia coli came to the conclusion that inmates employed at an onsite dairy had probably acquired the infection during work and exposed other inmates after they transported contaminated items into the main prison and kitchen. The onsite dairy provided milk to all state-run correctional facilities in the region. The US Centers for Disease Control and Prevention reminded all correctional authorities of the importance to 'consult with public health officials to design and implement effective infection control measures' (CDC 2012b: 149).

Professionals working in prisons should also be aware of prison specific reasons for foodborne disease. Botulism, a potentially fatal paralytic illness, is caused by food contaminated by Clostridium botulinum toxin. Several studies reported botulism caused by alcoholic drinks made illicitly in prisons (Vugia et al. 2009). The self-made alcohol is typically made of fruit, sugar, and water. Vegetables are sometimes added and in one case a 'baked potato saved from a meal served weeks earlier and added' to the alcoholic beverage was the suspected source of C. botulinum spores (CDC 2012a: 782). The outbreak led to prolonged hospitalization of several inmates. Knowledge of these environmental causes is important to be able to treat inmates rapidly and to reduce associated treatment costs.

In Australia, a study reports a prison outbreak of tonsillopharyngitis caused by foodborne group A streptococcus. Close to a third of all inmates of the same prison facility were affected. The pathogenic streptococcus species was isolated from throat swab specimens obtained from primary and secondary cases and was also identified in hand wounds and throat swab specimens from one of the food handlers. Inmates probably acquired the disease after the consumption of contaminated curried egg salad sandwiches prepared by the food handler suffering from infected hand wounds (Levy et al. 2003). The authors acknowledge that similar outbreaks have been described in nursing homes and military bases. However, it is important to remember the specific situation in prisons and to adopt particularly strict surveillance procedures. Inmates' income depends on their work, and many are hesitant to report minor wounds or illnesses because of their fear of loss of income during the time absent from work.

Outbreaks of other foodborne diseases such as hepatitis A and E have been described. In India, hepatitis E virus was identified as having caused a major outbreak. The suspected source of the infection was contaminated drinking water (Kar et al. 2000).

7.4 Nutrition and Non-Communicable Diseases

It has been known for many years that prisoners, particularly female inmates, often gain weight in prison due to unhealthy diet and lack of exercise (Shaw et al. 1985). For a long time, public health specialists have almost exclusively looked at transmissible diseases in prison. The driving motivation was the fear that diseases such as tuberculosis and HIV infection would spread to the non-prison community if left untreated in prisons. In 2012, a systematic analysis of BMI and diet in prison was published in the Lancet (Herbert et al. 2012) and received considerable attention (Arnold 2012; Kuester et al. 2012; Yuan et al. 2012). The new driving motivation to prevent not only communicable, but also non-communicable diseases is mostly related to a fear of rising costs. Herbert and colleagues systematically searched online databases for studies reporting 'data on body-mass index and physical activity among prisoners'. They identified 31 eligible studies that included 'more than 60,000 prisoners in 884 institutions in 15 countries'. According to the data, female detainees were more likely to be obese than non-incarcerated women in the USA and Australia and female mean calorie-intake was higher than recommended levels. Female and male prisoners had a sodium intake 2–3 times higher than recommended. This leads the authors to conclude:

> Contact with the criminal justice system is a public-health opportunity to promote health in this vulnerable population; the costs to the individual and to society of failing to do so are likely to be substantial (Herbert et al. 2012: 1975).

Apart from lifestyle factors such as exercise and smoking, diet is an important factor in preventing chronic diseases and improving cardiovascular health.

> In countries where the frequency and duration of incarceration are rising, the incidence and consequences of non-communicable diseases will inevitably increase in parallel with an ageing population in jail (Arnold 2012: 1932).

A study from the UK showed that prisoners' general health was compromised. Unhealthy behaviours included high sugar diets which are not only responsible for cardiovascular disease, diabetes and obesity, but also for caries. Not surprisingly, the study found that the oral health of the examined remand prisoners was poor: high levels of decay were found and prisoners showed high use of prison dental services. Poor oral health, which is contributed to by pre-prison lifestyles and health behaviours, causes considerable health care costs (Heidari et al. 2007).

7.5 Special Diet Requirements

An estimated 80,000 prisoners in the US are diabetic and need access to an appropriate diet as part of their medical treatment (American Diabetes Association 2007). Imprisonment is an unique opportunity for public health efforts concerning diabetic patients. Studies in the UK have shown that good metabolic control is possible in prison if rigid dietary regimens and compliance with treatment are ensured through structured diabetic care that should be offered in all prisons (MacFarlane et al. 1992). In France, a study showed that diabetic diets were available in only 61 % of the 115 prisons that responded to the survey. During a 10-year period, the authors counted 20 hospital admissions for diabetic ketoacidosis and 14 for hypoglycaemia (Petit et al. 2001).

In Japan, good diabetic control was documented in a prison where most prisoners work 8 h a day 5 days a week and consume a high dietary fibre diet including 'Mugimeshi', which consists of boiled rice with barley. The retrospective analysis of 4385 medical records over a 6 year period showed significantly decreased mean fasting plasma glucose and hemoglobin Alc (HbA1c) levels compared to values at prison entry. A total of 28 % of insulin treated patients and half of the patients treated with oral hypoglycemic agents 'were able to discontinue their treatment and maintain good metabolic control' (Hinata et al. 2007).

In the US, the 2nd U.S. Circuit Court of Appeals ruled that 'denial of dietary product isn't deliberate indifference' (Anonymous 1999: 10). A New York prison inmate had complained that the prison refused to provide a dietary supplement to him which he claimed was a necessary medical treatment. Due to his HIV infection he was suffering from weight loss and his CD-4 T cell count was decreasing. The detainee had refused antiviral treatment and wished to receive the supplement instead. The court argued that 'a difference of medical opinion does not constitute indifference or carelessness and therefore is not a constitutional violation' (ibid.).

Disagreement exists about the right of detainees to receive a diet that is in line with religious rules. In Arizona and Colorado, inmates have started court battles to fight for 'the right to receive kosher or vegetarian meals in prison'. Prison officials referred to the high costs of providing a special meal for only a few detainees within the institution. The Colorado Department of Corrections agreed to offer kosher meals to inmates under the conditions that the detainees 'paid 25 % of costs that exceeded the regular prison diet, which the department calculated to be $90 per month per inmate' (Stein 2000: 509). Others opposed kosher meals in prison because they considered it a 'potential display of favouritism that could cause friction among inmates and a hassle for foodservice employees who would have to prepare the food separately with special utensils' (Stein 2000: 509).

7.6 Diet and Aggressiveness

Several intervention studies were recently published in well-known scientific journals on the influence of vitamin, mineral and essential fatty acid supplements on prisoners' antisocial behaviour. One of them, a randomised, placebo-controlled trial, showed that compared with placebos, 'those receiving the active capsules committed on average 26.3 % (95 % CI 8.3–44.33 %) fewer offences (p = 0.03, two-tailed)' (Gesch et al. 2002). The authors concluded that 'antisocial behaviour in prisons, including violence, are reduced by vitamins, minerals and essential

fatty acids with similar implications for those eating poor diets in the community'
(Gesch et al. 2002: 22). In 2009, the journal Science reported that psychologist
Bernard Gesch is carrying out a 'more ambitious study than ever before' in order to
confirm results of his previous study on nutritional supplements. The article also
mentions a study within the Dutch prison service that, similar to Gesch's 2002
study, 'has also recently found that supplements reduce violence' (Bohannon 2009:
1614). The Dutch study, published in 2010 (Zaalberg et al. 2010), recommended a
cautious interpretation of data. It investigated 'the effects of food supplements on
aggression, rule-breaking, and psychopathology' among 221 young Dutch prisoners
aged 18–25 years who received either nutritional supplements (vitamins, minerals,
and essential fatty acids) or placebos. Treatment duration was 1–3 months. Similar
to the study by Gesch, incidents reported by prison guards were significantly
reduced ($p = .017$, one-tailed) in the 115 inmates who received the supplements,
as compared with the 106 prisoners who were treated with placebos. However, the
study found no significant improvements in several other (self-reported) outcome
measures (ibid.).

7.7 The Role of Food in Enhancing Compliance with Medical Treatment

'Bad' food in prison has been associated with insufficient compliance with HIV
treatment. A Spanish study investigated reasons for decreased treatment adherence
in prisoners with a focus on factors specific to the prison environment. The cross-
sectional study included all patients receiving antiretroviral treatment in three
Spanish prisons. In 54.8 % of cases, prisoners were non-compliant. Prisoners who
indicated difficulties in taking medication classified the food as 'bad', and those
suffering from anxiety or depression showed increased non-adherence to treatment
(Blanco et al. 2005).

Food has also been mentioned as promising incentive for prisoners to complete
tuberculosis treatment among Russian prisoners and ex-prisoners. The completion
of tuberculosis treatment was compromised because of social factors, drug and
alcohol addiction, and difficulties tolerating medications because of other diseases,
particularly HIV and hepatitis. 'Prisoners and former prisoners ranked help with
obtaining an internal passport and money, followed closely by food and a job, as the
most desirable incentives to completing TB treatment' (Fry et al. 2005: 1027).

7.8 Barriers to a Balanced Diet

Barriers to a balanced treatment are in part related to costs. In the US, but also
in some other regions, a tendency exists to give less weight to social determinants
of crime and to see prisoners as meriting punishment, i.e. prisoners don't deserve

vitamins (Mossberg and Anggard 1994) and to believe that food costs in prison should be kept minimal.

> How would you approach development of a food service plan—budgeted at less than $3 per person per day—for a growing population that included both men and women, the young and the elderly, the healthy and the chronically ill, vegetarians and meat eaters, and, very likely, at least one representative of each racial/ethnic group residing in the United States? (Stein 2000: 508)

Stein reports that across the United States 'the average amount budgeted for food-related expenses by state departments of corrections is $3.71 per inmate per day and may be as low as $2.05 per inmate per day in Mississippi and Florida. 'We are using public money to fund correctional food services, and the public wants us to feed inmates for the least amount of money possible' (Stein 2000: 508)

More than 10 years later, in spite of inflation, the amount is even lower. 'The current economic downturn has caused some states to consider serving inmates less food to save money' (Collins and Thompson 2012: 210). One study investigated the nutritional value of prison meals in South Carolina where meal costs were reported to have decreased to $1.13/day per inmate. In comparison to Dietary Reference Intake recommendations, prison meals 'revealed higher levels of cholesterol, sodium, and sugar and lower levels of fibre, magnesium, potassium, vitamin D, and vitamin E than recommended' (Collins and Thompson 2012: 210). The authors of the study urge that prisoners should be offered more fruits, vegetables and whole grains, while sodium and sugar should be reduced in inmate meals in order to 'improve health, decrease chronic disease, reduce medical costs, and benefit taxpayers' (Collins and Thompson 2012: 210).

Diet habits are formed during childhood. Food can fulfil different functions and is often one of few sources of pleasure, particularly in prison. Food is also sometimes used as a means to fight prison related depression and boredom. It is not sufficient to offer healthy food in prison if prisoners continue previously adopted bad health behaviours. Indeed, health inequalities are known to be associated with social factors: lower income and lower education usually imply poorer health. The diet and exercise habits of prisoners mirror the inequalities that exist in the community (Agozino and Volpe 2009). Prisoners come from populations with poor eating habits and poor access to food. In the UK, a study found that both white and black female prisoners demonstrated poor health and health behaviours overall. In comparison to white female prisoners, black female inmates ate more healthily, but were still more likely to be overweight and to have higher blood pressure (Shah et al. 2011). A study carried out among released prisoners in the US established that 37 % 'did not eat for an entire day in the past month'. The authors found also an association between not eating for an entire day and certain HIV risk behaviours (Wang et al. 2013).

Food offered in prison may be relatively healthy and still not be eaten because of its taste. Prisoners 'universally complain that meals are neither tasty nor fresh, and it's no wonder why. The food budget amounts to a few dollars per prisoner per day. And by the time it travels from the central kitchen facility, through the layers of security and up to each ward's dining area, foods such as fried potatoes are lukewarm and limp' (Bohannon 2009). A study from the UK found prison food to comply with dietary recommendations, except for low selenium contents. However, prisoners ate overall unbalanced diets because they preferred buying food in the prison store.

> Vitamin content exceeded recommendations, with the exception of niacin in the vegetarian menu (12.6 mg compared with the reference nutrient intake of 16.8 mg). Selenium content was low in all menus [. . .] Vitamin D intakes were low (3.4 and 3.3 microg in 1996 and 1997, respectively) compared with the recommendation (10 microg) for those with limited exposure to sunlight. Intakes of a number of minerals fell below recommendations, with some prisoners barely meeting the LRNI [Lower Reference Nutrient Intake]. This was particularly notable for selenium where 35 % of prisoners in 1996, and 60 % of prisoners in 1997 had intakes below the LRNI (Eves and Gesch 2003: 167).

In the UK and in many prisons in the US, prisoners have the opportunity to make a variety of food choices. Eves and Gesch (2003) demonstrated that most of the examined UK inmates ate too much fat. This was largely attributed to the fact that many prisoners used their small salaries to buy and consume unhealthy food from the prison shop. Similarly, a study from the US found that weight increase was due to unbalanced consumption patterns in jail cafeterias, which are characterised by a tendency of 'eating more and enjoying it less' (Shaw et al. 1985: 39)

Finally, another barrier could be that prison personnel are not a good model for eating habits. In the US, obesity levels among prison guards were higher than national averages. Among the obstacles related to health living and a balanced diet were elevated stress levels due to 'concerns about security, administrative requirements, and work/family imbalance'. High stress levels were associated with elevated levels of hypertension. Prison personnel, similar to detainees, are therefore at 'high risk for chronic disease and environmental changes are needed to reduce risk factors' (Morse et al. 2011).

7.9   Solutions

An interview study among female detainees in Spain demonstrated that food is perceived as one of the most important health issues in prison, next to HIV/AIDS infection and drugs. The prisoners proposed various ways how to increase healthy behaviour. Qualitative studies are important to explore the views of detainees (Ritter et al. 2011; Ritter et al. 2012; Ritter and Elger 2013). More information concerning the opinions of detainees about food in prisons is needed in order to ensure their participation in interventions designed to favour a more balanced diet (Paredes i Carbonell and Colomer Revuelta 2000).

The first step is to make prisoners fully aware of their individual health risks and of the importance of a balanced diet. Plugge and colleagues (2009) therefore examined 'the prevalence of five modifiable cardiovascular risk factors (smoking, physical activity, diet, body mass index and hypertension)' among 505 women prisoners. The first data set was obtained on entry to prison and a second measurement was carried out after 1 month of imprisonment. Measurements of blood pressure, height and weight as well as results of life-style questionnaires demonstrated prisoners to be at high risk of future cardiovascular disease. More than 80 % were smokers and did not sufficiently exercise. A total of '86 % did not eat at least five portions of fruit and vegetables each day and 30 % were overweight or obese' (Plugge et al. 2009: 334). The authors deplored that 1 month of imprisonment did not lead to substantial improvements and recommended 'systematic approaches which address these health issues within UK women's prisons' (ibid.).

Shaw and colleagues have concluded that weight gain and hypertension in prison could be improved by 'changing ingredients, preparation, and the role of food in the prisoners' life' (Shaw et al. 1985: 39). However major adjustments of food management will be needed in many prisons to offer an adequate and balanced diet to prisoners with specific health conditions such as diabetes and pregnancy.

Several studies have tested the outcome of interventions concerning prison diets. Gil-Delgado and colleagues assessed changes in cardiovascular risk and metabolic syndrome associated with inclusion in a nutritional program that consisted of health education and the offer of a balanced diet. The authors carried out a non-randomized prospective cohort study in a Spanish prison over a 1 year period. Anthropometric and blood biochemical variables were evaluated several times during the year to assess the results of diet changes in 139 prisoners, of whom 95 completed the program. The researchers found diet modifications in 86.3 % of the sample. They were able to demonstrate significant improvements in weight, body mass, fat mass, abdominal perimeter and diastolic blood pressure and an overall reduction of cardiovascular risk. They recommend similar interventions to health professionals in other prisons as 'a new tool in the [prison] health care repertoire' (Gil-Delgado et al. 2011).

Sioen and colleagues (2009) tested the effect of an alpha-linolenic-acid-enriched food supply on cardiovascular risk factors in a sample of 59 healthy male prisoners in Belgium. They carried out a single-blind field trial with pre- and post-measurements where the intervention was to supply a diet of commonly eaten food enriched in alpha-linolenic acid intake (around 5 g/day as opposed to 2.8 g/day in a normal diet) to obtain a decreased, i.e. more healthy, Omega 6 to Omega 3 ratio (n-6/n-3 ratio). While subjects' waist circumferences, weight, BMI, and systolic blood pressure remained unchanged, the diastolic blood pressure significantly decreased and the HDL-cholesterol level increased in non-smoking participants (Sioen et al. 2009). The study seems to indicate that healthy diets have positive outcomes and are feasible in prison if the financial and human resources to offer healthy food are provided.[1]

Finally, a study carried out by Loeb and Steffensmeier (2011) explored challenges to health promotion among inmates aged 50 years and older. Focus groups with 42 prisoners established that food concerns were among the factors challenging

---

[1]The study seems to contradict the principle of subsidiarity (Council of Europe 2005: Art. 20) because it could be carried out with a non-vulnerable (non-prisoner) population.

prisoners' ability to engage in a healthy life style. Inmates said they try to adopt self-care strategies which included 'staying positive, managing diet and weight, engaging in physical activity, and protecting self' (Loeb and Steffensmeier 2011: 185). The study identified factors that increase inmates' motivation:

> A key motivator for pursuing good health was to be respected and perceived as healthy and strong by fellow inmates (Loeb and Steffensmeier 2011: 185).

Further studies are needed to develop and test programs to enhance inmates' motivation to comply with health promotion goals including adherence to a balanced diet.

7.10   The Role of Health Care Practitioners

International recommendations mention a specific role of prison health personnel concerning diet and nutrition in prisons. Within the explanation about 'equivalence of care' the Council of Europe recommendations stipulate that control of appropriate diets in prison is part of the duties of a prison physician.

> The role of the prison doctor is firstly to give appropriate medical care and advice to all the prisoners for whom he or she is clinically responsible. [...] It should also imply advising the prison management on matters concerned with nutrition or the environment within which the prisoners are required to live, as well as in respect of hygiene and sanitation (Council of Europe 1998: IB15 and IIA24).

The explanatory memorandum seems to imply that physicians are obligated to inform about imbalanced diets, but remain powerless when the competent authorities refuse to improve food.

> From this point of view, health care staff must therefore also be attentive to hygiene, food, the minimum space available to prisoners, etc.; if one or other of these criteria is not fulfilled, the doctor has a duty to inform the competent authorities in order that they may remedy the situation (Council of Europe 1999: IIA23.).

Single prison health care professionals may not be in a position to have a state increase food budgets for prisons in order to grant a balanced diet for inmates that is in line with current dietary recommendations. They should, however, inform reluctant authorities that they have an obligation to disclose the inadequate prison diet to their professional organisations. Medical organisations have a duty to engage in favour of equivalence of care in prisons.

In most prisons, health care professionals have significant means to improve prisoners' diets and to decrease food-related morbidity and mortality. The first important step is to remain up-to-date concerning medical evidence and to support ongoing training of colleagues and of other prison professionals. This is important in order to make appropriate diagnosis and to identify rapidly causes of food-related diseases.

Prison health professionals have a number of possible ways to convince authorities to improve prison diets and to engage in health promotion activities for prisoners. Balanced diets are a public health measure and cost-effective because a small increase of the budget spent for food and food management can avoid huge health care related costs that are caused by outbreaks of food-borne diseases and the tremendous increase in the prevalence of chronic illness such as diabetes, obesity and cardiovascular disease. Prison administrations need to understand, for example, that the 'easiest and most cost-effective means to facilitate good outcomes in patients with diabetes is instituting a heart-healthy diet as the master menu' for all prisoners (American Diabetes Association 2007: S79).

Health care professionals have a duty to engage in health promotion through education of their patients and appropriate treatment of psychiatric comorbidities such as depression and anxiety that lead to 'self-treatment' by food-overconsumption. Both education and treatment of psychiatric disorders are key factors in reducing the barriers to healthy diets caused by the food shopping and consumption habits of prisoners. Health professionals trained in motivational approaches can actively encourage necessary behaviour changes. They should link with researchers to encourage and facilitate nutrition intervention studies and assist in finding appropriate solutions for improved diets in individual patients and correctional institutions.

References

Agozino, B., & Volpe, S. L. (2009). Health inequalities in correctional institutions: Implications for health inequalities in the community. *Journal of Correctional Health Care, 15*(4), 251–267. doi:10.1177/1078345809333407.

Ahoua, L., Etienne, W., Fermon, F., Godain, G., Brown, V., Kadjo, K., Bouaffou, K., Legros, D., & Guerin, P. J. (2007). Outbreak of beriberi in a prison in Cote d'Ivoire. *Food and Nutrition Bulletin, 28*(3), 283–290.

Ake-Tano, O., Konan, E. Y., Tetchi, E. O., Ekou, F. K., Ekra, D., Coulibaly, A., & Dagnan, N. S. (2011). Beriberi, recurrent nutritional disease in a detention house in Cote-d'Ivoire. *Bulletin de la Societe de Pathologie Exotique, 104*(5), 347–351. doi:10.1007/s13149-011-0136-6.

American Diabetes Association. (2007). Diabetes management in correctional institutions. *Diabetes Care, 30*(1), 77–84. doi:10.2337/dc07-S077.

Anonymous. (1999). Denial of dietary product isn't deliberate indifference. *AIDS Policy Law, 14*(15), 10.

Arnold, F. W. (2012). Non-communicable diseases in prisons. *Lancet, 379*(9830), 1931–1933. doi:10.1016/S0140-6736(12)60471-1.

Baillargeon, J., Pollock, B. H., Leach, C. T., & Gao, S. J. (2004). The association of neoplasms and HIV infection in the correctional setting. *International Journal of STD & AIDS, 15*(5), 348–351. doi:10.1258/095646204323012869.

Bennett, M., & Coninx, R. (2005). The mystery of the wooden leg: Vitamin C deficiency in East African prisons. *Tropical Doctor, 35*(2), 81–84. doi:10.1258/0049475054036896.

Blanco, J. M., Perez, I. R., de Labry Lima, A. O., Recio, J. M., Lopez, E. G., & Basanta, J. J. (2005). Adherence to antiretroviral treatment in prisons. *AIDS Research and Human Retroviruses, 21*(8), 683–688. doi:10.1089/aid.2005.21.683.

Bohannon, J. (2009). Psychology. The theory? Diet causes violence. The lab? Prison. *Science, 325*(5948), 1614–1616. doi:10.1126/science.325_1614.

Carpenter, K. J. (2006). Nutritional studies in Victorian prisons. *Journal of Nutrition, 136*(1), 1–8.

Centers for disease control and prevention (CDC). (2009). Clostridium perfringens infection among inmates at a county jail – Wisconsin, August 2008. *Morbidity and Mortality Weekly Report, 58*(6), 138–141.

Centers for Disease Control and Prevention (CDC). (2012a). Botulism from drinking prison-made illicit alcohol – Utah 2011. *Morbidity and Mortality Weekly Report, 61*(39), 782–784.

Centers for Disease Control and Prevention (CDC). (2012b). Outbreak of Shiga toxin-producing Escherichia coli O111 infections associated with a correctional facility dairy – Colorado, 2010. *Morbidity and Mortality Weekly Report, 61*(9), 149–152.

Cieslak, P. R., Curtis, M. B., Coulombier, D. M., Hathcock, A. L., Bean, N. H., & Tauxe, R. V. (1996). Preventable disease in correctional facilities. Desmoteric foodborne outbreaks in the United States, 1974–1991. *Archives of Internal Medicine, 156*(16), 1883–1888.

Collins, S. A., & Thompson, S. H. (2012). What are we feeding our inmates? *Journal of Correctional Health Care, 18*(3), 210–218. doi:10.1177/1078345812444875.

Council of Europe (1998). *Committee of Ministers Rec(1998)7 on the ethical and organisational aspects of health care in prison.* www.coe.ba/pdf/Recommendation_No_R_98_7_eng.doc. Accessed Apr 2011.

Council of Europe. (1999). *The ethical and organisational aspects of health care in prison: Recommendation no. R(98)7 adopted by the Committee of Ministers of the Council of Europe on 8 April 1998 and explanatory memorandum.* https://wcd.coe.int/com.instranet. InstraServlet?command=com.instranet.CmdBlobGet&InstranetImage=530914&SecMode= 1&DocId=463258&Usage=2. Accessed 7 Apr 2013.

Council of Europe. (2005). *Additional protocol to the convention on human rights and biomedicine, concerning biomedical research.* http://conventions.coe.int/Treaty/Commun/QueVoulezVous. asp?CL=GER&NT=195. Accessed 30 Jan 2012.

Davies, A. R., Ruggles, R., Young, Y., Clark, H., Reddell, P., Verlander, N. Q., Arnold, A., & Maguire, H. (2012). Salmonella enterica serovar Enteritidis phage type 4 outbreak associated with eggs in a large prison, London 2009: An investigation using cohort and case/non-case study methodology. *Epidemiology and Infection, 141*(5), 931–940.

de Montmollin, D., MacPhail, J., McMahon, J., & Coninx, R. (2002). Outbreak of beri-beri in a prison in West Africa. *Tropical Doctor, 32*(4), 234–236.

Eves, A., & Gesch, B. (2003). Food provision and the nutritional implications of food choices made by young adult males, in a young offenders' institution. *Journal of Human Nutrition and Dietetics, 16*(3), 167–179.

Fry, R. S., Khoshnood, K., Vdovichenko, E., Granskaya, J., Sazhin, V., Shpakovskaya, L., Zhemkov, V., Zhemkova, M., Rowhani-Rahbar, A., Funk, M., & Kozlov, A. (2005). Barriers to completion of tuberculosis treatment among prisoners and former prisoners in St. Petersburg, Russia. *The International Journal of Tuberculosis and Lung Disease, 9*(9), 1027–1033.

Gesch, C. B., Hammond, S. M., Hampson, S. E., Eves, A., & Crowder, M. J. (2002). Influence of supplementary vitamins, minerals and essential fatty acids on the antisocial behaviour of young adult prisoners. Randomised, placebo-controlled trial. *British Journal of Psychiatry, 181*, 22–28.

Gil-Delgado, Y., Dominguez-Zamorano, J. A., & Martinez-Sanchez-Suarez, E. (2011). Assessment of health benefits from a nutrition program aimed at inmates with cardiovascular risk factors at Huelva Prison. *Revista española de sanidad penitenciaria, 13*(3), 75–83. doi:10.1590/S1575-06202011000300002.

Greig, J. D., Lee, M. B., & Harris, J. E. (2011). Review of enteric outbreaks in prisons: Effective infection control interventions. *Public Health, 125*(4), 222–228.

Heidari, E., Dickinson, C., Wilson, R., & Fiske, J. (2007). Verifiable CPD paper: Oral health of remand prisoners in HMP Brixton, London. *British Dental Journal, 202*(2), E1. doi:10.1038/bdj.2007.32.

Heraut, L. A. (2008). Miranda de Ebro: Medical condition of the concentration camp in the autumn of 1943. *Histoire des Sciences Médicales, 42*(2), 205–214.

Herbert, K., Plugge, E., Foster, C., & Doll, H. (2012). Prevalence of risk factors for non-communicable diseases in prison populations worldwide: A systematic review. *Lancet, 379*(9830), 1975–1982. doi:10.1016/S0140-6736(12)60319-5.

Hinata, M., Ono, M., Midorikawa, S., & Nakanishi, K. (2007). Metabolic improvement of male prisoners with type 2 diabetes in Fukushima Prison, Japan. *Diabetes Research and Clinical Practice, 77*(2), 327–332. doi:10.1016/j.diabres.2006.10.008.

Kalk, W. J., Felix, M., Snoey, E. R., & Veriawa, Y. (1993). Voluntary total fasting in political prisoners–clinical and biochemical observations. *South African Medical Journal, 83*(6), 391–394.

Kar, P., Gangwal, P., Budhiraja, B., Singhal, R., Jain, A., Madan, K., Gupta, R. K., Barua, S. P., & Nath, M. C. (2000). Analysis of serological evidence of different hepatitis viruses in acute viral hepatitis in prisoners in relation to risk factors. *Indian Journal of Medical Research, 112*, 128–132.

Kuester, L. B., Flanigan, T. P., Clarke, J. G., & Fletcher, A. (2012). Risk factors for non-communicable diseases in prison populations. *Lancet, 380*(9849), 1226–1268.

Larkin, E. P. (1991). Food refusal in prison. *Medicine, Science, and the Law, 31*(1), 41–44.

Levy, M., Johnson, C. G., & Kraa, E. (2003). Tonsillopharyngitis caused by foodborne group A streptococcus: A prison-based outbreak. *Clinical Infectious Diseases, 36*(2), 175–182. doi:10.1086/345670.

Loeb, S. J., & Steffensmeier, D. (2011). Older inmates' pursuit of good health: A focus group study. *Research in Gerontological Nursing, 4*(3), 185–194. doi:10.3928/19404921-20100730-01.

MacFarlane, I. A., Gill, G. V., Masson, E., & Tucker, N. H. (1992). Diabetes in prison: Can good diabetic care be achieved? *British Medical Journal, 304*(6820), 152–155.

Marilov, V. V. (1998). Mental disorders in food deprivation under extreme conditions. *Zhurnal nevrologii i psikhiatrii imeni S.S.Korsakova, 98*(6), 57–61.

Mataev, S. I., Sukhovei Iu, G., Petrov, S. A., Popov, A. V., Unger, I. G., Vasil'kova, T. N., & Argunova, G. A. (2004). The peculiaries of the nutrition and immune status of people in the condition of penitentiary establishment. *Voprosy Pitaniia, 73*(3), 25–30.

Mathenge, W., Kuper, H., Myatt, M., Foster, A., & Gilbert, C. (2007). Vitamin A deficiency in a Kenyan prison. *Tropical Medicine & International Health, 12*(2), 269–273.

McRorie Higgins, P. (2006). The scurvy scandal at Millbank penitentiary: A reassessment. *Medical History, 50*(4), 513–534.

Morse, T., Dussetschleger, J., Warren, N., & Cherniack, M. (2011). Talking about health: Correction employees' assessments of obstacles to healthy living. *Journal of Occupational and Environmental Medicine, 53*(9), 1037–1045. doi:10.1097/JOM.0b013e3182260e2c.

Mossberg, L., & Anggard, E. (1994). Medical ethics behind bars. Should a child's murderer get vitamins when feeling tired? *Läkartidningen, 91*(28/29), 2690–2693.

Olubodun, J. O., Jayesimi, A. E., Olasode, O. A., & Sobowale, A. B. (1991). Severe clinical nutritional neurological damage in a young Nigerian detainee. *Tropical and Geographical Medicine, 43*(1/2), 231–233.

Olubodun, J. O., Akinsola, H. A., & Adeleye, O. A. (1996). Prison deprivation and protein nutritional status of inmates of a developing community prison. *European Journal of Clinical Nutrition, 50*(1), 58–60.

Paredes i Carbonell, J. J., & Colomer Revuelta, C. (2000). A hearing in prison: Health needs perceived by women deprived of freedom. *Atencion Primaria, 25*(8), 536–541.

Petit, J. M., Guenfoudi, M. P., Volatier, S., Rudoni, S., Vaillant, G., Hermant, C., Verges, B., & Brun, J. M. (2001). Management of diabetes in French prisons: A cross-sectional study. *Diabetic Medicine, 18*(1), 47–50.

Plugge, E. H., Foster, C. E., Yudkin, P. L., & Douglas, N. (2009). Cardiovascular disease risk factors and women prisoners in the UK: The impact of imprisonment. *Health Promotion International, 24*(4), 334–343. doi:10.1093/heapro/dap034.

Ranjbar, R., Hosseini, M. J., Kaffashian, A. R., & Farshad, S. (2010). An outbreak of shigellosis due to Shigella flexneri serotype 3a in a prison in Iran. *Archives of Iranian medicine, 13*(5), 413–416. doi:010135/AIM.008.

Ritter, C., & Elger, B. S. (2013). Second-hand tobacco smoke in prison: Tackling a public health matter through research. *Public Health, 127*(2), 119–124.

Ritter, C., Stöver, H., Levy, M., Etter, J. F., & Elger, B. S. (2011). Smoking in prisons: The need for effective and acceptable interventions. *Journal of Public Health Policy, 32*(1), 32–45. doi:10.1057/jphp.2010.47.

Ritter, C., Huynh, C. K., Etter, J. F., & Elger, B. S. (2012). Exposure to tobacco smoke before and after a partial smoking ban in prison: Indoor air quality measures. *Tobacco Control, 21*(5), 488–491. doi:10.1136/tc.2011.043356.

Robinson, M. (1999). The human right to food and nutrition. *SCN News, 18*, 17–18.

Shah, S., Plugge, E. H., & Douglas, N. (2011). Ethnic differences in the health of women prisoners. *Public Health, 125*(6), 349–356. doi:10.1016/j.puhe.2011.01.014.

Shaw, N. S., Rutherdale, M., & Kenny, J. (1985). Eating more and enjoying it less: U.S. prison diets for women. *Women and Health, 10*(1), 39–57. doi:10.1300/J013v10n01_04.

Sioen, I., Hacquebard, M., Hick, G., Maindiaux, V., Larondelle, Y., Carpentier, Y. A., & de Henauw, S. (2009). Effect of ALA-enriched food supply on cardiovascular risk factors in males. *Lipids, 44*(7), 603–611. doi:10.1007/s11745-009-3307-5.

Stein, K. (2000). Foodservice in correctional facilities. *Journal of the American Dietetic Association, 100*(5), 508–509. doi:10.1016/S0002-8223(00)00153-X.

Tharakan, T. (2010). Nutrition in warfare: a retrospective evaluation of undernourishment in RAF prisoners of war during World War II. *Medical Humanities, 36*(1), 52–56. doi:10.1136/jmh.2010.004051.

Tousignant, B., Brian, G., Venn, B. J., Gould, C., McKay, R., & Williams, S. (2013). Optic neuropathy among a prison population in Papua New Guinea. *Ophthalmic Epidemiology, 20*(1), 4–12. doi:10.3109/09286586.2012.742552.

United Nations. (1977). *Standard minimum rules for the treatment of prisoners*. http://www.unhcr.org/refworld/docid/3ae6b36e8.html. Accessed Dec 2012.

Vugia, D. J., Mase, S. R., Cole, B., Stiles, J., Rosenberg, J., Velasquez, L., Radner, A., & Inami, G. (2009). Botulism from drinking pruno. *Emerging Infectious Diseases, 15*(1), 69–71. doi:10.3201/eid1501.081024.

Wang, E. A., Zhu, G. A., Evans, L., Carroll-Scott, A., Desai, R., & Fiellin, L. E. (2013). A pilot study examining food insecurity and HIV risk behaviors among individuals recently released from prison. *AIDS Education and Prevention, 25*(2), 112–123.

Yuan, J., Mao, Q. C., & Tang, J. L. (2012). Risk factors for non-communicable diseases in prison populations. *Lancet, 380*(9849), 1227–1228. doi:10.1016/S0140-6736(12)61709-7.

Zaalberg, A., Nijman, H., Bulten, E., Stroosma, L., & van der Staak, C. (2010). Effects of nutritional supplements on aggression, rule-breaking, and psychopathology among young adult prisoners. *Aggressive Behaviour, 36*(2), 117–126. doi:10.1002/ab.20335.

Chapter 8
Doing Gender in Prisons: Sport as a Way of Creating Masculinity

Heino Stöver

Abstract Which opportunities are being left for prisoners to create masculinity? In this chapter practicing sport is given as an example for prisoners to regain power and take control over the creation and re-creation of themselves. The social inclusion of prisoners through sport demands a more inclusive approach which also deals with Prison as an ultramasculine world where nobody talks about masculinity.

Hegemonic masculinity cannot be created in the same way that it is on the outside. As dominance over women can not be lived out in custodial settings, the construction of masculinity can mainly be achieved by dominance over and violence against other inmates. Prison rape is a particular form of violence that constitutes a serious social problem in the many prison system worldwide. Additionally, one could argue that prison rape is a particularly interesting form of violence in prison because it is a different phenomenon in prison than it is on the outside.

Which opportunities are left for prisoners to create masculinity? In this chapter practicing sport is given as an example for prisoners to regain power and take control over the creation and re-creation of themselves. The social inclusion of prisoners through sport demands a more inclusive approach which also deals with fundamental problems relating to participation inequalities in other domains, such as education, work and leisure.

'Prison is an ultramasculine world where nobody talks about masculinity.' (Sabo, Kupers, and London 2001: 3)

H. Stöver (✉)
Faculty 'Health and Social Work', Frankfurt University of Applied Sciences, Nibelungenplatz 1, 60318 Frankfurt, Germany
e-mail: hstoever@fb4.fra-uas.de

© Springer Science+Business Media Dordrecht 2017
B.S. Elger et al. (eds.), *Emerging Issues in Prison Health*,
DOI 10.1007/978-94-017-7558-8_8

8.1 Introduction

'Doing gender' signifies a reciprocal, interactive and steady process, in which both sexes are involved in constructing masculinity or femininity. Several other aspects, of which the 'social milieu' or social environment is supposed to be the most dominant framing factor, determine this process.

Numerous authors have described the relationship between hegemonic masculinity and crime, concluding that cultural constructions of masculinity are correlated with crime and that male prison culture reifies hypermasculinity (Karp 2010). Crime, and particularly violent crime, is clearly gendered.

This chapter focuses on the relationship between masculinity and sports because almost 95 % of the global prison population (Walmsley 2011) are men. It is striking that there is very little debate on why this is the case. Messerschmidt (1993) argues that the social construction of gender can explain much of the discrepancy between male and female crime rates. Masculinity is not a unitary concept, and cultures will manifest multiple conceptions of masculinity – a dominant, 'hegemonic' masculinity is contrasted not only with femininity, but also with alternative 'subordinated' and 'oppositional' constructions of masculinity (Karp 2010).

In many cultures hegemonic masculinity is characterized by authority, control, independence, heterosexuality, aggressiveness, a capacity for violence, and dominance, particularly over women, but also over homosexual men, men supposed to be weak(er) etc. Thus this hegemonic construction of masculinity predisposes men to criminality and violence. How can this concept of masculinity be lived in closed settings like prisons?

8.2 Doing Gender in Prisons

Doing gender in prisons means that the available resources and opportunities of creating and constructing masculinity are drastically reduced in comparison to the outside world: 'The prisoner is separated from all resources for enacting manhood: women, money, clothing and weapons and access to goods and services' (Philipps 2001: 14). Goffman (1961: 14) refers to this process of forced dispossession and deconstruction as 'mortification of the self.' The inmate is 'shaped and coded into an object to be fed into the institutional machinery.' Men in prison live in an environment characterized by danger, deprivation, and subordination on the one hand and the construction and regaining of power on a small scale with necessary everyday goods on the other hand.

Indeed, the most common resources used by men outside prison to construct (hegemonic) masculinity are unavailable or limited in closed settings; examples include having a working career, acquiring status symbols, being a father or being successful in adult heterosexual relationships (Connell 1983: 22–26). However, there are expressions of masculinity possible that are far more detailed, for example being a reliable man, having a good reputation, not informing on other inmates, being in or leading a gang or an association, having comrades and supporting them, and being 'a man to count on' when it comes to resistance and gang violence. Each of these interactional displays asserts masculinity and enhances male status and reputation. 'Hegemonic masculinity is defined as the culturally-prescribed ideal, and therefore, accorded the highest status. Individual males vary in the resources they can bring to bare to achieve this status.' (Karp 2010: 65). This process is far more difficult to conduct in prisons as degrading behaviour towards women, for instance, is not possible, and it is only possible to create and maintain hegemonic masculinity in a reduced, limited, and homophobic institution within a gender-homogenousenvironment.

8.3 Homophobia and Hypermasculinity

Prisons are not only total institutions, but are also homosocial and homophobic total institutions at the same time.

The worldwide dominance of the concept of homophobia is striking. Homosexuality is perceived as weak and opposed to the mainstream construction of masculinity. Homosexual prisoners often hide their sexual preferences in order to avoid being targeted by the violence of other inmates. Although homophobia is a global concept and is especially being followed in prison settings there ar countries, e.g. in Africa, where homosexuality still is a criminal offence and thus leading to even more problems in prisons. In those countries, fears of being caught in the act are widespread; those convicted receive a punishment of up to 30 years in prison (e.g. in Kenya).

However, same-sex activities are prevalent among prisoners. These are often perceived as 'prison contextual' that means prison specific same-sex sexual activities, and most consist of unprotected sexual contacts. This means that a huge area is taboo, and prisoners are living parts of their emotional and sexual lives in an extremely clandestine atmosphere.

Rape and sexual aggression among male prisoners as well as between prison staff and prisoners have received little attention in most countries, although it is reported as a reality in prison and is of high importance when it comes to consequences of infectious diseases. Evidence suggests that in Southern Africa unprotected sexual activity is the most prominent HIV risk behaviour and responsible for the majority of infections, whereas sharing of razors, tattooing and piercing instruments and injection-drug use are less problematic (Goyer and Gow 2001; Simooya et al. 2001).

While multiple masculinities are present, the dominant construction intensifies several elements of hegemonic masculinity. "Although various types of masculinity are adopted to counter some aspects of marginalization (scholar, skilled tradesman, and expert in legal matters and prisoners' rights are common examples), an extreme construction of masculinity as an identity position is the most universal response to the imperative to conform to the lower working-class dominated prison culture" (Jewkes 2005: 61).

Hypermasculinity is reflected in the norms of inmates, which together are called the 'prison code' (Sabo et al. 2001: 10–11):

> 'Suffer in silence. Never admit you are afraid [...] Do not snitch [...] do not do anything that will make other prisoners think you are gay, effeminate, or a sissy. Act hard [...] Do not help the authorities in any way. Do not trust anyone. Always be ready to fight, especially when your manhood is challenged [...] One way to avoid a fight is to look as though you are willing to fight. As a result, prisoners lift weights compulsively, adopt the meanest stare they can muster, and keep their fears and their pain carefully hidden beneath a well-rehearsed tough-guy posture.'

The cultural model for establishing relationships among men in prison is characterized by an overlay of the requirement for comrades to stick together, powerlessness, and suspicion. The accepted strategy is 'trust no one' and 'watch your back.'

Inside prison, inmates have the lowest status in wider society, are without work (either jobless on the outside or without work in the prison), have little or no money, are unable to express heterosexuality, and have no distinctive clothing, little autonomy, and no freedom. 'Thus male inmates seeking interactional confirmation of their masculine status are much less able to exploit the standard cultural markers of hegemonic masculinity: socio-economic status, a reputable profession, fashionable clothing, independence, whiteness, and heterosexuality' (Karp 2010: 66). It becomes necessary to identify and apply alternative means of doing gender: physical and psychological violence, rape and highly tabooed same-sex activities (at least for men), hierarchical structures, including dominance and obedience, and sports are all ways of constructing masculinity in prisons. This process is of special interest for the health of prisoners. Some authors point out that these alternative means are risky for their health (e.g. belonging to a prison gang means fighting if someone in the gang is challenged). Others, like Sillitoe in his short story 'The Loneliness of the Long Distance Runner', used sports as a medium for protest and a demonstration of independence (Sillitoe 1959).

Several authors find a debilitating tension between the cultural demands of prison hypermasculinity and the personal needs of individual inmates for emotional self-expression and affiliation (see Sabo et al. 2001). This becomes clear when looking at the ageing process of prisoners, when strengths are lacking and the construction of a tough man can no longer be maintained. Here, issues of personal care might become more acceptable. Toch (1998: 174) argues that hypermasculinity may serve short-term goals in prison, but is unsustainable and ultimately counter-productive. 'Sooner or later, hypermasculine men must age and must face their decreased capacity and propensity for violence' As their hypermasculine resources diminish, inmates face depression and hopelessness, and may resort to violent and suicidal escapist fantasies – a 'pseudo-reparative script' – in which an inmate 'believes that he can save the meaning of his life by heroically losing it' (Toch 2010: 175).

8.4   The Re-Construction of Manhood in Prisons

The re-construction of manhood and the construction of hegemonic masculinity in prison represent adaptation to an environment of extreme social control and extremely limited resources. Men in prison are forced to reconstitute their identity and status using the available resources. Social and cultural behaviours shift to accommodate this sparse, controlled environment.

In a way, it is easier for men in prison to keep their role and identity: cultural rules among male prison inmates are potent and straightforward, and the consequences of neglecting or breaking the rules are ever-present (Philipps 2001). In the outside world rules and functions are becoming more and more complex and. Behaving as a typical man in a very traditional way outside prisons with the family or with the partner, on the job, or in public can easily cause problems and conflicts (e.g. requirements of 'modern life' expect participation from men in daily family issues, household, child care, obeying non-smoking areas etc.). In a pluralistic society, where issues of gender stereotyping play a considerable role in all areas with efforts towards political correctness men are forced to adapt to democratic mechanisms towards each other and towards women. In contrast, the custodial setting remains quite clear with the above mentioned prison code to obey. . owever, applying or maintaining a healthy lifestyle and surviving conditions of intramural scarcity means very clearly to be able to identify possible psychological and even physical threats caused by other inmates because they want everyone to follow the perceived gender rules.

Prison is a particularly illustrative environment in terms of the cultural structure of manhood. The rapid isolation from the outside world is followed by total indoctrination into a separate society within the prison walls. The prison's social system exerts a powerful shaping effect on the lives of inmates, thereby intensifying the enactment of masculinity. A collective acting out of manhood-enhancing behaviours enforces newly gendered transactions. The harsher the environment, the more accentuated the behaviour; the more depleted the resources for augmenting manhood, the higher the stakes for the accrual of honour. Ironically, men are sent to prison for the very behaviours that become essential to their survival behind prison walls.

8.5   Recouping Threatened Manhood

Once inside, inmates become part of a prison-based cultural system built around rules for recouping their threatened manhood. Life revolves around the seeking of minor privileges and small status symbols and the avoidance of punishment. Privileges emerge as powerful symbols of the reassertion of autonomy and status. In prison, there is also a hierarchical subculture that influences role models beyond the superficial adaptation to the rules of the institution. The modes of social organization are built around these dynamics and the available limited goods and services. Honour and status are sought in battles over small items such as fruit, a can of soup, tobacco and paper, legal and illegal drugs or a package of coffee.

Through a combination of behavioural cues and the very active flow of gossips, an unknown inmate is sized up as a man. When living in close and crowded quarters, especially when avoidance is not possible, a sense of urgency prevails among inmates to assess and locate everyone on a cognitive map of the types of men in prison according to length of sentence, and type of offence.

Associations are often transitory in nature. However, the construction of social relationships is a key survival strategy in prison. Social isolation and ostracism leave prisoners vulnerable. The building of associations, particularly throughout the various locales in the prison, represents a valuable resource for the construction of a reputation as a 'stand-up man'. Associates, and particularly close associates, are a potential pool for mobilization in time of conflict.

8.6   Violence and Rape as Health Risks in Prison

In mainstream society, the gender order consists of two main paradigms: a hierarchal system in which men are dominant over women and another hierarchal system in which higher-status men dominate over other men, particularly over men with lower status, weaker and/or homosexual men, men from other cultural backgrounds (Connell 1995). These two processes mirror and support one another, and violence is one way in which status is attained, maintained and re-attained (Connell 1995). As dominance over women cannot be lived out in custodial settings, the construction of masculinity can mainly be achieved by dominance and violence over other inmates.

Empirical findings show that masculinity plays a complex and crucial role in the phenomenon of prison rape (Carlson 2009). Prison rape, or any coercive sexual contact is one particular form of violence and a serious social problem in the many prison system worldwide. Additionally, one could argue that prison rape is an especially interesting form of violence in prison because it is a different phenomenon in correctional institutions than on the outside. While men are the most likely victims of homicide, robbery, and assault both inside and outside prison, experiencing rape is relatively unlikely on the outside but much more common for men on the inside.

The true rate and extent of prison rape is unknown. From the existing literature, a multitude of issues surround prison rape, and it becomes clear that there are several relevant themes and contextual definitions that permeate estimation. It is agreed by most researchers in this area that sexual assault in prisons is a serious preoccupation, estimates vary as to the actual rates of victimization among inmates. Estimates of sexual assault victimization have varied between 1 and 41 % dependent on what acts are included. The annual rate in US prisons seems to converge about 5 % or less (see. Pont et al. 2015). A thorough review and meta-analysis of studies of prison rape concluded that 1.9 % of inmates have experienced sexual victimization over a lifetime of incarceration (Gaes and Goldberg 2004). Recently, Wolff and Shi (2011) found that 4 % of male inmates and 22 % of female inmates reported prisoner-on-prisoner sexual victimization (most often abusive sexual contact like inappropriate touching) during the previous 6 months. Seven percent of male inmates and 8 % of female inmates reported at least one type of staff-on-prisoner sexual victimization. Non-consensual prisoner-on-prisoner sexual acts affected less than 2 % of prisoners per 6 months, while staff-on-prisoner non-consensual sexual acts constituted less than 1.1 %.

As such, the question of why there are such vastly different estimates of sexual assault remains an important one. Several reasons for the differing rates have been posited: these include the hypotheses that researchers have used inconsistent definitions to operationalize prison rape, that scholars use different methods to collect information on prison rape, and that prison rape is a particularly under-reported crime in the prison system.

The consensus is that prison rape occurs frequently enough to be a contributing factor to additional prison violence as well as to an overall climate of physical domination.

8.7 The Example of Sports

McNay (1992: 17) stated:

'(I)n many respects, masculine characteristics can be seen to be related to dominant perceptions of the male body, i.e. firmness, aggression, strength.'

Prisoners with few resources to do gender compensate in other ways, such as sports. Success in sports is an example of how men construct masculinity by doing gender with sports.

Johnsen (2001: 195f) states that

'by practising sport the prisoners create a space where they take control over the creation and re-creation of themselves and their own well-being. Such spaces can be labelled heterotopias, and by making the practice of sport into a heterotopia for the creation and re-creation of himself as a subject, a prisoner centres his construction of subjectivity on the body. Bodily performances can be interpreted as expressions of masculinity, and when these bodily expressions become a part of the prisoners subjectivity, the prisoners are empowered, which makes it easier for them to handle the imprisonment [. . .] The sport-practising prisoners must exercise considerable self-discipline in order to express this bodily ideal, and managing to create himself within this bodily ideal therefore results in self-worth.'

From this perspective, intensive sports exercise contributes to the empowerment of men.

To shape the body using an amount of time and an intensity that most men were probably never able to devote outside prison also gives them a positive self-image as attractive men waiting for the (heterosexual) outside world. Thus body shaping does not simply fulfil a function inside prisons in terms of other inmates and officers.

Sport and especially weight training and body building are ways to construct masculinity via shaped bodies visible to all. Weight training is still the most common sport activity in most prisons. Prisoners think that weight training, which is done in order to construct a large, strong and muscular body, might contribute to enhancing 'macho masculinities' among prisoners.

Sport is important from this perspective, and muscular bodies are 'read' as masculine bodies. Prisoners' connection of masculinity to the body is therefore understandable, especially if we consider that sport is perhaps the only 'common' discourse for constructing masculinity that exists in custodial settings (Johnsen 2001).

In many prisons discussions are taking place with regard to the appropriateness of such sport facilities. In some countries (e.g. Norway) team sports are supported by prison authorities because of the social and educational value provided by learning social skills and fellowship, which are supposed to be promoted by team sports (Johnsen 2001).

Caplan (1993) found that recreational sports programmes play an important role in the social control of male prisons. Other findings show that these programmes are beneficial to inmates during their incarceration in a number of ways. Most respondents in Caplan's study claimed that involvement in recreational sport reduced stress and/or frustration, alleviated boredom, increased self-esteem, helped in the establishment of goals and routine, and assisted inmates in developing friendships. The study found out that both inmates and staff concluded that prison recreational sports did not contribute to additional aggression and were essential components of the prison regime. Recreation can be seen as a fundamental component of any healthy lifestyle and, hence, it is argued that recreation opportunities should be provided for those incarcerated.

Johnsen (2001: 196) states:

'while the prison uses the sports activities to maintain control over the prisoners, the prisoners use the sports activities to resist this control. The prisoners have different strategies for how to resist this control. Common to all, however, is that their exercise of sport is related to resisting the psychological violence that they experience as embedded in the control. When using sport for this purpose the prisoners built resistance by the cultivation of their bodies. This means that the prisoners' bodies become the sites of the resistance.'

8.8 Social Inclusion and Avoidance of Health Inequalities – The Need to Increase Sport Activities

Access to sport in prison should be equivalent to that available in the community. This may be even more important for the prison setting as sport events and trainings can be viewed as contributing substantially to social inclusion, at least for some men. Social inclusion of prisoners through sport demands a more inclusive approach which also deals with fundamental problems relating to participation inequalities in other domains, such as education, work and leisure. Inmates should be actively involved in the planning, organisation, guiding and evaluation of sport programs (e.g., enable developmental opportunities in coaching, refereeing, volunteering, etc.). Collaboration with the sports sector outside prisons is crucial for the transition from detention to post-detention and facilitating a successful return to society. It appears that one of the primary needs is to respond to prisoners' demands and requests. They ask for socialisation, and sports are one of the major vectors of socialisation. Sport enables them to meet people who do not belong to the prison environment, as well as to learn the rules and understand their benefits (EAC SPORT 2012).

Looking at the few opportunities and very limited resources for male prisoners to express their masculinities, doing gender by sport is one possible way to help male prisoners maintain and strengthen their identity. The predominantly preferred way to do that is muscle training as visible form of masculinity. However, this again excludes many prisoners and it is high time to introduce other forms of team sports to make this type of physical activities more accessible and to permit all men to achieve identity building, team-related, physical as well as social goals through sports.

References

Caplan, A. (1993). *The role of recreational sports in the federal prison system*. B .A. (Honours), Acadia University, Thesis submitted in partial fulfilment of the requirements for the degree of Master of Arts in Sociology.

Carlson, M. (2009). *Man up or punk out: The role of masculinity in prison rape*. Dissertation http://udini.proquest.com/view/man-up-or-punk-out-the-role-of-pqid:1912228451/. Accessed 29 Mar 2013.

Connell, R. W. (1983). *Which way is up? Essays on sex, class and culture*. Sydney: Allen & Unwin.

Connell, R. W. (1995). *Masculinities*. Los Angeles: University of California.

EAC SPORT Preparatory Action. (2012). *'Prisoners on the move!'* http://www.prisonersonthemove.eu/. Accessed 29 Mar 2013.

Gaes, G. G., & Goldberg, A. L. (2004). *Prison rape: A critical review of the literature*. Washington, DC: National Institute of Justice.

Goffman, E. (1961). *Asylums: Essays on the social situation of mental patients and other inmates*. New York: Anchor Books.

Goyer, K., & Gow, J. (2001). Transmission of HIV in South African prisoners: Risk variables. *Society in Transition, 32*(1), 128–132.

Jewkes, Y. (2005). Men behind bars: 'Doing masculinity' as an adaptation to imprisonment. *Men and Masculinities, 8*, 44–63.

Johnsen, B. (2001). *Sport, masculinities and power relations in prison.* PhD thesis, Norwegian School of Sport Sciences, Oslo.

Karp, D. R. (2010). Unlocking men, unmasking masculinities: Doing mens's work in prison. *The Journal of Men's Studies, 18*(1), 63–83.

McNay, L. (1992). *Foucault and feminism.* Cambridge: Polity Press.

Messerschmidt, J. W. (1993). *Masculinities and crime: Critique and reconceptualization of theory.* Lanham: Rowman and Littlefield.

Philipps, J. (2001). Cultural construction of manhood in prison. *Psychology of Men & Masculinity, 2*(1), 13–23.

Pont, J., Stöver, H., Gétaz, L., Casillas, A., & Wolff, H. (2015, August). Prevention of violence in prison – The role of health care professionals. *Journal of Forensic and Legal Medicine, 34,* 127–132. http://www.jflmjournal.org/article/S1752-928X%2815%2900105-5/references

Sabo, D., Kupers, T. A., & London, W. (2001). *Prison masculinities.* Philadelphia: Temple University Press.

Sillitoe, A. (1959). *The loneliness of the long distance runner.* London: W. H. Allen Ltd.

Simooya, O. O., et al. (2001). 'Behind walls': A study of HIV risk behaviours and seroprevalence in prisons in Zambia. *Aids, 15*(13), 1741–1744.

Toch, H. (1998). Hypermasculinity and prison violence. In L. H. Bowker (Ed.), *Masculinities and violence* (pp. 168–178). Thousand Oaks: Sage Publications, Inc.

Walmsley, R. (2011). *World prison population list* (9th ed.). International Centre for Prison Studies. http://www.idcr.org.uk/wp-content/uploads/2010/09/WPPL-9-22.pdf. Accessed 15 Mar 2013.

Wolff, N., & Shi, J. (2011). Patterns of victimization and feelings of safety inside prison: The experience of male and female inmates. *Crime & Delinquency, 57,* 29.

Chapter 9
Psychiatric Problems in Prisoners: Screening, Diagnosis, Treatment, and Prevention

Annette Opitz-Welke

Abstract Prisoners have a high prevalence of mental disorders. Suicide is a leading cause of death in prison, and self-harming behaviour and suicide attempts are common. Therapeutic services should be organized according to the needs of prisoners with severe mental disturbances. This includes psychiatric inpatient care and psychiatric outpatient care. In general psychiatric care in prison should provide the same quality of psychiatric care as that available in the community. Psychiatrists working in prisons should insist on being able to offer psychiatric treatment without being implicated in the correction system.

9.1 Introduction

Prison psychiatry is performed away from public eyes and therefore little is known about its challenges (Krassner 2011). Although hospitalized psychiatric patients in prison resemble those in forensic psychiatric security hospitals in some aspects such as socio-demographic variables, a recent study of inpatient treatment in the psychiatric department of Berlin revealed that the distribution of psychiatric diagnoses was rather similar to that of the psychiatric department of a Berlin Community Hospital (Opitz-Welke and Konrad 2012). Besides training in psychiatric care, knowledge of the legal process is also essential for prison psychiatrists because they would have a deeper understanding of the stress that prisoners are exposed to during their incarceration. In general, prisoners in remand have the highest risk of developing depressive symptoms and disorders (Cassau and Goodwin 2012; Eytan et al. 2011). Among prisoners who failed to pay a fine, a high percentage had psychotic disorders (Konrad et al. 2007) and disorders due to substance abuse. Long-term confinement in general may be connected to feelings of resignation and severe social deprivation.

Prison psychiatrists can stabilize the conditions of the prisoners through legal proceedings and are, in this aspect, definitely part of the correctional system. This may lead to role conflicts. However, the role of prison psychiatry should be seen as

A. Opitz-Welke (✉)
Department of Psychiatry, Justizvollzugskrankenhaus Berlin, Saatwinkler Damm 1a, 13627 Berlin, Germany
e-mail: opitz-welke@web.de

© Springer Science+Business Media Dordrecht 2017
B.S. Elger et al. (eds.), *Emerging Issues in Prison Health*,
DOI 10.1007/978-94-017-7558-8_9

a clear treatment option and not as a support unit for correctional goals (Konrad 2010). Therefore, prison psychiatrists should adhere as closely as possible to a purely therapeutic role, which may mean having to endure the pressure that is placed on medical experts in the correctional system.

In general, working as a prison psychiatrist means facing a cluster of specific problems (Appelbaum 2011b; Barth 2012; Burki 2010) such as those connected to the specific burdens of psychiatric disorders in prisoners. Further problems arise from the correctional system itself and from the difficulties of establishing adequate treatment facilities inside a correctional institution. Prison psychiatrists also face problems when liaising with external mental healthcare workers. Despite increasing scientific interest in psychiatric work in prison, there is still a lack of methodically sound studies on the subject, because the circumstances of incarceration complicate or prevent scientific work.

9.2 Prevalence of Mental Disorders in Prison

There is strong evidence of a high and possibly increasing prevalence of mental disorders in prisoners. A methodically sound systematic review and meta-analysis of 33,588 prisoners (Fazel and Seewald 2012) showed a pooled prevalence of about 4 % for psychotic disorders (3.6 % in men and 3.9 % in women). Major depression was diagnosed in 10.2 % of the imprisoned men and 14.1 % of the imprisoned women. Fazel and Danesh (2002) found a pooled prevalence of personality disorder in 65.5 % of the incarcerated men and in 42 % of the incarcerated women, including 47.5 % with antisocial personality disorder for men and 21 % with anti-social personality disorder for women, in a systematic review and meta-analysis of 62 surveys of 23,000 prisoners. According to Fazel and Baillargeon (2011), drug and alcohol problems are common as well. About 17–30 % of men and 10–24 % of women were diagnosed with alcohol misuse or dependency and 10–48 % of men and 30–60 % of women misused or were dependent on illegal drugs. Applebaum (2011a) reported prevalence rates from 9 to 45 % for attention deficit hyperactivity disorder (ADHD) in adult prisoners. Prisoners on remand are at an especially high risk for not only health problems in general, but also for psychiatric disorders (Eytan et al. 2011).

There is a lively discussion about the reasons for the high prevalence of psychiatric disorders in prison, and some factors that clearly foster the incarceration of mentally disordered persons have emerged (Konrad 2002). First, there is an increasing tendency to criminalize socially disturbing behaviour and to emphasize personal responsibility regarding psychiatric disturbance. This is imbedded in a political climate where the costs for the care of mentally disturbed prisoners tend to be minimized. Second, we are at the end of a long period in which institutionalized psychiatric care was reduced to a minimum. Therefore, many long-term care units were closed and the average hospital stay in psychiatric inpatient care has been falling. This may be due to providers of psychiatric care outside of prison be-ing less willing to accept clients who are offenders and favouring the idea of placing offenders with psychiatric illnesses in prison.

Due to the high prevalence of psychiatric disorders in prisoners, psychiatric facilities in prison have to deal with clients who often show a combination of severe psychiatric illness with substance misuse or personality disorder and who often have a high degree of social deprivation.

Prison psychiatrists are currently discussing whether adult ADHD should be treated with stimulants, but the discussion has not been conclusive. Based on clinical experience, a confirmation of the diagnosis of ADHD is recommended before starting medication and care should be taken when treating individuals with a psychiatric disorder because of the possibility of substance abuse.

9.3 Suicide

Suicide is the leading cause of death in prison, and the suicide rate in prison is several times higher than that of the general population (Konrad et al. 2007). However, the prison population is not a representative sample of the general population, because groups with an especially high risk of suicide are overrepresented in prison. Factors associated with increased risk for suicide are recent suicidal ideation, a history of attempted suicide, a present psychiatric diagnosis (especially psychosis and depression), substance abuse, pre-trial status, and solitary confinement (Fazel et al. 2011; Felthous 2011; Hayes 2010). To what extent these factors respectively contribute to differences between the general population and the prison population remains unknown, although it is safe to assume that the suicide rate in prison does not reflect the suicide rate in the general population (Fazel et al. 2011).

Prisoners are at the highest risk for suicidal behaviour in the first few days of incarceration. This may be partly due to the stress from simply being incarcerated, when prisoners are first faced with the reality of being separated from relatives and friends, the surrender to the prison system with its strict regulations and loss of personal freedom, as well as possible feelings of shame and guilt, which may emerge as a reaction to the actual charge (Fazel et al. 2011; Konrad 2006). Therefore, interventions to prevent suicide should start immediately after incarceration. Instruments have been established for the screening of prisoners who are at a very high risk for suicidal behaviour (Konrad 2006). If this screening becomes a routine procedure, there may be a reasonable chance of reducing prison suicide by promptly referring the persons at risk to medical and psychological service. Unfortunately, standardized screening instruments are not widely used, which leaves most of the burden of identifying prisoners at risk for suicidal behaviour to the prison healthcare service. The provision of psychiatric service for people with acute suicidal ideation may help to decrease suicide rates (Felthous 2011; Opitz-Welke and Konrad 2012). For places where no constant psychiatric service is available, a psychiatric consultation-liaison service, which helps the general healthcare service in prison to improve their strategies in handling suicidal behaviour, should be offered.

9.4   Suicide Attempts and Self-harming Behaviour

Self-harming behaviour and suicide attempts are common in prison and can often be construed as attempts to gain control (Konrad et al. 2007). In general, male prisoners with antisocial or sociopathic personality disorders often exhibit repeated severe self-harming, possibly because of their problems in dealing with prison routine. However, although some cases of self-harming behaviour are connected to true suicidal ideation, in other cases, they may be covert attempts at escape or carried out with other untold and/or unwanted motives (Knoll 2010). For example, the prisoner may engage in self-harming in order to be transferred into medical care inside prison, which may be deemed to have a more relaxed atmosphere than a regular prison ward. Indeed, self-harming behaviour has been found to decrease and even stop when the person is transferred to a unit where the atmosphere is more relaxed and more "caring," which supports the thesis that self-harming behaviour is a form of protest and a call for attention (Lohner and Konrad 2006). Therefore, there may be a need to put a prisoner under psychiatric observation after an episode of severe self-harm to determine the cause for the behaviour, for example, whether it is an expression of severe psychiatric disorder or personality disorder, or a type of malingering/exaggeration. At the same time, staff working with self-harming prisoners require support and supervision as these prisoners may interpret the attitude of health professionals toward repetitive self-harm as hostile (Marzano et al. 2012).

9.5   Malingering and Exaggeration

Malingering is generally considered a typical problem of psychiatric work in prison. Malingering/exaggeration may follow an episode of severe illness, probably to lengthen the stay in the prison hospital or to continue to benefit from the advantages one may have had during illness. According to existing literature, 10–25 % of male prison inmates show malingering (Walters 2011). Indeed, most psychiatric disorders are diagnosed clinically and may therefore be more prone to be-ing feigned. Although screening instruments for malingering/exaggeration for psychiatric symptomatology exist, research conducted on clinical findings did not find any categorical distinction between malingerers and the genuinely disturbed (Walters 2011). This information is relevant in the training of healthcare workers in prison, because prison healthcare workers often tend to debate futilely over whether a symptomatology is genuine. Thus, it is important to understand symptomatology in terms of personal strategy or coping with the adverse effect of in-carceration.

9.6 Providing Psychiatric Care in Prison

Psychiatric care for prisoners is often subject to wide regional variations. This is especially true for inpatient treatment. In Germany, only a few prison hospitals have psychiatric departments, but most of the prisons offer a psychiatric outpatient service, which is part of the general healthcare system in prison. Although not all prisons offer psychiatric services regularly (Witzel 2009), it is generally easier to get an appointment with a psychiatrist inside a prison rather than outside. Access to psychiatric services is easier for patients in prisons probably because of the high risk of suicide in prisoners in remand. This facilitates the detection of persons at risk, which will undeniably help to save lives. Therefore, psychiatric care in prisons offer diagnostic approaches to clients who may have never seen a psychiatrist before entering prison, although they may have severe mental disorders. Psychiatric service inside prison should be seen as part of society's general health care, which offers the option of preventing chronic mental disorder (Fazel and Baillargeon 2011). Most of the clients of psychiatric outpatient services in prison have adjustment disorders with depressive symptoms, and some may be suicidal. As mentioned previously, it would be advantageous if a comprehensive screening of prisoners' suicide risk could be implemented into the routine of the correctional system (Konrad et al. 2007).

In addition, substance withdrawal symptoms are common and complicate underlying adjustment problems. As stated above, many prison hospitals do not have psychiatric departments, making treatment for prisoners with psychiatric disorders difficult. However, some prisons cooperate with local forensic security hospitals (Konrad 2006), while elsewhere, psychiatric patients are typically cared for in other departments of prison hospital care, usually in the departments of General Medicine or Internal Medicine. This offers opportunities for sharing knowledge about psychiatric disorders (Diefenbacher 2004). Ideally, this cooperation will increase understanding of the needs of the mentally ill and help to fight discrimination against mentally ill patients. In this context, prison hospitals may also function as a place for advanced training, where knowledge about psychiatric disorders and psychiatric care can be imparted to prison healthcare workers.

Psychiatric inpatient care that resembles that of a psychiatric ward in a community hospital is available for male prisoners in Berlin Prison Hospital. In addition, the hospital is mostly open during daytime, which is useful for people requiring diagnostic and therapeutic services. This also facilitates the detection of malingering/exaggeration. In some cases, it may be difficult to transfer prisoners back to prison owing to the severity of their diseases. Consequently, these patients remain in psychiatric inpatient care for a long time, sometimes even for years. Therefore, to solve this problem, the Berlin Prison Hospital has opened a ward for intermediate care in cooperation with a high security prison.

9.7 Adjustment Disorder

As mentioned above, the majority of patients in psychiatric outpatient care in prison are diagnosed with adjustment disorder. These symptoms may have been induced by the act of incarceration itself or through adverse decisions of the court, and may be signs of the client asking for help. For deeper understanding of the clients' situations, prison psychiatrists should be aware of the legal proceedings in which pressure is imposed upon the client. Therefore, a prison psychiatrist should have a sound forensic training in order to provide adequate treatment.

Most prisoners with an adjustment-disorder show mild to moderate depressive symptoms, which should be treated in accordance with the treatment standards of general psychiatry – with a combination of supportive psychotherapy and antidepressive medication. Owing to the high prevalence of substance abuse, tranquilizers are not recommended for outpatient care. It should also be emphasized that recovery is generally quicker when the patient has the opportunity to be active during daytime, for example, when going to school or to work. On the other hand, symptoms tend to persist when the prisoner is kept in solitary confinement. A recent study on Berlin Prison Hospital showed a lower than expected rate of suicide attempts among pre-trial detainees, which may be partly due to their being outdoors for most of the day (Opitz-Welke and Konrad 2012).

9.8 Psychotic Disorders

Most of the clients who have a severe mental illness and who are receiving psychiatric inpatient service have a psychotic disorder. This may be explained by the increased risk of these people being victimized in the prison subculture, which leads to an increased risk of decompensation (Konrad and Lau 2010). In Germany, there has traditionally been a distinction between 'real' psychotic disorders and disorders caused by incarceration ('Haftpsychose'). However, nowadays, prison psychiatrists agree that a psychotic disorder due to incarceration does not exist. Rather, prisoners with psychotic disorders either had a psychotic disorder before incarceration or were psychotically ill for the first time because of the stress incarceration puts on them (Gössling and Konrad 2004). Additionally, prisoners may present with symptoms that are interpreted as psychotic but are in fact a result of a severe adjustment disorder caused by incarceration. The (traditional) diagnosis of a psychotic disorder caused by incarceration might have been the result of former prison rules, which in Germany included strict isolation as part of rehabilitation; it was previously thought that criminal behaviour is a misbehaviour that is learnt and can be overcome by the enforced separation of the criminals from each other. The finding that severe self-harm tends to decrease or stop when the person is transferred to a more relaxed setting corresponds with the observation that the paranoid symptoms of adjustment disorder disappear when the prisoner is transferred to a less strict and less stressful setting.

The prison system itself is characterized by a combination of social stress and deprivation. The condition of prisoners with pre-existing psychiatric disorders tends to deteriorate (Konrad 2010; Metzner and Fellner 2010). This is even more likely when current medication is interrupted, which is probable because the relationships with former caregivers are disrupted. Hence, psychiatric care in prison should follow the principle of equivalence, meaning that the therapeutic standard outside prison should be the benchmark of psychiatric care in prison (Konrad 2010). Consequently, as psychiatric care outside of prison does not recommend solitary confinement, this should not be used with prisoners with severe mental illness as well.

In many countries, medical services in prison provide treatment for the mentally ill who have fallen out of community healthcare (Fazel and Baillargeon 2011). Therefore, many of the mentally ill are diagnosed and treated for the very first time in prison. Discussions on whether these people should be treated in or out of prison have been inconclusive and controversial. The arguments for transferring mentally ill prisoners to the community health service (Bauer and Chernes 2010; Brooker et al. 2010) are often ethical in nature and emphasize that the mentally ill should not be placed in prison. On the other hand, a psychiatric hospital unit in prison offers the option to treat the mentally ill under maximum security, which would be difficult if the patient is transferred to a psychiatric hospital outside of prison.

9.9 Female Prisoners

Female prisoners are a minority in prison, but seem to be an extremely vulnerable group, with high rates of reported self-harm, suicide ideation, and suicide at-tempts (Marzano et al. 2010, 2011). Psychotic disorders, major depression, and personality disorders are more common in female prisoners than in male prisoners (Fazel and Baillargeon 2011). As gender separation in prisons usually extends to clinical practice, it is difficult to provide psychiatric inpatient care for female prisoners with severe mental disorders, because of the small size of this group. As female prisoners may need to be transferred to an external psychiatric hospital or a forensic psychiatric security hospital, close cooperation be-tween the general health care system in prison, the psychiatric specialist, and the prison administration is essential. As mentioned above, a comprehensive screen-ing for suicide risk would be very helpful, as decisions about therapeutic approaches could then be made in time.

9.10 Planning for the Release of Prisoners with Severe Mental Disorders

Studies from Europe, Australia, and the USA revealed a high mortality of ex-prisoners after their release (Binswanger et al. 2007; Kariminia et al. 2007b; Rosen et al. 2008). Most deaths of released prisoners were caused by suicide, homicide, and drug overdose (Kariminia et al. 2007a). In many countries, prisons provide opportunities for diagnosis, treatment, counselling, and disease management education for the mentally ill, who have slipped through the community healthcare system (Fazel and Baillargeon 2011; Konrad 2002). Therefore, re-entering the community generally offers an opportunity to reintegrate these people into the community healthcare system. A good transition management would not only have potential public health benefits but may also reduce recidivism rates (Fazel and Seewald 2012). Released prisoners often face a combination of different problems, and among these, the need for money and housing may take more priority over the need for psychiatric care. This may explain why prisoners with psychiatric disorders have severe difficulties in adhering to their medication and disease management strategies upon release (Binswanger et al. 2011). Thus, close cooperation between the providers of public mental healthcare and prison administration is necessary to improve this situation. General psychiatric care is community-based in Germany, and every ex-convict with a severe mental disorder has the right to participate. However, health professionals who work in prisons sometimes meet strong prejudice when contacting these services. Therefore, professional healthcare providers in prisons, and especially social workers, should be prepared for these challenges. On the one hand, they have to stay in contact with healthcare providers in the community and anticipate the problems that may emerge when a prisoner attempts to access community psychiatric care. On the other hand, they have to be prepared for working with the psychiatrically ill in general and should expect that, in some instances, ex-convicts with severe mental disorders may not be able to access community psychiatric care owing to their conditions. Therefore, to meet these needs, healthcare providers in Berlin Prison Hospital stay in close contact with local psychiatric community hospitals and providers of integrated psychiatric care. The social workers working in Berlin Prison Hospital also undergo special training to become sensitized to the needs of our clients. In some cases, ex-convicts with severe mental illnesses return for inpatient care, especially in cases where a high competency in psychiatric care is needed.

References

Appelbaum, K. L. (2011a). Stimulant use under a prison treatment protocol for attention-deficit/hyperactivity disorder. *Journal of Correctional Health Care, 17*(3), 218–225.

Appelbaum, P. S. (2011b). Lost in the crowd: Prison mental health care, overcrowding, and the courts. *Psychiatric Services, 62*(10), 1121–1123.

Barth, T. (2012). Relationships and sexuality of imprisoned man in the German penal system – A survey of inmates i a Berlin prison. *International Journal of Law and Psychiatry, 35*(3), 153–158.

Bauer, A., & Chernes, Y. (2010). The proper place for the committer of a crime is prison custody not psychiatric hospital inpatient care. *The Israel Medical Association Journal, 12*(10), 633–644.

Binswanger, I. A., Stern, M. F., Deyo, R. A., Heagerty, P. J., Cheadle, A., Elmore, J. G., & Koepsell, T. D. (2007). Release from prison-a high risk of death for former inmates. *The New England Journal of Medicine, 356*(2), 157–165.

Binswanger, I. A., Nowels, C., Corsi, K. F., Long, J., Booth, R. E., Kutner, J., & Steiner, J. F. (2011). 'From the prison door right to the sidewalk, everything went downhill', a qualitative study of the health experiences of recently released inmates. *International Journal of Law and Psychiatry, 34*(4), 249–255.

Brooker, C., Flynn, J., & Fox, C. (2010). Trends in self-inflicted deaths in prison in England and Wales (2001–2008): Towards targeted interventions. *Journal of Aggression, Conflict and Peace Research, 2*(4), 191–195.

Burki, T. (2010). Grasping the nettle of mental illness in prisons. *Lancet, 376*(9752), 1529–1530.

Cassau, J., & Goodwin, D. E. (2012). The phenomenology and course of depressive syndromes in pre-trial detention. *International Journal of Law and Psychiatry, 35*(3), 231–235.

Diefenbacher, A. (2004). Consultation-liaison psychiatry in Germany. *Advances in Psychosomatic Medicine, 26*, 1–19.

Eytan, A., Haller, D. M., Wolff, H., Cerutti, B., Sebo, P., Bertrand, D., & Niveau, G. (2011). Psychiatric symptoms, psychological distress and somatic comorbidity among remand prisoners in Switzerland. *International Journal of Law and Psychiatry, 34*(1), 13–19.

Fazel, S., & Baillargeon, J. (2011). The health of prisoners. *Lancet, 377*(9769), 956–965.

Fazel, S., & Danesh, J. (2002). Serious mental disorder in 23000 prisoners. A systematic review of 62 surveys. *Lancet, 359*(9306), 545–50.

Fazel, S., & Seewald, K. (2012). Severe mental illness in 33.588 prisoners worldwide: Systematic review and meta-regression analysis. *The British Journal of Psychiatry, 200*, 364–373.

Fazel, S., Grann, M., Kling, B., & Hawton, K. (2011). Prison suicide in 12 countries: An ecological study of 861 suicides during 2003–2007. *Social Psychiatry and Psychiatric Epidemiology, 46*(3), 191–195.

Felthous, A. R. (2011). Suicide behind bars: Trends, inconsistencies, and practical implications. *Journal of Forensic Science, 56*(6), 1541–1555.

Gössling, J., & Konrad, N. (2004). Zur Entität der sogenannten Haftpsychose. *Recht und Psychiatrie, 22*(3), 123–129.

Hayes, L. M. (2010). National study of jail suicides: 20 years later. *National Jail Exchange.*

Kariminia, A., Butler, T. G., Corben, S. P., Levy, M. H., Grant, L., Kaldor, J. M., & Law, M. G. (2007a). Extreme cause-specific mortality in a cohort of adult prisoners-1988 to 2002: A data-linkage study. *International Journal of Epidemiology, 36*(2), 310–316.

Kariminia, A., Law, M. G., Butler, T. G., Corben, S. P., Levy, M. H., Kaldor, J. M., & Grant, L. (2007b). Factors associated with mortality in a cohort of Australian prisoners. *European Journal of Epidemiology, 22*(7), 417–428.

Knoll, J. L. (2010). Suicide in correctional settings: Assessment, prevention, and professional liability. *Journal of Correctional Health Care, 16*(3), 188–204.

Konrad, N. (2002). Prisons as new asylums. *Current Opinion in Psychiatry, 15*, 583–587.

Konrad, N. (2006). Psychiatrie des Strafvollzuges. In H.-L. Kröber, D. Dölling, N. Leygraf, & H. Sass (Eds.), *3 Psychiatrische Kriminalprognose und Kriminaltherapie* (pp. 234–241). Darmstadt: Steinkopff.

Konrad, N. (2010). Ethical issues in forensic psychiatry in penal and other correctional facilities. *Current Opinion in Psychiatry, 23*(5), 467–471.

Konrad, N., & Lau, S. (2010). Dealing with the mentally ill in the criminal justice system in Germany. *International Journal of Law and Psychiatry, 33*(4), 236–240.

Konrad, N., Daigle, M. S., Daniel, A. E., Dear, G., Frottier, P., Hayes, L. M., Kerkhof, A., Liebling, A., & Sarchiapone, M. (2007). Preventing suicide in prisons. Part II. International comparison of suicide prevention services in correctional facilities. *CRISIS, 28*(3), 122–130.

Krassner, D. (2011). Personal accounts: A day in the life of a prison psychiatrist. *Psychiatric Services, 62*(4), 350–351.

Lohner, J., & Konrad, N. (2006). Deliberate self-harm and suicide attempt in custody: Distinguishing features in male inmates' self-injurious behaviour. *International Journal of Law and Psychiatry, 29*, 370–385.

Marzano, L., Fazel, S., Rivlin, A., & Hawton, K. (2010). Psychiatric disorders in women prisoners who have engaged in near-lethal self-harm: Case–control study. *The British Journal of Psychiatry, 197*(3), 219–226.

Marzano, L., Hawton, K., Rivlin, A., & Fazel, S. (2011). Psychosocial influences on prisoner suicide: A case–control study of near-lethal self-harm in women prisoners. *Social Science & Medicine, 72*(6), 874–883.

Marzano, L., Ciclitira, K., & Adler, J. (2012). The impact of prison staff responses on self-harming behaviours: Prisoners' perspectives. *British Journal of Clinical Psychology, 51*(1), 4–18.

Metzner, J. L., & Fellner, J. (2010). Solitary confinement and mental illness in U.S. prisons: A challenge for medical ethics. *Journal of the American Academy of Psychiatry and the Law, 38*(1), 104–108.

Opitz-Welke, A., & Konrad, N. (2012). Inpatient treatment in the psychiatric department of a German prison hospital. *International Journal of Law and Psychiatry, 35*(3), 240–243.

Rosen, D. L., Schoenbach, V. J., & Wohl, D. A. (2008). All-cause and cause-specific mortality among men released from state prison, 1980–2005. *American Journal of Public Health, 98*(12), 2278–2284.

Walters, G. D. (2011). Screening for malingering/exaggeration of psychiatric symptomatology in prison inmates using the PICTS Confusion and Infrequency scales. *Journal of Forensic Sciences, 56*(2), 444–449.

Witzel, J. G. (2009). Psychiatrischer Konsiliardienst. In K. Keppler & H. Stöver (Eds.), *Gefängnismedizin* (pp. 208–222). Stuttgart: D. Thieme.

Chapter 10
Drug Services and Harm Reduction Practice in Prisons

Heino Stöver

Abstract A wide range of drug services should be available to prisoners, based on local and individual needs. Interdisciplinary staff and multi-professional teams should offer psycho-social as well as pharmacological treatment, stimulating and enhancing self-help potential of prisoners.

Estimates suggest that half the prisoners in the European Union have a history of drug use, many with problematic, injecting drug use. Drug use is one of the main problems facing prison systems, threatening security, dominating the relationships between prisoners and staff and leading to violence, bullying and mobbing for both prisoners and often their spouses and friends in the community. The prevalence of infectious diseases (particularly HIV and Aids, hepatitis B and C, and tuberculosis) is often much higher in prisons than outside, often related to injecting drug use. Drug dependence services and measures to address infectious diseases in prisons should be equivalent to the services provided outside prisons. This can best be achieved through close co-operation and communication between prison and community services and by integrating prison drug and BBV strategies into the national drug and BBV strategy. Continuity of treatment for prisoners entering and leaving prison necessitates close co-operation between prisons and external agencies. Relapse to drug use and fatal overdoses after release are widespread, and these risks need to be addressed during the time of imprisonment.

A wide range of drug services should be available to prisoners, based on local and individual needs. Interdisciplinary staff and multi-professional teams should offer psycho-social as well as pharmacological treatment, stimulating and enhancing self-help potential of prisoners. There should be training for prison staff and prisoners on drugs and related health problems. Drug strategies in prisons require actions to be taken both on the level of individual behavioural change and on the structural level. Although targeting programmes at individual prisoners or groups of prisoners is important, there is also a need for more structurally oriented measures to run

H. Stöver (✉)
Faculty 'Health and Social Work', Frankfurt University of Applied Sciences, Nibelungenplatz 1, 60318 Frankfurt, Germany
e-mail: hstoever@fb4.fra-uas.de

© Springer Science+Business Media Dordrecht 2017
B.S. Elger et al. (eds.), *Emerging Issues in Prison Health*,
DOI 10.1007/978-94-017-7558-8_10

concurrently, to comprehensively address necessary improvements in the living conditions of the prisoners and the working conditions of prison staff. National and international networking and exchange of good practice models seems to be a valuable method for all prison systems to engage in. In addition, international networks need to disseminate internationally available good practice models and knowledge about evidence-based strategies into the prison settings and/or on the level of prison administration. Guidelines and detailed protocols are needed on how exactly certain treatment options can and have to be implemented to support prison doctors/nurses and prison administration in delivering adequate health care services (e.g. for substitution treatment to opiate dependent prisoners). Drug services in prisons should be subject to monitoring and evaluation.

10.1 Introduction

10.1.1 Drug Use and the Consequences for Prisoners, Prisons and Prison Health Care

Drug use and blood-borne virus infections (BBVs) (including HIV/Aids and viral hepatitis) are serious health problems in prison populations and wider criminal justice systems. This makes these places important settings for the provision of effective, evidence-based drug-related and BBV services to help reduce the damage that drug use does to health, prison safety and security, and the community at large (through increased re-offending and infections on release).

Large proportions of people who enter the criminal justice system and prison have a history of drug use and injecting. Many continue to use drugs while in prison. The prison environment may impact positively on some drug users, helping them to stop or reduce drug use or to use less frequently, but for others prison will be an environment where they switch to more harmful patterns of use.

Prisons are risk environments because they are often overcrowded, stressful, hostile and sometimes violent places in which individuals from poor communities and from ethnic and social minorities are overrepresented, including people who use drugs, and migrants. Furthermore they often do not provide the same size and quality of prevention and treatment services as applied in the community.

A European study on health problems arising in prison highlighted three main issues: substance abuse, mental health problems and communicable diseases (Tomasevski 1992). These three problem areas are closely interrelated. Some of the harms associated with drug users in the criminal justice system include: High rates of HIV and viral hepatitis infection (imprisonment is associated with higher rates of blood-borne virus infection among injecting drug users); high rates of tuberculosis in some countries; restricted access to harm reduction services and treatment for drug dependence and BBVs; increased risk of death by overdose on release; increased risk of passing on infections acquired in prison; and increased risk of re-offending on release.

Although alternatives to imprisonment have been developed and introduced in many countries, the number of people who have used or still use drugs who enter prison settings is still increasing. Only a limited number of drug users are in prison as a result of a conviction for a drug offence. Most drug users are imprisoned for other drug-related offences.

Generally, in many countries the number of drug users with problematic consumption patterns in prison has dramatically increased over the last two decades. Problematic drug use is defined as 'injecting drug use or long duration/regular use of heroin/cocaine and/or amphetamines' (EMCDDA 2011). This definition can also include other opioids such as methadone. Furthermore, drug consumption is deemed to be problematic if this behaviour is joined with other risk behaviour, causes damage to other persons or produces negative social consequences. Every sixth prisoner is thought to be a problematic drug user (Hedrich and Farrell 2012). Thus, people who use drugs are over-represented in prisons throughout Europe. Several factors have contributed to this, including poverty, migration, violence and the fact that increased incarceration is often politically expedient. Ultimately, however, repressive legislation against drugs in the context of increasing drug consumption in the community has often played an important role.

This fact inevitably affects life in penal institutions. Drugs have become a central theme: a dominating factor in the relationships between prisoners and between prisoners and staff. Many security measures are aimed at controlling drug use and drug trafficking within the prison system. Daily prison routines are in many respects dictated by drug-dependent inmates and drug-related problems: drug-related deaths, drug-induced cases of emergency, increase in the number of people who use drugs, dealer hierarchies, debts, mixed drugs, drugs of poor quality, incalculable purity of drugs and risks of infection (particularly HIV and hepatitis) resulting from the sharing of contaminated syringes and paraphernalia. Drugs become the central medium and currency in prison subcultures. An important proportion of inmates' routine activities is dedicated to the acquisition, smuggling, consumption, sale and financing of drugs.

Prison management is faced with increased public pressure to keep prisons drug-free. Few prison managers talk frankly and in public about drug use in prisons, establish adequate drug services and develop new drug strategies. People who confess that drug use is prevalent in prisons and that prison is a risk environment are frequently blamed for failing to maintain prison security. The number of prison managers who deny or ignore drug use in prison therefore remains great. Furthermore, many prison physicians believe they can cure inmates' drug problems by temporarily forcing them to stop using drugs. It therefore becomes obvious why dealing with people who are dependent on drugs in detention is difficult. The goal of rehabilitating prisoners must be pursued, but prison managers in many countries face rising drug consumption among inmates and political and economic circumstances that make the drug problem even more difficult to solve. The current situation of judicial authorities is paradoxical. They have to find a solution to a problem that is not supposed to exist: drugs in prisons.

10.2 Definition of 'Drug Users'

Throughout Europe, prison systems report that drug users are a significant and extremely problematic part of the total prison population, but only a few countries have developed and apply clear definitions of a drug user. Few countries apply common diagnostic instruments for the classification of diseases (ICD-10 or DSM-IV) and few have a comprehensive system to quantify the scale of this problem, even though most countries assume that 'drug users' comprise a significant part of criminal justice and prison populations. Variations in the definition used for a problem drug user exist throughout Europe, e.g. whether drug use was restricted to dependence or included problematic use without dependency. Several questions arise:

(a) Who establishes who is a drug user? The doctor on admission, based on certain drug-related symptoms such as abscesses, puncture marks or positive urine testing? Or staff members, or the prison administration? Or users themselves when self-reporting drug use?
(b) On what basis are people considered to be drug users? Because of the type of criminal offence committed, as noted in the prisoner's personal file (violating the drug law and/or other laws in order to finance drug use)?
(c) Which types of drugs are included? Illegal drugs only or also legal drugs such as alcohol?
(d) What are the criteria? Lifetime prevalence, drug use prior to incarceration (4 weeks, 1 year?), drug use within prison, occasional drug use, frequency, quantity, setting, problematic drug use, multiple drug use or supplementary use of pharmaceutical products such as benzodiazepines or barbiturates? Which route of administration: injecting, smoking or inhaling?
(e) Are occasional drug users distinguished from people addicted to drugs?

10.3 Nature and Prevalence of Drug Use and Related Risks in Prisons and on Release

Many drug users in prison come from the more disadvantaged groups in society, with a high prevalence of low educational attainment, unemployment, physical or sexual abuse, relationship breakdown or mental disorder. They lead chaotic lives and experience a range of issues with housing, employment, education and health that need to be addressed. Most never had access to health care and health promotion services before imprisonment. The health care services therefore offer an opportunity to improve their health and personal well-being (The Patel Report 2010).

According to the EMCDDA (2012) every sixth prisoner in Europe is a problem drug user. Drug use in prison takes place in extreme secrecy, and drug seizure statistics, the confiscation of needles/syringes and positive urine test rates only indicate a part of the full story of drug use behind bars. The patterns of drug use vary considerably between different groups in the prison population. For instance, drug use among women differs significantly from that among men, with different drugs, levels and types of misuse and different motivations and behavioural consequences. Studies show that substances available outside prison can also be found inside prison, with the same regional variation in patterns of use. The quality of these drugs is often poor compared with that of drugs in the community.

Some prisoners use drugs in prison to counter boredom and to help them deal with the hardships of prison life or to overcome a crisis situation, such as bad news, conviction and sentencing or violence. Imprisonment thus sometimes seems to provide reasons for taking drugs or continuing the habit, or causes relapse after a period of withdrawal.

Many countries report changes in the patterns of drug use (volume and type of drug) when the preferred drugs are scarce. Studies and observations of prison officers indicate that switching to alternative drugs (such as from opiates to cannabis) or to any substitute drugs with psychotropic effects regardless of their potential damage (illegal drugs and/or medicine) is widespread. Due to a lack of access to the preferred drug or because of controls (such as mandatory drug testing), some prisoners seem to switch from cannabis to heroin, even if on an experimental basis, because cannabis may be detected in urine up to 30 days after use.

In many prisons, the most commonly used drug besides tobacco is cannabis, which is used for relaxation purposes. Some studies have shown that more than 50 % of prisoners use cannabis while in prison: prevalence at entry vary between 38 % in France and 81 % in Scotland (Stöver et al. 2008). Studies indicate that both prison staff and inmates believe that cannabis gives psychological relief and has a positive impact on the social ambiance in the particular setting of prison. Therefore, tackling cannabis use in prison needs to take into account those effects, and include harm reduction measures tailored to individual users and their therapeutic needs. Generally, this means that alternatives to substance use have to be developed in order to favour a calm and safe environment in prison (Ritter et al. 2013).

A much smaller percentage of prisoners reports injecting drugs in prison. The extent and pattern of injecting and needle sharing vary significantly among prisons. Prisoners who use drugs on the outside usually will reduce their levels of use in prison and only a minority of prisoners use drugs daily. This may be due to the reduced supply of drugs or it may reflect the ability of drug-using inmates to reduce or stop drug use while in prison. However, according to various studies undertaken in Europe, between 16 % and 60 % of people who injected on the outside continue to inject in prison (Stöver et al. 2008).

Although injecting less frequently than outside, prisoners are much more likely to share injecting equipment than drug injectors in the community and with a greater number of people (Jürgens et al. 2009). Many were accustomed to easy and anonymous access to sterile injecting equipment outside prison and start sharing injecting equipment in prison because they lack access to it.

Thus, each episode of injecting is far more dangerous than outside due to the lack of sterile injecting equipment, the high prevalence of sharing and already widespread infectious diseases. Prisons are high risk environments for the transmission of HIV and other blood-borne virus (BBV) infections for several reasons, including the following: a disproportionate number of inmates coming from and returning to backgrounds where the prevalence of HIV and BBV infection is high; authorities not officially acknowledging HIV and BBV, thus hindering education efforts; activities such as injecting drug use and unsafe sexual practices (consensual or otherwise) continuing to occur in prison, with clean injecting equipment and condoms rarely being provided to prisoners; tattooing and piercing using non-sterile equipment being prevalent in many prisons; epidemics of other sexually transmitted infections such as syphilis, coupled with their inadequate treatment, leading to a higher risk of transmitting HIV through sexual activity.

In the first documented outbreak of HIV within a prison population in 1993, 43 % of inmates reported injecting within the prison – and all but one of these individuals had shared injecting equipment within the prison (Taylor and Goldberg 1996). The high rates of injecting drug use, if coupled with lack of access to evidence-based prevention measures, can result in a frighteningly rapid spread of HIV and hepatitis B and C. There were early indications that HIV could be transmitted extensively in prisons. HIV outbreaks in prison have been documented in a number of countries, demonstrating how rapidly HIV can spread in prison unless effective action is taken to prevent transmission.

Studies also show the following (Stöver et al. 2008): Although smoking heroin ('chasing the dragon') plays an increasing and significant role all over Europe, this route of administration is not widespread in prisons because drugs are so expensive in prisons and injecting maximizes the effect of a minimal amount of drugs, and is not as easily detectable as smoking (both for prison staff and other prisoners; Stöver and Schäffer 2014). A substantial number of drug users report having first started to inject while in prison. Studies of drug users in prison suggest that between 3 and 26 % first used drugs while they were incarcerated and up to 21 % of injectors initiated injecting while in prison. In addition to illegal drugs, legal drugs, alcohol and prescribed pharmaceuticals often contribute to the substance dependence and related health problems of prisoners. Many prisoners have a long history of regular use of legal drugs. Poly-drug use is common among offenders entering custody, co-dependent on any combination of alcohol, opiates, stimulants and benzodiazepines. Dual diagnosis or the co-existence of mental health and substance use problems has also increased in recent years. Some prisoners may also discover new substances while in prison (medicines or tablets) or develop habits of mixing certain drugs they did not mix outside.

The vulnerability of drug-using prisoners to suicide and self-harm in prison is followed for many prisoners upon release from prison, which is a very critical time. In the week following release, prisoners are 37 times more likely to die of a drug overdose than other members of the public due to diminished opioid tolerance (women are 69 times more likely to do so) (Farrell and Marsden 2005).

Prisoners who have not taken drugs frequently during detention often have difficulty in adapting to the new situation after release. They return to old habits and consume drugs in the same quantity and quality as before prison. After release, many injecting drug users continue with their habit. A study indicates that 63 % of those who injected before prison inject again in the first 3 months after release (Stöver et al. 2008). Prison, therefore, cannot be seen as providing a short- or longer-term solution to individuals' problems with drugs. The transition from life inside prison to the situation in the community is an extremely sensitive period. The longer a drug user stays in prison, the more difficult adapting to life outside prison will be. Even a prison sentence of just several weeks, during which no drugs are consumed, poses a considerable risk to released drug users; because of a reduced tolerance for opiates, even small quantities can be life-threatening.

10.4 Guiding Principles and Goals of Drug Services in Prisons

In general, drug services in prisons can be divided into: assessment, prevention, counselling, medication-assisted and abstinence-oriented treatment, self-help groups and peer-driven interventions, harm reduction measures and pre-release and aftercare programmes.

It is essential to recognise that drug dependence (whether opiates, cocaine, tobacco, alcohol or other drugs) is a chronic disease (not a criminal or hedonistic behaviour), characterised by a long process of relapses and attempts at stabilisation. It is a disorder that consequently requires a continuing care and support approach. It should be treated in the same manner as other chronic illnesses (including diagnosis, treatment plan, control of progress, monitoring etc.). The following aspects are important: it is vital that any drug treatment and intervention strategies in the community and in prison are not developed in isolation, but linked to other relevant initiatives and strategies. Prison drug strategy should be part of, and in line with, the national drug strategy. All drug services available in the community should also be available in prisons, in the same quality, size and accessibility. Guidelines developed by the World Health Organization's (WHO) Health in Prisons Project and the Council of Europe's Pompidou Group and its principles for the provision of healthcare services in prisons (2001) state that: 'There should be health services in prisons which are broadly equivalent to health services in the wider community' (WHO 2001). Drug strategies and interventions in prisons require actions to be taken both on the level of individual behavioural change and on the structural level. Although targeting programmes at individual prisoners or groups of prisoners is important, there is also a need for more structurally oriented measures to run concurrently, to comprehensively address necessary improvements in the living conditions of the prisoners and the working conditions of prison staff. Drug dependent prisoners should be given a choice, an appropriate 'menu of services', including medical treatment, psychosocial interventions, harm reduction and broader social care that promotes resettlement and recovery. Interdisciplinary, multi-professional drug services should combine psycho-social and pharmacological approaches on the basis of stimulation of self-help potentials. Only a comprehensive approach is promising for tackling the complex phenomenon of drug dependence. The different services should be interconnected with each other and should offer the possibility of a transition by the choice of the patient from one module to the other (e.g. from medication assisted treatment to abstinence oriented). A balanced treatment system is vital to ensure that drug dependent prisoners get access to the types of treatment that is appropriate to their changing needs and circumstances. It is vital that drug treatment and interventions are matched to individual need and appropriate to individuals at the time that they are within the criminal justice system e.g. making sure that the right people, get the right intervention, at the right time. With regard to prevalent somatic or psychiatric co-morbidity among drug users, drug services should be linked to respective services in prisons (psychiatric services and general health service). In order to prevent treatment gaps on the edge of community prison and prison community, drug services should be organised in close relationship with community services (continuity of care of drug treatment within and between prisons and community services after release). Local partnerships should be established in order to develop routines and integrated care pathways (between prisons and community services that support the treatment and interventions that are most effective, targeted at the right users with abstinence-based treatment for some, medically assisted treatment for others). Apart from the specific drug treatment, lasting changes can only be achieved with help and support from outside the treatment system (family and friends, peer support/mutual aid networks, access to housing, and education and employment opportunities). Emphasis is also needed on developing life skills to help prevent relapse into drug use and offending, and a lot of importance placed on crisis support, peer support and daytime activities to help make the transition to a normal life. The needs of particular groups (women, minority ethnic groups, people with dual diagnosis (mental health and substance use problems) must be considered. It is vital that the service user's 'voice' is heard and their experiences are taken into account. According to health promoting strategies, active involvement of drug users, their families and local communities is pivotal. The involvement of service users should be encouraged and facilitated through regular consultation and service user satisfaction surveys. Service users should be involved in making decisions on how services are developed, designed and delivered. Clear and consistent standards for monitoring and evaluating drug-related and BBV services should be established to improve the quality of health care that is available. This should include standardised data collection (including gender disaggregated data) so that the measurement and quality of data within a country and between different countries is harmonised, information dissemination is improved, and quality criteria are implemented. The allocation of sufficient and sustained funding (in the form of both financial and human resources) is of critical importance and continued lobbying and advocacy work is crucial in helping to secure the provision of high quality drug-related and BBV services in prisons and criminal justice systems.[1]

The above mentioned goals of drug services in prisons must be, as a minimum, protecting prisoners to leave prison in a healthier state than upon arrival and, as a maximum, psycho-socially stabilising prisoners and encouraging them to continue treatment after release. Thus, the ultimate goal of all treatment of drug dependency on an individual level is to achieve abstinence from their drug – or drugs – of dependency either with or without medically assisted treatment. On a systemic or institutional level, reducing re-offending and improving health and rehabilitation are the overarching twin aims (the outcome could be measured with four topics, which need to take into account the situation after release), in particular: reduced drug use; reduced re-offending; improved health and social functioning; and increased employment and enhanced workforce skills (The Patel Report 2010: 13ff).

10.4.1   What Works?

Given the enormous investment in criminal justice system interventions for drug dependent prisoners, we know remarkably little about what works, for whom, in which period of his/her sentence and drug career. It is difficult to transfer results of evidence-based interventions into the custodial setting. However, taking into account the lack of funds for many prison administrations, only those interventions should be supported which have proven evidence, are effective and efficient. Furthermore, it can be stated that 'positive experience from in-prison treatment helps inmates to continue treatment after release, reduce relapse rates and related health risks, and also reduce delinquency recidivism' (Uchtenhagen 2006).

Apart from the necessary continuity of care, research evidence shows that treatment success largely depends on the duration of the intervention (the longer the intervention, the better the outcome) and its connection with additional services: e.g. the provision of immediate help and support on and after release, with aftercare being increasingly seen as an important component of an integrated treatment programme offered to drug-using prisoners.

It is well established that adequate drug treatment for prisoners can reduce both drug use and rates of re-offending. Especially opioid substitution treatment, intensive psycho-social support/supervision on release but also 12-step abstinence-based programmes and therapeutic communities have particularly strong evidential support. That means that pharmacological and psychosocial as well as other supportive 'wraparound' interventions are promising strategies to stabilise prisoners. Especially the importance of having integrated medical and psychosocial services within a comprehensive package, including a range of offers that meet the needs of drug dependent prisoners is critical for effective drug services.

---

[1] For an overview see Stöver (2012).

The Patel Report (2010) puts it this way:

> One of the overall themes to emerge is that people need to feel they have choices. This is as important when deciding about treatment and interventions options and in choosing their own route to recovery i.e. working toward abstinence. The reality of supported self-change is vital in a recovery-focused treatment system in order to raise aspirations and create opportunities for further self-change and personal development.

Isolated interventions, not linked with offers of psychosocial or pharmacological treatment, are not promising ways to reduce drug use or drug-related risks e.g. there is not a great deal of evidence, either within or outside prisons, on the effectiveness of substance misuse related advice and information.

10.5   Guiding Principles for Harm Reduction and Treatment Services in Prisons

These guiding principles are the outcome of a European research project – 'Good Practice in Preventing Drug Misuse and Related Infections in Criminal Justice Systems in Europe' (Connections Project 2011).

- Clear and transparent protocols and guidelines (which are accessible at all times and regularly updated) should be put in place for health professionals and other members of staff working in the area of harm reduction and drug treatment in prisons and criminal justice systems.
- Staff working with drug users and those at risk of infection should be committed to providing a healthy and safe environment. They should be provided with the relevant training and support to achieve this (including training on treatment goals), which should help to promote positive attitudes and reduce discrimination.
- An interdisciplinary approach to drug treatment programmes should be adopted and all staff involved in delivering these programmes should adhere to best clinical practice.
- Staff responsible for delivering health services to individuals in police custody and prisons should be able to demonstrate their independence from security staff. This will help them to promote trust and confidence in the medical care they provide.
- Each prisoner should be provided with information about his/her rights (which should be the same as the rights of individuals who are treated by community drug services) and about any obligation the clinician treating them has to a third party. They should also receive advice on medical confidentiality before their treatment commences.

- Treatment and harm reduction programmes for prisoners in different facilities should be harmonised and there should be comparable standards for drug users and those at risk of infections which are based on meeting individual needs.
- Drug users and those at risk of infection should be provided with continuity of care and treatment (harm reduction programmes, substitution treatment, detoxification or drug-free treatment); when they come into police custody or prison; on transfer to and from police custody; between prisons; and on release into the community. This should be provided at a consistent level in all custodial settings and should include taking steps to reduce the risk of overdose on release, by assessing who is most at risk and providing appropriate treatment and counselling prior to release, which is then continued on release. Preparing individuals for release should commence at the beginning of their sentence as part of the sentence planning process.
- In addition to addressing the immediate health needs of drug users and those at risk of infection, other issues such as, employment, education, financial matters, family ties, housing and social support should be addressed to help prevent relapse on release. This should include education for family members about overdose and safe storage of medication at home.
- A system should be set up to facilitate close co-operation between professionals working in police custody, prisons and the community so that the treatment offered to individuals is sustainable and the benefits of continuity of care are achieved. The important role that non-governmental organisations play in the provision of services should be recognised and prison staff should have regular contact with local community services and encourage greater involvement of non-governmental organisations in prisons so that their expertise can be used to benefit prisoners.
- Drug users should be offered the option of a first assessment within 24 h of entering prison.
- To reduce the prevalence of infectious diseases, harm reduction material (including information on sexual risk behaviours and the provision of condoms and lubricants) should be distributed to all those in police custody and prison.
- Prisoners who use drugs and those who are at risk of infection should be given information that explains what type of services the prison health service can provide and how to manage an illness in prison. This should be disseminated in a format that enables those with poor literacy skills or language difficulties to access it.
- Prisoners should be encouraged to take part in peer-related initiatives which help to inform and educate them about the effects of drug use, infectious diseases and high risk behaviours. Peer led initiatives should be encouraged.
- Opioid substitution treatment (using medication such as methadone, buprenorphine, and sustained-release morphine) as well as detoxification and drug-free

programmes should be available to opiate dependent prisoners. These should be based on individual needs and available for an appropriate length of time. Where medication is prescribed, prisoners should be given the option of receiving the same medication they were prescribed in the community and it should be given at the correct dose (in line with national guidelines).

- The clinician responsible for treating a detainee should clearly explain the advantages and disadvantages of all treatment options, including the length and type of programmes available.
- Prison-based needle exchange programmes should be available in prisons which are assessed as containing a risk of infection transmission through sharing needles and drug using equipment along with comprehensive treatment services, and counselling to encourage the reduction of injecting drug use.
- All drug using prisoners should be offered anonymous testing (with pre- and post-test counselling) for BBVs on entry to prison.
- An immunisation programme for hepatitis A and B should be put in place for all prisoners on entry to prison. Agreement should also be reached on the practicality and feasibility of adopting a short duration immunisation programme (to enable maximum participation) and on the feasibility of testing prisoners on release.

10.6 Assessment of Drug Problems and Related Infectious Diseases

In almost all prisons, the prison doctor sees every incoming prisoner within 24 h of admission for a medical check. Nearly all prisons have a health unit comprising doctors, nurses and psychologists. Smaller prisons often rely on private contract doctors. The size of the team varies according to the prisons and their capacities. Cases with special health needs are referred to the prison hospital.

Nearly every European prison prepares treatment plans tailored to the specific needs of every prisoner for the duration of the prison sentence. This plan should also cover the drug treatment and psychosocial support measures to be taken after release. Treatment plans include steps towards social rehabilitation and health promotion to strengthen personal competencies and skills. If necessary, treatment measures are included and staff or special treatment boards will review progress. Although throughcare planning is perceived as inevitable to deliver adequate services to drug users, this is harder to achieve but nevertheless necessary for those with a short-term sentence.

As best practice the integrated counselling, assessment, referral, advice and throughcare services model in England and Wales comprehensively links different services that fall apart in some other European countries: prisons, community services and probation (Stöver and Kastelic 2014).

10.7 Best Practice Examples of Services to Drug Users

10.7.1 Psycho-Social Drug Treatment and Pharmacological Approaches as Complementary Orientations in a Comprehensive Package of Drug Services

An integrated drug treatment system, as developed for instance in England (Marteau et al. 2010), is needed in order to comprehensively respond to the complex phenomenon of drug dependence in custodial settings. Drug-free as well as pharmacological interventions together with self-help stimulation are the key for successful drug services: psychosocial drug treatment and clinical substance dependence management have to be integrated and harmonised. Thus, drug-free orientation and pharmacological treatment are no longer contradictory strategies, but on the contrary can ideally complement each other.

10.7.2 Opioid Substitution Treatment (OST)

Hedrich et al. (2012) showed in their systematic review that OST was significantly associated with reduced heroin use, injecting and syringe-sharing in prison if doses were adequate. Pre-release OMT was significantly associated with increased treatment entry and retention after release if arrangements existed to continue treatment. There was limited evidence that pre-release OST reduces post-release mortality. But one of the most striking results was that disruption of OST continuity, especially due to brief periods of imprisonment, was associated with very significant increases in HCV incidence.

The authors conclude that the benefits of prison OST are similar to those in community settings and that OST presents an opportunity to recruit problem opioid users into treatment, to reduce illicit opioid use and risk behaviours in prison, and potentially minimise overdose risks on release. If liaison with community-based programmes exists, prison OST facilitates continuity of treatment and longer-term benefits can be achieved. For prisoners in OST before imprisonment, prison OST provides treatment continuity (Kastelic et al. 2008; Stöver and Kastelic 2014).

10.7.3 Harm Reduction Services

In their broadest sense, harm reduction policies, programmes, services and actions work to reduce the health, social and economic harms to individuals, communities and society that are associated with the use of drugs. The 'Status Paper on Prisons, Drugs and Harm Reduction (WHO 2005) defined harm reduction measures in prisons:

In public health relating to prisons, harm reduction describes a concept aiming to prevent or reduce negative health effects associated with certain types of behaviour (such as drug injecting) and with imprisonment and overcrowding as well as adverse effects on mental health.

Harm reduction acknowledges that many drug users cannot totally abstain from using drugs in the short term and aims to help them reduce the potential harm from drug use, including by assisting them in stopping or reducing the sharing of injecting equipment in order to prevent HIV or hepatitis transmission that, in many ways, is an even greater harm than drug use. A 'harm reduction approach' recognises that a valid aim of drug interventions is to reduce the relative risks associated with drug misuse.

In addition, the definition WHO adopted acknowledges the negative health effects imprisonment can have. These include the impact on mental health, the risk of suicide and self-harm, the need to reduce the risk of drug overdose on release and the harm resulting from inappropriate imprisonment of people requiring facilities unavailable in prison or in overcrowded prisons.

All drug treatment services should provide a distinct harm reduction element to reduce the spread of blood-borne viruses and risk of drug-related deaths in the treatment they provide. Specific harm reduction interventions to reduce the spread of blood-borne viruses and to reduce overdose include:

– Needle exchange services i.e. the provision and disposal of needles and syringes and other clean injecting equipment (e.g. spoons, filters, citric acid) in a variety of settings (Lines et al. 2006; UNODC 2014)
– Advice and (peer) support on safer injection and reducing injecting and reducing initiation of others into injecting (Stöver and Trautmann 2001)
– Advice and information to prevent transmission of BBVs (particularly hepatitis A, B and C and HIV) and other drug use-related infections
– Hepatitis B vaccination (Farrell et al. 2010)
– Access to testing and treatment for hepatitis B, C and HIV/AIDS
– Counselling relating to HIV/hepatitis testing (pre- and post-test)
– Advice and support on preventing risk of overdose
– Risk assessment and referral to other treatment services.

In the last past 25 years harm reduction measures have been successfully implemented also in custodial settings as a supplementary strategy to existing drug-free oriented treatment programmes. Harm reduction does not replace the need for other interventions but adds to them and should be seen as a complementary component of wider health promotion strategies. The following hierarchy of goals should guide drug policy, in prisons as outside: Securing survival; securing survival without contracting irreversible damage; and, finally, stabilizing the addict's physical and social condition (Stöver et al. 2007).

10.7.4 Psychosocial Drug Treatment and Rehabilitation

Within prisons, the use of illegal drugs is a criminal offence, and therefore abstinence-based interventions are generally viewed as compatible with the goal of prison systems to seek to eradicate drug use inside prison. Abstinence is compatible with, and re-inforces, the aim of custody in general, and is seen to enable prisoners to lead a life without committing criminal offences after release.

Prisons run a variety of rehabilitation programmes for drug users based on different therapeutic approaches and assumptions. The programmes are designed to reduce the risk of re-offending through alleviating prisoners' substance use problems. Three main approaches and types of programmes can be distinguished. First, *Cognitive behavioural therapy* (CBT) is available at different levels of intensity (low/medium intensity programme; gender specific and short duration). The aim is to gain social learning experiences, and to understand and treat drug-related problem behaviour associated with substance-related offending. Second, the *12-step programme* is based on social learning within a peer approach, with new group members given instructions in the means to a drug-free life by more established prisoners. It works on the assumption that addiction is a lifelong illness that can be controlled but not necessarily completely cured. The programmes are high intensity for highly dependent prisoners, no matter which specific drug they are dependent on (programmes may last for 15–18 weeks). The third available therapy is the so called *Structured therapeutic community*. Therapeutic communities are based on hierarchical treatment and aims to teach new behaviours, attitudes and values, reinforced through peer and therapeutic community support. It is available for adult prisoners with a medium or high risk of reconviction and level of dependence on drugs (The Patel Report 2010).

The referral to these programmes is based on individual risks and needs. The different approaches allow the individual to be directed towards the treatment that is most suited to the severity of their problem and fits with their personal characteristics and circumstances. Some of the CBT programmes are suitable for people who are stabilised on opioid substitution programmes either as part of the process of working towards abstinence or towards a better stabilisation, while the 12-step and therapeutic community models require participants to be entirely drug-free before commencing the programme. 'The factors which are rated as being good include the quality of relationships, ease of access and experiencing a transformation in which drug users describe their life as having being 'turned around" (The Patel Report 2010: 29).

These approaches can additionally be matched with, on the one hand, voluntary drug testing which intends to provide an incentive for prisoners to stay drug free – either because they are recovering from drug dependence or because they wish to continue receiving particular privileges, such as a release on temporary licence or a more desirable job within the prison. On the other hand, having something meaningful to do, including employment, education and structured programmes, seems to be a key determinant in remaining drug-free.

10.7.5 Abstinence-Oriented Treatment and Therapeutic Communities in Prisons

Abstinence-oriented treatment for prisoners is provided predominantly in special facilities (therapeutic communities). Most of the Council of Europe countries have abstinence-based programmes. Therapeutic communities are intensive treatment programmes for prisoners with histories of severe drug dependence and related offending, who have a minimum of 12–15 months of their sentence left to serve. They are drug-free environments that implement an intensive treatment approach that requires 24-h residential care and comprehensive rehabilitation services. Residents are expected to take between three and 12 months to complete the programme.

In general, therapeutic community treatment models are designed as total-milieu therapy, which promotes the development of pro-social values, attitudes and behaviour through positive peer pressure. Although each therapeutic community differs in terms of services provided, most programmes are based on a combination of behavioural models with traditional group-based, confrontational techniques. As a high intensity, often multi-stage programme, therapeutic communities are provided in a separate unit of the prison. Many in-prison therapeutic communities ensure a continuum of care by providing community-based aftercare, which is closely connected to the specific therapeutic community and part of the correctional system.

Little research has been done on the effectiveness of therapeutic communities and the sustainability of abstinence. The problem not solved is that therapeutic communities are often not linked with interventions of 'safer-drug use' and prophylaxis of mortality after relapse on release. New research has been carried out on training of prisoners before release and handing them out the antidote Naloxone in England (N-Alive) and other parts of the world. Thus it is strongly suggested that the treatment experiences should be followed up after release.

10.7.6 Contract Treatment Units and Drug-Free Units

Drug-free units (or wings or contract treatment units) aim to allow the prisoner to keep their distance from the prison drug scene and market and to provide a space to work on dependence-related problems. The focus in these units is on drug-free living. Prisoners stay in these units voluntarily. They commit themselves (sometimes with a contract) to abstinence from drugs and to not bringing in any drugs and agree to regular medical check-ups often associated with drug testing. Prisoners staying in these units sometimes enjoy a regime with more favours and privileges, such as additional leave, education or work outside, excursions and more frequent contact with their families. Drug-free units (often called drug-free zones) do not necessarily include a treatment element. They aim to offer a drug-free environment for everyone who wants to keep their distance from drug-using inmates.

The purpose of staying in a contract treatment unit is that the inmate will remain drug-free or at least become motivated for continued treatment after imprisonment. Attempts will be made to motivate the inmate to strengthen his or her health and personality, to participate in work routines and to maintain and strengthen his or her social network.

The treatment principles in the units reflect a fundamental concept that the inmates can be supported in their decision to stop drug use by offering close personal contact and talks with drug dependence experts. Thus, a person is attached to each inmate in a contact person scheme in the units. The contact person is responsible for the inmate's treatment plan and for handling general casework concerning the inmate. Moreover, treatment includes sessions with supervisors: external people with a theoretical and practical background as therapists. The contact person, the supervisor and the inmate hold regular sessions, tripartite talks to investigate the inmate's development and consider the course of the future treatment. Another part of the treatment is the group dynamics. This consists of motivating the inmates to support each other in the everyday life in the unit. Group dynamics are developed by creating good physical surroundings and an open environment in the units and by both staff and inmates participating in a series of activities inside and outside the unit. Finally, the units work with the concept of the consequential teaching procedure, which means that an inmate caught using drugs or counteracting the principles of the unit is expelled from the unit. The treatment plans take into account the treatment needs of the individual. They set out targets for the inmates' stay in the unit, and decisions are made on any further treatment outside.

10.7.7 Peer Support and Peer-Driven Interventions

Peer education and peer support can be defined as the process by which trained people carry out informal and organised educational activities with individuals or small groups in their peer group (people belonging to the same societal group, such as of the same age or prisoners). Peer education has the overall aim of facilitating improvement in health and reduction in the risk of transmitting HIV or other blood-borne diseases, targeting individuals and groups that cannot effectively be reached by existing services. Peer-driven interventions make systematic use of the high and authentic value of peers.

Based on the data available and extrapolating from the literature on community-based programmes, education programmes in prisons – as in community settings – are more likely to be effective if peers develop and deliver them. As Grinstead and colleagues (1999) stated:

> When the target audience is culturally, geographically, or linguistically distinct, peer education may be an effective intervention approach. Inmate peer educators are more likely to have specific knowledge about risk behaviour occurring both inside and outside the prison. Peer educators who are living with HIV may also be ideal to increase the perception of personal risk and to reinforce community norms for safer sexual and injection practices.

Peer education has the additional advantage of being cost-effective and, consequently, sustainable. Inmate peer educators are always available to provide services as they live alongside the other inmates who are their educational target.

Peer educators can play a vital role in educating other prisoners, since most of the behaviour that puts prisoners at risk of HIV, hepatitis and overdose in prisons involves illegal (e.g. injecting drug use) or forbidden (e.g. same sex sexual activity (in some countries) and tattooing) and stigmatized (e.g. same sex sexual activity) practices. Peers may therefore be the only people who can speak candidly to other prisoners about ways to reduce the risk of contracting infections. Peer educators' input is also not likely to be viewed with the same suspicion as the information provided by the prison hierarchy. Peer educators are more likely to be able to realistically discuss the alternatives to risk behaviour that are available to prisoners and can better judge which educational strategies will work within their prison and the informal power structure among prisoners. Finally, peer-led education has been shown to be beneficial for the peer educators themselves: individuals who participate as peer educators report significant improvements in their self-esteem.

However, as with other education programmes, preventive education among peers is difficult when prisoners have no means to adopt the changes that would lead to healthier choices. Peer support groups need to be adequately funded and supported by staff and prison authorities, and need to have the trust of their peers, which can be difficult when the prison system appoints prisoners as peer educators because it trusts them, rather than because the prisoners trust them.

10.7.8 Pre-release Units

Prisoners should begin to be prepared for release on the day the sentence starts as part of the sentence planning process. All staff should be involved in preparing prisoners for release. Good release planning is particularly important for drug-using prisoners. The risks of relapse and overdose are extremely high. Measures taken in prison to prepare drug-using prisoners for release include, first, implementing measures to achieve and maintain drug-free status after release; a second measure is to grant home leave and to provide conditional release, both integrated into treatment processes. Third, co-operating with external drug services or doctors in planning a prisoner's release is important. Fourth, self-help groups in the release phase should be involved. Last, but not least, effective measures should be taken in prison, such as the provision of naloxone and training, to prevent prisoners from dying of a drug overdose shortly after release.

The challenge for prison services in facilitating a successful return to the community is not only to treat a drug problem but also to address other issues, including employability, educational deficits and maintaining family ties.

Harm reduction information needs to be provided to reduce the risk of a relapse to heroin or multiple drug use after leaving the prison. Few prisons speak frankly and proactively about relapse. Many prisons undertake efforts to reduce relapse and to provide social reintegration. Protocols are therefore sometimes set up with drug treatment centres from the national and community health networks. In Portugal, for instance, some projects focus on preparing for freedom and that getting a life means getting a job. Moreover, peer groups are developed to support treated drug addicts to prevent relapse.

10.7.9   Throughcare

The drug strategy of the HM Prison Service for England and Wales (Parliament 1999) defines the term throughcare as follows: 'By throughcare we mean the quality of care delivered to the offender from initial reception through to preparation for release establishing a smooth transition to community care after release'. The aims are to understand the pressures and fears affecting people's judgement on entry to prison and to ease the transition process between the community and prison and back to the community for drug users.

The ultimate goal is to provide continuity, for those receiving treatment and support in the community on arrival in prison, on transferring between prisons and on returning to the community.

10.7.10   Aftercare

Several studies show that intensive and effective aftercare for drug-using prisoners is essential to maintain gains made in prison-based treatment. Nevertheless, prisoners often have difficulty in accessing assessments and payment for treatment on release under community care arrangements. The following conclusions are drawn from a multi-country survey on aftercare programmes for drug-using prisoners in several European countries (Fox 2000):

– Aftercare for drug-using prisoners significantly decreases recidivism and relapse rates and saves lives.
– Interagency co-operation is essential for effective aftercare. Prisons, probation services, drug treatment agencies and health, employment and social welfare services must join to put the varied needs of drug-using offenders first.
– Drug treatment workers must have access to prisoners during their sentence to encourage participation in treatment and to plan release.
– Short-sentence prisoners are most poorly placed to receive aftercare and most likely to re-offend. These prisoners need to be fast-tracked into release planning and encouraged into treatment.
– Ex-offenders need choice in aftercare. One size does not fit all in drug treatment.

- Aftercare that is built into the last portion of a sentence appears to increase motivation and uptake.
- In aftercare, housing and employment should be partnered with treatment programmes.
- Unemployed and homeless ex-offenders are most likely to relapse and re-offend.

10.7.11 Working with Families and Maintaining Family Ties

The European Health Committee (established in 1954 by the Committee of Ministers of the Council of Europe) stated in 1998:

> One of the inevitable consequences of imprisonment is the temporary weakening of social contacts. It is true that family ties are not broken off completely, in the sense that in most cases a visit of at least one hour per week is permitted; nevertheless the prisoners' relationships suffer enormously from the confinement. A large number of wives, husbands and children of detainees feel punished themselves to a similar extent as their convicted spouses and fathers. Besides, and worse still, in many cases the marriage is bound to fail or be ruined.

Social contacts in general also suffer as a consequence of imprisonment. In some countries such as Denmark and Switzerland, prisoners are given the opportunity to see their partners without supervision (conjugal visits). Working with families of prisoners is a central part of rehabilitation and social reintegration in many countries. In some countries (such as Scotland), special family contact development officers are employed to help families keep or initiate contact with prisoners' relatives, to help to work on relatives' drug problems, to inform families about drug problems in prison and outside, and to enhance family visits.

10.7.12 Counselling and the Involvement of Community Health Structures

Counselling is a direct, personalized and client-centred intervention designed to help initiate behaviour change – keeping off drugs, avoiding infection or, if already infected, preventing transmission to other inmates or partners – and to obtain referral to additional health care, disease prevention, psychosocial and other needed services in order to remain healthy.

Health care employees require different information than guards or surveillance staff; inmates have their own specific background, subculture and language. Disease prevention material from the outside cannot simply be transferred to the prison setting; the relevant target groups require prison-adapted versions. This requires input from different groups based on interviews and focus-group discussions. Initial drafts and design need to be tested and approved. Both prison staff and prisoners greatly influence any prison environment. Both groups should therefore participate actively in developing and applying effective preventive measures and in disseminating relevant information.

Involvement and support from municipal health structures should have priority; non-governmental drug service, HIV and Aids organisations have especially valuable expertise and networks that can contribute to enhancing the quality of material development and sustaining this as an ongoing activity. Some prisons even have their own advisory bureau on drug issues, and the social workers in some prisons take care of these problems. In contrast to internal workers, prisoners more widely accept and trust external workers because the outsiders have a duty to maintain confidentiality and have the right to refuse to give evidence. Moreover, the external workers are more experienced and know about the content of, and requirements for, the various support services offered. Counsellors on drug issues in prison should primarily provide information about the various support services and programmes available inside and outside prisons. In a second step, their efforts should focus on motivating prisoners to overcome their drug use. A major advantage of external drug counselling is that it links life inside and outside the prison and thus is very helpful for continuing treatment that was started in prison.

In the past decade, approaches have developed and grown substantially to divert individuals away from prison and into treatment alternatives as well as a range of services within prisons. Specific legislation in several countries has attempted to enhance links between the criminal justice system and health services to reduce the number of drug users entering prison. Despite this development, the number of prisoners with drug dependence has continued to grow. As drug users often serve short sentences, they return into their communities and many return to their old drug-using habits. Support services need to be continued in order to sustain successes that may be achieved while in custody. This indicates that criminal justice agencies need to link better with drug services.

10.7.13 Vocational Training

Both doctors and prison staff confront multiple drug use in their everyday work. Use of tobacco, cannabis, alcohol, benzodiazepines and opioids is widespread, and withdrawal and craving are relatively frequent. Nevertheless, physicians and prison personnel know too little about the issues and problems related to drug use. It is vital, therefore, that staff receive adequate training to tackle the problems connected with drug use in prisons and to move towards a more treatment-focused approach. Prison staff needs training and regular updating on all aspects concerning HIV, hepatitis and drug abuse, especially on medical, psychological and social aspects, in order to feel secure themselves and be able to give prisoners appropriate guidance and support.

Also, human rights and medical ethics in prisons are important issues (Lehmets and Pont 2014).

10.8 Specific Groups

The diverse needs of drug users and those at risk of infection in police custody and prison should be recognised and the type of services offered to them should be responsive to their particular needs and delivered without discrimination. These groups include: women, members of ethnic and cultural minorities, foreign language speaking offenders, older prisoners, juveniles/young offenders and those with psychiatric co-morbidities and cognitive impairments. Three aspects are of particular importance: first, services that are responsive to and meet the specific needs of female drug users and women at risk of infection are required because in some countries women still face barriers to treatment. These should include more services and treatment opportunities, and services that have been designed specifically to meet their needs (van den Bergh et al. 2009). Second, services that meet the specific needs of juveniles/young offenders who are drug users or may be at risk of infection are needed. Third, foreign nationals who use drugs or are at risk of infection should be given equal access to treatment, care and support when entering police custody or prison to ensure that their health needs are addressed while they are detained. They should also be provided with information (in an accessible format and a language that they understand) about what is available to them on their release (including what is available if they are deported on release) or on transfer to another jurisdiction.

10.9 Summary: Key Points

- Estimates suggest that half the prisoners in the European Union have a history of drug use, many with problematic, injecting drug use.
- Drug use is one of the main problems facing prison systems, threatening security, dominating the relationships between prisoners and staff and leading to violence, bullying and mobbing for both prisoners and often their spouses and friends in the community.
- The prevalence of infectious diseases (particularly HIV and Aids, hepatitis B and C, and tuberculosis) is often much higher in prisons than outside, often related to injecting drug use.
- Drug dependence services and measures to address infectious diseases in prisons should be equivalent to the services provided outside prisons. This can best be achieved through close co-operation and communication between prison and community services and by integrating prison drug and BBV strategies into the national drug and BBV strategy.
- Continuity of treatment for prisoners entering and leaving prison necessitates close co-operation between prisons and external agencies.
- Relapse to drug use and fatal overdoses after release are widespread, and these risks need to be addressed during the time of imprisonment.

- A wide range of drug services should be available to prisoners, based on local and individual needs. Interdisciplinary staff and multi-professional teams should offer psycho-social as well as pharmacological treatment, stimulating and enhancing self-help potential of prisoners.
- There should be training for prison staff and prisoners on drugs and related health problems.
- Drug strategies in prisons require actions to be taken both on the level of individual behavioural change and on the structural level. Although targeting programmes at individual prisoners or groups of prisoners is important, there is also a need for more structurally oriented measures to run concurrently, to comprehensively address necessary improvements in the living conditions of the prisoners and the working conditions of prison staff.
- National and international networking and exchange of good practice models seems to be a valuable method for all prison systems to engage in. In addition, international networks need to disseminate internationally available good practice models and knowledge about evidence-based strategies into the prison settings and/or on the level of prison administration.
- Guidelines and detailed protocols are needed on how exactly certain treatment options can and have to be implemented to support prison doctors/nurses and prison administration in delivering adequate health care services (e.g. for substitution treatment to opiate dependent prisoners).
- Drug services in prisons should be subject to monitoring and evaluation.

References

Connections Project. (2011). *Good practice in preventing drug misuse and related infections in criminal justice systems in Europe*. University of Kent, Kent, UK

EMCDDA. (2011). *Estimates of prevalence of problem drug use at national and subnational level: Bibliographic references. Table PDU-0*. Luxembourg: Publications Office of the European Union.

EMCDDA. (2012). *Drug use in prison: The problem and responses*. It is European Monitoring Centre for Drugs and Drug Addiction (EMCDDA) in Lisbon/Portugal, Special Issue. Lisbon.

European Health Committee. (1998). *The organisation of health care services in prisons in European Member States*. Strasbourg: Council of Europe Pub.

Farrell, M., & Marsden, J. (2005). Drug-related mortality among newly-released offenders 1998 to 2000. *Home Office Online Report, 40*(5). http://library.npia.police.uk/docs/hordsolr/rdsolr4005.pdf. Accessed 22 June 2012.

Farrell, M., Strang, J., & Stöver, H. (2010). Hepatitis B vaccination in prisons; A much needed targeted intervention. *Addiction 105,* 189–190. http://www3.interscience.wiley.com/cgi-bin/fulltext/123236973/PDFSTART. Accessed 22 Mar 2013.

Fox, A. (2000). *Prisoners' aftercare in Europe: A four-country study*. London: ENDHASP.

Grinstead, O., Zack, B., Faigeles, B., Grossman, N., & Blea, L. (1999). Reducing post-release HIV risk among male prison inmates: A peer-led intervention. *Criminal Justice and Behaviour, 26*(4), 453–465.

Hedrich, D., & Farrell, M. (2012). Opioid maintenance in European prisons: Is the treatment gap closing? *Addiction, 107,* 461–463.

Hedrich, D., Alves, P., Farrell, M., Stöver, H., Möller, L., & Mayet, S. (2012). The effectiveness of opioid maintenance treatment in prison settings: A systematic review. *Addiction, 107*(3), 501–517. http://www.ncbi.nlm.nih.gov/pubmed/21955033. Accessed 22 Mar 2013.

Jürgens, R., Ball, A., & Verster, A. (2009). *Lancet Infect Disease, 9*(1), 57–66.

Kastelic, A., Pont, J., & Stöver, H. (2008). *Opioid substitution treatment in custodial settings: A practical guide*. Oldenburg: BIS-Verlag. http://gesundinhaft.eu/wp-content/uploads/2008/04/2117_5_ost-in-custodial-settings.pdf. Accessed 22 Mar 2013.

Lehmets, A., & Pont, J. (2014). Prison health care und medical ethics. *CoE Manual*. http://www.coe.int/t/dgi/criminallawcoop/Presentation/Documents/Publications_HealthCaremanual_Web_A5_E.pdf

Lines, R., Jürgens, R., Betteridge, G., Laticevschi, D., Nelles, J., & Stöver, H. (2006). *Prison needle exchange: a review of international evidence and experience*. Montreal: Canadian HIV/AIDS Legal Network. http://www.aidslaw.ca/publications/interfaces/downloadFilephp?ref=1173. Accessed 22 Mar 2013.

Marteau, D., Palmer, J., & Stöver, H. (2010). Introduction of the Integrated Drug Treatment System (IDTS) in English prisons. *International Journal of Prisoner Health, 6*(3), 117–124.

Parliament of the United Kingdom. (1999). *Memorandum by HM prison service: Drugs and prison*. http://www.publications.parliament.uk/pa/cm199899/cmselect/cmhaff/363/363ap02htm. Accessed 29 June 2012.

Ritter, C., Broers, B., & Elger, B. S. (2013). Cannabis use in a Swiss male prison: Qualitative study exploring detainees' and staffs' perspectives. *The International Journal on Drug Policy, 24*(6), 573–578. doi:10.1016/j.drugpo.2013.05.001. Epub 14 June 2013.

Stöver, H. (2012). Drug treatment and harm reduction in prisons. In P. Jones (Ed.), *Interventions in criminal justice: A handbook for counsellors and therapists working in the criminal justice field* (pp. 97–128). Hove: Pavilion Publishing.

Stöver, H., & Kastelic, A. (2014). Drug treatment and harm reduction in prisons. In: WHO (S. Enggist, L. Moller, G. Galea, & C. Udesen (Eds.), *Prisons and health* (2nd ed., pp. 113–133). http://www.euro.who.int/en/health-topics/health-determinants/prisons-and-health/who-health-in-prisons-programme-hipp

Stöver, H., & Schäffer, D. (2014, June 27). *SMOKE IT! Promoting a change of opiate consumption pattern – From injecting to inhaling*. In: 2014, 11:18 (27 June 2014) http://www.harmreductionjournal.com/content/11/1/18

Stöver, H., & Trautmann, F. (2001). *Manual on risk reduction for drug users in European prisons*. http://www.harm-reduction.org/ru/images/stories/doc/Sekc/RU_Harm%20reduction%20in%20prisons/RISK%20REDUCTION%20FOR%20DRUG%20USERS%20IN%20PRISONS. PDF. Accessed 22 Mar 2013.

Stöver, H., MacDonald, M., & Atherton, S. (2007). *Harm reduction for drug users in European Prisons*. Oldenburg: BIS-Verlag.

Stöver, H., Weilandt, C., Zurhold, H., Hartwig, C., & Thane, K. (2008). Final report on prevention, treatment, and harm reduction services in prison, on reintegration services on release from prison and methods to monitor/analyse drug use among prisoners. European Commission, Directorate – General for health and Consumers. Drug policy and harm reduction. SANCO/2006/C4/02, page 58 http://ec.europa.eu/health/ph_determinants/life_style/drug/documents/drug_frep1.pdf

Taylor, A., & Goldberg, D. (1996). Outbreak of HIV infection in a Scottish prison: Why did it happen? *Canadian HIV-AIDS Policy & Law Newsletter, 2*(3), 13–14.

The Patel Report. (2010). *Prison drug treatment strategy review group: Reducing drug-related crime*. http://www.drugsandalcohol.ie/13941/1/Patel_report_prison_drug_treatment.pdf. Accessed 22 Mar 2013.

Tomasevski, K. (1992). *Prison health: International standards and national practices in Europe*. Helsinki: Helsinki Institute for Crime Prevention and Control.

Uchtenhagen, A. (2006). *The Lisbon agenda for prisons. All on drugs and public health in prisons*. http://www.encod.org/info/IMG/pdf/The_Lisbon_Agenda_for_Prisons_RS_PW.pdf. Accessed 22 Mar 2013.

UNODC. (2014). *A handbook for starting and managing needle and syringe programmes in prisons and other closed settings.* ADVANCE COPY. http://www.unodc.org/documents/hiv-aids/publications/Prisons_and_other_closed_settings/ADV_COPY_NSP_PRISON_AUG_2014.pdf

van den Bergh, B. J., Gatherer, A., & Moller, L. F. (2009). Women's health in prison: Urgent need for improvement in gender equity and social justice. *Bulletin of the World Health Organization, 87*(6), S. 406.

WHO Regional Office for Europe. (2005). *Status paper on prisons, drugs and harm reduction.* http://www.euro.who.int/__data/assets/pdf_file/0006/78549/E85877.pdf. Accessed 22 Mar 2013.

WHO and Council of Europe. (2001). *Prison, drugs and society.* http://www.euro.who.int/__data/assets/pdf_file/0003/99012/E81559.pdf. Accessed 22 Mar 2013.

Chapter 11
Hepatitis C Viral Infection in Prisons

Geert Robaeys, Amber Arain, and Heino Stöver

Abstract Worldwide, several million people spend time in prisons each year. Illicit drug use is very common in inmates. In order to use drugs without prison staff noticing, there is high rate of sharing of drug use equipment such as needles, which constitutes the most important risk factor for hepatitis C infection (HCV). Hepatitis C is becoming an important issue in custodial settings, and the prevalence of hepatitis C infection is higher in prisons than in general population.

International organisations agree that all blood-borne virus prevention, treatment and care interventions available in the community must also be available to prisoners.

Many inmates re-enter the community having had different unmanaged conditions during imprisonment. Among inmates, similar rates of HCV treatment completion and success (SVR) to those in the general population have been recorded.

However, in reality, screening for HCV infection and uptake of antiviral treatment are low in custodial settings. Correctional institutions are important settings for health interventions such as diagnosis, prevention, and treatment of HCV infection.

G. Robaeys (✉)
Department of Gastroenterology and Hepatology, Ziekenhuis Oost Limburg, Schiepse Bos, 6, 3600 Genk, Belgium

Department of Hepatology UZ Leuven, Leuven University, Herestraat 49, 3000 Leuven, Belgium

Limburg Clinical Research Program, Faculty of Medicine and Life Sciences, Hasselt University, Martelarenlaan 42, 3500 Hasselt, Belgium
e-mail: geert.robaeys@zol.be

A. Arain
Limburg Clinical Research Program, Faculty of Medicine and Life Sciences, Hasselt University, Martelarenlaan 42, 3500 Hasselt, Belgium
e-mail: amber.arain@uhasselt.be

H. Stöver
Faculty 'Health and Social Work', Frankfurt University of Applied Sciences, Nibelungenplatz 1, 60318 Frankfurt, Germany
e-mail: hstoever@fb4.fra-uas.de

© Springer Science+Business Media Dordrecht 2017
B.S. Elger et al. (eds.), *Emerging Issues in Prison Health*,
DOI 10.1007/978-94-017-7558-8_11

11.1 Introduction

Globally, over 10 million people are held in prisons and other places of detention at any given time (Open Society Foundations 2011). Due to the high turnover rate in the prison population, it is estimated that over 30 million people spend time in prisons each year. Drug users in particular often spend relatively short periods in prisons and then return to the community, to their partners and families.

The majority of people held in prisons have severe problems associated with drug use, together with related health and social disadvantages. Those categorised as problematic drug users (PDUs) constitute a substantial proportion of prison populations in Europe. Taking only the number of sentenced prisoners with drug offences as the main offence in penal institutions in the European Union, Croatia, Turkey and Norway (on 1 September 2008) '15 of the 26 countries for which information is available report proportions over 15 %, indicating that drug-related crime is an important category of custodial offence in many European countries' (Carpentier et al. 2012). The number of drug users in prisons is even higher. A systematic review of international studies – with a predominance of studies conducted in the United States – found that 10–48 % of men and 30–60 % of women were dependent on or used illicit drugs in the month before entering prison (Fazel et al. 2006). In the European Union, it has been estimated that about half of the prison population have used illicit drugs at some time in their lives (Zurhold et al. 2005).

Hepatitis C viral (HCV) infection, which is both preventable and treatable, is a major concern in correctional settings. Very close relationships exist between illicit drug use, HCV infection, and imprisonment (Hunt and Saab 2009). Injecting drug users (IDUs) have high rates of imprisonment which are predominantly due to the criminalization of their drug use, and the tendency to fund drug use through crime (see the Chap. 10).

The consequence of chronic viral infection is the possible development of cirrhosis of the liver and development of liver cancer (hepatocellular carcinoma – HCC) and eventually death (Haber et al. 1999; Vlahov et al. 1993). In general, 80 % of HCV-infected individuals will develop chronic HCV. Of these, 10–15 % will develop liver cirrhosis (Spaulding et al. 1999) and 3–4 % of patients with cirrhosis develop HCC every year (Vescio et al. 2008; Macalino et al. 2004). Worldwide, 25 % of liver cancer cases are attributable to HCV infection (Baillargeon et al. 2003).

The mortality rate for HCV-induced liver disease is high. Chronic liver disease -related deaths accounted for 16 % of deaths. HBV or HCV were identified as a causal factor in more than a third (34 %) of chronic liver disease-related deaths (Harzke et al. 2009).

11.2 Transmission of HCV and Risk Factors

All modes of HCV transmission that occur in the community also occur in prisons. In particular, HCV/HBV and HIV are transmitted in prisons through the sharing of non-sterile needles and syringes as well as contaminated injecting equipment (e.g. spoons, filter, water, lighter etc.) among people who inject and/or use drugs, unsafe sexual contact, unsafe skin penetration (such as piercing and tattooing, sharing of razors, blood sharing/'brotherhood' rituals) and the improper sterilisation or reuse of medical or dental instruments (WHO et al. 2009). Some prisoners continue to use opioids, including by injection, and a few even initiate injecting in prison (Hedrich et al. 2012). About half of all imprisoned people who inject drugs continue to inject drugs in prison (Hepatitis Australia 2011).

Imprisonment is an independent risk factor for HCV infection in community-based IDUs (van Beek et al. 1998; Butler et al. 2007; Hellard et al. 2004; Hennessey et al. 2009; Miller et al. 2009; Poulin et al. 2007).

One of the most important risk factors for HCV infection is intravenous drug use while in prison (Hellard et al. 2004; Poulin et al. 2007). In a meta-analysis of 30 studies in different countries, there was a clear association between the prevalence of HCV infection in prisoners and the history of IDU and a weaker association with female gender and tattooing. The results showed that HCV seroprevalence was approximately 11 % higher among already detained inmates, as opposed to inmates entering prison. A strong association of HCV infection with the period spent in prison was also seen, which could be explained by intra-prison transmission of HCV (Vescio et al. 2008).

The prevalence of HCV infection among prison inmates is many times higher in most custodial settings than in the general population (Haber et al. 1999; Vlahov et al. 1993), mainly because of the high proportion of injecting drug users (IDU) (Spaulding et al. 1999) who are known to be at high risk of infection. In the general population the prevalence is approximately 1 in 100 in Western Europe but higher in Southern and Eastern Europe (respectively 2.5 and 6 %) (Esteban et al. 2008).

Different studies from Europe, Australia and the United States suggest that hepatitis C prevalence rates in prisons range from 8 % to 57 % (Backmund et al. 2003; Baillargeon et al. 2003; Burek et al. 2010).[1]

Data on HCV antibody prevalence among injecting drug users in European prisons between 2005 and 2010 were reported by five countries, with prevalence ranging from 11.5 % in Hungary to 90.7 % in Luxembourg (EMCDDA 2012: 14).

Among female prisoners the prevalence is 2 in 3. Among female IDUs the prevalence can be even higher, ranging from 49 % to 88 % (Viitanen et al. 2011).

The incidence of HCV infection in prison varies from 18.2 to 34.2 per 100 person years (Crofts et al. 1994; Dolan et al. 2010).

---

[1]For more information see also, Christensen et al. (2000), Gore et al. (1999), Hellard et al. (2004), Long et al. (2001), Macalino et al. 2004, Maher et al. 2004, Ogilvie et al. (1999), Solomon et al. (2004), Weild et al. (2000).

Patterns of hepatitis C prevalence in custodial settings include (i), an increasing prevalence with age, (ii) a higher prevalence among female prisoners, and (iii) an increasing prevalence with multiple admissions to prisons (AIHW 2010).

11.3   Equivalence of Health Care and HCV

Prisoners are entitled, without discrimination, to a standard of health care equivalent to that available in the outside community, including preventive measures. This principle of equivalence is fundamental to the promotion of human rights and best health practice within prisons, and is supported by international guidelines on prison health and prisoners' rights, as well as national prison policy and legislation in many countries.

Numerous laws and related declarations demand humane treatment in detention with availability, accessibility, acceptability and adaptability of adequate health services (UN General Comment on the Right to Health).

The standards and norms outlined in these documents reflect established international human rights instruments and good public health practice, and should guide the development of appropriate, ethical, and effective responses to hepatitis and other infectious diseases in prisons. Cooperation and action should be inclusive, intersectoral and evidence-based (UNODC et al. 2006).

People should not leave custody in a worse condition, or with poorer health than when they entered (Hepatitis Australia 2011). The period of incarceration should be viewed as a public health window of opportunity, including HCV testing, treatment care and support (MACASHH 2008). There is consensus among international organisations that all blood borne virus (BBV) prevention, treatment and care interventions, including harm reduction interventions, available in the community must also be available to prisoners (UNAIDS 1997; UNODC et al. 2006; WHO 1993).[2]

11.4   Multiple HCV Infections

Multiple infections are defined as infection with more than one strain of HCV. Multiple infection is sub-classified into mixed infection (infection by two or more heterologous viruses either simultaneously or within a narrow time period), superinfection (detection of infection by an HCV strain distinct from the primary infecting strain in subjects with persistent viremia), and reinfection (infection by a distinct HCV from the primary strain following viral clearance). A strain switch is determined when two or more distinct viruses were detected during follow-up.

---

[2]For more on the principle of equivalence of care, see the Chap. 13.

Different studies have demonstrated the occurrence of multiple HCV infections caused by the large degree of HCV genomic variation, the lack of protective immunity generated by HCV infection, and frequent opportunities for re-exposure through ongoing injection behaviours (Aitken et al. 2008; Fujimura et al. 1996; Herring et al. 2004; van de Laar et al. 2009; Kao et al. 1996; Widell et al. 1995). Multiple infections are classified as either mixed infection (also sometimes referred to as co-infection), superinfection, and/or re-infection (Blackard and Sherman 2007; Pham et al. 2010). A study of multiple infections occurring in prison inmates detected a high cumulative prevalence (24.4 %) of multiple infections within this IDU prisoner cohort; HCV RNA levels were shown to be a major factor influencing the outcome of mixed infection (Pham et al. 2010).

11.5 Screening

Screening for HCV infection and uptake of antiviral therapy is low in prisons. In a nationwide survey in the USA, only one state reported routine screening and only one reported conducting a seroprevalence study in custodial care (Spaulding et al. 1999). Of 3034 new prisoners at Dartmoor Prison (England), 12 % were screened, with 16 % of these being seropositive. Seventy-nine percent of seropositive prisoners with a positive polymerase chain reaction result were confirmed as cases of positive viremia, and 27 % of these prisoners had a biopsy. Two prisoners were eligible for treatment (Horne et al. 2004).

11.5.1 Barriers to Testing

Many inmates enter prison with social, medical, and mental health conditions and re-enter the community with few of these conditions having been addressed while incarcerated. Hepatitis C is one such condition, and its management challenges both the correctional and public health systems.

Qualitative research has described barriers to testing, such as lack of proactive approaches to offering testing, prisoners' fears and lack of knowledge about HCV, low motivation for testing and concerns about confidentiality and stigma, which may mean fewer people are tested (Khaw et al. 2007). More work is needed to increase the level of testing in prisons.

11.6 HCV Treatment

Previous studies indicate that, with good adherence to treatment regimens, sustained virological response (SVR) rates for prison patients treated with combination therapy (peg-interferon and ribavirin) are comparable to those observed in non-inmate patients at similar stages of disease (Chew et al. 2009; Farley et al. 2005; Sterling et al. 2004). Encouraging rates of HCV treatment completion (feasibility) and success (SVR) were registered in the correctional population, and were similar to those reported in community samples (Bate et al. 2010; Boonwaat et al. 2010; Farley et al. 2005). The re-infection rate after successful antiviral treatment in prisons is low (7 %) (Bate et al. 2010), and comparable to re-infection rates outside prison.

Antiviral treatment in prison may be cost effective. Treatment resulted in both decreased costs and improved quality of life. In prisoners between 40 and 49 years of age, treatment saved $41,321 and increased Quality-Adjusted-Life-Years (QALYs) by 0.75. For prisoners between 50 and 59 years of age, treatment decreased costs by $33,445 and increased QALYs by 0.69. In prisoners between 60 and 69 years of age, treatment produced $11,637 in savings and a gain of 0.5 in QALYs (Tan et al. 2008).

Several groups argued that correctional institutions are an important setting for health interventions such as screening, diagnosis, prevention, and treatment of HCV infection (Chew et al. 2009; Hammett 2001; Spaulding et al. 2006). One of the reasons is that in prison it is possible to monitor adherence to treatment and the availability of substance use treatment more closely, and to closely monitor and address side effects and provide psychiatric care as necessary (De Groot et al. 2001). A second reason is that prisons provide an opportunity to engage with a 'hard-to-reach' population, because incarceration may be the first or only time that many inmates intersect with the healthcare system. A third reason is that medical management and adherence to antiviral therapy require lifestyle stability, which can be provided by incarceration, particularly for offenders with a history of mental illness or substance abuse (Spaulding et al. 2006).

11.7 The Hepatitis Nurse Model

However, as the standard peg-interferon (weekly injections) and ribavirin (daily per os administration) combination treatments for hepatitis C are quite costly, averaging at approximately $15,000–20,000 per patient for a full course of treatment; helping the patient get access to this costly medication involves a coordinated process. This can best be done via a 'hepatitis nurse', a model that has been implemented in several countries. The nurse can have a coaching role to support the patient in decision-making, and during the treatment itself. This could be done as follows: before beginning treatment, the hepatitis nurse meets with the patient at the hepatologist's clinic for a patient training session during which the nurse and the patient will usually discuss (i) the goals of treatment, (ii) what medications he/she is currently taking, (iii) the negative effect of alcohol consumption and smoking during treatment, (iv) the importance of using two methods of birth control until at least 6 months post-treatment to prevent pregnancy (this is because ribavirin causes birth defects), (v) the treatment he/she is about to begin and how it works, (vi) the side effects of the treatment and the adapted response in case of need, and (vii) the process of determining responsiveness to the treatment and conditions for continuing or discontinuing treatment (Cheong-Lee 2011).

Once the treatment has started, the hepatitis nurse teaches patients how to precisely self-administer the interferon-based injections and safely handle the needles. The weekly injections are administered under the skin (subcutaneously) of the abdomen or the thighs. The patient is provided with as much guidance and support as he/she requires until he/she is comfortable doing the injections on his/her own. The patient is also instructed about the dosage of ribavirin and when to take the tablets.

11.8 General Recommendations

The following recommendations can be made regarding hepatitis C prevention, screening and treatment in prisons:

- Close collaboration between prison and public (or community) health services is needed. Ensure continued hepatitis C treatment and care when movements between custodial settings occur, and re-entry to the community (Hepatitis Australia 2011; Spaulding et al. 2006; Vescio et al. 2008).
- Incarcerated persons with risk factors for HCV infection should be screened for viral hepatitis infections (Spaulding et al. 2006; Weinbaum et al. 2003)
- HCV-infected persons should be counselled on how to avoid HCV transmission to others (CDC 1998)
- Provide prisoners with substance abuse treatment (Spaulding et al. 2006). Opiate agonist therapy (methadone, buprenorphine or diacetylmorhpine) (Hedrich et al. 2012) should be administered to opiate dependent subjects with hepatitis B and C infections in order to reduce the risks of transmission, re-infection and the progression of liver disease.
- There is a need to provide sterile injecting equipment and other harm reduction measures to those who inject while in prison (Lines 2005; Stöver and Nelles 2003).
- There is a need to develop approaches to increase the uptake of testing by raising awareness amongst prisoners about HCV infection, optimising testing pathways that support appropriate testing at appropriate times during a prisoner's stay in prison, ensuring adequate pre- and post-test discussion, and by developing care pathways for HCV that enable seamless continuity of care (Khaw et al. 2007). Proven nurse-lead intervention models as presented above could be transferred into the prison setting in order to guarantee guidance.
- Community follow-up of treatment, including ongoing substance abuse treatment, life-skills support, and health education, is needed for drug treatment and

harm reduction to be most effective. (ECDC and EMCDDA 2011; Spaulding et al. 1999). Health education activities (including peer education) can be carried out, in particular for persons with no or minimal prior health education (Broadhead et al. 2002; Edlin et al. 2005).

- Depression and psychosis, which are common in prison settings, occur with interferon treatment. It is essential to provide psychiatric evaluation of patients prior and during treatment, in order to avoid/control the possible appearance of mental side effects (Hauser et al. 2002; Spaulding et al. 2006)
- HCV-positive prisoners who may benefit from treatment should be identified (Spaulding et al. 2006).
- A multidisciplinary approach through the collaboration of addiction specialists, hepatologists, infectious disease experts, clinical psychologists, nurses and prison physicians should be adopted (Belfiori et al. 2009).
- If possible a directly observed treatment (DOT) strategy, which ensures supervision of oral therapy administration and the injection of subcutaneous therapy by healthcare professionals, should be used, as occurs in anti-HIV and tuberculosis treatment in prison inmates (Haber et al. 1999).

11.9 Staff Training and Support Recommendations

Staff training is important because all people working in prisons should be blood–aware and be informed about prevention possibilities, their risks for infection and the universal and special precautions that should be taken. Informing staff about transmission risks gives them an understanding of all BBVs and enables them to differentiate between the different diseases and to be cautious in daily prison routines.

- Provide education on hepatitis and other communicable diseases, routes of transmission in the workplace, confidentiality, drug use, hepatitis prevention measures, hepatitis testing and treatment opportunities, drug dependence treatment, universal precautions and use of protective equipment, and the rationale for and content of prison rules and policies related to hepatitis to all prison staff as part of their initial training, and update this training on a regular basis during the course of employment.
- Ensure that all staff receive regular training.
- Consult with staff on the development of educational materials and programmes and the methods of delivering training programmes, and encourage and support the development of peer education initiatives and materials by and for prison staff.
- Ensure that the training of prison staff addresses hepatitis-related discrimination and homophobia, reduces staff opposition to the provision of hepatitis prevention measures to prisoners, emphasises the importance of confidentiality and non-disclosure of hepatitis status and medical information, and promotes the compassionate treatment of prisoners living with hepatitis.

- Ensure that the content of all training is specific to the duties and responsibilities of the various categories of prison staff (i.e. security staff, medical and nursing staff, etc.) and that it is relevant to the specific realities of the prison environment.
- Provide regular training to prison health care workers to enable them to maintain and improve their skills and knowledge current with developments in all health areas, in particular drug dependence treatment and BBV prevention, care, and treatment.
- Implement policies and training to minimize the risk of workplace exposure (i.e. needle-stick injuries while searching cells for example).
- Provide mechanisms to ensure a safe physical environment such as hand washing stations, health waste management and disposal, appropriate ventilation systems (especially for the accommodation of patients with smear positive tuberculosis), and utilizing universal precautions.
- Ensure that all prison staff are provided with hepatitis B vaccinations at no cost.
- Ensure that in the event of potential workplace exposure to hepatitis, prison staff have access to appropriate post-exposure prophylaxis and counselling.
- Ensure that health insurance plans for prison staff include coverage for antiretroviral treatments.

References

AIHW. (2010). *The health of Australia's prisoners*. http://www.aihw.gov.au/publication-detail/?id=6442468371&tab=2. Accessed 30 Mar 2013.

Aitken, C. K., Lewis, J., Tracy, S. L., Spelman, T., Bowden, D. S., Bharadwaj, M., Drummer, H., & Hellard, M. (2008). High incidence of hepatitis C virus reinfection in a cohort of injecting drug users. *Hepatology, 48*(6), 1746–1752.

Backmund, M., Meyer, K., Wächtler, M., & Eichenlaub, D. (2003). Hepatitis C virus infection in injection drug users in Bavaria: Risk factors for seropositivity. *European Journal of Epidemiology, 18*(6), 563–568.

Baillargeon, J., Wu, H., Kelley, M. J., Grady, J., Linthicum, L., & Dunn, K. (2003). Hepatitis C seroprevalence among newly incarcerated inmates in the Texas correctional system. *Public Health, 117*(1), 43–48.

Bate, J. P., Colman, A. J., Frost, P. J., Shaw, D. R., & Harley, H. A. (2010). High prevalence of late relapse and reinfection in prisoners treated for chronic hepatitis C. *Journal of Gastroenterology and Hepatology, 25*, 1276–1280.

Belfiori, B., Ciliegi, P., Chiodera, A., Bacosi, D., Tosti, A., Baldelli, F., & Francisci, D. (2009). Peginterferon plus ribavirin for chronic hepatitis C in opiate addicts on methadone/buprenorphine maintenance therapy. *Digestive and Liver Disease, 41*(4), 303–307.

Blackard, J. T., & Sherman, K. E. (2007). Hepatitis C virus co-infection and superinfection. *Journal of Infectious Diseases, 195*, 519–524.

Boonwaat, L., Haber, P. S., Levy, M. H., & Lloyd, A. R. (2010, May 3). Establishment of a successful assessment and treatment service for Australian prison inmates with chronic hepatitis C. *The Medical Journal of Australia, 192*(9), 496–500.

Broadhead, R. S., Heckathorn, D. D., Altice, F. L., van Hulst, Y., Carbone, M., Friedland, G. H., O'Connor, P. G., & Selwyn, P. A. (2002). Increasing drug user's adherence to IV treatment: Results of a peer-driven intervention feasibility study. *Social Science and Medicine, 55*(2), 235–246.

Burek, V., Horvat, J., Butorac, K., & Mikulić, R. (2010). Viral hepatitis B, C and HIV infection in Croatian prisons. *Epidemiology and Infection, 138*(11), 1610–1620.

Butler, T., Boonwaat, L., Hailstone, S., Falconer, T., Lems, P., Ginley, T., Read, V., Smith, N., Levy, M., Dore, G., & Kaldor, J. (2007). The 2004 Australian prison entrants' blood-borne virus and risk behaviour survey. *Australian and New Zealand Journal of Public Health, 31*(1), 44–50.

Carpentier, C., Royuela, L., Noor, A., & Hedrich, D. (2012). Ten years of monitoring illicit drug use in prison populations in Europe: Issues and challenges. *The Howard League of Criminal Justice, 51*(1), 37–66.

CDC. (1998). Recommendations for prevention and control of hepatitis C virus (HCV) infection and HCV-related chronic disease. *MMWR, Recommendations and Reports, 47*(RR-19), 1–39.

Cheong-Lee, C. (2011). *Hepatitis nurse. What to expect with Hepatitis C treatment and how Hepatitis nurses can help*. Presentation on the 2nd international symposium on hepatitis care in substance users. Brussels.

Chew, K. W., Allen, S. A., Taylor, L. E., Rich, J. D., & Feller, E. (2009). Treatment outcomes with pegylated interferon and ribavirin for male prisoners with chronic hepatitis C. *Journal of Clinical Gastroenterology, 43*(7), 686–691.

Christensen, P. B., Krarup, H. B., Niesters, H. G., Norder, H., & Georgsen, J. (2000). Prevalence and incidence of blood-borne viral infections among Danish prisoners. *European Journal of Epidemiology, 16*(11), 1043–1049.

Crofts, N., Hopper, J. L., Milner, R., Breschkin, A. M., Bowden, D. S., & Locarnini, S. A. (1994). Blood-borne virus infections among Australian injecting drug users: Implications for spread of HIV. *European Journal of Epidemiology, 10*(6), 687–694.

De Groot, A. S., Stubblefield, E., & Bick, J. (2001). Hepatitis C. a correctional-public health opportunity. *Medscape Infectious Diseases, 3*, 1–14.

Dolan, K., Teutsch, S., Scheuer, N., Levy, M., Rawlinson, W., Kaldor, J., et al. (2010, February). Incidence and risk for acute hepatitis C infection during imprisonment in Australia. *European Journal of Epidemiology, 25*(2), 143–148. doi:10.1007/s10654-009-9421-0.

ECDC, & EMCDDA. (2011). Prevention and control of infectious diseases among people who inject drugs. *Guidance in brief*. http://www.emcdda.europa.eu/publications/ecdc-emcdda-guidance. Accessed 30 Mar 2013.

Edlin, B. R., Kresina, T. F., Raymond, D. B., Carden, M. R., Gourevitch, M. N., Rich, J. D., Cheever, L. W., & Cargill, V. A. (2005). Overcoming barriers to prevention, care and treatment of hepatitis C in illicit drug users. *Clinical Infectious Diseases, 40*(5), 276–285.

EMCDDA. (2012). *Prisons and drug sin Europe: The problem and responses*. http://www.emcdda.europa.eu/publications/selected-issues/prison. Accessed 30 Mar 2013.

Esteban, J. I., Sauleda, S., & Quer, J. (2008). The changing epidemiology of hepatitis C virus infection in Europe. *Journal of Hepatology, 48*(1), 148–162.

Farley, J., Vasdev, S., Fischer, B., Haydon, E., Rehm, J., & Farley, T. A. (2005). Feasibility and outcome of HCV treatment in a Canadian Federal Prison Population. *American Journal of Public Health, 95*, 1737–1739.

Fazel, S., Bains, P., & Doll, H. (2006). Substance abuse and dependence in prisoners: A systematic review. *Addiction, 101*(2), 181–191.

Fujimura, Y., Ishimoto, S., Shimoyama, T., Narita, N., Kuze, Y., Yoshioka, A., Fukui, H., Tanaka, T., Tsuda, F., Okamoto, H., Miyakawa, Y., & Mayumi, M. (1996). Genotypes and multiple infections with hepatitis C virus in patients with haemophilia a in Japan. *Journal of Viral Hepatitis, 3*(2), 79–84.

Gore, S. M., Bird, A. G., Cameron, S. O., Hutchinson, S. J., Burns, S. M., & Goldberg, D. J. (1999). Prevalence of hepatitis C in prisons: WASH-C surveillance linked to self-reported risk behaviours. *Quarterly Journal of Medicine, 92*(1), 25–32.

Haber, P., Parson, S., Harper, S., White, P. A., Rawlinson, W. D., & Lloyd, A. R. (1999). Transmission of hepatitis C within Australian prisons. *Medical Journal of Australia, 171*(1), 31–33.

Hammett, T. M. (2001). Making the case for health interventions in correctional facilities. *Journal of Urban Health, 78*, 236–240.

Harzke, A. J., Baillargeon, J., Paar, D. P., Pulvino, J., & Murray, O. J. (2009). Chronic liver disease mortality among male prison inmates in Texas, 1989–2003. *American Journal of Gastroenterology, 104*(6), 1412–1419.

Hauser, P., Khosla, J., Aurora, H., Laurin, J., Kling, M. A., Hill, J., Gulati, M., Thornton, A. J., Schultz, R. L., Valentine, A. D., Meyers, C. A., & Howell, C. D. (2002). A prospective study of the incidence and open-label treatment of interferon-induced major depressive disorder in patients with hepatitis C. *Molecular Psychiatry, 7*(9), 942–947.

Hedrich, D., Alves, P., Farrell, M., Stöver, H., Möller, L., & Mayet, S. (2012). The effectiveness of opioid maintenance treatment in prison settings: A systematic review. *Addiction, 107*(3), 501–517.

Hellard, M. E., Hocking, J. S., & Crofts, N. (2004). The prevalence and the risk behaviours associated with the transmission of hepatitis C virus in Australian correctional facilities. *Epidemiology and Infection, 132*(3), 409–415.

Hennessey, K. A., Kim, A. A., Griffin, V., Collins, N. T., Weinbaum, C. M., & Sabin, K. (2009). Prevalence of infection with hepatitis B and C viruses and co-infection with HIV in three jails: A case for viral hepatitis prevention in jails in the United States. *Journal of Urban Health, 86*(1), 93–105.

Hepatitis Australia. (2011). *Consensus statement: Addressing hepatitis C in Australian custodial settings.* http://www.hepatitisaustralia.com/__data/assets/pdf_file/0008/2123/Prisons-consensus-statement.pdf. Accessed 30 Mar 2013.

Herring, B. L., Page-Shafer, K., Tobler, L. H., & Delwart, E. L. (2004). Frequent hepatitis C virus superinfection in injection drug users. *Journal of Infectious Diseases, 190*(8), 1396–1403.

Horne, J. A., Clements, A. J., Drennan, P., Stein, K., & Cramp, M. E. (2004). Screening for hepatitis C virus in the dartmoor prison population: An observational study. *Journal of Public Health, 26*(4), 372–375.

Hunt, D. R., & Saab, S. (2009). Viral hepatitis in incarcerated adults: A medical and public health concern. *The American Journal of Gastroenterology, 104*(4), 1024–1031.

Kao, J. H., Chen, P. J., Wang, J. T., Yang, P. M., Lai, M. Y., Wang, T. H., & Chen, D. S. (1996). Superinfection by homotypic virus in hepatitis C virus carriers: Studies on patients with post-transfusion hepatitis. *Journal of Medical Virology, 50*, 303–308.

Khaw, F., Stobbart, L., & Murtagh, M. (2007). 'I just keep thinking I haven't got it because I'm not yellow': A qualitative study of the factors that influence the uptake of hepatitis C testing by prisoners. *BioMed Central Public Health, 7*(1), 98.

Lines, L. (2005). Taking action to reduce injecting drug-related harms in prisons: The evidence of effectiveness of prison needle exchange in six countries. *International Journal of Prisoner Health, 1*, 49–64.

Long, J., Allwright, S., Barry, J., Reynolds, S. R., Thornton, L., Bradley, F., & Parry, J. V. (2001). Prevalence of antibodies to hepatitis B, hepatitis C, and HIV and risk factors in entrants to Irish prisons: A national cross sectional survey. *British Medical Journal, 323*, 1209–1213.

Macalino, G. E., Vlahov, D., Sanford-Colby, S., Patel, S., Sabin, K., Salas, C., & Rich, J. D. (2004). Prevalence and incidence of HIV, hepatitis B virus, and hepatitis C virus infections among males in Rhode island prisons. *American Journal of Public Health, 94*(7), 1218–1223.

MACASHH. (2008). *Hepatitis C prevention, treatment and care: Guidelines for Australian custodial settings evidence base for the guidelines.* http://www.health.gov.au/internet/main/publishing.nsf/content/9F632131D38B580CCA257505007C1A70/$File/prison-guidelines-evidence.pdf. Accessed 30 Mar 2013.

Maher, L., Chant, K., Jalaludin, B., & Sargent, P. (2004). Risk behaviours and antibody hepatitis B and C prevalence among injecting drug users in southwestern Sydney, Australia. *Journal of Gastroenterology and Hepatology, 19*, 1114–1120.

Miller, E. R., Bi, P., & Ryan, P. (2009). Hepatitis C virus infection in South Australian prisoners: Seroprevalence, seroconversion, and risk factors. *International Journal of Infectious Diseases, 13*(2), 201–208.

Ogilvie, E. L., Veit, F., Crofts, N., & Thompson, S. C. (1999). Hepatitis infection among adolescents resident in Melbourne Juvenile Justice Centre: Risk factors and challenges. *Journal of Adolescent Health, 25*, 46–51.

Open Society Foundations. (2011). *Improving health in pretrial detention: Pilot interventions and the need for evaluation*. http://www.soros.org/initiatives/health/focus/ihrd/articles_publications/publications/pretrial-detention-health-20110531. Accessed 29 Mar 2013.

Pham, S. T., Bul, R. A., Bennett, J. M., Rawlinson, W. D., Dore, G. J., Lloyd, A. R., & White, P. A. (2010). Frequent multiple hepatitis C virus infections among injection drug users in a prison setting. *Hepatology, 52*, 1564–1572.

Poulin, C., Alary, M., Lambert, G., Godin, G., Landry, S., Gagnon, H., Demers, E., Morarescu, E., Rochefort, J., & Claessens, C. (2007). Prevalence of HIV and hepatitis C virus infections among inmates of Quebec provincial prisons. *Canadian Medical Association Journal, 177*(3), 252–256.

Solomon, L., Flynn, C., Muck, K., & Vertefeuille, J. (2004). Prevalence of HIV, syphilis, hepatitis B, and hepatitis C among entrants to Maryland correctional facilities. *Journal of Urban Health, 81*, 25–37.

Spaulding, A. C., Greene, C., Davidson, K., Schneidermann, M., & Rich, J. (1999). Hepatitis C in state correctional facilities. *Preventive Medicine, 29*, 92–100.

Spaulding, A. C., Weinbaum, C. M., Lau, D. T., Sterling, R., Steff, L. B., Margolis, H. B., & Hoofnagle, J. H. (2006). A framework for management of hepatitis C in prisons. *Annals of Internal Medicine, 144*, 762–769.

Sterling, R. K., Hofmann, C. M., Luketic, V. A., Sanyal, A. J., Contos, M. J., Miles, A. S., & Shiffman, M. L. (2004). Treatment of chronic hepatitis C virus in the Virginia department of corrections: Can compliance overcome racial differences to response. *American Journal of Gastroenterology, 99*, 866–872.

Stöver, H., & Nelles, J. (2003). Ten years of experience with needle and syringe exchange programmes in European Prisons. *International Journal of Drug Policy, 14*(5/6), 437–444.

Tan, J. A., Joseph, T. A., & Saab, S. (2008, November). Treating hepatitis C in the prison population is cost-saving. *Hepatology, 48*(5), 1387–1395. doi:10.1002/hep.22509. PMID: 18924228, Review.

UNAIDS. (1997). *Prisons and AIDS: UNAIDS point of view*. Geneva: UNAIDS.

UNODC, WHO, & UNAIDS. (2006). *HIV/AIDS prevention, care, treatment and support in prison settings. A framework for an effective national response*. New York/Vienna/Geneva: United Nations Office on Drugs and Crime, World Health Organization and Joint United Nations Programme on HIV/AIDS.

van Beek, I., Dwyer, R., Dore, G. J., Luo, K., & Kaldor, J. M. (1998). Infection with HIV and hepatitis C virus among injecting drug users in a prevention setting: Retrospective cohort study. *British Medical Journal, 317*(7156), 433–437.

van de Laar, T. J., Molenkamp, R., van den Berg, C., Schinkel, J., Beld, M. G., Prins, M., Coutinho, R. A., & Bruisten, S. M. (2009). Frequent HCV reinfection and superinfection in a cohort of injecting drug users in Amsterdam. *Journal of Hepatology, 51*, 667–674.

Vescio, M. F., Longo, B., Babudieri, S., Starnini, G., Carbonara, S., Rezza, G., & Monarca, R. (2008). Correlates of hepatitis C virus seropositivity in prison inmates: A meta-analysis. *Journal of Epidemiology and Community Health, 62*(4), 305–313.

Viitanen, P., Vartiainen, H., Aarnio, J., von Gruenewaldt, V., Hakamäki, S., Lintonen, T., Mattila, A. K., Wuolijoki, T., & Joukamaa, M. (2011). Hepatitis A, B, C and HIV infections among Finnish female prisoners – Young females a risk group. *Journal of Infection, 62*(1), 59–66.

Vlahov, D., Nelson, K. E., Quinn, T. C., et al. (1993). Prevalence and incidence of hepatitis C virus infection among male prison inmates in Maryland. *European Journal of Epidemiology, 9*, 566–569.

Weild, A. R., Gill, O. N., Bennett, D., Livingstone, S. J., Parry, J. V., & Curran, L. (2000). Prevalence of HIV, hepatitis B, and hepatitis C antibodies in prisoners in England and Wales: A national survey. *Communicable Disease and Public Health, 3*, 121–126.

Weinbaum, C., Lyerla, R., & Margolis, H. S. (2003). Prevention and control of infections with hepatitis viruses in correctional settings. *MMWR, Recommendations and Reports/Centers for Disease Control, 52,* 1–36.

WHO. (1993). *WHO guidelines on HIV infection and AIDS in prisons.* Geneva: WHO (WHO/GPA/DIR/93.3).

WHO, UNODC, & UNAIDS. (2009). *Technical guide for countries to set targets for universal access to HIV prevention, treatment and care for injecting drug users.* Geneva.

Widell, A., Mansson, S., Persson, N. H., Thysell, H., Hermodsson, S., & Blohme, I. (1995). Hepatitis C superinfection in hepatitis C virus (HCV)-infected patients transplanted with an HCV-infected kidney. *Transplantation, 60,* 642–647.

Zurhold, H., Haasen, C., & Stöver, H. (2005). *Female drug users in European prisons: A European study of prison policies, prison drug services and the women's perspectives.* Oldenburg: Bibliotheks- und Informationssystem der Carl von Ossietzky Universität.

Chapter 12
Confidentiality in Prison Health Care – A Practical Guide

Bernice S. Elger and David M. Shaw

Abstract Medical confidentiality is universally recognized as an essential component of healthcare. However, preserving and protecting the confidentiality of prisoner patients is challenging in several ways. In this chapter we explore the general importance of medical confidentiality, and some of the challenges that arise in the wider context, before explaining and discussing some of the particular dilemmas that arise in the context of providing healthcare for prisoners. Overall, although healthcare professionals have the same obligations regarding confidentiality in the context of prisons, the conflicts of interest posed by their competing obligations to prison authorities often make it very difficult to strike the right balance between respecting patient confidentiality and protecting prisoners and others. We conclude by suggesting potential solutions for some of these difficult situations.

The importance of medical confidentiality is obvious to anyone who has ever been a patient, and protecting private information about patients is one of the key responsibilities of healthcare professionals. However, maintaining the confidentiality of patients who are incarcerated in prisons poses several ethical challenges. In this chapter we explain the importance of confidentiality in general, and the dilemmas that doctors sometimes face with regard to it, before describing some of the specific difficulties encountered by prison doctors. Although healthcare professionals working in prisons have the same duty to respect confidentiality as those working in the wider community, the conflicts of interest caused by their dual loyalty to prisoners and to prison authorities can make it very difficult to strike the right balance between respecting confidentiality and protecting prisoners and third parties. We illustrate some of the dilemmas facing prison doctors with a series of case discussions before providing suggestions for resolving these difficult situations. Ideally, a combination of great ethical and legal sensitivity on the part of healthcare professionals and general respect for prisoners' rights on the part of other prison staff enables most issues to be resolved without the need to compromise patients' confidentiality.

B.S. Elger (✉) • D.M. Shaw
Institute for Biomedical Ethics, University of Basel, Bernoullistrasse 28, 4056 Basel, Switzerland
e-mail: b.elger@unibas.ch; david.shaw@unibas.ch

© Springer Science+Business Media Dordrecht 2017
B.S. Elger et al. (eds.), *Emerging Issues in Prison Health*,
DOI 10.1007/978-94-017-7558-8_12

12.1 Confidentiality: A Fundamental Principle in Health Care

Medical confidentiality should be guaranteed and respected with the same rigour [in prisons] as in the population as a whole (Council of Europe 1998b: C.13).

When examining how to respect medical confidentiality in prison, the principle of equivalence applies: prisoners are entitled to the same standard of health care as is available to non-incarcerated citizens. Therefore, the main aspects of medical confidentiality must be summarized before turning to more specific cases in the prison context.

Confidentiality is a cornerstone of health care ethics (Elger 2009, 2010). Both the famous Hippocratic Oath and its more modern form, the World Medical Association's Declaration of Geneva, stipulate its importance:

I will respect the secrets that are confided in me, even after the patient has died (World Medical Association 1948).

It is also important to mention that Article 8 of the European Convention on Human Rights establishes the state's obligation to protect citizens against unlawful communication of sensitive information:

1. Everyone has the right to respect for his private and family life, his home and his correspondence. 2. There shall be no interference by a public authority with the exercise of this right except such as is in accordance with the law and is necessary in a democratic society in the interests of national security, public safety or the economic well-being of the country, for the prevention of disorder or crime, for the protection of health or morals, or for the protection of the rights and freedoms of others (Council of Europe 1950).

Two important ethical foundations for confidentiality in health care should be kept in mind: first, the principle of respect for patients' autonomy implies that they should be able to control information about their health, just as they have the right to control what happens to their bodies. They should have the right to decide whether and to whom any such information is communicated. Second, the principle of confidentiality can also be justified in terms of consequences. Respect for medical secrecy is generally beneficial not only for individual patients but also for society in general (Baird 2008; Bourke and Wessely 2008).

There is a clear public good in having a confidential medical service. The fact that people are encouraged to seek advice and treatment, including for communicable diseases, benefits society as a whole as well as the individual. Confidential medical care is recognised in law as being in the public interest (General Medical Council 2009b: 16).

In order to illustrate public health benefits, examples of various types of infectious diseases are usually cited. Patients who suffer from a sexually transmitted disease are more likely to see a doctor and to seek treatment if they know that confidentiality will be respected. Confidentiality can also be of significant importance in order to protect possible victims against violence or sexual abuse by dangerous psychiatric patients. In such cases, as in those involving infectious diseases, patients need to be able to trust that stigmatizing information about their disease will be kept confidential. Only if confidentiality is granted will they be likely to consult a psychiatrist and receive appropriate treatment that helps to prevent violence due to untreated psychiatric disease (Beck 1998).

It is well established that confidentiality plays a crucial role in psychiatry (Brahams 1988), not only because of its ethical, but also because of its practical relevance. Psychiatric patients are particularly vulnerable to stigma and discrimination if information about their diseases is transmitted to third parties (Appelbaum 2002). In order to build and maintain patient trust, the exceptions to confidentiality must remain scarce and should be clearly defined in ethical guidelines and the law. For example, if a patient poses a clear risk to another person, it might be necessary to breach confidentiality in order to protect this third party (Tarasoff 1974). Most importantly, patients should be informed about confidentiality rules: in most cases their explicit consent is needed to authorize transmission of information. They should also be informed about the exceptions to confidentiality, i.e. when a physician has to balance conflicting interests and is obligated to breach confidentiality even in the absence of consent. This information has to be provided transparently from the very beginning of any health care encounter.

12.2 General Aspects of Confidentiality in Prison

In prisons[1] worldwide, health care personnel are under particular pressure when it comes to medical confidentiality. This pressure forms part of the conflicts caused by the dual loyalties of health care personnel which exist not only in the context of detention, but also in occupational medicine and the military (Benatar and Upshur 2008; Clark 2006; Heikkinen et al. 2007). Dual loyalty means that health care personnel have not only loyalties towards their patients, but also a duty to maintain security in detention facilities, or at least not to interfere with or threaten security. This implies that they have to respect orders from the prison administration concerning security measures in the prison itself. In addition, health personnel have a responsibility towards individuals who live outside the detention facilities, if a health care provider receives information from a patient that a former or future victim might be in danger.

Some general conflicts are not fundamentally different from those faced by every health care professional. All physicians have to balance their obligation to protect medical confidentiality with conflicting values such as the health of relatives if a patient is suffering from a serious infectious disease or the safety of third person if a psychiatric patient is dangerous to others. In the prison context, however, such conflicts are particularly frequent.

---

[1] The word prison is used in a global sense in order to indicate any kind of detention facility such as jails, prisons, police custody (etc.). Similarly, 'prisoner' refers to any person detained in such facilities.

Health care personnel in prison often face the criticism that straightforward application of the principle of equivalence to confidentiality is overly idealistic because of a number of persistent problems. One example is the fact that patients are usually brought to medical consultations by prison guards. Due to increased promiscuity in prisons, security personnel and often other detainees are able to observe whether a detainee is ill and whether he or she is seeing a psychiatrist or another specialist. Prisoners have also complained about the lack of confidentiality during the distribution of medication. Bystanders are able to observe whether detainees take medication regularly and can even read the name on the medication package; both these opportunities can enable others to draw conclusions about the type of disease affecting the patient (Condon et al. 2007).

The fact that confidentiality is not granted in many prison health care settings has negative consequences for medical treatment as a whole. Detainees in Europe have voiced serious concerns that insufficient medical secrecy and the lack for respect for patient autonomy in prisons are the principal barriers that interfere with adequate medical treatment of prisoners. As a result, health problems are insufficiently diagnosed and treated in many prisons (Condon et al. 2007).

Whether tailored to general medicine (General Medical Council 2009b), psychiatry (Council of Europe 2004), or prison medicine (SAMW 2012), guidelines often present only general guidance. We will therefore first summarize existing guidance with a focus on specific guidelines on confidentiality in prison health care, and second present practical guidance through the presentation and analysis of cases.[2]

12.3 International Recommendations and Guidelines Concerning Confidentiality in Prison

The principle of equivalence implies that prisoners have the right to receive health care of the same quality as that provided to patients living outside prisons in the same country. In line with the principle of equivalence, confidentiality should be applied in prison with the same rigor as outside prisons, as stated in international and national legal and ethical regulation (Council of Europe 1998a, b; SAMW 2012).

The recommendations of the Council of Europe and the Committee for the Prevention of Torture (CPT) reports represent 'soft law', which means that they are not binding. However, they are of high importance and parts of them have acquired binding status because the European Count of Human Rights has quoted soft law in court decisions. The recommendations of the Council of Europe and the guidelines ('standards') published by the CPT address a number of general and specific situations related to confidentiality that health care personnel must know and are therefore reported here in detail.

---

[2]For more information, see the Chap. 13, pp. 201–215.

The recommendations of the Council of Europe explicitly mention a number of situations to underline how confidentiality in prison should be handled. Particular caution is necessary concerning the transfer of medical records:

> All transfers to other prisons should be accompanied by full medical records. The records should be transferred under conditions ensuring their confidentiality. Prisoners should be informed that their medical record will be transferred. They should be entitled to object to the transfer, in accordance with national legislation. All released prisoners should be given relevant written information concerning their health for the benefit of their family doctor (Council of Europe 1998b: Paragraph 18).

The Explanatory Memorandum to the Recommendations of the Council of Europe adds that consent to medical treatment and confidentiality are an 'essential aspect of medical ethics' because both are 'almost unanimously accepted in professional and general ethics and in law' (Council of Europe 1998a: IC13.). The Memorandum also mentions the importance of storing medical records in protected places.

> Freedom of consent to medical treatment and confidentiality are not only fundamental rights of the individual, but also the 'cement' of the necessary relationship of trust between doctor and patient, especially in prisons, where prisoners are not usually able to choose their doctor freely. Not only should the doctor and nursing staff carry out consultations on a confidential basis, but they should also see that sick prisoners' medical records are kept in a place where protection of the confidentiality of medical documents can be guaranteed. For example, medical records may be kept in a place to which only the medical and nursing staff have access, or they may be placed in a locked cupboard used only by the health care staff (Council of Europe 1998a: IC13).

The Memorandum underlines that professional training of prison health care staff is necessary to educate personnel how to act in the case of a 'conflict between respecting confidentiality and protecting the interests of the prison community' (Council of Europe 1998a: IID34). It mentions confidentiality further with respect to HIV infection and AIDS (Council of Europe 1998a: IIIA37).

> In view of the often irrational fears and reactions aroused by this infectious disease, it is essential that the voluntary nature of HIV screening and the confidentiality of the result of the examination be respected. Any exception to the voluntary nature of screening should be made only in accordance with the law (Council of Europe 1998a: IIIA37).

The correct attitude of health care personnel towards transmissible diseases is also summarized in a separate recommendation on prison and criminal aspects of transmissible diseases, including AIDS:

> Voluntary testing for HIV/AIDS infection, together with counselling before and after the test, should be made available. Health staff should, under the responsibility of a doctor, explain to prison inmates the consequences of test results prior to undergoing such tests, and inform them of the results, in full confidentiality, unless he/she declines to receive such information (Council of Europe 1993: IA3.)

Recommendations on the control of transmissible diseases address how physicians should act in situations of conflict. Prisoners' medical data is confidential, and a doctor can only share information with other health care professionals or the prison authorities when it is 'strictly necessary for the treatment and care of the prisoner or in order to examine the health of the prisoners and staff, with due regard to medical ethics and legal provisions' (Council of Europe 1993: IA8). If communication of confidential details is planned because it is beneficial for the care of the prisoner 'this should take place with the consent of the person concerned' (ibid.). The recommendations also state that 'HIV/AIDS serological status is not generally considered necessary information' (ibid). The document does not provide specific guidance on how to deal with situations of conflict where a detainee does not provide consent to the communication of information, but mentions equivalence as guiding principle.

> Disclosure of information should follow the same principles as those applied in the general community (Council of Europe 1993: IA8).

A special section deals with confidentiality in the context of human subject research in prison. This is a particularly sensitive issue, as prisoners might feel pressured to participate in such research by the prison authorities.

> Ethical principles concerning research on human subjects must be strictly applied, particularly in relation to informed consent and confidentiality [. . .]. Publication and communication of the results of research studies must ensure absolute confidentiality concerning the identity of prisoners who have participated in such studies (Council of Europe 1993: IA16).

Finally, the recommendations insist that medical records can only be transferred from one medical prison service to another.

> HIV/AIDS infection should not prevent a prisoner from being transferred on the basis of a bilateral agreement or of the Council of Europe Convention on the Transfer of Sentenced Persons. The medical report on a sentenced person transferred to his/her country of origin should be sent directly by the prison medical services in the sentencing state to the prison medical service in the enforcing state, since the report is protected by medical confidentiality (Council of Europe 1993: IA25).

In the State of the Art report 'Standards of the CPT' (European Committee for the Prevention of Torture), confidentiality is also mentioned as a cornerstone of testing for HIV and other infectious diseases:

> It must also be stressed that appropriate information and counselling should be provided before and - in the case of a positive result - after any screening test. Further, it is axiomatic that patient-related information should be protected by medical confidentiality. As a matter of principle, any interventions in this area should be based on the informed consent of the persons concerned (CPT 2006: 26).

The CPT, similar to the Council of Europe (see above), underlines that respect for confidentiality is a fundamental right of the individual and that it is 'essential to the atmosphere of trust which is a necessary part of the doctor/patient relationship, especially in prisons, where a prisoner cannot freely choose his own doctor' (CPT 2006: IIIc.45, p. 33). The CPT adds further that it is the doctor's responsibility, not the task of other prison personnel such as guards, to keep and store patients' medical records (CPT 2006: IIIc.50, p. 34).

An important detail is provided in the CPT report concerning confidentiality during medical examinations.

All medical examinations of prisoners (whether on arrival or at a later stage) should be conducted out of the hearing and – unless the doctor concerned requests otherwise – out of the sight of prison officers. Further, prisoners should be examined on an individual basis, not in groups (CPT 2006: IIIc.51, p. 34).

The CPT recommends that prison staff receive on-going training about 'preventive measures to be taken and the attitudes to be adopted regarding HIV-positivity' and instructions on non-discrimination and respecting confidentiality (CPT 2006: IIIc.55, p. 34).

Finally, the CPT adds that criteria provided in the sections on prison health services on confidentiality 'also apply to involuntary placement in psychiatric establishments' (CPT 2006: VA26, p. 51).

12.4 Respecting Confidentiality in Difficult Situations: A Case-Based Approach to Prison Medicine

What makes it so difficult to ensure confidentiality in prisons? Confidentiality is obviously affected by the specific conditions of imprisonment, and particularly by dual loyalty conflicts of health care personnel, lack of privacy due to promiscuity[3] and the fact that security personnel play a gatekeeper role for access to health care or even work as health care assistants in many prisons.

In most cases, conflict arises in the prison context because of two assumptions. The first is that communication of information protected by medical confidentiality is judged to be necessary to protect security. The second, which occurs frequently, is a misunderstanding of roles: health care should be provided by health care personnel and not by prison wardens or guards. Although international guidance requires that medical care be truly independent of the prison administration and legal authorities (Council of Europe 1998b), in many prisons, the provision of health care and security are not clearly separated. The reason for this is generally that it is perceived to be less expensive to have prison guards who are already on the spot distribute medication or supervise psychiatrically ill patients. In order to ensure that confidentiality is respected appropriately, it is important to provide relevant information to all types of prison personnel, including health care providers and administrative and security personnel. This is crucial to avoid misunderstandings and unnecessary conflicts and to ensure that staff are fully aware of and respect the ethical obligations of different professional groups working in prison. If all prison staff are aware of prisoner's rights, they are less likely to put pressure on prison physicians to breach confidentiality.

---

[3] As detainees share cells – which regularly do have toilets in the room without further shielding - and eat together and many of their activities are supervised by prison guards it is almost impossible to hide medication intake or disease symptoms.

To decide which attitude is professionally and ethically correct with respect to confidentiality, health care personnel first need to balance the involved interests. In order to be able to find the right balance between the duty to respect confidentiality and other possibly conflicting interests, in general or in a particular case, the first step is to evaluate the resulting consequences of each option. 'What will lead to a better outcome?' is an empirical question. Is it really the case that potential victims are better protected if patients know that health personnel do not respect confidentiality? Data seem to suggest the opposite, indicating that the outcome is better if health care personnel opt for strict confidentiality. Respecting confidentiality prevents in most cases harm to all involved stakeholders which includes the protection of potential victims (Reilly 2008; Rodriguez et al. 1998, 2001).

Independently of the consequences of actions there is also a deontological question to be asked: 'What is the right action?' Most people have beliefs about what would be 'just'. For example, imagine that a detainee tells his physician that he has committed a crime many years ago, which is not known to the justice system. Many would think that it is 'just' to punish the detainee for this crime, even if knowledge about the yet unknown crime does not change the overall evaluation of the detainee's dangerousness. This evaluation would remain unchanged if, for example, the crime in the past was less severe than later crimes for which the detainee is at present incarcerated. However, according to most ethical guidelines (e.g. SAMW 2012) in most jurisdictions, confidentiality would be considered more important than a duty to denounce crimes in the absence of any immediate danger to others (Kottow 1986). This means that health care personnel are not obligated to denounce past crimes as long as that information is not needed to prevent serious danger to third persons in the future. Jurisdictions vary with regard to the protection of particularly vulnerable victims. While federal law in Switzerland contains general dispositions that allow physicians to denounce crimes against minors but do not stipulate any obligations in general,[4] this is not the case in some cantons in Switzerland and some states in the US. The latter have adopted laws that render the declaration of crimes mandatory if the victims are minors. In some states, the duty to denounce also extends to abused sexually abused women and abused elders of both male or female gender (Rodriguez et al. 2006), or even more generally to all patients who are victims of gunshot wounds (Gupta 2007; Houry et al. 2002; Mathews and Kenny 2008). In the United Kingdom, the police must be notified of any gunshot or stab wounds (GMC 2009a), and the General Medical Council states that there are several other circumstances in which physicians must disclose confidential information:

> Confidential medical care is recognised in law as being in the public interest. However, there can also be a public interest in disclosing information: to protect individuals or society from risks of serious harm, such as serious communicable diseases or serious crime; or to enable medical research, education or other secondary uses of information that will benefit society over time (GMC 2009b).

---

[4]See, Art. 364 Swiss criminal Code.

While there is little disagreement over which diseases are serious and communicable, what constitutes a 'serious crime' is open to debate. For example, many health professionals in the UK regard social security fraud as serious (which it technically is), yet the GMC presumably intends the phrase to refer to violent crime, where denunciation is necessary to prevent future bodily harm. In regions where legal obligations exist to denounce certain types of crimes, physicians have repeatedly made the criticism that legal duties not only conflict with their professional and ethical obligations towards confidentiality, but also that they have adverse consequences because victims forgo medical care for fear of breaches of confidentiality (Malv 2006; Rodriguez et al. 1999).

The following cases are anonymised versions of real cases that have occurred in a prison health care service during the past 30 years. They have been chosen to explain the criteria that should be used for decision-making and to illustrate how to balance values in order to find practical solutions in prison health care. All the cases concern a conflict between the duty to protect confidentiality and the duty to prevent bodily harm, either to the patient or to third parties.

When discussing the cases we will also refer to the responses of prison health professionals with whom the cases were discussed during a recent interview study among prison health care professionals (Elger et al. 2014, 2015a, b).[5] Our aim is here not to provide a comprehensive report of the study results, which will be published elsewhere. The objective is instead to enrich the theoretical analysis by referring to the views of experienced prison physicians. The results of the study are generalisable to prisons in other countries, as we interviewed health care professionals in different regions, with different prison regulations. Indeed, cantons in Switzerland's federal structure have a high degree of autonomy and regulations vary significantly between cantons as well as between prisons. A recent study by legal scholars has shown that some cantonal laws in Switzerland contradict the professional obligation of medical confidentiality, which is regulated in the federal criminal law code (Art. 321). In one Canton, the law stipulates that a prison director is to be informed about the health status of detainees (Sprumont et al. 2009:70), which is not compatible with medical secrecy. Two other cantons have an agreement concerning a jointly used prison which foresees communication with the prison director about the health of every detainee, and the medical exam at entry is obligatory, which means it could be enforced and carried out without the detainee's consent. That agreement mentions only that prisoners have the right to refuse laboratory screening tests (Sprumont et al. 2009: 71–73). Several interviewees

---

[5]The aim of the study was to explore health professionals' experiences with confidentiality. After approval by the competent research ethics committee, 24 mental health professionals working in Swiss prisons were interviewed in 2008 and 2009. They were selected from different regions and backgrounds, and varied in nationality, gender, professional experience, therapeutic orientation and cultural context. Interviews were transcribed and anonymised. At the beginning of the interview, participants were asked to describe difficult cases they had experienced and if cases similar to those discussed below were not spontaneously mentioned, the interviewer described them and asked how the heath professional would react and why.

reported that they had to deal with such contradictions; similar regulations which contradict the principle of medical confidentiality exist in other countries (Elger 2008).

12.5   Case 1: Violence Against a Detainee

During a medical consultation, the physician finds several fresh bruises and small round wounds from burning. The detainee tells the physician that his roommates burn him regularly with their cigarettes and beat him. He asks the physician to keep the information confidential because the co-detainees have threatened to will kill him if he tells anyone about the violence.

A disclosure that is made to protect a legally competent patient without his consent usually falls within the range of unjustified paternalism. Several interviewed prison health care professionals indicated that dealing with such situations is difficult, and some adopted a paternalistic approach. The interviews showed that they often did not have enough information to determine whether disclosure or non-disclosure would cause more harm. Health professionals have a tendency to underestimate the risks posed to detainees by whistle blowing. Their duty is to inform patients adequately and to encourage them to make decisions that are in their own interests. During the interviews, some health professionals reported that they would try to solve the problem in a confidential way that protects the victim. They would contact a prison warden in their confidence and ask him to move the victim to a different cell without giving any reasons. The importance in such cases is that the prison physician can trust the warden to provide an organizational reason for the cell change and to keep the health care professional's request to change cells fully confidential. There could also be non-paternalistic arguments in favour of disclosure, i.e. arguments that do not refer to the benefit of a competent patient, but to the protection of third parties. This is the case if the health care professional has reasons to believe that the aggressors may also harm other persons. If the aggressors are judged dangerous because of psychiatric problems that require treatment, the health professional should try to arrange a medical consultation with them while keeping information obtained from the victim confidential. The situation is different, and disclosure without consent may be justified, if the patient lacks the capacity to consent or if it is not possible to seek consent for other reasons.

In one region, the health care professionals had adopted a preventive approach to situations where the detainee has been a victim of inappropriate treatment from the police or prison guards. If the detainee does not consent to the transmission of the medical report about the injuries to the chief of police or the prison director, an anonymous reporting procedure is chosen. This means that the chief of the police or director receives monthly summaries of reported violence that indicate as many details as possible without making detainees identifiable. This approach has led to a reduction in the number of identified violent acts by the police (Bertrand et al. 1995; Elger 2008, 2011).

In the UK, there is some tension between medical guidelines and the law with regard to confidentiality and protecting patients. The GMC states that

> It may be appropriate to encourage patients to consent to disclosures you consider necessary for their protection, and to warn them of the risks of refusing to consent; but you should usually abide by a competent adult patient's refusal to consent to disclosure, even if their decision leaves them, but nobody else, at risk of serious harm (GMC 2009b: 21).

In Scotland, however, health boards are required by legislation (Adult Support and Protection Act 2007) to report to local authorities 'if they know or believe that an adult is at risk of harm (but not necessarily incapacitated) and that action needs to be taken to protect them' (GMC 2009b: 40). The Act also stipulates that certain public bodies and office-holders co-operate with local authorities when inquiries about adults at risk are carried out and provides 'powers to examine health records for related purposes' (GMC 2009b: 40). These legal requirements actually place an obligation on physicians both in prisons and the wider community to breach confidentiality, potentially placing them in a difficult position.

12.6 Case 2: A Suicidal Detainee

A detainee confesses that he has been considering suicide for the past 2 weeks. He faces lifelong detention and already attempted suicide 5 days ago. He was rescued by chance because a co-detainee came back earlier than planned from a visit with his lawyer and was able to free the detainee who had hanged himself using his belt. The detainee has been able to obtain heroin and a syringe and plans to take an overdose once he gets back to his cell.

The case describes a detainee who presents with a high risk of suicide and requires transfer to a psychiatric hospital. During the interviews, many health professionals reported spontaneously that confidentiality is particularly problematic when dealing with suicidal detainees. This is the case because prison administrations tend to require them to report suicidal detainees and health professionals experience it as difficult to find the right balance between respect for confidentiality and the wish to protect the detainee from harm. Health professionals explained that for all prison personnel, including guards, a completed suicide is very traumatising and is generally seen as "their fault" as it is their duty to detect and treat suicidal inmates. They also feel under pressure to avoid too many transfers of detainees to psychiatric hospitals because they are costly in terms of financial and human resources, including security personnel who have to be mobilized to accompany the transfer. Therefore, although this is not in line with the principle of equivalence, they try to find intermediate solutions where patients at risk are transferred into cells where they have a roommate and are closely observed by prison guards, who are the personnel most directly in contact with the inmates. A general perception seemed to be that – death being irreversible – the common interest in preventing it brings different professionals closer, i.e. that the honourable common goal of preventing suicide justified less strict informational boundaries between health care professionals and other prison personnel.

However, in line with the principle of equivalence, confidentiality should be handled in the same way as outside prison. In the present case, where the risk of suicide is high and hospital transfer is indicated, there is no justification to transmit any information to non-medical personnel, except that they should call an ambulance to enable transfer to a hospital. The duty of prison wardens is to decide whether security considerations require that a police car follows the ambulance.

In many countries, prison administrations interfere with the equivalent treatment of suicidal detainees. In the US, there are few appropriate non-prison mental health facilities (American Psychiatric Association 2007). Therefore, in a former draft guideline, the American Psychological Association (APA) announced that in 'correctional settings, professionals must carefully balance the potential threat of self-harm with the potential harm caused by reporting. In prisons, threats of self-harm are generally not met simply with understanding and reassurance. Inmates who report thoughts or attempts at self-harm may be strip-searched and placed in segregation. Hence, your responsibility as a professional is increased to ensure that all potential harms are considered in reporting' (Elger 2008: 242). In recent guidelines on patient records that are kept in institutions including prisons, the APA acknowledges that confidentiality policies in prisons may be in conflict with the psychologists' code of ethics and recommends that those conflicts be addressed.

> In the event that there are conflicts between an organization's policies and procedures and the Ethics Code, psychologists clarify the nature of the conflict, make their ethical commitments known, and to the extent feasible, resolve the conflict consistent with those commitments (American Psychological Association 2007: 1000).

In previous years, the APA made efforts to remind prison health professionals about how to insist on ethically acceptable ways of maintaining confidentiality. Psychologists should be aware that confidentiality issues may not be clear to some prison administrators, who therefore may not abide by these limits and 'try to pressure you to violate confidentiality of your patient. Be polite but firm in stating your reporting obligations to administrators' (Elger 2008, p. 243). It is also important to make sure that prisoners feel able to communicate any thoughts of self-harm or suicide without fear of being overheard. The APA makes the following recommendations:

> When conducting an evaluation, be sure to get as private a space (within the constraints of security) as possible. This communicates respect to your patient, in addition to just being good ethical practice. Instead of having an officer in the room during the assessment, check to see if the officer could sit outside the room and look in through the window. This will be dictated entirely by security practices and if this is not possible, you will need to decide whether to conduct the assessment (American Psychological Association 2000, quoted in Elger 2008: 243).

The best way to solve conflicting obligations is for the health professional to explain to a detainee that he is worried about the detainee's risk of committing suicide and that it is in his/her best interest to inform the prison guards. In many cases, especially if prison inmates are treated with respect (e.g. segregation and strip searches are avoided) and believe that prison personnel truly act in their interests, information can be transmitted with the detainee's consent.

Individual health care professionals may not always succeed in convincing prison administrations to respect medical confidentiality. Professional organisations and state health departments should offer to be contacted in such cases to support the implementation of adequate confidentiality policy in the prison setting. This includes provisions that grant access for suicidal detainees to appropriate inpatient facilities that offer equivalent psychiatric care.

12.7 Case 3: Threats to Third Parties

During his visit to the prison physician, a detainee reports violent fantasies. He is angry with a prison guard and has imagined different methods of revenge, including stabbing the guard with a knife that the detainee plans to steal from the prison kitchen where he works.

The interviewed prison health professionals reported different thresholds for determining when risks of harm to third parties should be disclosed and how decisions about disclosure should be made. Several of them think that such decisions should always be made in a team, and should therefore be discussed with health care colleagues working in the same prison, and if possible with those who know the patient (except in urgent cases that do not permit consultation of colleagues). In the quantitative study, where a similar case vignette was tested among medical and legal professionals, differences were found. Medical professionals valued confidentiality more than legal professionals did. The interviews showed that one possible explanation for this is that prison psychiatrists are aware that fantasies do not automatically imply a risk that the detainee will put them into action. Therefore, they favour thorough psychiatric evaluation and would only report detainees perceived as dangerous where no other means exists to prevent the danger. In contrast, legal professionals might not be sufficiently familiar with evaluations of dangerousness and believe that fantasies in themselves prove dangerousness. Interviewed professionals were aware that thresholds of disclosure vary between colleagues and some recommended that each prison medical service should discuss those thresholds and try to adopt a consistent approach. This is important because the aim must be to inform detainees not only that confidentiality will be applied strictly with the same rigor as outside prisons, but also to inform them about the limits to confidentiality. In order to establish a trusting physician-patient-relationship, detainees should be informed from the very beginning. They must know for example that in the case of mandatory psychiatric treatment health care professionals are under an obligation to provide reports to legal authorities, and should also know how much detail a physician will need to include in such reports.

Respecting medical confidentiality does not mean an absence of communication between health professionals and other prison staff. Interviewees reported that they are regularly pressured by prison guards to reveal psychiatric diagnoses or other medical details of detainees who guards perceive as 'strange' or 'crazy'. The participants had a feeling of loyalty towards prison guards; they believed they had a duty to protect and educate them, and that this education was also in the interest of the detainee. While some struggled with balancing their duties, others presented valuable approaches to harmonising their different duties. They would routinely educate prison guards about the general symptoms of psychiatric disease and strategies of de-escalation for use with aggressive patients. If guards requested information about individual detainees they would not release any diagnostic or treatment information, but instead describe how guards should deal with patients in a respectful way that minimizes risks to themselves and to the patients. It is important that prison health professionals build a trusting relationship with prison guards so that the latter know the requirements and limitations of medical confidentiality. This implies that prison health professionals will carry out thorough evaluations of dangerousness, but that psychiatric skills do not permit the prediction of dangerousness with 100 % precision. Therefore, guards and health care professionals need to apply routine preventive strategies.

12.8 Conclusions and Recommendations

In all jurisdictions, legal provisions provide scope for balancing benefits and harms in each individual case, and an obligation to do so. Many exceptions to medical confidentiality are optional and acquire ethical and legal weight only when there is an existing serious and imminent danger to third parties. Health care professionals must evaluate for each case whether a breach of confidentiality is justified or even required. Three cumulative elements justify divulging information to others: (1) the probability of serious danger is high, meaning that the detainee has the means to be violent and is likely to carry out a threat; (2) the danger concerns identifiable victims (as opposed to vague threats), and (3) there are no means to prevent the danger from occurring other than through breaching confidentiality. In all cases, a health care professional should explain to the patient his/her ethical and legal obligations to protect others or to protect the detainee from abuse or self-harming behaviour. If the doctor has been able to build a trust-based relationship with the patients and takes the time to explain issues in a caring way, it will be possible in a large majority of cases to make the detainee aware of his/her own interests and to either convince him/her to declare relevant facts himself, e.g. render a weapon to the prison administration, or to obtain consent for the communication of information. In many cases, explanation of the fact that the doctor will be obligated to disclose information even if consent is not given will be sufficient to obtain consent from the prisoner because the latter will understand that it is in his interest to prevent further harm (including punishment for another crime) to him and to others. Even in cases where consent cannot be obtained, an approach based on information and explanations helps to reduce the negative consequences of un-consented to disclosures.

Medical personnel in prisons need appropriate training not only about legal requirements and ethical balancing, but also about practically useful strategies for action in typical situations. Chief physicians in prisons should be on call to provide advice for more junior colleagues in difficult cases. We offer the following recommendations:

- At the beginning of the therapeutic relationship, health care personnel in prisons should devote sufficient time to explaining to their patients the equivalence principle, and confidentiality provisions and their foreseeable limits.
- Health care professionals should exchange their opinions about thresholds for disclosure and define acceptable practice based on case examples both within the team and within professional organisations, e.g. through detailed guidelines.
- In cases where breaches of confidentiality are justified or required, professionals should explain their ethical and legal duties and ask for patient consent. In most cases this enables identification of a solution and avoids a serious conflict with the patient, which could interfere with future medical treatment and trust. However, it is of utmost importance to carry out a diligent evaluation as to whether a patient provides consent freely without being influenced by direct or indirect coercion.
- If the patient is incompetent and at risk of self-harm, the physician has an obligation to protect the best interests of the patient. This is best accomplished if confidentiality is respected and the patient agrees to any measures.
- If a patient presents a danger to third parties that cannot be avoided except through a breach of confidentiality, the case should be discussed with colleagues that are part of the health care team if time permits. The case should be anonymised if health colleagues are not part of the treating team. Even within a team, potentially stigmatizing information should be shared only if necessary.
- Decisions to breach confidentiality and the reasoning that led to them should be reported in the medical record. Training about legal requirements and ethical reasoning provides important skills that enable appropriate record keeping.
- An important question remains regarding how extensively health personnel should report symptoms and details about the patient's life that become known during a consultation, whether in medical records or reports that will be sent to legal authorities. In the case of written expert reports, a physician should consider what level of detail is necessary to facilitate the justice system's decisions. In our study, health care professionals' opinions varied and different solutions were proposed. One solution was for medical records to be written in a detailed way. In order to protect patients from abuse of this information, the treating physicians had obtained an agreement with the legal authorities that forensic experts would not obtain access to the records. Instead, the treating physicians would send a summary of the therapeutic encounter and treatments to the expert. The second solution consisted in keeping concise medical records and only writing down the details that were absolutely necessary to understand treatment decisions. In regions where physicians reported adherence to this solution, forensic experts are given full access to medical records.

- In all cases, patients should have the right to refuse access to their medical records. However, they should be informed that such refusals are likely to influence forensic evaluations. Forensic evaluations should not be confused with situations of mandatory treatment. In the former situation, the expert informs the individual who is to be evaluated that all information revealed during the consultation will be transmitted to the justice system. In the latter case, it is important to maintain a therapeutic relationship. Therefore, while the detainee should be informed that regular reports will be written for the detaining authorities and that these reports will include details revealed during consultations, patients should retain the right to refuse disclosure of reports after being informed that refusals are likely to impact on the evaluation.
- Finally, the most important requirement - in both prison health care and health care outside prisons - is to inform patients transparently, even in purely therapeutic encounters, about the possibility that experts may request access to their medical records at a later date: 'You must inform patients about disclosures for purposes they would not reasonably expect, or check that they have already received information about such disclosures' (GMC 2009a, b: Art. 7). Doing so may compromise trust to some extent, but is essential if patients' autonomy is to be respected.

References

Adult Support and Protection (Scotland) Act. (2007). http://www.legislation.gov.uk/asp/2007/10/contents. Accessed 28 Mar 2016.

American Psychiatric Association. (2007). *Use of jails to hold persons with criminal charges who are awaiting civil psychiatric hospital beds.* http://www.psychiatry.org/advocacy--newsroom/position-statements. Accessed 2 Apr 2013.

American Psychological Association. (2000). *Draft forensic mental health standards and guidelines.* Presented to the New York State Conference of Local Mental Hygiene Directors. http://clmhd.org/itemfiles/Standards_Final_Printable.PDF. Accessed 20 Oct 2007.

American Psychological Association. (2007). *Record keeping guidelines.* http://www.apa.org/practice/guidelines/record-keeping.pdf. Accessed 30 Mar 2013.

Appelbaum, P. S. (2002). Privacy in psychiatric treatment: Threats and responses. *American Journal of Psychiatry, 159*(11), 1809–1818.

Baird, G. (2008). Confidentiality: What everyone should know, or, rather, shouldn't. *British Journal of General Practice, 58*(547), 131–133.

Beck, J. C. (1998). Legal and ethical duties of the clinician treating a patient who is liable to be impulsively violent. *Behavioral Sciences & the Law, 16*(3), 375–389.

Benatar, S. R., & Upshur, R. E. (2008). Dual loyalty of physicians in the military and in civilian life. *American Journal of Public Health, 98*(12), 2161–2167.

Bertrand, D., La Harpe, R., Martin, J. L., & Plaut, O. (1995). Constatation des violences chez les personnes arrêtées ou détenues: Rôle préventive du Médecin. *Bulletin de criminology, 2*, 9–19.

Bourke, J., & Wessely, S. (2008). Confidentiality. *British Medical Journal, 336*(7649), 888–891.

Brahams, D. (1988). A psychiatrist's duty of confidentiality. *Lancet, 2*(8626–8627), 1503–1504.

Clark, P. A. (2006). Medical ethics at Guantanamo Bay and Abu Ghraib: The problem of dual loyalty. *Journal of Law, Medicine & Ethics, 34*(3), 570–580.

Condon, L., Hek, G., Harris, F., Powell, J., Kemple, T., & Price, S. (2007). Users' views of prison health services: A qualitative study. *Journal of Advanced Nursing, 58*(3), 216–226.

Council of Europe. (1950). The European convention on human rights. http://www.hri.org/docs/ECHR50.html. Accessed 20 June 2010.

Council of Europe. (1993). *Recommendation No. R(93) 6 of the Committee of Ministers to member states concerning prison and criminological aspects of the control of transmissible diseases including AIDS and related health problems in prison.* http://www.prison.eu.org/article.php3?id_article=. Accessed 30 Jan 2008.

Council of Europe. (1998a). *Committee of Ministers Rec(1998)7 on the ethical and organisational aspects of health care in prison, explanatory memorandum.* http://www.unav.es/cdb/ccoerec98-7exp.html. Accessed 30 Aug 2008.

Council of Europe. (1998b). *Committee of Ministers Rec(1998)7 on the ethical and organisational aspects of health care in prison.* http://www.coe.ba/pdf/Recommendation_No_R_98_7_eng.doc. Accessed Apr 2011.

Council of Europe. (2004). *Rec(2004)10 des Ministerkomitees für Mitgliedsstaaten bezüglich des Schutzes von Menschenrechten und der Würde von Personen mit psychischen Krankheiten.* Strasbourg: COE.

CPT. (2006). *European Committee for the Prevention of Torture and Inhuman or Degrading Treatment or Punishment (CPT) The CPT standards.* http://www.cpt.coe.int/en/documents/eng-standards-prn.pdf. Accessed 30 Mar 2013.

Elger, B. S. (2008). Medical ethics in correctional healthcare: An international comparison of guidelines. *Journal of Clinical Ethics, 19*(3), 234–249.

Elger, B. S. (2009). Violations of medical confidentiality: Opinions of primary care physicians. *British Journal of General Practice, 59*(567), 344–352. doi:10.3399/bjgp09X472647.

Elger, B.S. (2010). *Die ärztliche Schweigepflicht im Strafvollzug – praktische, ethische und rechtliche Aspekte. Fünfte europäische Konferenz zur Gesundheitsförderung in Haft, Dokumentation der Konferenz in Hamburg.* Berlin: Conrad GmbH.

Elger, B. S. (2011). Prison medicine, public health policy and ethics: The Geneva experience. *Swiss Medical Weekly, 141*, 13273. doi:10.4414/smw.2011.13273.

Elger, B. S., Handtke, V., & Wangmo, T. (2014). Disclosure of past crimes: An analysis of mental health professionals' attitudes toward breaching confidentiality. *Journal of Bioethical Inquiry, 11*, 347–358. Epub ahead of print.

Elger, B. S., Handtke, V., & Wangmo, T. (2015a). Informing patients about limits to confidentiality: A qualitative interview study of health professionals. *International Journal of Law and Psychiatry, 41*, 50–57. doi:10.1016/j.ijlp.2015.03.007. Epub 7 Apr 2015.

Elger, B. S., Handtke, V., & Wangmo, T. (2015b). Paternalistic breaches of confidentiality in prison: Mental health professionals' attitudes and justifications. *Journal of Medical Ethics, 41*(6), 496–500. doi:10.1136/medethics-2013-101981. Epub 13 Jan 2015.

General Medical Council. (2009a). *Confidentiality: reporting gunshot and knife wounds.* http://www.gmc-k.org/Confidentiality_reporting_gunshot_wounds_2009.pdf_27493825.pdf. Accessed 2 Apr 2013.

General Medical Council. (2009b). *Confidentiality.* http://www.gmc-uk.org/static/documents/content/Confidentiality_0910.pdf. Accessed 2 Apr 2013.

Gupta, M. (2007). Mandatory reporting laws and the emergency physician. *Annals of Emergency Medicine, 49*(3), 369–376.

Heikkinen, A. M., Wickstrom, G. J., Leino-Kilpi, H., & Katajisto, J. (2007). Privacy and dual loyalties in occupational health practice. *Nursing Ethics, 14*(5), 675–690.

Houry, D., Sachs, C. J., Feldhaus, K. M., & Linden, J. (2002). Violence-inflicted injuries: Reporting laws in the fifty states. *Annals of Emergency, 39*(1), 56–60.

Kottow, M. H. (1986). Medical confidentiality: An intransigent and absolute obligation. *Journal of Medical Ethics, 12*(3), 117–122.

Malv, H. (2006). Confidentiality threatened if physicians are to report drivers who pose a danger to traffic. *Läkartidningen, 103*(14), 1125–1126.

Mathews, B., & Kenny, M. C. (2008). Mandatory reporting legislation in the United States, Canada, and Australia: A cross-jurisdictional review of key features, differences, and issues. *Child Maltreatment, 13*(1), 50–63.

Reilly, D. R. (2008). Breaching confidentiality and destroying trust: The harm to adolescents on physicians' rosters. *Canadian Family Physician, 54*(6), 834–839.

Rodriguez, M. A., Craig, A. M., Mooney, D. R., & Bauer, H. M. (1998). Patient attitudes about mandatory reporting of domestic violence. Implications for health care professionals. *Western Journal of Medicine, 169*(6), 337–341.

Rodriguez, M. A., McLoughlin, E., Bauer, H. M., Paredes, V., & Grumbach, K. (1999). Mandatory reporting of intimate partner violence to police: Views of physicians in California. *American Journal of Public Health, 89*(4), 575–578.

Rodriguez, M. A., McLoughlin, E., Nah, G., & Campbell, J. C. (2001). Mandatory reporting of domestic violence injuries to the police: What do emergency department patients think? *Journal of the American Medical Association, 286*(5), 580–583.

Rodriguez, M. A., Wallace, S. P., Woolf, N. H., & Mangione, C. M. (2006). Mandatory reporting of elder abuse: Between a rock and a hard place. *The Annals of Family Medicine, 4*(5), 403–409.

SAMW. (2012). *Swiss Academy of Medical Sciences: The exercise of medical activities with respect to detained persons (with addendum from 2012).* http://www.samw.ch/en/Ethics/Guidelines/Currently-valid-guidelines.html. Accessed 31 Dec 2012.

Sprumont, D., Schaffter, G., Hostettler, U., Richter, M., & Perrenoud, J. (2009). *Pratique médicale en milieu de détention. Effectivité des directives de l'Académie suisse des sciences médicales sur 'L'exercice de la médecine auprès de personnes détenues'.* Neuchâtel: Institut du Droit de la Santé.

Tarasoff v Regents of the University of California. 529 P 2d 55 (California, USA 1974).

World Medical Association. (1948). *Declaration of Geneva.* http://www.wma.net/en/30publications/10policies/g1/. Accessed 15 Mar 15 2013.

Chapter 13
Preventing Human Rights Violations in Prison – The Role of Guidelines

Bernice S. Elger and David M. Shaw

Abstract It is common knowledge that the human rights of prisoners are often not respected. But can guidelines help to prevent such violations? In this chapter we explore this topic and examine how to help healthcare professionals navigate the conflicts of interest that can make it difficult to ensure that patients' rights are respected. To do so, we explain the role of guidelines – both clinical and ethical – for non-incarcerated patients outside prisons and for those within prisons. Within such institutions, the main challenges are ensuring that patients receive healthcare that is equivalent to that available outside prison, and ensuring patient autonomy in healthcare decisions. Despite the good practices set out in many national and international guidelines, physicians (both inside and outside prisons) are often unfamiliar with this guidance. Both greater awareness of existing guidelines and development of further guidelines are required.

It is well known that prisoners' human rights are often violated. In this chapter we examine whether guidelines can be effective in preventing such violations and in helping physicians resolve the significant conflicts of interest that they often face in trying to protect prisoners' rights. We begin by explaining the role of clinical and ethical guidelines outside prisons, in the context of healthcare for non-incarcerated prisoners, and then the specific role of such guidelines within prisons, where the main concerns are ensuring respect for the principle of equivalence of care, and for a prisoner patient's autonomy in health care decisions. After reviewing and analysing various national and international guidelines, we review the literature and assess whether the good practices set out in these guidelines actually translate into changes in professional behaviour and consequent benefits for prisoners. It emerges that physicians both outside and within prisons tend to be insufficiently familiar with the relevant guidelines, and that they too infrequently use the guidance to make decisions, preferring instead to use personal codes of conduct. Guidelines designed specifically for the prison context are important to ensure equivalence of care and should be better known by health care personnel and other professional groups

B.S. Elger (✉) • D.M. Shaw
Institute for Biomedical Ethics, University of Basel, Bernoullistrasse 28, 4056 Basel, Switzerland
e-mail: b.elger@unibas.ch; david.shaw@unibas.ch

© Springer Science+Business Media Dordrecht 2017
B.S. Elger et al. (eds.), *Emerging Issues in Prison Health*,
DOI 10.1007/978-94-017-7558-8_13

working in prison. Further guidelines should be developed that describe challenging situations and provide concrete guidance as to how to deal with them.

13.1 Introduction

Human rights violations in prison[1] are not infrequent. The range of violations is considerable, and in a substantial number of cases health care personnel are involved in the violations. International human rights law, as well as non-binding 'soft law' and court decisions (in particular those of the European Court of Human Rights) stipulate more or less explicitly the framework of rights that should be granted to prisoners. In the centre of this framework sits the principle of equivalence of care (Birmingham et al. 2006; Council of Europe 1998; Elger 2008b). Prisoner patients should have access to the same care that is available to non-imprisoned patients in the same country. Medical ethics in prison should follow the same rules inside prisons as outside, i.e. respect for patient autonomy, including confidentiality and informed consent, should govern medical practice and be applied with the same rigor as outside prisons (CPT 1993, 2004).

Two examples of the human rights violations that typically occur in prisons are violation of the right to privacy, i.e. failure to respect medical confidentiality, and lack of access to equivalent health care (Anonymous 1999a, b). The latter can take different forms: employment of prison physicians and other health care personnel who are less well trained than those outside prison; unavailability of medical specialists in prison; limitations in provision of transfers to hospitals despite inpatient treatment being indicated; lack of appropriate health care resources and health care facilities in prison; and delays in accessing a physician because the request passes through a prison guard who is the first person to 'evaluate' prisoners' health needs. Many of these violations are insufficiently recognized and have become routine in the prison health care setting. In a country or prison where the principle of equivalence is not respected, health care personnel face different choices. Should they refuse to work in prisons? Or should they agree to work there, given that health care for prisoners might be even worse if less qualified personnel were to provide prison health care?

Violations of the principle of informed consent can also occur in prison without being recognized. While the experiments carried out by Nazi physicians without patient consent seem to lie in the remote past in the perception of many health care personnel working in prison today, violations may still be part of routine practice. For example, force feeding of hunger strikers is practiced in many countries (Gilmore 1983; Guilbert 2001). Less obvious violations occur when patients are insufficiently informed because of lack of time in prison or if physicians do not

---

[1] The term 'prison' is used to indicate any place of detention; 'prisoner' or 'detainee' means any person who is deprived of his or her liberty.

pay sufficient attention to the fact that prisoners might not dare to refuse medical treatment in prison because they are under pressure from prison authorities in general.

O'Connor pointed out that a 'significant minority of the tortured prisoners who survive report that a doctor was present during their torture' (O'Connor 2009: 426). He makes the criticism that 'few medical practitioners are ever criminally prosecuted or even disciplined by their regulatory bodies' (ibid.), and wonders how it is possible that such evident violations of medical ethics and human rights are first ignored and then go unpunished. One factor that could contribute to physicians' impunity is that physicians often act upon orders from state and prison authorities (although this is obviously no excuse for allowing violations to occur); another is that health personnel themselves do not sufficiently recognize violations. In many cases the role of health personnel is to examine prisoners in order to evaluate their 'capacity to withstand the torture or resuscitate them to allow torture and interrogation to continue' (O'Connor 2009: 426). O'Connor argues 'that the de facto immunity which complicit doctors currently appear to enjoy must be stripped away and replaced by effective processes to detect and then prosecute criminal behaviour'(ibid.). S. Miles and colleagues carried out a multilingual web search of the 'records of international and national courts, military tribunals, medical associations (licensing boards and medical societies), medical and non-medical literature databases, human rights groups and media stories for reports of physicians who had been punished for complicity with torture or crimes against humanity that were committed after World War II (Miles et al. 2010: 23). They found 56 physicians in eight countries who 'had been punished for complicity with torture or crimes against humanity.'

> Courts punish crimes. Medical societies punish ethics violations. Fifty-one physicians (85 %) had been punished by the medical associations of five countries. Eleven (18 %) had been punished by domestic courts (Miles et al. 2010: 23).

To what extent such punishment has a preventive effect remains unclear. How health care personnel should be punished for working in prisons where the principle of equivalence is not respected also remains to be defined. S. Miles points out the 'need for clear ethics norms requiring physicians and other clinicians to prevent the mistreatment of prisoners' (Miles 2007b: 5).

> Army investigation and the corresponding interrogation log show clinical supervision, monitoring and treatment during an interrogation that employed dogs, prolonged sleep deprivation, humiliation, restraint, hypothermia and compulsory intravenous infusions. The interrogation and the involvement of a psychologist, physician and medics violate international and medical norms for the treatment of prisoners (Miles 2007b: 5).

While routine education that addresses explicitly human rights violations of detained persons is urgently needed in medical schools, additional educational efforts should extend to health care personnel who are 'at risk' (O'Connor 2009), including those working in prisons.

> [Education] should address professional behaviour which tolerates or even protects cultures of abuse. A code of professional conduct would assist 'doctors at risk' to resist overtures for

them to become complicit in torture, Medical Practice Acts should include statements on respecting human rights when defining good professional conduct (O'Connor 2009: 426).

As the prison context is shaped by ethical dilemmas related to different perceptions of obligation and dual-loyalty conflicts of interest, guidelines could be an efficient and simple way to help health care personnel make the right decisions and to prevent human rights violations. In this chapter we will give an overview of the different guidelines that are valuable for health care personnel in prison, and examine the role played by codes of conduct and guidelines in correctional health care. In line with the principle of equivalence, we will first examine the role of guidelines outside prisons to help define their role for health care personnel in prisons.

13.2 Different Types of Guidelines

Regular calls for guidelines can be observed in medical practice both in and outside prisons. The most obvious situations that trigger a perceived need for guidelines are related to new diseases, new technology and/or to disagreement about the appropriate conduct of health care personnel (ACOG 2006; Basu et al. 2005; Eysenbach 2000; FIGO Committee 2006; O'Brien 1989; Price 2005; South African Medical Association 2002). A distinction can be made between clinical and ethical guidelines, although many clinical guidelines contain more or less explicit ethical guidance and ethical guidelines may contain reference to best clinical practice.

13.3 Benefits and Harms of Clinical and Ethical Guidelines

The usefulness of clinical and ethical guidelines is debated (Woolf et al. 1999). Clinical guidelines can benefit patients if they ensure that physicians prescribe appropriate treatments, and can benefit health care personnel if they provide support (Pettifor et al. 2001) by reducing uncertainty regarding how to proceed with patient care. Clinical guidelines may also cause harm if they describe treatment paths for 'average' patients and do not permit sufficiently personalized treatment for individual patients.

Criteria have been developed to evaluate the quality of clinical and ethical guidelines (Strech and Schildmann 2011). It is not yet clear whether ethical guidelines are associated with benefits and harms similar to clinical guidelines. One problem that is clearly relevant for both ethical and clinical guidelines is the existence of contradictory recommendations in different guidelines and policies (Eriksson et al. 2008; Geppert 2007; Matheson et al. 2012; Tangwa 2004). It is therefore particularly important to strive for harmonization and compliance with international standards and to ensure that guidelines are applicable to multicultural contexts (Pedersen 1989).

Few studies have tried to evaluate whether guidelines actually affect physicians' behaviour. The actual or perceived legal status of guidelines may influence health professionals' knowledge of and compliance with them. The Swiss Academy of Medical Sciences (SAMS) is known worldwide for its intensive guideline-writing activity. Most SAMS guidelines are not legally binding in a direct way, but they acquire considerable legal significance because the Swiss federal court referred to the guidelines as the standard of diligent professional care in cases of dispute; this also the case for guidelines issued by National Institute for Health Clinical Excellence (NICE) in the United Kingdom. According to a recent study, the vast majority of respondents to a survey of Swiss physicians (72.2 %) 'considered themselves to be completely familiar' with the guidelines on the determination of death in the context of organ transplantation (Pfister and Biller-Adorno 2010: 160). This guideline is binding as it is mentioned in the federal legal dispositions on transplantation. In contrast, in the case of other guidelines included in the study (one on end-of-life decision making, and another on palliative care) only less than 20 % of respondents indicated that they were 'completely familiar' with the content, 31 % had already heard of them and 34 % reported they knew some of their contents. These guidelines were perceived as useful by many practitioners. Although they 'cannot provide precise instructions on how to act and decide in the individual case [. . .] they serve as decision-making aids in clinical practice and provide orientation in legally unregulated medical areas' (Pfister 2009: 581).

D.C. Malloy and colleagues carried out focus groups with physicians 'from six culturally distinct countries to explore their perception of formalized, written ethical guidelines' (Malloy et al. 2009: 373).

> The most commonly occurring theme found in our focus groups (23.7 % of comments) was a lack of awareness of the content of domestic medical codes of ethics and other explicit ethical documents pertaining to their practice (e.g., hospital value statements). While there was a general knowledge of medical codes and statements, few physicians were able to identify specific content (Malloy et al. 2009: 376).

Furthermore, the physician's comments indicated that guidelines had no influence on their actual behaviour; although they considered them to be philosophically interesting, 'in terms of pragmatic use, they failed' (Malloy et al. 2009: 377). Other physicians complained about 'marginal utility in ethical guidelines'. For them, a major weakness of guidelines was that their generalized content meant that 'they could not address particular ethical dilemmas' (Malloy et al. 2009: 378).

A major finding of the study was that physicians indicated their major source of guidance to be personal codes of ethics and personal values. Still, a substantial minority of responses indicated strong support for formal 'cosmopolitan' codes of ethics.

These findings are confirmed by two other studies carried out in different contexts. Goulding and colleagues (2003) investigated the level of compliance with guidelines among UK researchers in the field of genetics.

The survey showed that 81 % of researchers had consulted one or more sets of formal guidelines in relation to their research. But interviewees frequently considered them overly abstract, lacking in practical feasibility and of secondary importance compared with their own attitudes and experience. This suggests that if there were a conflict between the codified consensus contained in such guidelines and a circumstance where it felt appropriate to do otherwise, then the guidance would be ignored (Goulding et al. 2003: 118).

Osborn and colleagues (2009) used focus groups and in-depth interviews with 56 practicing physicians in Australia and New Zealand to explore their attitudes towards the Royal Australasian College of Physicians (RACP) Guidelines for ethical relationships between physicians and the pharmaceutical industry.

Most physicians were aware of the RACP ethical Guidelines (3rd edition, 2006), but only a few used them to resolve ethical dilemmas or to influence their decision-making in relation to interacting with the pharmaceutical industry. Ethical standards used or approaches to decision-making practices related to interactions with the pharmaceutical industry were most likely to have been developed through past experiences, peer pressure or decisions that were considered to be 'in the best interests of their patients' (Osborn et al. 2009: 800).

13.4   Clinical and Ethical Guidelines in Prison

In the prison environment guidelines are discussed in a variety of different contexts. Clinical guidelines can be used to ensure equivalence of care. Some discussion exists about the extent to which clinical guidelines established in a non-prisoner population are fully valid in prison. Indeed, prisoners suffer from a wide range of health problems and 'in many cases [of disease] prevalence is greater than in the general population' (Sakelliadis et al. 2009). This means that pre-test probability (CEBM 2013)[2] may differ in a prisoner population from that in patients outside prisons. Wherever such differences are significant, clinical guidelines would need to be adapted to the prison context. In a number of areas, existing clinical guidelines have been used in prison medicine and adapted or newly written for the treatment of prisoners. Guideline activities are a mirror of the disease burden in prisons and of controversies regarding resource distribution. Most guidelines concern public health and are related to infectious diseases (Safyer et al. 1988), particularly HIV (Bollini et al. 2002; Harding 1995), hepatitis (Almasio et al. 2011; Neff 2003), and tuberculosis (Dara et al. 2009; Mendelson 1996; Skolnick 1989; WHO 2000). Another theme of guidelines is the practice of psychiatry in prison (Doyle and Logan 2012), with a particular focus on the treatment of substance abuse (Chalke 1978;

---

[2]Pretest Probability is important for the interpretation of the results of diagnostic tests and for the decision regarding which diagnostic test should be selected. It is defined as the 'probability of the target disorder before a diagnostic test result is known' and 'represents the probability that a specific patient [e.g. a 50 year old prisoner], with a specific medical history [e.g. drug abuse and hypertension], who presents to a specific clinical setting [e.g. an emergency consultation in a prison health service], with specific symptoms, say retrosternal chest pressure, dyspnoea and diaphoresis, has a specific diagnosis, such as acute myocardial infarction' (CEBM 2013).

Dejgaard 2007; Michel and Maguet 2005; Sharon 1984) and health care for juvenile detainees (Olivan-Gonzalvo 2002).[3]

Some guidelines address ethical issues related to research with prisoners in the context of HIV infection (Collins et al. 1995; De Groot et al. 2001; Lazzarini and Altice 2000; South African Medical Association 2002) and psychiatric disease (Kalmbach and Lyons 2003).

A number of international guidelines from the United Nations, the Council of Europe and the Committee for the Prevention of Torture (CPT) address ethical issues in prison medicine; most of these constitute 'soft law', i.e. non-binding recommendations (Council of Europe 1998; CPT 1993; United Nations 1982, 1984, 1985, 1988, a, b, c, 1991). Ethical guidelines have been published by the World Medical Association (WMA 1975, 1981, 1993, 2004), as well as different professional associations, including the Swiss Academy of Medical Sciences (SAMS 2002), and US associations of prison physicians (NCCHC 2002, 2007, 2009, 2013), psychiatrists and psychologists (Elger 2008a; Sakelliadis et al. 2009). While most of the guidelines mentioned above address ethical problems specific to the prison context, it should be added that clinical and ethical guidelines that apply to clinical care outside prisons are also valid in prison in line with the principle of equivalence; these will not be specifically discussed here.

While studies that evaluate the impact of clinical practice guidelines and pathways outside prisons are becoming more frequent, they remain scarce in the prison context. This is probably because prison physicians are often not affiliated with any research association and research in prison is cumbersome and requires more time and resources than other types of research. However, we have been able to identify two studies which evaluated clinical guidelines in prisons. Marco and colleagues analysed Spanish health care professionals' adherence to the 'Guidelines for the treatment of HIV-infected adults' among HIV-infected prison inmates in 2010. They found that in 86 % of cases the guidelines were followed. In 43 % of cases where the guidelines were not respected, this was because the patient refused antiretroviral therapy. Where guidelines were applied fully, a higher percentage of patients had an undetectable viral load (Marco et al. 2013). Lehman and colleagues (2012) examined compliance with the Occupational Safety and Health Administration (OSHA) Blood-borne Pathogens (BBPs) Standard at eight correctional facilities. Their aim was 'to identify potential barriers to compliance and [...] to discuss steps to address these barriers.' The authors found that facility compliance 'was less than 50 % for four activities: updating exposure control plans, implementing

---

[3]International organisations have been very active in producing clinical guidelines. For drug abuse in prison, see United Nations Office on Drugs and Crime (UNODC): http://www.unodc.org/unodc/en/hiv-aids/prison-settings.html; for WHO guidance on prisons and health, see: http://www.euro.who.int/en/what-we-do/health-topics/health-determinants/prisons-and-health; for WHO general clinical guidance that should be used in prisons in line with the principle of equivalence of care, see the Evidence for Action Series: http://www.who.int/hiv/pub/idu/evidence_for_action/en/. This chapter does not provide exhaustive references concerning clinical guidelines; for evidence based guidance concerning specific health topics in prison see the other chapters in this volume.

use of appropriate safer medical devices, soliciting employee input on selection of safer devices, and training medical staff when such devices are implemented' (Lehman et al. 2012: 29). They concluded that 'inconsistent compliance may be due to difficulties in applying the standards in the correctional health care work setting' and recommended more targeted training of personnel and tailoring of health communication activities to the correctional facility setting (Lehman et al. 2012: 29).

We are not aware of any published studies that examine compliance with ethical guidelines in prison. Data from a qualitative (Elger et al. 2014, 2015a, b) and quantitative (Bruggen et al. 2012) study in Switzerland that explored knowledge of and compliance with the SAMS guidelines regarding confidentiality in prison is currently being analysed with respect to the role of guidelines. The preliminary results show that prison health personnel have limited knowledge of the guidelines and that compliance with and interpretation of the guidelines varies widely in different cantons.

In none of the aforementioned studies concerning clinical and ethical guidelines is there any evaluation and comparison of behaviour before and after use of guidelines. Future research should investigate this issue further.

13.5   Guidelines in Prison: Lessons for Health Care Practitioners

The principle of equivalence requires health care professionals to follow general clinical guidelines when they treat patients who are deprived of their liberty. Physicians have a duty to examine carefully whether guidelines that 'have been adapted to the prison context' should be followed. The adaptation is justified if it correctly integrates epidemiological differences between prisoner populations and non-incarcerated patient populations. Guidelines designed and enacted by state authorities in order to limit resources for prisoner health care or to impose distinct ethical standards in prison in a way that contradicts the principle of equivalence should immediately trigger a reaction by health personnel through their medical associations. Indeed, it is the responsibility of professional associations of health care personnel to ensure that their members work in conditions where they are able to act according to international standards of medical ethics and human rights.

More empirical studies investigating the implementation and use of clinical guidelines in prison are needed. Such studies are beneficial in that they make guidelines more widely known and encourage practitioners to follow them. Epidemiologists should also be involved in this research in order to ensure clinically meaningful adaptations of guidelines to the unique characteristics of the prisoner population.

The implementation of ethical guidelines in prison encounters similar barriers to those affecting medical care outside prisons: there is a lack of knowledge and lack of compliance because priority is given to experience and personal ethics. However, studies have also shown that international guidance is valued by many health care professionals. Therefore, it is of crucial importance that local medical associations refer to the current international guidance (Miles and Freedman 2009) and use available mechanisms to monitor and encourage professional behaviour among prison physicians. In the prison context it is not unusual for health professionals to feel isolated; they lack specific guidance because guidelines describe conflicting values without spelling out how the balancing of values should take place in typical cases. Medical associations should assist prison physicians in reporting abuses (Miles 2007a) and in clarifying ethically acceptable approaches to frequently observed standard cases. In this regard, it should be noted that there is remarkable disregard for the principle of equivalence of care in the United States, where it is 'never mentioned in court cases and emerges only rarely in professional guidelines' (Elger 2008a: 244). Indeed, in countries such as the US where state law and individual prison policy stipulate a different set of medical ethics for prisoners, the guidelines of professional organisations such as the American Psychological Association actually contradict the principle of equivalence of care. Prison health personnel need the support of their medical associations and from a human rights perspective it is unacceptable that guidelines claim that general professional ethics might need to be partly abandoned in the prison context, due to state pressure (Elger 2008a). This lack of support for prisoners' rights puts prison physicians in the United States in a particularly difficult position. While encouraging changes have occurred, as shown by a comparison of ACP guidelines (ACP 2001, 2012), it is important that different professional associations in the US, including NCCHC, APA and ACP, join forces and harmonize their guidelines fully with international standards.

Guidelines are typically written when responsible groups and medical associations are aware about controversies and examples of unacceptable behaviour by their members (Solomon 1989). When CPT reports indicated that physicians in Switzerland had prescribed tranquillizers to facilitate deportations of prisoners by plane, the SAMS reacted and published guidelines that clarified medical obligations and prohibited use of medication without clinical indications. Medical associations have a duty to react to situations where physicians violate international recommendations and rules of professional conduct. Clark (2006) refers to examples from the Guantanamo Bay detention facility in Cuba and Abu Ghraib prison in Iraq, pointing out that the 'United States military medical system failed to protect detainee's human rights', 'violated the basic principles of medical ethics and ignored the basic tenets of medical professionalism' (Clark 2006: 570). Guidelines for prison physicians will make a difference to health care professionals' behaviour if the licensing medical associations enforce them strictly so that physicians will lose their right to practice if they do not follow them, whether because of lack of knowledge or personal preferences. However, enforcement of guidelines among health care professionals is not enough.

To discourage victimization of physician whistle-blowers on detainee abuse, domestic medical associations should pressure their respective governments to explicitly endorse their codes of ethics. Domestic medical communities should regard it as their ethical duty to pressure their respective governments to accede to the Optional Protocol to the Convention Against Torture and Other Cruel, Inhuman, or Degrading Treatment or Punishment, if their governments have not already done so. They should also regard it as their ethical duty to pressure their governments to afford 'prisoner of war' status to persons they detain. If faced with a conflict between following national policies and following universally accepted, multilateral principles of international law and ethics, military physicians should consider themselves ethically bound to follow the latter (Singh 2007: 15).

This illustrates that health care professionals should not be left in isolation. Many violations of human rights and of principles of medical ethics in prison are avoidable without causing negative repercussions for health care professionals. In addition to asking governments to endorse medical association's guidelines, we would suggest that prison authorities (and particularly governors) should be mandated to familiarise themselves with all relevant guidelines on prisoners' healthcare. If the prison authorities themselves understand prisoners' rights in the context of health care, they will be less likely to apply pressure on physicians to violate those rights.

There are also cases in which the neutrality of medical personnel is seriously threatened. Human rights crises can create ethical dilemmas where the international community as a whole must react.

In Bahrain, physicians have recently received harsh prison terms, apparently for treating demonstrators who clashed with government forces. In Syria, physicians are under the same political pressure to avoid treating political demonstrators or to act as informants against their own patients, turning them in to government authorities. This pressure has been severe, to the point that some physicians have become complicit in the abuse of patients who were also political demonstrators (Hathout 2012: 1).

This is not the only time and place where physicians are being 'used as both political pawns and political weapons in clear violation of Geneva Convention and World Medical Association guidelines' (Hathout 2012: 1). Physicians who are treating detained persons or state enemies find themselves in an extreme dilemma.

[Physicians] are being forced to choose between their own safety and well-being and that of their patients – a negative sum scenario wherein there is no optimal choice (Hathout 2012: 1).

The prevention of human rights violations in the context of imprisonment calls for different actions, including United Nations inquiries and the involvement of medical associations to protect the neutrality of medical care and personnel in any situation of dual loyalty. The implementation and enforcement of the use of clinical and ethical guidelines in prison is a first step towards protecting health care professionals and the rights of patients. Physicians and other health care professionals should increase their efforts to enhance knowledge about existing guidelines among health care personnel and prison administrations, to draft new or more specific guidelines where needed, and to comply fully with the general standards of medical ethics in prison health care.

References

ACOG. (2006). ACOG Committee Opinion No. 352: Innovative practice: Ethical guidelines. *American Journal of Obstetrics and Gynaecology, 108*(6), 1589–1595.

ACP. (2001). American College of Physicians – American Society of Internal Medicine. Correctional Medicine. *Public Policy Paper.* http://www.acponline.org/hpp/pospaper/correct_med. pdf. Accessed on 30 Oct 2007.

ACP. (2012). *American college of physicians.* Correctional Health Care. http://www.acponline. org/acp_policy/policies/correctional_facilities_healthcare_delivery_compendium_2012.pdf. Accessed 30 Mar 2013.

Almasio, P. L., Babudieri, S., Barbarini, G., Brunetto, M., Conte, D., Dentico, P., Gaeta, G. B., Leonardi, C., Levrero, M., Mazzotta, F., Morrone, A., Nosotti, L., Prati, D., Rapicetta, M., Sagnelli, E., Scotto, G., & Starnini, G. (2011). Recommendations for the prevention, diagnosis, and treatment of chronic hepatitis B and C in special population groups (migrants, intravenous drug users and prison inmates). *Digestive and Liver Disease, 43*(8), 589–595. doi:10.1016/j.dld.2010.12.004.

Anonymous. (1999a). Nearly one-third of prison inmates aren't getting proper care. *AIDS Policy Law, 14*(20), 7.

Anonymous. (1999b). New medical report confirms 'abysmal' care in Mississippi prison. *AIDS Policy Law, 14*(13), 4.

Association, S. A. M. (2002). SAMA ethical guidelines on HIV research, education, prison life and public campaigns. *South African Medical Journal, 92*(7), 508.

Basu, S., Smith-Rohrberg, D., Hanck, S., & Altice, F. L. (2005). HIV testing in correctional institutions: Evaluating existing strategies, setting new standards. *AIDS Public Policy, 20*(1–2), 3–24.

Birmingham, L., Wilson, S., & Adshead, G. (2006). Prison medicine: Ethics and equivalence. *British Journal of Psychiatry, 188*, 4–6. doi:10.1192/bjp.bp.105.010488.

Bollini, P., Laporte, J. D., & Harding, T. W. (2002). HIV prevention in prisons. Do international guidelines matter? *European Journal of Public Health, 12*(2), 83–99.

Bruggen, M. C., Eytan, A., Gravier, B., & Elger, B. S. (2012). Medical and legal professionals' attitudes towards confidentiality and disclosure of clinical information in forensic settings: A survey using case vignettes. *Medicine, Science and the Law.* doi:10.1258/msl.2012.012045.

CEBM. (2013). *Centre for evidence based medicine.* Pre-test Probability. http://www.cebm.net/ index.aspx?o=1041. Accessed 31 Mar 2013.

Chalke, F. C. (1978). Prison psychiatrists: A survey of ethical guidelines. *Psychiatric Annals, 8*(1), 29–63.

Clark, P. A. (2006). Medical ethics at Guantanamo Bay and Abu Ghraib: The problem of dual loyalty. *The Journal of Law, Medicine & Ethics, 34*(3), 570–580.

Collins, A., Baumgartner, D., & Henry, K. (1995). U.S. prisoners' access to experimental HIV therapies. *University of Minnesota Medical Bulletin, 78*(11), 45–48.

Committee, F. I. G. O. (2006). Ethical guidelines on sex selection for non-medical purposes. FIGO committee for the ethical aspects of human reproduction and women's health. *International Journal of Gynaecology and Obstetrics, 92*(3), 329–330.

Council of Europe. (1998). *Committee of Ministers on the ethical and organisational aspects of health care in prison.* http://www.coe.ba/pdf/Recommendation_No_R_98_7_eng. doc. Accessed Apr 2011.

CPT. (1993). *European Committee for the prevention of torture and inhuman or degrading treatment or punishment: Third general report 1993.* http://www.cpt.coe.int/en/annual/rep-03. htm. Accessed 1 Dec 2012.

CPT. (2004). *The CPT standards 'Substantive' sections of the CPT's general reports.* http://www. cpt.coe.int/en/documents/eng-standards-scr.pdf. Accessed 30 Jan 2008.

Dara, M., Grzemska, M., Kimerling, M. E., Reyes, H., & Zagorskiy, A. (2009). Tuberculosis Coalition for Technical Assistance (USAID, TBCTA) and International Committee of the

Red Cross. *Guidelines for Control of Tuberculosis in Prisons*. http://pdf.usaid.gov/pdf_docs/ PNADP462.pdf. Accessed 1 Apr 2013.

De Groot, A. S., Bick, J., Thomas, D., & Stubblefield, E. (2001). HIV clinical trials in correctional settings: Right or retrogression? *The AIDS Reader, 11*(1), 34–40.

Dejgaard, B. (2007). Guidelines for acute detoxication and substitution treatment in persons unknown or only superficially known to the physician. *Ugeskrift for Laeger, 169*(10), 936.

Doyle, M., & Logan, C. (2012). Operationalizing the assessment and management of violence risk in the short-term. *Behavioral Sciences and the Law, 30*(4), 406–419.

Elger, B. S. (2008a). Medical ethics in correctional healthcare: An international comparison of guidelines. *Journal of Clinical Ethics, 19*(3), 234–259.

Elger, B. S. (2008b). Towards equivalent health care of prisoners: European soft law and public health policy in Geneva. *Journal of Public Health Policy, 29*(2), 192–206.

Elger, B. S., Handtke, V., & Wangmo, T. (2014). Disclosure of past crimes: An analysis of mental health professionals' attitudes toward breaching confidentiality. *Journal of Bioethical Inquiry, 11*, 347–358. Epub ahead of print.

Elger, B. S., Handtke, V., & Wangmo, T. (2015a). Informing patients about limits to confidentiality: A qualitative interview study of health professionals. *International Journal of Law and Psychiatry, 41*, 50–57. doi:10.1016/j.ijlp.2015.03.007. Epub 7 Apr 2015.

Elger, B. S., Handtke, V., & Wangmo, T. (2015b). Paternalistic breaches of confidentiality in prison: Mental health professionals' attitudes and justifications. *Journal of Medical Ethics, 41*(6), 496–500. doi:10.1136/medethics-2013-101981. Epub 13 Jan 2015.

Eriksson, S., Hoglund, A. T., & Helgesson, G. (2008). Do ethical guidelines give guidance? A critical examination of eight ethics regulations. *Cambridge Quarterly of Healthcare Ethics, 17*(1), 15–29. doi:10.1017/S0963180108080031.

Eysenbach, G. (2000). Towards ethical guidelines for e-health: JMIR theme issue on eHealth ethics. *Journal of Medical Internet Research, 2*(1), E7. doi:10.2196/jmir.2.1.e7.

Geppert, C. M. (2007). Medical education and the pharmaceutical industry: A review of ethical guidelines and their implications for psychiatric training. *Academic Psychiatry, 31*(1), 32–39. doi:10.1176/appi.ap.31.1.32.

Gilmore, A. (1983). Medicine behind bars: Treatment or torture? *Canadian Medical Association Journal, 129*(8), 867–872.

Goulding, N. J., Waddell, H. C., & Doyal, L. (2003). Adherence to published ethical guidelines by the UK genetics research community. *Nature Genetics, 34*(2), 117–119. doi:10.1038/ng0603-117.

Guilbert, P. (2001). Le jeune de protestation en médecine pénitentiaire: épidémiologie genevoise et analyse de la prise en charge en Suisse et dans des pays européens. *Thèse de la Faculté de médecine de Genève N, 10180*, 2001.

Harding, T. (1995). HIV infection in prisons. What about the WHO guidelines? *BMJ, 310*(6989), 1265.

Hathout, L. (2012). The right to practice medicine without repercussions: Ethical issues in times of political strife. *Philosophy, Ethics, and Humanities in Medicine, 7*, 11. doi:10.1186/1747-5341-7-11.

Kalmbach, K. C., & Lyons, P. M. (2003). Ethical and legal standards for research in prisons. *Behavioral Sciences and the Law, 21*(5), 671–686. doi:10.1002/bsl.533.

Lazzarini, Z., & Altice, F. L. (2000). A review of the legal and ethical issues for the conduct of HIV-related research in prisons. *AIDS Public Policy, 15*(3–4), 105–135.

Lehman, E. J., Huy, J. M., Viet, S. M., & Gomaa, A. (2012). Compliance with blood-borne pathogen standards at eight correctional facilities. *Journal of Correctional Health Care, 18*(1), 29–44. doi:10.1177/1078345811421466.

Malloy, D. C., Sevigny, P., Hadjistavropoulos, T., Jeyaraj, M., McCarthy, E. F., Murakami, M., Paholpak, S., Lee, Y., & Park, I. (2009). Perceptions of the effectiveness of ethical guidelines: An international study of physicians. *Medicine, Health Care and Philosophy, 12*(4), 373–383. doi:10.1007/s11019-009-9212-0.

Marco, A., Gallego, C., Blanco, X. R, Puig, A., Arguelles, M. J., & Moruno, L. (2013). An analysis of adherence to the Recommendations for the treatment of human immunodeficiency virus-infected adults in a penitentiary in Barcelona. *Enfermedades infecciosas y microbiología clínica*. doi:10.1016/j.eimc.2012.12.006.

Matheson, F. I., Forrester, P., Brazil, A., Doherty, S., & Affleck, L. (2012). Incentives for research participation: Policy and practice from Canadian corrections. *American Journal of Public Health, 102*(8), 1438–1442. doi:10.2105/AJPH.2012.300685.

Mendelson, D. (1996). Government guidelines issued for TB control in correctional facilities. *Nevada RNformation, 5*(2), 19.

Michel, L., & Maguet, O. (2005). Guidelines for substitution treatments in prison populations. *Encephale, 31*(1 Pt 1), 92–97.

Miles, S. H. (2007a). Human rights abuses, transparency, impunity and the Web. *Torture, 17*(3), 216–221.

Miles, S. H. (2007b). Medical ethics and the interrogation of Guantanamo 063. *American Journal of Bioethics, 7*(4), 5–11. doi:10.1080/15265160701263535.

Miles, S. H., & Freedman, A. M. (2009). Medical ethics and torture: Revising the declaration of Tokyo. *Lancet, 373*(9660), 344–348. doi:10.1016/S0140-6736(09)60097-0.

Miles, S. H., Alencar, T., & Crock, B. N. (2010). Punishing physicians who torture: A work in progress. *Torture, 20*(1), 23–31.

NCCHC. (2002). National Commission on Correcitonal Health Care. Public health and corrections. Connecting care, connecting communities. *Ethical Decision Making, 4.* http://www.coach.aed. org/pubs/factsheets/phc-policy.pdf. Accessed 20 Oct 2007.

NCCHC. (2007). *National Commission on Correctional Health Care. Position statement. Correctional Health Care Professionals Response to Inmate Abuse.* http://www.ncchc.org/correctional-health-care-professionas'-response-to-inmate-abuse. Accessed 20 Mar 2013.

NCCHC. (2009). *National Commission on Correctional Health Care Standards. 2003 standards for health services in prisons. 2003 standards for health services in jails. 2004 standards for health services in Juvenile detention and confinement facilities. A summary guide to the revisions.* http://www.ncchc.org/resources/stds_summary/intro.html. Accessed Apr 2009.

NCCHC. (2013). National Commission on Correctional Health care. *Clinical guidelines.* http:// www.ncchc.org/clinical-guidelines. Accessed 20 Mar 2013.

Neff, M. J. (2003). CDC updates guidelines for prevention and control of infections with hepatitis viruses in correctional settings. *American Family Physician, 67*(12), 2620–2625.

O'Brien, M. (1989). Mandatory HIV antibody testing policies: An ethical analysis. *Bioethics, 3*(4), 273–300.

O'Connor, M. (2009). Can we prevent doctors being complicit in torture? Breaking the serpent's egg. *Journal of Law and Medicine, 17*(3), 426–438.

Olivan-Gonzalvo, G. (2002). Delinquent adolescents: Health problems and health care guidelines for juvenile correctional facilities. *Anales de Pediatría, 57*(4), 345–353.

Osborn, M., Day, R., Komesaroff, P., & Mant, A. (2009). Do ethical guidelines make a difference to decision-making? *Internal Medicine Journal, 39*(12), 800–805. doi:10.1111/j.1445-5994.2009.01954.x.

Pedersen, P. (1989). Developing multicultural ethical guidelines for psychology. *International Journal of Psychology, 24*(1–5), 643–652. doi:10.1080/00207594.1989.10600073.

Pettifor, J., Crozier, S., & Chew, J. (2001). Recovered memories: Ethical guidelines to support professionals. *Journal of Child Sexual Abuse, 10*(2), 1–15.

Pfister, E. (2009). Do ethical guidelines provide assistance in clinical practice? *Therapeutische Umschau, 66*(8), 581–584. doi:10.1024/0040-5930.66.8.581.

Pfister, E., & Biller-Adorno, N. (2010). The reception and implementation of ethical guidelines of the Swiss Academy of Medical Sciences in medical and nursing practice. *Swiss Medical Weekly, 140*(11/12), 160–167. doi:smw-12647.

Price, D. D. (2005). New facts and improved ethical guidelines for placebo analgesia. *Journal of Pain, 6*(4), 213–214. doi:10.1016/j.jpain.2005.01.348.

Safyer, S. M., Alcabes, P., & Chisolm, S. (1988). Protecting public health in U.S. Jails: A call for the development of guidelines for managing communicable disease outbreaks. *American Journal of Infection Control, 16*(6), 267–271.

Sakelliadis, E. I., Spiliopoulou, C. A., & Papadodima, S. A. (2009). Health care provision in prisons: A review on European and international guidelines. *Acta Clinica Belgica, 64*(5), 399–405.

SAMS. (2002). Swiss Academy of Medical Sciences. *The exercise of medical activities with respect to detained persons.* http://www.samw.ch/en/Ethics/Guidelines/Currently-valid-guidelines.html. Accessed 31 Dec 2012.

Sharon, L. (1984). Benzodiazepines: Guidelines for use in correctional facilities. *Psychosomatics, 25*(10), 784–788. doi:10.1016/S0033-3182(84)72966-5.

Singh, J. A. (2007). Treating war detainees and terror suspects: Legal and ethical responsibilities of military physicians. *Military Medicine, 172*(12 Suppl), 15–21.

Skolnick, A. (1989). Government issues guidelines to stem rising tuberculosis rates in prisons. *JAMA, 262*(23), 3249–3253.

Solomon, S. D. (1989). We need ethical guidelines for promotion of prescription drugs to physicians. *The New England Journal of Medicine, 320*(25), 1700.

Strech, D., & Schildmann, J. (2011). Quality of ethical guidelines and ethical content in clinical guidelines: The example of end-of-life decision-making. *Journal of Medical Ethics, 37*(7), 390–396. doi:10.1136/jme.2010.040121.

Tangwa, G. B. (2004). Between universalism and relativism: A conceptual exploration of problems in formulating and applying international biomedical ethical guidelines. *Journal of Medical Ethics, 30*(1), 63–67.

United Nations. (1982). *Principles of medical ethics relevant to the role of health personnel.* Adopted by General Assembly resolution 37/194. http://www2.ohchr.org/english/law/medicalethics.htm. Accessed 30 Nov 2012.

United Nations. (1984). *Safeguards guaranteeing protection of the rights of those facing the death penalty.* Approved by Economic and Social Council resolution 1984/50. http://www2.ohchr.org/english/law/protection.htm. Accessed Dec 2012.

United Nations. (1985). *Standard minimum rules for the administration of Juvenile Justice* (The Beijing Rules). Adopted by United Nations General Assembly Resolution 40/33. http://www.un.org/documents/ga/res/40/a40r033.htm. Accessed on Dec 2012.

United Nations. (1988). *Body of principles for the protection of all persons under any form of detention or imprisonment.* Adopted by General Assembly resolution 43/173 of 9 December 1988: http://www.un.org/documents/ga/res/43/a43r173.htm. Accessed Dec 2012.

United Nations. (1990a). *Basic principles for the treatment of prisoners.* Adopted and proclaimed by General Assembly resolution 45/111. http://www2.ohchr.org/english/law/basicprinciples.htm. Accessed Sept 2012.

United Nations. (1990b). *United Nations rules for the protection of Juveniles deprived of their liberty.* Adopted by General Assembly resolution 45/113. http://www2.ohchr.org/english/law/res45_113.htm. Accessed Dec 2012.

United Nations. (1990c). *United Nations standard minimum rules for non-custodial measures* (The Tokyo Rules. Adopted by General Assembly resolution 45/110). http://www2.ohchr.org/english/law/tokyorules.htm. Accessed Dec 2012.

United Nations. (1991). *United Nations manual on the effective prevention and investigation of extra-legal, arbitrary and summary executions.* http://www1.umn.edu/humanrts/instree/executioninvestigation-91.html. Accessed 8 Oct 2010.

WHO. (2000). *World Health Organisation. Tuberculosis control in prisons.* A manual for programme managers. http://www.who.int/tb/publications/prisons_tb_control_manual/en/index.html. Accessed 1 Apr 2013.

WMA. (1975). *World Medical Association Declaration of Tokyo.* Guidelines for medical doctors concerning torture and other cruel, inhuman or degrading treatment or punishment in relation to detention and imprisonment. Adopted in Tokyo, Japan.

WMA. (1981). *World Medical Association. Resolution on physician participation in capital punishment.* Adopted in Lisbon, Portugal, and amended by in Edinburgh, Scotland, October 2000 and in Seoul, Korea, October 2008.

WMA. (1993). *World Medical Association statement on body searches of prisoners.* Adopted in Budapest, Hungary.

WMA. (2004). *World Medical Association. Doctors working in prisons: Human rights and ethical dilemmas. A web-based course for health care personnel working in prison.* http://www.wma.net/e/webcourse_2004.htm. Accessed 30 June 2005.

Woolf, S. H., Grol, R., Hutchinson, A., Eccles, M., & Grimshaw, J. (1999). Clinical guidelines: Potential benefits, limitations, and harms of clinical guidelines. *BMJ, 318*(7182), 527–530.

Chapter 14
Immigration Detention and Health in Europe

Barbara Rijks, Caroline Schultz, Roumyana Petrova-Benedict, and Mariya Samuilova

Abstract In Europe, irregular migrants and rejected asylum-seekers still face detention. This chapter examines the most important aspects related to health in the context of immigration detention in Europe. Reviewing the literature and drawing on field evidence from IOM projects, it identifies the main health conditions of migrants in detention and looks into the common EU standards set in the Return Directive and the Reception Condition Directive as well as the relevant non-binding resolutions of the Council of Europe. The main finding is that despite these policies being in place, conditions typically found in European migrant detention facilities pose risks both to the physical and mental health of migrants as well as to immigration officials and health professionals working with detainees. Health conditions in detention facilities need to be improved by avoiding over-crowding and prison-like conditions as well as training staff to the specific requirements of immigration detention.

In Europe as well as world-wide, significant numbers of migrants and asylum-seekers are detained in former warehouses, prisons, military barracks and other facilities, on the grounds of their migration status, often without contact to the outside world and in conditions that negatively affect their health. This chapter highlights some of the important aspects related to health in the context of immigration detention

Opinions as stated are those of the authors, and not those of the Organization.

B. Rijks (✉)
Migration Health Division, International Organization for Migration,
Route de Morillons 17, 1211 Geneva, Switzerland
e-mail: BRIJKS@iom.int

C. Schultz
Expert Council of German Foundations on Integration and Migration,
Neue Promenade 6, 10178 Berlin, Germany
e-mail: schultz@svr-migration.de

R. Petrova-Benedict • M. Samuilova
Migration Health Division, International Organization for Migration,
Rue Montoyer 40, 1000 Brussels, Belgium
e-mail: rpetrovabenedict@iom.int; msamuilova@iom.int

© Springer Science+Business Media Dordrecht 2017
B.S. Elger et al. (eds.), *Emerging Issues in Prison Health*,
DOI 10.1007/978-94-017-7558-8_14

in Europe, which often resemble and sometimes exacerbate health conditions frequently prevalent in prisons. Reviewing the existing literature and evidence from project activities, it identifies the main health conditions of migrants in detention, presents relevant policies in place in Europe, and concludes with recommendations on how to improve health conditions in detention facilities. Existing evidence shows that the conditions commonly found in immigration detention have detrimental effects on the physical and mental health of migrants, and that there are significant gaps in health service delivery. In addition, immigration detention puts immigration and border officials and health professionals, who work with detainees, under stress and in ethical dilemmas, which can result in anxiety and depression. The chapter picks up the recommendation by international human rights bodies to progressively abolish immigration detention. In the meantime, the negative health effects of immigration detention should be attenuated by improving the physical environment of the detention facilities (e.g. avoiding over-crowding and a prison-like atmosphere), having culturally-sensitive, well-trained staff available (both immigration officials and health workers), and avoiding 'dual loyalty' problems, where health professionals have to report to detention authorities while being responsible for health care provision for staff and migrants in detention facilities.

14.1 Introduction

In Europe and world-wide, significant numbers of migrants[1] and asylum-seekers[2] are detained in former warehouses, prisons, military barracks and other 'recycled' facilities on the grounds of their particular immigration status; often without contact to the outside world, let alone conditions adequate for their health.[3]

This chapter aims to highlight some of the important aspects related to health in the context of immigration related detention in Europe. It first identifies the main health conditions of migrants in detention, presents the policies in place that inter alia address health in migrant detention facilities in the European sphere, and concludes with recommendations how to improve health services in detention

---

[1]The term irregular migrant describes a person who, owing to unauthorized entry, breach of a condition of entry, or the expiry of his or her visa, lacks legal status in a transit or host country (IOM Glossary 2011a).

[2]An asylum seeker is a person who seeks safety from persecution or serious harm in a country other than his or her own and awaits a decision on the application for refugee status under relevant international and national instruments (IOM Glossary 2011a).

[3]The EU Return Directive (2008/115/EC) specifies the reasons that justify immigration detention in preparation of returning illegally staying third-country-nationals as follows: 'Unless other sufficient but less coercive measures can be applied effectively in a specific case, Member States may only keep in detention a third-country national who is the subject of return procedures in order to prepare the return and/or carry out the removal process, in particular when: (a) there is a risk of absconding or (b) the third-country national concerned avoids or hampers the preparation of return or the removal process.'

facilities and the training for both border officials and health professionals dealing with migrants in detention.

Immigration-related detention is fundamentally different from prisons: the persons detained are migrants and asylum-seekers who have been detained for administrative reasons, since their legal status does not conform to the national laws of the host country. As pointed out by the Special Rapporteur on the human rights of migrants, François Crépeau, irregular entry or stay should never be considered criminal offences: they are not crimes against persons, property or national security. It is important to emphasize that irregular migrants are not criminals per se and should not be treated as such.[4,5] Immigration-related detention can be defined as 'the deprivation of liberty of non-citizens because of their immigration status' (Flynn 2011; see also Andalusian School of Public Health (EASP) and International Organization for Migration (IOM) (2010).[6]

Nevertheless, facilities for the detention of irregular migrants and asylum-seekers[7] more often than not resemble prisons; they 'generally tend to have similar infrastructure, environment, and administrative procedures to prison facilities' (EASP and IOM 2010; see also European Parliament 2008; IOM 2010a; Migreurop 2012). Most detention centres operate with fixed times for meals, recreation hours and mandatory night curfews, which leads detainees 'to feel as if they are in prison' (Jesuit Refugee Service (JRS) 2010). Above all, many countries use criminal facilities (jails, prisons, police lock-ups) for administrative immigration detention, including the use of security guards, fences, etc. and some hold administratively detained migrants alongside criminal detainees (Flynn 2011). Migrants in detention often lack social activities and contact to the outside world (IOM 2010a), and 'a major distress factor for detained persons seems to be the uncertainty on their stay in detention and the overall lack of information and support' (IOM 2010a). Thus, detention is one of the administrative sanctions for migrants which 'mimic criminal ones', according to a report by the Commissioner for Human Rights of the Council of Europe (2010).

---

[4]United Nations General Assembly (UNGA) (2012). Report of the Special Rapporteur on the human rights of migrants, François Crépeau).

[5]Note, however, that in some countries illegal entry is considered a criminal offense (UN GA 2012).

[6]This definition is used by the Global Detention Project, which is 'an inter-disciplinary research endeavour that investigates the role detention plays in states' responses to global migration, with a special focus on the policies and physical infrastructures of detention. The project, which was initiated in October 2006 [. . .], is based at the Graduate Institute's Programme for the Study of Global Migration' (http://www.globaldetentionproject.org/).

[7]In the following, the term 'migrants in detention' is meant to refer to both irregular migrants and asylum-seekers in immigration-related detention.

14.1.1 Detention Facilities in Europe

According to a study commissioned by the European Parliament (EP) Committee on Civil Liberties, Justice and Home Affairs based on field studies in 25 European Union (EU) member states, conditions in immigration detention facilities are very variable in the different countries (2008).

In general, there are different types of detention facilities, and many centres have multiple functions. In addition, many countries have set up transit or induction centres close to border checkpoints or at airports or sea ports (EP 2008).

The exact number of detention facilities in Europe is unknown, as 'not all operating centres are officially listed' (EP 2008: 178). Migreurop[8] estimates that there were 473 detention centres in Europe and in neighbouring Mediterranean countries in 2012, a number which has increased significantly from 324 in 2001. Most of them have been set up in already existing facilities that were 'recycled' for the purpose of immigration detention, like 'former barracks, other military buildings [...] and hangars and abandoned warehouses', all equipped with 'fences, barbed wire and other security measures' (EP 2008: 178).

According to Migreurop (2012), 'the number of holding sites [to detain migrants] is constantly increasing.' They estimate that the total capacity of holding centres in the EU and neighbouring countries is about 37,000, of which two thirds are located within the EU (Migreurop 2012).[9]

14.1.2 Statistics on Migrants Detained in Europe

No reliable data are available for the total numbers of migrant detainees in European countries (on data limitations, see for instance IOM, Hollings et al. 2012). Although different countries are obviously differently affected by irregular migration flows, individual country data from the Global Detention Project (2012) gives an idea of numbers: In Spain, 11,573 persons were detained on immigration-related grounds in

---

[8] 'Migreurop is a network of organisations, activists and researchers both from several European Union member states, Sub-Saharan, Maghreb and Near-East countries. It aims at identifying, denouncing and spreading information concerning European policies that marginalise migrants (detention, expulsions, and externalization of migratory controls) as 'unwanted' on European territory, and concerning the consequences of such policies for Southern countries. Since 2002 Migreurop denounces the generalization of migrants' detention and the multiplication of detention sites in Europe and beyond. The Encampment Map is the cornerstone of this work. Migreurop calls on all governments of EU Member States and its neighbours to stop using detention to control migration, to stop approaching asylum and immigration policies from a security perspective and, instead, to promote the right to move as a fundamental right' (Capodanno 2013).

[9] A map of the European continent and surrounding areas across the Mediterranean Sea portrays detention centres and internment camps for undocumented immigrants and asylum seekers (Migreurop 2012).

2009. In Belgium, 6902 migrants were detained in 2008 (down from 9101 persons in 2003). France detained 35,008 migrants in 2007 (up from 28,220 in 2003). In Italy, the number of migrant detainees totalled 7735 in 2011; in the Netherlands 8585 in 2008; in Malta 1864 in 2009; in Slovenia 408 in 2009 and in Sweden 1645 in 2008. Amnesty International (2013) estimates that '600,000 men, women and children are detained in Europe every year for migration control purposes.'

Data on the average length of detention is not available for all European countries. There seems to be a wide range, with for instance an average of 10.17 days in France (2007), 24.2 days in Finland (2008), 2.2 to 35.8 days in Belgium depending on the respective detention facility (2008), and six months in Bulgaria (2011). In Sweden, men were detained on average for 22.1 days, women for 15.6 days, and children for 1.6 days (Global Detention Project 2013).

According to the International Detention Coalition (IDC 2012),[10] the UK is the only European Union (EU) country that continues to practice indefinite detention. It also has one of the largest immigration detention estates (i.e. capacity of detention facilities) in Europe. In 2011, around 27,000 persons were detained on immigration-related grounds (28,000 in 2009 and 26,000 in 2010). More than 50 % of them are held for less than 60 days (Silverman and Hajela 2012).

A study commissioned by the European Parliament (2008) found accompanied minors in closed detention facilities in almost all of the 25 European countries investigated, although there is little reliable data on the exact numbers of minors in detention in Europe. In the UK, the number of children among detainees declined significantly in the last few years, from 1000 children having been detained with their families in 2009, to 400 in 2010 and about 100 in 2011 (Silverman and Hajela 2012). The Convention on the Rights of the Child states in Article 37(b) that '[n]o child shall be deprived of his or her liberty unlawfully or arbitrarily. The arrest, detention or imprisonment of a child shall be in conformity with the law and shall be used only as a measure of last resort and for the shortest appropriate period of time.'

According to EU law, both '[u]naccompanied minors and families with minors shall only be detained as a measure of last resort and for the shortest appropriate period of time' (Directive 2008). There are several rulings by the European Court of Human Rights (ECHR) on immigration-related detention of both unaccompanied and accompanied children. In the Kanagaratnam v. Belgium case in 2009, the Court recalled the extreme vulnerability of children, and found that the detention of Ms. Kanagaratnam and her three children aged 8, 11, and 13 at the time of detention was unlawful in violation of article 5.1 (right to liberty and security) of the European

---

[10] 'The IDC is an international coalition with a membership base of more than 250 non-governmental organizations, faith-based groups, academics, practitioners and individuals working in 50 countries globally. Coalition members research, advocate and provide direct services to and on behalf of refugees, asylum-seekers and migrants.' See http://idcoalition.org/. Accessed 5 March 2013.

Convention on Human Rights because of having remained in detention for an extended period of time (January to May 2009) in a facility not designed for families (ECHR 2011).

Given the scope and severity of immigration detention, there are concerns that this collides with the universal human right to health.[11] Especially in Southern EU countries, human rights organizations have repeatedly highlighted the inhuman conditions of detention in for instance Malta, Greece, and Italy (see for instance HRW 2010a, 2012; MSF 2011). The same applies to countries neighbouring the EU, for instance the Ukraine (HRW 2010b).

14.2 Main Health Issues Associated with Immigration Detention

14.2.1 Migration and Health – The Bigger Picture

Vulnerabilities for migrants exist even before they are apprehended or detained in an immigration detention facility. It is estimated that about 1.9 to 3.8 million irregular migrants reside in EU Member States (Karl-Trummer et al. 2010). No population-based health status data are available regarding irregular migrants in Europe, but interviews with care providers in several countries suggests that the most (between one-third and one-half of irregular migrants seeking services) common health care needs involved mental health problems, infectious and sexually transmitted diseases, and reproductive health (PICUM 2007). Another 25 % had work-related diseases or accidents. Irregular migrants lack access to prevention and health care services due to a variety of factors including fear of being reported, lack of information about their rights, lack of legal entitlements, the cost of services, discriminatory attitudes among health professionals, and other barriers related to language, culture and gender (Biffl and Altenburg 2012). In addition, because irregular migrants are often exposed to risk factors related to their precarious living and working conditions including exploitation and substance abuse (IOM 2010b), the prevalence of conditions of public health concern might be high in this population before detention, and therefore their confinement might represent a high risk for themselves, for other detainees, and the people who work in such facilities.

---

[11] The right to the highest attainable standard of physical and mental health was first enunciated in the Constitution of the WHO (1946), and later reiterated in the Universal Declaration of Human Rights, Article 25 (1948), as well as in several other legally binding international human right treaties. The International Covenant on Economic, Social and Cultural Rights (ICESCR 1966, Art 12) delineates the steps to be taken by states to achieve the full realization of the right to health. The Committee on Economic, Social and Cultural Rights explicitly states that 'the Covenant rights apply to everyone including non-nationals, such as refugees, asylum-seekers, stateless persons, migrant workers' (General Comment No. 20).

Therefore, from a public health perspective, guaranteeing migrants' equitable access to health care and health promotion is both sound and practical – it is cost-effective and improves public health outcomes. Promoting migrants' use of primary health care and early treatment, and including them into disease-control programmes, will reduce the need for costly emergency care and related high costs for the health system.

These principles are widely recognized and reflected in the 2008 World Health Assembly adopted Resolution WHA 61.17 Health of Migrants, which calls upon Member States of the World Health Organization 'to promote migrant-sensitive health policies' and 'to promote equitable access to health promotion and care for migrants [. . .].' In follow up to this Resolution, the World Health Organization (WHO), the International Organization for Migration (IOM) and the Government of Spain organized a Global Consultation on the Health of Migrants in Madrid in 2010, which saw the participation of Governments, UN Agencies, IOs, NGOs and Academia, resulting in the identification of four key priority areas for action:

- Monitoring migrant health
- Policy and legal frameworks
- Migrant-sensitive health systems
- Partnerships, networks, and multi-country frameworks

IOM has been promoting, in close partnership with WHO, governments and other stakeholders the implementation of these priority actions.

Although there is some literature on general detention conditions of migrants, specific research on their impact on health has been scarce (Hollings et al. 2012). Available studies or anecdotal evidence, indicate mostly negative health effects through higher risks of communicable and non-communicable diseases, including adverse mental and psychosocial health effects.

14.2.2 Health Issues in Detention Centres

14.2.2.1 Communicable Diseases

For all stakeholders (migrants, border officials, health professionals, and the public), the concern and fear of communicable diseases is evident, resembling the situation in prisons and refugee camps. A joint report of the European Centre for Disease Prevention and Control (ECDC) and the World Health Organization (WHO) published in 2011 on the situation of migrants detained at the Greek-Turkish border, however, argues that the heightened risk for the spread of communicable diseases in detention centres is 'mainly linked to severe overcrowding, lack of hygiene, lack of basic supplies (e.g. blankets, shoes, soap, etc.), lack of the possibility for outdoor activities and the long duration of detention', all of which favour the spread of infectious diseases such as tuberculosis, diarrhoea, upper respiratory infections etc.

Data by Médecins Sans Frontières (MSF) on Greek detention centres shows that of the 1809 migrant detainees treated by MSF doctors between December 2010 and March 2011, more than 63 % were diagnosed with respiratory tract infections, body pains, diarrhoea, gastrointestinal disorders, psychological complaints and skin diseases (MSF 2011).

14.2.2.2 Mental Health

While the fear of communicable diseases is dominating the discussions, non-communicable conditions, such as mental and psychosocial health, is often a more critical issue for migrants in detention. Several studies and reports highlight the negative effect of detention on mental and psychosocial health.

For instance, results of the project Increasing Public Health Safety Alongside the New Eastern European Border Line (PHBLM)[12] focused inter alia on health in immigration detention in three Eastern EU Member States, Hungary, Poland and Slovakia, and found that the living environment in the centres (a 'bare prison-like atmosphere', lack of social activities, education opportunities and lack of contact to the outside world) had a deteriorating effect on the already fragile mental health condition on the migrants detained (Hollings et al. 2012; IOM 2010a). A study conducted by the Jesuit Refugee Service (JRS 2010) found that the average detainee (in the 23 EU member states surveyed) perceived the detention as a form of punishment rather than a mere administrative procedure.[13] A paper by MSF on the impact of detention on migrants' health identifies uncertainty about the future as one of the greatest stressors and recounts the experience of MSF staff working in Belgian detention centres from 2004 to 2007, where they encountered that '[n]early all the migrants were suffering from stress-related psychosomatic problems, for example sleep problems, stomach-ache and lack of appetite' (MSF 2010: 5). Other health conditions reported by MSF in detention centres in Greece, Malta, Belgium and Italy include depression, anxiety, and post-traumatic stress disorder (PTSD) (MSF 2010). The fact that detained migrants sometimes seek to 'claim their rights through violence, suicide attempts, self-harm or hunger strikes' (EP 2008: 172) is taken as evidence for their negative state of mental health linked to isolation and confinement. As the United Nations (UN) Special Rapporteur on the Human Rights of Migrants, Mr François Crépeau, summed up, '[r]esearch

---

[12]This project, shortly PHBLM, was implemented between 2007 and 2010, co-funded under the European Commission's 1st Public Health Programme and coordinated by IOM's regional office in Brussels.

[13]For more reports on the impact of immigration detention on migrants' mental health, see for instance: Hodes 2010; Toselli and Gualdi-Russo 2008; Bean et al. 2006; Procter 2005.

shows that immigration detention has widespread and seriously damaging effects on the mental (and sometimes physical) health of detainees' (UN General Assembly 2012: 12).

Impacts on mental health are particularly of concern for vulnerable groups such as children (UN General Assembly 2010), pregnant women (Siva 2013), and victims of torture (UN General Assembly 2012). A study commissioned by the European Parliament (2008) cautioned that detention (which is often combined with a lack of recreational facilities, access to education, health care and a feeling of safety and trust important for the development of a child) is 'particularly harmful' for minors and can lead to 'psychological disorders.' Even when minors are detained together with family members, these relatives are often in an unstable psychological state themselves, and hence less able provide adequate care for the child.

14.2.3 Health Services in Detention Facilities

A study commissioned by the European Parliament (EP) Committee on Civil Liberties, Justice and Home Affairs based on field studies in 25 EU countries (EP 2008) found significant gaps in health service delivery for migrants in detention. According to their findings, all in all, in EU countries' detention centres, no systematic medical and psychological examinations are done, neither when people are arrested nor before they are being deported (see also Siva 2013).

Similar findings are made by the PHBLM project. All in all, the situational analysis finds that '[t]he lack of standardized medical screening of irregular migrants and unavailability of migrant health-related statistics limit the assessment of migrant's health conditions and increases related risks for the border population and staff, especially in case of epidemiological outbreak' (IOM 2010a: 80). The analysis found that even if medical screening is performed on entry in the detention centre, the quality of such is 'uncertain', and difficult to assess, which is inter alia due to the 'lack of standardized screening and data collection procedure; communication barriers and issues of miscommunication, and preconceptions and cultural gaps' (IOM 2010a: 65).

In addition, in general, '[m]edical services are available in limited capacities in relation to the number of people involved' (EP 2008: 172). Access to specialized health care services is often difficult (IOM 2010a). The infrastructure at some border checkpoints in the three EU countries visited, as part of the PHBLM project, was described as 'poorly designed from a public health perspective' (IOM 2010a: 70), with for instance isolation rooms located close to snack machines and even complete lack of a room specifically dedicated for medical examinations.

In conclusion, the conditions that are commonly found in immigration detention have detrimental effects on the physical and mental health of migrants detained. The ECHR (2008) also recognized that detention of migrants can particularly affect their health in a judgment in April 2010 (case of Tehrani and others v. Turkey). It ruled that 'the State must ensure that a person is detained in conditions which are compatible with respect for his human dignity, [. . .] and that, given the practical demands of imprisonment, the individual's health and well-being are adequately secured.'

The following section looks into European regulations on immigration detention and what they say on health, and on factors that determine the health of migrants in detention.

14.3 Policies Related to Health in Migrant Detention Facilities

While the EU is progressing towards common standards on immigration policy and integrated border management, there is still no harmonized approach towards migration and health (Hollings et al. 2012). The EU, however, has set some ground rules on the use of immigration detention, including on health. The most important EU legal guidelines on detention are the Return Directive and the Reception Conditions Directive.

14.3.1 Return Directive

Directive 2008/115/EC on common standards and procedures in Member States for returning illegally staying third-country nationals was adopted by the EP and the Council of the EU in 2008. It contains several paragraphs regulating the conditions of detention to be implemented by EU Member States in the context of return to the country of origin or to a 'safe third country.'[14] The Directive states that 'Member States may only keep in detention a third-country national who is the subject of return procedures in order to prepare the return and/or carry out the removal process, in particular when: (a) there is a risk of absconding or (b) the third-country national concerned avoids or hampers the preparation of return or the removal process' (Art. 15(1)) and that '[t]he use of detention for the purpose of removal should be limited', requesting each Member State to set a limited time period for detention, which cannot exceed six months (Art. 15(5)). However, in exceptional circumstances, Member States are allowed to detain migrants for up to 18 months (Art. 15(6)). Regarding health, Art. 5 requests Member States to 'take due account of [. . .] the state of health of the third-country national concerned' when implementing the directive. Art. 16 lays down the conditions of detention, and holds that '[p]articular attention shall be paid to the situation of vulnerable persons. Emergency health care and essential treatment of illness shall be provided.'

---

[14]Denmark, the UK and Ireland opted out of this Directive and are hence not bound by it.

14.3.2 Reception Conditions Directive

The EU Council Directive 2003/9/EC lays down minimum standards for the reception of asylum seekers which also allows for the detention of asylum seekers in limited cases (Art. 7(3)).[15] In June 2011, the European Commission published a proposal to amend this so-called Reception Conditions Directive. In October 2012, the Council adopted a political agreement for a new reception directive, which at the time of writing still needed to be formally adopted. If the new directive is adopted, EU Member States will have to transpose the new rules to national law.[16] The proposal for the new directive provides inter alia 'that detention is only possible on the basis of an individual assessment which has to show that other less coercive alternative measures cannot be applied effectively' (Art 8, para. 43 of the Proposal for a Directive of the European Parliament and of the Council laying down minimum standards for the reception of asylum seekers).[17]

Moreover, the new 'provisions on health care explicitly include essential treatment of serious mental disorders and, where needed, appropriate mental health care', and there will be a 'more specific regime concerning the assessment of special reception needs of vulnerable persons such as minors and victims of torture' (EU Press Release 2012). While this seems to be a step in the right direction, the directive is only applicable to asylum seekers and not to detained migrants in general.

14.3.3 Council of Europe Resolutions

Several times, the Parliamentary Assembly of the Council of Europe (CoE) took a firm stance on the issue of irregular migrants and asylum seekers in detention. Although these Resolutions are non-binding, the CoE constitutes an important voice in the European international political sphere. Resolution 1637 (2008) on Europe's boat people lays down some conditions that should be met for immigration detention and calls on Mediterranean member states of the CoE inter alia to 'guarantee to irregular migrants, refugees and asylum seekers not only emergency health care [. . .], but also basic health care, including essential dental care. Psychological assistance should also be provided for those with particular needs, such as victims of torture and violence, including sexual violence' (Art. 9.13). Resolution 1707 (2010) on the Detention of asylum seekers and irregular migrants in Europe acknowledges

---

[15]Denmark and Ireland opted out.

[16]Denmark, Ireland and the UK will opt out of this new Directive (EU Press Release 2012).

[17]Available at: http://eur-lex.europa.eu/LexUriServ/LexUriServ.do?uri=CELEX:52008PC0815.: EN:HTML. Accessed 5 March 2013.

that sometimes appalling conditions and strict regimes in detention centres have 'a negative impact on the mental and physical well-being of persons detained both during and after detention.' Member states of the CoE are encouraged to ensure inter alia that 'the detention authorities shall safeguard the health and well-being of all detainees in their care.' In Resolution 1810 (2011) on unaccompanied children in Europe: issues of arrival, stay and return, the Parliamentary Assembly of the CoE stated furthermore that unaccompanied minors should never be detained.

Regardless of these directives, resolutions and various Court rulings mentioned earlier, policies and practices on immigration detention still vary highly between different European countries. As the International Detention Coalition (IDC 2012) states, '[s]ome countries like Malta, the Netherlands and Greece, are continuing to regard detention as one of the most effective migration management tools, and some like Belgium, Denmark, and Sweden are increasingly identifying and implementing 'Alternatives to Detention.' France uses different detention practices in its overseas territories than on its European mainland.[18] In line with its external migration policy, the EU and its Member States also engage third countries in immigration control (see European Commission 2011). As has been pointed out repeatedly by academics and human rights activists, this practice can legitimize and possibly increase the use of detention – often in substandard conditions – in these third countries. The most commonly known example probably constitutes the cooperation on immigration control of Italy with Libya, which was formalized in several bilateral agreements regardless of the systematic arbitrary arrests and the construction of camps to detain migrants in 'deplorable' conditions (Global Detention Project: Libya Detention Profile 2009; Paoletti and Pastore 2010). Another example is the Ukraine: In light of the EU-Ukrainian readmission agreement,[19] in 2011 the EU funded the construction of nine detention centres in the Ukraine, even though Ukraine has been criticized by NGOs and the UN High Commissioner for Refugees (UNHCR) for its arbitrary detention practices (Global Detention Project: Ukraine Detention Profile 2012).[20]

---

[18]For instance, 'there were over 5000 children placed in immigration detention in Mayote in 2011, although France has a clear policy against child immigration detention' (IDC 2012).

[19]Readmission agreements between countries facilitate deportation and return of irregular migrants to a country of origin or transit. It is one of the core migration management tools that the EU currently employs (see The Global Approach to Migration and Mobility, European Commission 2011).

[20]For instance, Human Rights Watch (HRW) found in 2010 that '[n]ot only has Ukraine been unable or unwilling to provide effective protection to refugees and asylum seekers, it has also subjected some migrants returned from neighboring EU countries to torture and other inhuman and degrading treatment' (HRW 2010b).

14.4 Recommendations on Health in Immigration-Related Detention

The available evidence suggests that immigration-related detention inevitably has a negative impact on the physical and mental health of detained migrants and asylum-seekers, who often face uncertainty and isolation. It also puts immigration and border officials and health professionals that work with detainees under stress and ethical dilemmas, which can result in occupation-related anxiety and depression. The conditions of detention, the health facilities available, the quantity of available staff and the training that these professionals receive greatly determine the extent of health risks in detention for all stakeholders concerned. The following recommendations address some of these identified risk factors.

The first recommendation has to be a general one, i.e. to make greater use of the alternatives of detention, i.e., non-custodial measures (IOM 2011b). For instance, the Working Group on Arbitrary Detention (1998) recommended that 'alternative and noncustodial measures should always be considered before resorting to detention.'[21] Several states have already established a presumption in favour of liberty in their national immigration policies or practices.[22] Progressively abolishing the use of immigration detention and resorting to non-custodial measures instead is not only in line with recommendations by international human rights bodies, but also makes economic sense: As the Special Rapporteur on the human rights of migrants, François Crépeau, has stated, '[t]he alternatives [to detention] have also proved to be considerably less expensive than detention, not only in direct costs but also when it comes to longer-term costs associated with detention, such as the impact on health services, integration problems and other social challenges' (UN General Assembly 2012). The deportation of people with medical conditions is especially challenging and can impose a high cost on both the person detained and the society, if for instance medical escorts are needed.

In the meantime, several measures can be taken that can significantly improve the situation in detention centres. The recommendations below are based on the ones provided in the Situational Analysis Report of the PHBLM project (IOM 2010a: 81–84) and include aspects related to the physical environment of detention facilities, access to health services, ethical issues and training.

14.4.1 Improve Health Services in Detention Facilities

Standardized health assessments of detained migrants (with a focus on communicable diseases, vaccine-preventable diseases, maternal and child health, mental health,

---

[21] This Working Group was set up in 1991 by the UN Commission on Human Rights (see http://www2.ohchr.org/english/about/publications/docs/fs26.htm. Accessed 5 March 2013).

[22] Sampson et al. (2011: 21) quote the following states: Argentina, Venezuela, Peru, Uruguay, Brazil, Austria, Germany, Denmark, the Netherlands, Slovenia and the United Kingdom.

and chronic conditions) should comply with international ethical practices, which include informed consent by the migrant, the confidentiality of medical results, and providing migrants with access to counselling and follow-up treatment and support services. It is important however that standardized health assessments are carried out regularly, to monitor the health of migrants and to collect and analyse relevant migrant health-related data.

In addition, referral systems between the different stakeholders need to be put in place and strengthened to ensure adequate care for migrants when needed. Therefore, it is good practice to improve the coordination between the border officials and relevant public health services as well as to employ social workers and involve humanitarian organizations who can play an important role in this regard. Another key issue is the continuity of care when detained migrants return to their country of origin. In this case, adequate mechanisms should be established to ensure the continuity of health care in the country of return, through relevant referrals at destination. This applies to individuals with known chronic, yet stable, health conditions requiring lasting medical care (e.g. insulin dependent diabetes, complicated hypertension, seizure disorders, etc.), as well as those requiring the continuity of an on-going treatment initiated in the country of immigration and for whom interruption of the treatment could have a significant public health impact (e.g. tuberculosis, AIDS).

Further, favourable physical conditions in detention facilities should be created, including for instance physical activity, recreation facilities, telecommunication facilities, wall decorations and the avoidance of bars on windows, amongst other. The IOM Guidelines for border management and detention procedures involving migrants: a public health perspective (IOM 2010c) provide detailed recommendations regarding the conditions of detention for different groups of migrant detainees, disaggregated by gender, age, language, and religion, and with specific reference to particularly vulnerable cases. They cover a broad range of issues including sleeping accommodation, sanitation, clothing, diet, daily activities and health education.

Migrants in detention should have access to primary and specialized health care, including psychological care and mental health services, provided by trained and independent staff. To provide health promotion and care to migrants in detention, a bond of trust between medical staff and patients is indispensable. It is therefore concerning that health professionals were found to face a 'possible conflict of interest rising from their reporting to MoI [Ministry of Interior]/detention authorities and being responsible for both the staff and the migrants' in some of the countries studied (IOM 2010a). This 'dual loyalty' is an 'ethical dilemma' in administrative detention and criminal prison health care alike (Pont et al. 2012). It was also found by IOM (2010a) and MSF that in many detention centres across Europe, '[o]ften, the psychologists had a dual role [. . .]: for example, they might be deputy director and psychologist at the same time' (MSF 2010: 6) and are meant to respond to both guards and to migrants needs. According to MSF (2010: 6), this can be considered 'a serious obstacle to the creation of a trusting relationship between doctor and patient, which is crucial for provision of effective treatment.'

14.4.2 Need for Training and Capacity building of Border/Immigration Officials

The IOM Information Note on International standards on immigration detention and non-custodial measures[23] states that 'the officials working in this type of facilities [i.e., detention centres] should be trained in human rights, cultural sensitivity, and age and gender considerations' (IOM 2011b).

The health of staff and host communities in the vicinity of detention facilities is seldom addressed in the research and literature on immigration detention. Yet, especially the training of border and immigration officials on health issues, their preparedness for emergency response and the provision of quality occupational health services are paramount for the sake of themselves, the detainees, and the public (IOM 2010a).

The PHBLM study addressed also this research gap and found that '[a]lthough border guards are mainly young men who perceive themselves in good health and receive regular check-ups from the occupational health services, they face significant environmental and mental health risks at work' (IOM 2010a: 80). The study also detected significant knowledge gaps on migration health and occupational health matters of border and immigration officials in the three EU countries. For instance, the border officials received only very basic training on first aid during their basic education training, whilst situations where provision of first aid is crucial would arise while patrolling isolated border areas. Knowledge about the International Health Regulations[24] and health related application of Schengen procedures was found to be insufficient, and many officials were unaware of any provisions in place for how to deal with victims of trafficking.

Moreover, one third of the border officials in the three countries investigated claimed that the occupational health services were not easily accessible at their work site. Yet, many shared a fear of becoming infected with communicable diseases through their work, which contributed to the perceived anxiety and stress of border and immigration officials (IOM 2010a). While Personal Protective Equipment (PPE), such as gloves and masks, was found to usually be available, there are gaps in quantity and quality of this. Moreover, with few exceptions, 'there is no written guidance nor training on when and how to use' this equipment (IOM 2010a).

---

[23]The Information Note is meant to be a tool to make those who are dealing with the issue of detention of migrants and non-custodial measures acquainted with international instruments setting the standards to be respected by States in this field.

[24]'The International Health Regulations (IHR) are an international legal instrument that is binding on 194 countries across the globe, including all the Member States of WHO. Their aim is to help the international community prevent and respond to acute public health risks that have the potential to cross borders and threaten people worldwide' (WHO 2016).

14.4.3 Need for Training and Capacity Building of Health Professionals

The PHBLM project's Situational Analysis also found a general shortage of medical staff in quantity as well as types of specializations, and the almost non-existence of social workers in the migration detention context in the three countries investigated (IOM 2010a). Similar observations were made in reports on other European countries (MSF 2010).

This shortage of medical staff results in a shortage of time for providing care for each individual detainee. Moreover, health professionals seldom know foreign languages and do not receive training on how to work with people from different cultural backgrounds. It is thus difficult for medical staff to 'interpret signs, symptoms, and perceptions of illnesses of their foreign patients' (MSF 2010: 65). Interpreters are not always available, which is why fellow migrant detainees have to help—which can lead to problems of possible miscommunication and neglected confidentiality.

In the context of mental and psychosocial health, it is all the more important that adequate health professionals are in place and are trained and aware about the cultural particularities and the possible past experiences that their foreign patients might have had to go through, in order to detect and treat a wide range of mental health issues they might be suffering from. These range from confusion, anxiety and depression to Post Traumatic Stress Disorder (PTSD). A special concern in this regard is whether children in detention receive adequate psychosocial and education support (Human Rights Watch 2010a; Siva 2013). The PHBLM study found that this was not the case in the three new EU countries (IOM 2010a).

Both health professionals and border officials should have access to regular training and been given the possibility to take foreign language courses. The curriculum for trainings could include the following: 'communication skills and how to handle with prejudices and cultural gaps and work with people from different cultural and risk backgrounds; understanding of global migration patterns [. . .]; knowledge on the public health implications of migration, related public and individual health hazards; practical skills in recognizing health emergencies and cases requiring transfer to health professionals, as well as self- protection and occupational health issues; sensitization to physical and mental health issues of vulnerable persons, including victims of trafficking, smuggled migrants and minors; would be beneficial for better health services to migrants' (IOM 2010a: 82).

14.5 Conclusion

The purpose of this chapter was to present some of the key health issues around immigration-related detention, including the impact of immigration detention on the health of migrants and asylum-seekers and the availability of health services in detention facilities across Europe. Research by different individuals, academic groups, NGOs, political bodies and international organizations has shown that immigration detention generally tends to carry significant risks of adverse physical and mental health for all stakeholders, and that there are significant gaps in health service delivery for migrants in detention.

Two major barriers in improving conditions in immigration detention are the limited availability of standardized, comparable data on detention facilities and on the characteristics of detained migrants (age, gender, country of origin etc.), and the relative laxness of policies on the provision of health services in detention facilities in Europe. Especially for migrants in detention, Directive 2008/115/EC only provides for 'emergency health care and essential treatment of illness' (Art. 16, para. 3, of the Directive), not for specialized care and mental care. While the review of Directive 2003/9/EC could be considered a step in the right direction by including 'essential treatment of serious mental disorders' (Para. 87 of the Proposal for a new Directive) and, for applicants with special needs, appropriate mental health care where needed (Para 88 of the Proposal for a new Directive), this only applies to asylum seekers. In addition, the external migration policies of the EU and its Member States, legitimizing and encouraging the detention of migrants in third countries that reportedly employ sub-standard detention conditions, are reason for concern for the health of migrants in detention, including women and children.

While the overall recommendation remains the progressive abolishment of immigration detention, in the meantime the negative health effects of immigration detention should be attenuated by improving the conditions of detention (the physical environment of the detention facilities, e.g. avoiding overcrowding and a prison-like atmosphere), the quantity of available culturally and human rights sensitive, well-trained staff (both immigration officials and health workers), and the avoidance of 'dual loyalty' in health care provision.

References

Amnesty International. (2013). *In detention in Europe – FACTS*. http://www.whenyoudontexist.eu/in-detention-in-europe-facts-and-figures/. Accessed 5 Mar 2013.

Andalusian School of Public Health (EASP), & International Organization for Migration (IOM). (2010). *Guidelines for border management and detention procedures involving migrants: A public health perspective*. Brussels: International Organization for Migration (IOM).

Bean, T., Eurelings-Bontekoe, E., Mooijaart, A., & Spinhoven, P. (2006). Factors associated with mental health service need and utilization among unaccompanied refugee adolescents. *Administration and Policy in Mental Health and Mental Health Services, 33*, 342–355.

Biffl, G., & Altenburg, F. (2012). Migration and health in Nowhereland – Access of undocumented migrants to work and health care in Europe. http://www.donau-uni.ac.at/de/department/migrationglobalisierung/publikationen/id/17566/index.php. Accessed 5 Mar 2013.

Capodanno, A. (2013). *Personal email to authors regarding the encampment map*. Accessed 18 Jan 2013.

Directive 2003/9/EC of the European Council. (2003). Laying down minimum standards for the reception of asylum seekers. *Official Journal, 31*, 18–25. http://eur-lex.europa.eu/LexUriServ/LexUriServ.do?uri=OJ:L:2003:031:0018:0025:EN:PDF. Accessed 5 Mar 2013.

Directive 2008/115/EC of the European Parliament and of the Council. (2008). Common standards and procedures in member states for returning illegally staying third-country nationals. *Official Journal, 348*, 98–107. http://eur-lex.europa.eu/LexUriServ/LexUriServ.do?uri=OJ:L: 2008:348:0098:0107:EN:pdf. Accessed 5 Mar 2013.

EU Press Release. (2012). *Reception conditions for asylum seekers: Better and more harmonised living standards and more effective rules for fighting abuse.* http://europa.eu/rapid/press-release_PRES-12-415_en.htm. Accessed 5 Mar 2013.

European Parliament. (2008). *The conditions in centres for third country national (detention camps, open centres as well as transit centres and transit zones) with a particular focus on provisions and facilities for persons with special needs in the 25 EU member states.* http://www.libertysecurity.org/IMG/pdf_eu-ep-detention-centres-report.pdf. Accessed 5 Mar 2013.

European Centre for Disease Prevention and Control (ECDC) and World Health Organization Regional Office for Europe. (2011). *Mission report: Increased influx of migrants at the Greek–Turkish border.* http://www.ecdc.europa.eu/en/publications/publications/1105_mir_joint_who_greece.pdf. Accessed 5 Mar 2013.

European Commission. (2011). *Communication: The global approach to migration and mobility.* http://ec.europa.eu/home-affairs/news/intro/docs/1_EN_ACT_part1_v9.pdf. Accessed 5 Mar 2013.

European Court of Human Rights (ECHR). (2008). *Case of Tehrani and others v. Turkey.* http://www.irainc.org/newsdb/src/CASE%20OF%20TEHRANI%20AND%20OTHERS%20v. %20TURKEY.pdf. Accessed 5 Mar 2013.

European Court of Human Rights. (2011). *Unlawful detention of a mother and her children.* http://www.codexnews.lu/codex/contents.nsf/WNPPrintArticles/ 6676D164C0E62F6AC2257967006CEB5F/$file/Chamber+judgment+Kanagaratnam+and+ others+v.+Belgium,+13.12.2011.pdf. Accessed 5 Mar 2013.

Flynn, M. (2011). *An introduction to data construction on immigration-related detention*, Global Detention Project. http://www.globaldetentionproject.org/fileadmin/publications/GDP_ data_introduction_v2.pdf. Accessed 5 Mar 2013.

Global Detention Project (GDP). (2009). *Libya detention profile.* http://www. globaldetentionproject.org/fileadmin/docs/Libya_Detention_Profile_2009.pdf. Accessed 5 Mar 2013.

Global Detention Project (GDP). (2012). *Ukraine detention profile.* http://www. globaldetentionproject.org/fileadmin/docs/Ukraine_detention_profile_2012.pdf. Accessed 5 Mar 2013.

Global Detention Project (GDP). (2013). *Programme for the study of global migration.* http://www. globaldetentionproject.org/. Accessed 5 Mar 2013.

Guild, E. (2010). *Criminalisation of migration in Europe: Human rights implications.* Issue Paper commissioned and published by Thomas Hammarberg, Council of Europe Commissioner for Human Rights. https://wcd.coe.int/ViewDoc.jsp?p=&id=1579605&direct=true. Accessed 21 Mar 2016.

Hodes, M. (2010). The mental health of detained asylum seeking children. *European Child and Adolescent Psychiatry, 19*(7), 621–623.

Hollings, J., Samuilova, M., & Petrova-Benedict, R. (2012). Health, migration and border management: Analysis and capacity-building at Europe's borders. *International Journal of Public Health, 57*(2), 363–369.

Human Rights Watch. (2010a). *Greece: End inhumane detention conditions for migrants – Transfer detainees; Protect and properly accommodate unaccompanied children.* http://www.hrw. org/news/2010/12/06/greece-end-inhumane-detention-conditions-migrants. Accessed 5 Mar 2013.

Human Rights Watch. (2010b). *Buffeted in the Borderland: The treatment of Asylum seekers and migrants in Ukraine.* http://www.hrw.org/de/reports/2010/12/16/buffeted-borderland-0. Accessed 22 Sept 2012.

Human Rights Watch. (2012). *Malta: Migrant detention violates rights government should stop detaining unaccompanied children, end blanket detention.* http://www.hrw.org/news/2012/07/18/malta-migrant-detention-violates-rights. Accessed 5 Mar 2013.

International Detention Coalition (IDC). (2012). *First EU workshop on immigration detention.* http://idcoalition.org/first-eu-workshop-on-immigration-detention/. Accessed 5 Mar 2013.

International Organization for Migration (IOM). (2010a). *Increasing public health safety alongside the New Eastern European border – An overview of findings from the situational analysis.* http://www.iom.int/jahia/webdav/shared/shared/mainsite/activities/health/PHBLM-SAR-Public-Report-2010.pdf. Accessed 5 Mar 2013.

International Organization for Migration (IOM). (2010b). *Drug use among asylum seekers from Georgia in Switzerland.* http://www.ch.iom.int/publikationen.html. Accessed 5 Mar 2013.

International Organization for Migration (IOM). (2010c). *Guidelines for border management and detention procedures involving migrants: a public health perspective.* http://www.iom.int/jahia/webdav/shared/shared/mainsite/activities/health/Guidelines-Border-Management-and-Detention-Procedures-Public-Health-Perspective.pdf. Accessed 5 Mar 2013.

International Organization for Migration (IOM). (2011a). *Glossary on migration; International migration law.* http://www.iom.int/jahia/webdav/site/myjahiasite/shared/shared/mainsite/published_docs/serial_publications/Glossary_eng.pdf. Accessed 5 Mar 2013.

International Organization for Migration (IOM). (2011b). *IML Information note on international standards on immigration detention and non-custodial measures.* http://www.iom.int/files/live/sites/iom/files/What-We-Do/docs/IML-Information-Note-Immigration-Detention-and-Non-custodial-Measures.pdf. Accessed 5 Mar 2013.

Jesuit Refugee Service (JRS). (2010). *Becoming vulnerable in detention, civil society report on the detention of vulnerable asylum seekers and irregular migrants in the European Union* (The DEVAS Project). http://www.europarl.europa.eu/document/activities/cont/201110/20111014ATT29338/20111014ATT29338EN.pdf. Accessed 5 Mar 2013.

Karl-Trummer, U., Novak-Zezula, S., & Metzler, B. (2010). Access to health care for undocumented migrants in the EU: A first landscape of Now Hereland. *Eurohealth, 16*(1), 13–16. http://www.euro.who.int/__data/assets/pdf_file/0013/122710/Eurohealth_Vol-16-No-1.pdf. Accessed 5 Mar 2013.

Médecins sans Frontières (MSF). (2010). *The impact of detention on migrants' health*, Briefing Paper. http://www.msf.ch/fileadmin/msf/pdf/2010/04/091209_MSF%20in%20detention%20centres%20for%20migrants_FIN.pdf. Accessed 5 Mar 2013.

Médecins sans Frontières (MSF). (2011). *Greece: Detention centres make migrants more ill.* http://www.msf.org.uk/Greece_migrants_160611_20110616.news. Accessed 5 Mar 2013.

Migreurop. (2012). *Encampment map.* http://www.migreurop.org/IMG/pdf/Carte_Atlas_Migreurop_8012013_Version_anglaise_version_web.pdf. Accessed 5 Mar 2013.

Paoletti, E., & Pastore, F. (2010). Sharing the dirty job at the southern front? Italian-Libyan relations on migration and their impact on the European Union. *IMI Working Paper Series, 29*.

Platform for International Cooperation on Undocumented Migrants (PICUM). (2007). *Access to health care for undocumented migrants in Europe.* http://picum.org/picum.org/uploads/file_/Access_to_Health_Care_for_Undocumented_Migrants.pdf. Accessed 5 Mar 2013.

Pont, J., Stöver, H., & Wolff, H. (2012). Dual loyalty in prison health care. *American Journal of Public Health, 102*(3), 475–480.

Procter, N. G. (2005). They first killed his heart (then) he took his own life. *International Journal of Nursing Practice, 11*, 286–291.

Resolution 1637 of the Parliamentary Assembly of the Council of Europe. (2008). *Europe's boat people: mixed migration flows by sea into southern Europe.* http://assembly.coe.int/Main.asp?link=/Documents/AdoptedText/ta08/ERES1637.htm. Accessed on 5 Mar 2013.

Resolution 1707 of the Parliamentary Assembly of the Council of Europe. (2010). *The detention of asylum seekers and irregular migrants in Europe.* http://assembly.coe.int/Mainf.asp?link=/Documents/AdoptedText/ta10/ERES1707.htm. Accessed 5 Mar 2013.

Resolution 1810 of the Parliamentary Assembly of the Council of Europe. (2011). *Unaccompanied children in Europe: issues of arrival, stay and return.* http://assembly.coe.int/Mainf.asp?link=/Documents/AdoptedText/ta11/ERES1810.htm. Accessed 5 Mar 2013.

Sampson, R., Mitchell, G., & Bowring, L. (2011). *There are alternatives: A handbook for preventing unnecessary immigration detention.* Melbourne: The International Detention Coalition.

Silverman, S. J., & Hajela, R. (2012). *Immigration detention in the UK: Migration observatory briefing.* Oxford: COMPAS, University of Oxford.

Siva, N. (2013). Time in detention, *The Lancet, Vol. 381.* http://www.thelancet.com/journals/lancet/article/PIIS0140-6736(13)60007-0/fulltext?rss=yes. Accessed 5 Mar 2013.

Toselli, S., & Gualdi-Russo, E. (2008). Psychosocial indicators and distress in immigrants living in Italian reception centers. *Wiley Inter Science, 24*(4), 327–334.

United Nations General Assembly Human Rights Council. (2010). *Report of the Special Rapporteur on the human rights of migrants,* Jorge Bustamante. http://daccess-ods.un.org/TMP/9621322.75104523.html. Accessed 5 Mar 2013.

United Nations General Assembly Human Rights Council. (2012). *Report of the Special Rapporteur on the human rights of migrants, François Crépeau.* http://daccess-dds-ny.un.org/doc/UNDOC/GEN/G12/125/96/PDF/G1212596.pdf?OpenElement. Accessed 5 Mar 2013.

Working Group on Arbitrary Detention. (1998). *Report on the visit to the United Kingdom on the issue of immigrants and asylum seekers.* http://www.unhcr.org/refworld/country NCHR.GBR.4562d8b62.45377b810.0.html. Accessed 5 Mar 2013.

World Health Assembly (WHA). (2008). *Health of Migrants, WHA Resolution 61.17,* http://apps.who.int/gb/ebwha/pdf_files/WHA61-REC1/A61_REC1-en.pdf. Accessed 5 Mar 2013.

World Health Organization (WHO). (1946). *Preamble to the constitution of the World Health Organization as adopted by the International Health Conference.* http://www.who.int/governance/eb/who_constitution_en.pdf. Accessed 5 Mar 2013.

WHO. (2016). *International Health Regulations.* http://www.who.int/cholera/health_regulations/en/. Accessed 21 Mar 2016.

Chapter 15
Detained Migrants in Conditions of Extreme Danger: How Does the European Human Rights System Protect them?

Clara Burbano-Herrera

Abstract Interim measures in the European human rights system may be defined as a tool, the purpose of which is to prevent irreparable harm to persons who are in a situation of extreme gravity and urgency. Interim measures result in immediate protection being offered by the member state to beneficiaries in compliance with the order issued by the European Court. This chapter explores which typologies of cases have lead the former European Commission of Human Rights and the former and current European Court of Human Rights to apply or reject provisional measures in cases related to persons deprived of their liberty. The cases concern situations in which (a) their own nationals and non–national prisoners urgently need medical attention and (b) non–nationals with an order of expulsion or extradition whose life or health would be in serious danger in case of deportation from the member state. In the circumstances mentioned above, the adoption of interim measures for detained people imply the opportunity to be examined by a doctor, to receive medical treatment in the prison hospital or in a specialised institution, or imply the suspension of the expulsion or extradition order while the European Court has the opportunity to examine their case. Through an analysis of the case law, this contribution describes the circumstances the petitioners are in, the order issued by the European supervisory organs in those situations, the State's compliance and the possibility that interim measures will be lifted.

Mr Ilaşcu was detained in the breakaway territory of Transnistria for eight years from 1993 until his release in May 2001, in very strict isolation: he had no contact with other prisoners, no news from the outside (since he was not permitted to send or receive mail) and no right to contact his lawyer or receive regular visits from his family. His cell was unheated, even in severe winter conditions, and had no natural light source or ventilation. The evidence shows that Mr Ilaşcu was also deprived of food as a punishment and that in any event, given

C. Burbano-Herrera (✉)
FXB Center for Health and Human Rights, Harvard University, Cambridge, MA, USA

Max Planck Institute for Comparative Public Law and International Law, Heidelberg, Germany

Human Rights Centre, Ghent University, Ghent, Belgium
e-mail: cburbano@hsph.harvard.edu

© Springer Science+Business Media Dordrecht 2017
B.S. Elger et al. (eds.), *Emerging Issues in Prison Health*,
DOI 10.1007/978-94-017-7558-8_15

the restrictions on receiving parcels, even the food he received from outside was often unfit for consumption. The applicant could take showers only very rarely, often having to wait several months between one and the next.[1]

15.1 Introduction

The European Convention for the Protection of Human Rights and Fundamental Freedoms (hereafter referred to as: the ECHR or the European Convention) is an international treaty under which the member States promise to guarantee civil and political rights to their own citizens and to everyone within their jurisdiction.[2] Anyone who proves that he/she is in a situation of extreme gravity and urgency and who is a potential victim of a violation of a right set forth in the ECHR may be protected by so-called 'provisional or interim measures', issued by the European Court of Human Rights,[3] an permanent international court which sits in Strasbourg and rules on private or state complaints alleging violations of the aforementioned civil and political rights set out in the European Convention (hereafter referred to as: European Court or Court). Provisional or interim measures in the European Human Rights System may be defined as a mechanism whose purpose is to prevent irreparable harm to persons who are in a situation of extreme gravity and urgency, which a favorable final judgment could therefore not undo:

> [. . .] where there is plausibly asserted to be a risk of irreparable damage to the enjoyment by the applicant of one of the core rights under the Convention, the object of an interim measure is to preserve and protect the rights and interests of the parties in a dispute before the Court, pending the final decision.[4]

The mechanism of provisional measures is not contemplated in the European Convention on Human Rights itself but (only) in the Rules of Court. Rule 39(1) of the current Rules holds:

> The Chamber or, where appropriate, its President may, at the request of a party or of any other person concerned, or of its own motion, indicate to the parties any interim measure which it considers should be adopted in the interests of the parties or of the proper conduct of the proceedings before it.

---

[1] See Ilascu and Others v Moldova and Russia at para 438.

[2] The European Convention on Human Rights was signed on 4 November 1950 in Rome and entered into force in 1953. Currently, there are 47 member States, i.e. all European states (except Belarus and the Holy See). Negotiations are under way to allow the European Union to adhere to the European Convention on Human Rights.

[3] Originally, the monitoring system under the European Convention consisted of a non-permanent European Commission on Human Rights and a non-permanent European Court of Human Rights. In 1998 the European Commission on Human Rights was abolished and the part-time European Court of Human Rights was replaced by a full-time and thus permanent European Court of Human Rights. The decisions and judgments of the European Court and most decisions and reports of the former European Commission can be found at http://www.echr.coe.int, through the HUDOC search engine.

[4] Paladi v Moldova at para 89; Ben Khemais v Italy at para 81; Grori v Albania at para 184.

All persons may request interim measures without any exaggerated formalities in situations of extreme gravity and urgency. Nonetheless, it is imperative that the person requesting an interim measure follows the instructions in a Practice Direction issued by the President of the European Court.[5] The request for interim measures may be presented at any moment of the proceedings. The request of maximum 2–3 pages, preferably in English or French (and where possible in one of the official languages of the Member States), have to be sent to the European Court via fax, e-mail or courier (but not by standard post). The e-mail/fax or letter should be marked in bold with 'Rule 39 — Urgent'[6] on the first page, in order to allow staff to identify the application with the necessary urgency. In addition to the data that identify the alleged victim, it must contain a brief summary of the facts (which should be related to a situation of extreme gravity and urgency), and the rights that are deemed to be violated following the imminent State action or omission (demonstrating a risk of irreparable damage). The petitioner must, according to the President's Practice Direction, 'in particular specify the grounds on which his or her particular fears are based and the nature of the alleged risks.' It is also essential that the request is accompanied by the documents (especially relevant national decisions, medical results and other decisions or material) that support the claim. It must also contain the applicant's address or place of detention. Both the original information as well as eventual changes to these details should be communicated as soon as possible to the European Court. Interim measures result in immediate protection being offered by the Member State to the beneficiaries in compliance with the order issued by the European Court.

The case law reveals that the beneficiaries of interim measures in the European Human Rights system are on many occasions nationals in a situation of custody in deplorable conditions who need urgent medical attention, and aliens in custody under an imminent order of deportation or extradition who want to avoid leaving the State party because once in the receptor State (normally their country of origin which is not a State party to the European Convention) they could run some type of risk. In these circumstances, the cases submitted for consideration to the organs of protection mostly describe situations where the 'right to life' (Art.2), the 'prohibition of the death penalty' (Art.1 Protocols 6 and 13) and the 'prohibition of torture, inhuman and degrading treatment or punishment' (Art.3) are in danger. In this context, the purpose of this contribution is to examine how the European supervisory organs work in the area of prevention of violations of human rights through interim measures in relation to persons who are in detention. In order to comply with the objective, I will first describe the circumstances the petitioners are

---

[5]Practice Direction concerning 'requests for provisional measures', 5 March 2003, meanwhile replaced by Practice Direction 'requests for interim measures'. http://www.echr.coe.int. Accessed 16. Oct 2009.

[6]Reference should be made in the following way: 'Rule 39 – Urgent; Person to contact (name and contact details): [in deportation and extradition cases]; Date and Time of removal and destination.'

in. Second, I will refer to the order given by the European organs in those situations. Third, I will refer to the State's compliance, and fourth I will indicate when the interim measures are lifted. Finally, I will give some conclusions.

15.2 People in a Situation of Custody: 'Two Categories'

15.2.1 Category 1: Prisoners Who Urgently Need Medical Attention

Category 1 is comprised of prisoners who urgently need medical attention. Most of the people in this group are nationals of the State Party who ask for protection due to the fact that (a) the prison conditions are deplorable and made them ill (unhealthy conditions). Usually the detained people arrive at the prison in good health but become sick after a very long period in a jail that faces problems of overcrowding, limited quantities of food, and cells with no toilets, no water and no natural light. For example, in the Ilascu and Others v Moldova and Russia case, the European Court noted that the applicants were beaten regularly and received practically nothing to eat or drink. The applicants were not able to wash themselves or change their clothes. The toilets were along the corridor, and the prisoners were taken there only once a day by guards accompanied by an Alsatian dog. They had only 45 s in which to relieve themselves, knowing that the dog would be set on them if they took longer. Since they were taken to the lavatory only once a day under the conditions described above, the applicants had to relieve themselves in their cells. Of course, the applicants' conditions of detention have deleterious effects on their health, which deteriorated in the course of the many years they spent in prison.[7]

In this category we also find a second group composed of (b), persons who contracted an illness before being in prison and whose health conditions have deteriorated since their arrest. This deterioration can be the result of the regular course of the sickness and/or because of bad conditions in the prison. In such cases, the illness usually requires special medical attention but the national authorities failed to take sufficient care. This category is illustrated in the Aleksanyan v Russia case. Upon his arrest in April 2006, the applicant was examined by prison doctors who established, inter alia, that he had serious sight problems, with floaters in the right eye and overall impairment of visual acuity. During his arrest the applicant also developed photophobia and in September 2006, he was found for the first time to be HIV-positive. Over the following months medical exams showed a further deterioration in his medical condition as a result of the HIV infection.[8] Another subcategory is (c) detainees who become ill because they maintained a hunger

---

[7]See supra note 2 Ilascu and Others at para 199.

[8]See Aleksanyan v Russia at paras 47–52.

strike, sometimes in order to protest against their prison conditions,[9] and on other occasions because they consider that they were denied due process.[10] In still other cases, for example in the Panagiotis Vakalis v Greece case, the petitioner started a hunger strike because he was kept in preventive detention for 4 years.[11]

In these cases the States normally claims that the prison hospital has all the necessary medication, that the conditions of detention are satisfactory, and that the applicant has received medical assistance in full.[12]

15.2.2 Category 2. Foreigners Detained in Closed Centres for Immigrants or in Normal Prisons with an Order of Expulsion or Extradition

This category can be divided in two groups; the first is composed of foreigners detained in closed centres for immigrants and the second includes foreigners who are in normal prisons. The situation in both groups cannot become more critical since the applicants are in the final step before being compulsorily returned to a third State.[13] Generally, those in the first group have asked for a residence permit, thereby invoking humanitarian grounds or requested asylum fearing persecution for political, racial or religious reasons, and the state authorities have refused the applicant's request.[14] In these cases the persons concerned are afraid to go back to the third State or to the receptor State that is usually their State of origin (a non-State Party). There are two main reasons why they ask for adoption of interim measures and each reason corresponds to one concrete situation. The first situation concerns (a) ill persons who are receiving medical treatment in the State Party, but claim that in the case of expulsion or extradition, the receptor State could not provide the medical treatment they need. For example, in D v United Kingdom, the applicant was living in the United Kingdom and receiving the treatment he required as a terminally ill patient with AIDS. He was in a critical state of health and the medical

---

[9] See Taner Tanyeri and Others v Turkey.

[10] See Ilijkov v Bulgaria at para 50.

[11] See Panagiotis Vakalis v Greece.

[12] In the Istratiin case the Government held that the conditions in the Centre for Fighting Economic Crime and Corruption in Chişinău (CFECC) remand centre were appropriate. A doctor was employed there. In case of an emergency, detainees could be taken to a nearby hospital. There was no obligation under the Court's case-law to transfer detainees outside their places of detention if they were offered appropriate medical assistance there. See Istratii and Others v Moldova at para 43. See also supra note 9 Aleksanyan at para 53.

[13] Denial of a request for asylum, if not accompanied or followed by an order to leave the country, is therefore insufficient to justify an interim measure.

[14] See supra note 2 Ilascu and Others. See also Babar Ahmad and Others v The United Kingdom; Rrapo v Albania and Abdulkhakov v Russia.

facilities for his situation in his native country, the small island of St. Kitts, were completely inadequate.[15]

In other circumstances we find (b) people that are actually in good health and in well-maintained prison conditions, but who allege that in case of expulsion or extradition, there is a very strong probability that they will be submitted to treatment contrary to the European Convention in the receptor State because they will suffer torture in prison for religious, political, or ethnical motives or be condemned to death, or because the prison conditions in the receptor State are miserable. That was the situation of Yang Chu Jian, a Chinese man detained in Hungary facing an order of extradition. He alleged that if he was sent back to China he would suffer treatment contrary to Article 3 of the European Convention because of the bad prison conditions and also because he could receive the death penalty.[16]

15.3   What Does the European Court Order?

For the first category of detained prisoners who need urgently medical attention, the organs of the European system generally only request States to allow the petitioners to undergo a medical examination.[17] The aim of the interim measures is to ensure that the petitioners will have medical care. The examination must usually be conducted in the prison with the doctor chosen by the State authorities.[18] However, when circumstances dictate that medical attention can only be granted in a specialised institution, the organs ask to transfer the petitioners from jail to a hospital that would offer adequate medical treatment. For example, in the Popov v Russia case, Russia was asked, apart from refraining from requiring the petitioner to do any physical activity, including working or exercising in prison, to allow him be examined by an independent doctor in a specialized institution. The petitioner in this case suffered from cancer of the urinary blander.[19] Recently, in Aleksanyan v Russia, the Russian Government was invited to immediately provide

---

[15] D. v United Kingdom.

[16] See Yang Chun, Jian v Hungary. The same situation was described in the case of Ismoilov and Others v Russia and Shamayev and 12 Others v Russia and Georgia at paras 6–7. Information Note no. 47 at 41 and 74. In Petrit Elezi and Others, the petitioners believed that if they were returned to their country they would be in danger due to, among other reasons, the armed conflict and the support that they had given to one of the parties, specifically 'The Kosovo Liberation Army'. See Petrit Elezi and Others v Sweden.

[17] Popov v Russia. See also Information Note no. 88 and Arsim Haziri and Others v Sweden.

[18] See supra note 10 Taner Tanyeri and Others; supra note 11 Ilijkov and Bhuyian v Sweden.

[19] See supra note 18 Popov. See also Vaja Ghvaladze v Georgia; supra note 5 Paladi and Grori v Albania.

by appropriate means, in-patient treatment for the applicant in a hospital specializing in the treatment of AIDS and related diseases.[20]

The Court has also sometimes asked States to keep the petitioner in hospital because it is necessary that he or she continues to receive medical treatment. In this kind of situation, the interim measures were adopted after the State had sent the petitioner to the hospital. The aim of the request in these cases is to prevent a petitioner going back to prison because his life is still in danger and the necessary treatment is not available in the place of detention.[21] In situations where petitioners are on a hunger strike, the Strasbourg monitoring organs have imposed an obligation on them to stop the strike, i.e. ordered them to no longer refuse to eat.[22] For example, in the Ilijkov v Bulgaria case, where the applicant complained about the totally unhygienic conditions in which he was being force-fed by non-qualified prison staff during his hunger strike, the Commission requested the State to undertake every effort to protect the health of the applicant and at the same time requested the applicant to cease his hunger strike.[23]

Some special considerations are relevant to this group. For example, a doctor or medical treatment is not always what the petitioner wants. Indeed, sometimes the petitioners ask that the examination should be conducted by a doctor of their choice. Depending on the specific circumstances of the case, the Court could decide affirmatively, but in any case this is a prisoner's right. In this sense, the applicant in the Soysal v Turkey case, one of the leaders of the Kurdish separatist movement PKK, complained about his prison conditions and asked the Court to apply Rule 39 in order to request Turkey to guarantee him, inter alia, free choice of a doctor. Even though the applicant had not been given permission to be examined by a doctor of his choice, it appeared that he was detained under a normal, common law prison regime, and in consequence he had been examined at regular intervals by a doctor and had received medical treatment. Therefore, in this case, the Court did not adopt interim measures.[24]

It is also important to emphasise that in this human rights system protection is always individual. The European organs have exclusively protected concrete persons. There is a huge difference between this and the Inter-American system where the monitoring organs have already ordered the protection of groups of

---

[20] See supra note 9 Aleksanyan.

[21] In the Paladi case the Court adopted interim measures under Rule 39, stating that the applicant should not be transferred from the Republican Neurological Centre to prison with the proposal to ensure the applicant's continued treatment until the Court had had the opportunity to examine the case. See, supra note 5 Paladi.

[22] In the Mashiur Rahman Bhuyian case the Commission asked the petitioner to commit no further suicide attempts and to no longer refuse to eat. See, supra note 19 Bhuyian. See also supra note 2 Ilascu and Others at paras 10, 448, supra note 10 Taner Tanyeri and Others.

[23] See supra note 11 Ilijkov.

[24] Soysal v Turkey and Moldova. See also Information Note no. 13 at 27–28, 282.

people.[25] The case law also reveals that the European Court has never requested improvements to general prison conditions, in contrast with the Inter-American Court.[26] The organs of the European system generally only request that States in these circumstances allow the petitioners to undergo a medical examination[27] and sometimes that they transfer them from jail to a hospital that would offer adequate medical treatment.[28] The European organs very rarely order the release of the applicant; in fact we found only one such case.[29] This was in relation to the Patane v Italy case, where the Commission requested Italy to take the necessary measures as quickly as possible to protect the health of the applicant, a severely depressed woman who had been sentenced to 5 years' imprisonment and whose medical report indicated that her condition had deteriorated to such an extent that her life was in danger. The Commission asked the Italian authorities to transfer the woman either to an institution where she could receive better medical treatment or 'to release her'.[30] In this case we can observe that the Commission in any case gave two possibilities to the State.

For the second category of foreigners detained in closed centres for immigrants or in normal prisons with an order of expulsion or extradition, the Court and the former Commission normally ask to suspend the order of extradition or expulsion while the situation is examined. The practical consequence is that the petitioner remains in the State party. Additionally, the States are requested to make every effort to protect the health of the applicant and, depending of the situation, to authorize the beneficiaries to be examined by independent doctors and have the results sent to Strasbourg. The aim is to provide the Court with access to reliable information that would permit it to reach an objective opinion on the petitioner's state of health and/or what his/her situation would be in case of expulsion or extradition.[31] In the Arsim Haziri and Others v Sweden case, the petition of the applicant to extend the residence permits of himself and his family had been refused because (according to the authorities)

---

[25] Proof of belonging to the group of alleged victims is given by using objective criteria; such as the ties of belonging and the type of risk that allow individualization of the beneficiaries at the time of execution of the measures. See Penitentiaries of Mendoza v Argentina at paras 7, 13–14. See also Urso Branco Prison v Brazil.

[26] See supra note 26 Urso Branco Prison. See also Internado Judicial de Monagas (La Pica) v Venezuela.

[27] See, supra note 11 Ilijkov.

[28] See, supra note 18 Popov and supra note 20 Vaja Ghvaladze.

[29] In the Absandze case the Court refused to adopt the interim measures requested by the applicant's lawyer to release the applicant, a former Cabinet minister who had been remanded in preventive custody on the grounds of the conditions in which he was held in custody and his rapidly deteriorating health, even though this was substantiated by a number of medical reports. See Absandze v Georgia. In the same sense see also, Wemhoff v Germany and supra note 11 Panagiotis Vakalis at para 226–227.

[30] Patane v Italy.

[31] See supra note 15 Rrapo v Albania and Abdulkhakov v Russia. See also Salkic and Others v Sweden, and Patrick Muliira v Sweden.

they did not need protection due to their health problems, as these problems could not be considered as a threat to life or a serious incapacity, which was required in order to grant them asylum for humanitarian reasons. The State was requested by the Court to stay the order of deportation and allow the beneficiaries to be examined by an independent doctor.[32]

In contexts where the applicants alleged that the prison conditions are awful or the situation is generally insecure in the third State, the Court has asked the State Party to examine what the real conditions are in the receptor States. In these cases information from NGOs has been very useful. For example, after an investigation in the D v United Kingdom case, the Red Cross of Antigua and Aruba reported that if the petitioner was expelled, he had no possibility of receiving adequate treatment on St Kitts. In the same case, the High Commissioner for the Caribbean States reported that the petitioner would not receive the necessary medical attention if he were imprisoned in that country.[33] Finally, it is important to mention that analysis of the case law reveals that the fact that the circumstances of the beneficiaries in the receptor State are generally less favorable than those that are enjoyed in a State party is not decisive to obligate a State to maintain a person in its territory.[34] Except, of course, if the situation can affect the scope of Article 2 or Article 3 of the ECHR.

15.4 Means Used to Protect the Beneficiaries

In most cases the State parties have complied with the interim measures and the beneficiaries have received effective protection. From the standpoint of compliance, it is necessary to differentiate direct and indirect effects. Direct effects relate to the immediate consequence of the implementation of the order, and indirect effects are those collateral consequences and actions which, although they were not requested by the supervisory organs of the system, were implemented by the States with important consequences for the beneficiaries and for the examination of the petition. As a direct effect on category 1, i.e. prisoners who urgently need medical attention, and category 2, i.e. foreigners detained in closed centres for immigrants or in normal prisons with an order of expulsion or extradition, compliance has involved improving the prison conditions of the beneficiaries, authorizing medical examinations or treatments and providing the Court with certain information. In the case of measures that have been directed to the petitioners the action involved suspending hunger strikes. In addition, in category 2, most of the actions taken by the States have consisted in suspending a decision of a national authority (orders of extradition or deportation) while the monitoring organs of the system examined the petition.

---

[32]See supra note 18 Arsim Haziri and Others.

[33]See supra note 16.

[34]The fact that the conditions in Algeria were less favorable was not a determining factor to obligate the State party to accept the claimant. See Bensaid v United Kingdom at paras 16–17; See also Mahin Ayegh v Sweden, and N. v United Kingdom.

As an indirect effect for alien beneficiaries, the compliance with interim measures supposes the possibility of remaining in the territory of a State party while their petition is examined. From a legal perspective, the adoption of measures in those cases means the suspension of the legal effect of judicial and/or administrative decisions of the national authorities. When the beneficiaries were nationals of the State party, in some cases the measures permitted those who were incarcerated to recover their health,[35] to preserve their life[36] and/or to have the opportunity that their case be reviewed to ascertain whether they were given due process.[37] In other situations, it allowed conservation and/or acquisition of evidence.[38] Compliance with the measures implies protecting rights at risk of being violated, such as the right to life and to physical integrity.

15.5 When Does the Court Decide to Lift the Interim Measures?

It is normally not possible to determine in advance how long interim measures will remain in effect, as this depends on the evolution and all the circumstances of each situation, which may last for days,[39] months[40] or even one,[41] two[42] or more years.[43] Usually, the measures lose their effect when the Court deems that the situation of extreme gravity and urgency and danger of irreparable harm to the rights of the beneficiaries have disappeared. This means in certain circumstances that the beneficiaries are in good health, or, although they are not perfectly fine,

---

[35]See, supra note 18 Popov, and supra note 17 Arsim Haziri and Others.

[36]Denmark, Norway, Sweden and Netherlands v Greece. See also Einhorn v France, and Fraydun Ahmet Kordian v Turkey.

[37]See supra note 17 Shamayev and 12 Others.

[38]See supra note 18 Arsim Haziri and Others.

[39]See supra note 37 Einhorn. The measures were maintained for 7 days; supra note 17 Shamayev and 12 Others. The measures concerning Russia were valid for 15 days; supra note 32 Salkic and Others. The measures were in effect for 7 days.

[40]Bodika v France. The measures were lifted after 5 months. Kazin Useinov v Netherlands. The measures were in effect for 5 months. Faig Osmanov and Jale Osmanova v Sweden. The measures were in effect for 10 months.

[41]Paez v Sweden. The measures were in effect for 22 months. Cardoso and Johansen v United Kingdom. The measures were lifted after 17 months. Francis Gomes v Sweden. The measures were in effect for 16 months.

[42]Chahal v United Kingdom. The measures were in effect for 26 months; Abdelnasser Saleh Moussa Shloun v Sweden. The measures were in effect for 2 years; see also supra note 35 Bensaid. The measures were in effect for 27 months.

[43]Bahaddar v Netherlands. The measures were in effect for 38 months. Salah Sheekh v Netherlands. The measures were in effect for 3 years. See, supra note 10 Taner Tanyeri and Others. The measures were in effect for more than 4 years.

their life or personal integrity is not really at risk and in others, that the petitioners are not obligated to leave the State. In the majority of cases, it is possible to see that the danger has disappeared when the Court declares the petition inadmissible (if it considers that the risk does not exist anymore),[44] resolves to strike the case out of the list,[45] (for example following a friendly settlement or when the authorities grant the applicants permanent residence permits), or when the Court decides the case on the merits. In the last situation, if the Court in category 1 (prisoners detained who need urgently medical attention) arrives at the conclusion that the State did not do enough to protect the life or personal integrity of the petitioner, it will indicate mainly in the final judgment that the State is responsible for the violation of Art. 3 and/or Art. 34 ECHR on account of the lack of proper medical assistance or in respect of the conditions of detention.[46] In the second category, in cases where the petitioners allege that their life or personal integrity will be in danger in case of extradition or expulsion, the Court can decide to lift the interim measures if the third State provides diplomatic guarantees or promises that it will treat the applicant well, i.e. according to the European Convention standards. Some third States that have manifested their commitment to respect the petitioners' rights in case of return to their territory are Ecuador,[47] the United States,[48] India,[49] Morocco,[50] Peru,[51] Russia,[52] Israel[53]

---

[44] See, supra note 19 Bhuyian. In the Fraydun case, once the US authorities promised that the death penalty would not be imposed on the petitioner, the Court declared the petition inadmissible and lifted the interim measures. See supra note 37 Fraydun Ahmet Kordian.

[45] In the Vakalis case, after the applicant was released, the Commission judged that the dispute had been resolved and that there were no grounds of general interest to pursue the case. The case was struck from the list. See supra note 12 Panagiotis Vakalis. In the Patane case the Commission decided to strike the application from the list; subsequently the State informed that its courts had suspended the enforcement of the punishment. See, supra note 31 Patane.

[46] In the Aleksanyan case, in the final analysis, the Court considered that the national authorities failed to take sufficient care of the applicant's health to ensure that he did not suffer treatment contrary to article 3 of the ECHR, at least until his transfer to an external hematological hospital. See supra note 9 Aleksanyan. In the Popov case, although the State complied with the measures, the Court held that Russia had violated articles 3, 6 and 34 because of the prison conditions of the petitioner, the lack of medical assistance and due process and for having been intimidated during the examination of the case. See, supra note 18 Popov. See also supra note 2 Ilascu and Others, and supra note 5 Paladi.

[47] The Court, in view of the guarantees offered by Ecuador and Spain, lifted the interim measures. See, Peñafiel Salgado v Spain. See also, Information Note no. 41.

[48] In the following cases the interim measures were lifted following the promise of the US authorities that the death penalty would not be imposed. See supra note 37 Einhorn. See also Nivette v France, and supra note 37 Fraydun Ahmet Kordian.

[49] See supra note 43 Chahal.

[50] Ismaili v Germany.

[51] Olaechea Cahuas v Spain.

[52] In the Shamayev case the measures were lifted when Russia promised that the petitioners would enjoy due process, access to medical treatment and legal support. See supra note 17 Shamayev and 13 Others.

[53] Eskinazi and Chelouche v Turkey.

and Uzbekistan.[54] The purpose of this offer is to give a guarantee that the rights of the petitioners will not be affected. Usually those States promise that they will provide adequate medical treatment to the applicant, that they will respect the life and integrity[55] of the beneficiary, or that they will not impose certain punishments such as the death penalty.[56] In this sense, in case of extradition of a person to a non-State Party of the European Convention where the death penalty is still enforced, no interim measure will be granted if it is clear from the extradition order that the extraditing country has received a firm guarantee from the receptor country that the person concerned will not be sentenced to death or that the death penalty will not be enforced. In the cases regarding the United States, these assurances usually (with some exceptions, for example in Soering v United Kingdom) have been accepted.[57] It is paradoxical that a country such as the United States, which has not accepted the contentious jurisdiction of the Inter-American Court nor the American Convention, has agreed on several occasions to adapt its domestic law to the European Convention in specific situations.

However, international case law also shows that organs have been quite cautious in accepting the promises of States. This is why the Court has decided to reject those assurances on many occasions. Sometimes interim measures were adopted notwithstanding the promise made by some States, such as Uzbekistan (Ismoilov and Others v Russia),[58] Morocco (Ismaili v Germany),[59] Peru (Olaechea Cahuas v Spain),[60] India (Chahal v UK)[61] and Russia (Shamayev and 12 Others v Georgia)[62] in order to guarantee the rights of the petitioners under the European Convention. Thus, before making a decision in this regard, the European organs examine the

---

[54] See Mamatkulov and Askarov v Turkey at para 104 and supra note 17 Ismoilov and Others.

[55] See supra note 48 Peñafiel Salgado, and supra note 16 Ismoilov and Others.

[56] See supra note 17 Ismoilov and Others; supra note 37 Fraydun Ahmet Kordian; supra note 37 Einhorn, and supra note 51 Ismaili.

[57] Soering v United Kingdom. See also supra note 49 Nivette; supra note 51 Ismaili, and supra note 37 Fraydun Ahmet Kordian.

[58] In the Ismoilov and Others case, in spite of the promise of the receptor State to respect the rights of the petitioners, the Court adopted interim measures to protect 13 Uzbekis, all of whom were Muslim and accused of belonging to an illegal organization and of possessing and disseminating subversive material. The State had explicitly promised that the applicants would not be sentenced to death, or tortured or subjected to any type of inhuman treatment. Their right to defense would also be respected and they would not be tried for political reasons. In its judgment on the merits, the Court held that there would be a violation of Article 3 in the event of expulsion. See, supra note 17 Ismoilov and Others at paras 116–128.

[59] In the Ismaili case, notwithstanding the promise of Morocco not to impose the death penalty on the petitioner, who was accused of having killed a policeman, the Court adopted interim measures. It ultimately declared the petition inadmissible and held that the deportation would not violate Article 3. See supra note 51 Ismaili.

[60] See supra note 52 Olaechea Cahuas.

[61] See supra note 43 Chahal.

[62] See, supra note 17 Shamayev and 12 Others.

concrete situation and the seriousness of the commitment. In cases where the petitioners allege that in the third State they run a risk due to political, religious or ethnic motives, the Court will strike the case out of the list if the State party decides to grant the applicants resident or asylum.[63]

15.6 Conclusion

The Strasbourg case-law shows that interim measures have been adopted in relation to detained people to protect Europeans and non-Europeans in a situation of deprivation of liberty, who have a well-founded fear that their life or integrity is in danger. Principally, the Court decides to order protection for those people because they are seriously ill and the States do not give them sufficient or adequate medical care, or because although they are in good health and under satisfactory detention conditions, in case of extradition or expulsion they will be submitted to treatment contrary to Article 2 or Article 3 of the European Convention in the receptor State. In the circumstances mentioned above, the adoption of interim measures provide for detained people the opportunity to be examined by a doctor, and to receive medical treatment in a prison hospital or in a specialised institution while the Court has the opportunity to examine the case. In this regard, it is relevant to mention that interim measures do not in any way prejudge the merits of the matter and are not an international declaration of State responsibility. Usually the Court takes a decision on the basis of very prima facie evidence that the person concerned might reasonably be expected to suffer harm (not all proof of the facts). It should be noted that, although in principle aliens who have completed their sentence and have received an order to leave the country cannot request to remain in the territory of a State party to the ECHR in order to continue to benefit from medical, social or any other care offered by the State during their stay in prison. On very exceptional occasions and when the health of the petitioners is seriously threatened, interim measures may be adopted for humanitarian reasons and to protect rights under Articles 2 and 3 of the European Convention. While it is true that some individuals have had their rights affected because Member States did not comply with the interim measures issued

---

[63]The Commission, after previously having refused to issue an interim measure requesting France not to proceed with the deportation of a Kurd to Turkey, reconsidered its earlier decision after the applicant had informed it that "un arrêté de reconduite à la frontière" had been issued and ordered the requested interim measure. The case was struck out of the list after the applicant was given refugee status in France and the "arrêté de reconduite à la frontière" had been revoked. See, D. v France. See also Information Note no. 50. In the same sense, in the Petrit Elezi and Others case, the petitioners, a couple with two children who were nationals of the former Yugoslav Republic of Macedonia but were of Albanian ethnic origin presented a petition in 2005 requesting the adoption of interim measures to stay orders of deportation after their requests for asylum were denied (since 2001), and after having exhausted domestic remedies. The State not only immediately complied but 11 months later asked that the case be struck out of the list since it had granted permanent residency to the petitioners. See supra note 17 Petrit Elezi and Others.

under the European System, the study of the case law makes it possible to conclude that interim measures, although they have not always been able to avoid violations, have often given the beneficiaries effective protection and are therefore consistent with the idea that rights recognized in international treaties can be effective and concrete in difficult situations, and are not illusory or theoretical. Of course, interim measures do not act miraculously and do not always prevent violations of rights that in fact occur, since a legal instrument per se is not sufficient to transform reality, but the manner in which the European Court and the former Commission have used interim measures has at least resulted in important consequences from the standpoint of some of the cases that have reached the European system on Human Rights.

References

Abdelnasser Saleh Moussa Shloun v Sweden, App. no. 17185/04. Eur. Ct. H.R. (4 Apr 2006).
Abdulkhakov v Russia, App. no. 14743/11. Eur. Ct. H.R. (2 Oct 2012).
Absandze v Georgia, App. no. 57861/00. Eur. Ct. H.R. (20 July 2004).
Aleksanyan v Russia, App. 46468/06. Eur. Ct. H.R. (22 Dec 2008).
Arsim Haziri and Others v Sweden, App. no. 37468/04. Eur. Ct. H.R. (5 Sept 2006).
Babar Ahmad and Others v The United Kingdom, App. nos. 24027/07, 11949/08, 36742/08, 66911/09 and 67354/09. Eur. Ct. H.R. (4 Sept 2012).
Bahaddar v Netherlands, App. no. 25894. Eur. Comm'n H.R. (19 Feb 1998).
Ben Khemais v Italy, Appl. No. 246/07. Eur. Ct. H.R. (21 Feb 2009).
Bensaid v United Kingdom, App. no. 44599/98. Eur. Ct. H.R. (6 Feb 2001).
Bhuyian v Sweden. App. no. 26516/95. Eur. Comm'n H.R. (14 Sept 1995).
Bodika v France, App. no. 48135/99. Eur. Ct. H.R. (12 Oct 1999).
Cardoso and Johansen v United Kingdom, App. no. 47061/99. Eur. Ct. H.R. (5 Sept 2000).
Chahal v United Kingdom, App. no. 22414/93. Eur. Ct. H.R. (15 Nov 1996).
D. v France, App. no. 19794/92. Eur. Comm'n H.R. (7 July 1992).
D. v United Kingdom, App. no. 30240/96. Eur. Ct. H.R. (2 May 1997).
Denmark, Norway, Sweden and Netherlands v Greece, App. nos. 3321/67, 3322/67, 3323/67 and 3344/67. Eur. Comm'n H.R. (5 Nov 1969).
Einhorn v France, App. no. 71555/01. Eur. Ct. H.R. (16 Oct 2001).
Eskinazi and Chelouche v Turkey, App. no. 14600/05. Eur. Ct. H.R. (13 Dez 2005).
Faig Osmanov and Jale Osmanova v Sweden, App. no. 30977/05. Eur. Ct. H.R. (27 June 2006).
Francis Gomes v Sweden, App. no. 34566/04. Eur. Ct. H.R. (7 Feb 2006).
Fraydun Ahmet Kordian v Turkey, App. no. 6575/06. Eur. Ct. H.R. (4 July 2006).
Grori v Albania, Appl. No. 25336/04. Eur. Ct. H.R. (7 July 2009).
Ilascu and Others v Moldova and Russia, App. 48787/99. Eur. Ct. H.R. (8 July 2004).
Ilijkov v Bulgaria, App. no. 33977/96. Eur. Comm'n. H.R. (20 Oct 1997) and Eur.Ct. H.R. (26 July 2001).
Information Note no. 13, Eur. Ct. H. R.
Information Note no. 41, Eur. Ct. H.R.
Information Note no. 47, Eur. Ct. H.R.
Information Note no. 50, Eur. Ct. H.R.
Information Note no. 88, Eur. Ct. H.R.
Internado Judicial de Monagas (La Pica) v Venezuela, Provisional Measures Order. Int. Ct. H.R. (24 Nov 2009).
Ismaili v Germany, App. no. 58128/00. Eur. Ct. H.R. (15 March 2001).
Ismoilov and Others v Russia, App. no. 2947/06. Eur. Ct. H.R. (24 Apr 2008).

Istratii and Others v Moldova, App. nos. 8721/05, 8705/05 and 8742/05. Eur. Ct. H.R. (27 March 2007).

Kazin Useinov v Netherlands, App. no. 61292/00. Eur. Ct. H.R. (11 Apr 2006).

Mahin Ayegh v Sweden, App. no. 4701/05. Eur. Ct. H.R. (7 Nov 2006).

Mamatkulov and Askarov v Turkey, App. nos. 46827/99 and 46951/99. Eur. Ct. H.R. (4 Feb 2005).

N. v United Kingdom, App. no. 26565/05. Eur. Ct. H.R. (27 May 2008).

Nivette v France, App. no. 44190/88. Eur. Ct. H.R. (3 July 2001).

Olaechea Cahuas v Spain. App. no. 24668/03. Eur. Ct. H.R. (10 Aug 2006).

Paez v Sweden, App. no. 29482/95. Eur. Ct. H.R. (30 Oct 1997).

Paladi v Moldova, Appl. No. 39806/05. Eur. Ct. H.R. (10 March 2009).

Panagiotis Vakalis v Greece, App. no. 19796/92. Eur. Comm'n H.R. (15 Jan 1993).

Patane v Italy, App. no. 29898/96. Eur. Ct. H.R. (3 Jan 2001).

Patrick Muliira v Sweden, App. no. 7260/05. Eur. Ct. H.R. (23 May 2006).

Peñafiel Salgado v Spain, App. no. 65964/01. Eur. Ct. H.R. (16 Apr 2002).

Penitentiaries of Mendoza v Argentina, Provisional Measures Order. Int. Ct. H.R. (22 Nov 2004).

Petrit Elezi and Others v Sweden, App. no. 4244/05. Eur. Ct. H.R. (17 Jan 2006).

Popov v Russia, App. no. 26853/04. Eur. Ct. H.R. (13 July 2006).

Rrapo v Albania, App. no. 58555/10. Eur. Ct. H.R. (25 Sept 2012).

Salah Sheekh v Netherlands, App. no. 1948/04. Eur. Ct. H.R. (1 Nov 2007).

Salkic and Others v Sweden, App. no. 7702/04. Eur. Ct. H.R. (29 June 2004).

Shamayev and 12 Others v Russia and Georgia, App. no. 36378/02. Eur. Ct. H.R. (12 Apr 2005).

Soering v United Kingdom, App. no. 14038/88. Eur. Ct. H.R. (7 July 1989).

Soysal v Turkey and Moldova. App. no. 50091/99. Eur. Ct. H.R. (23 Jan 2001; 3 May 2007).

Taner Tanyeri and Others v Turkey. App. no. 74308/01. Eur. Ct. H.R. (6 Dec 2005).

Urso Branco Prison v Brazil, Provisional Measure Order. Int. Ct. H.R. (25 Nov 2009).

Vaja Ghvaladze v Georgia, App. no 42047/06. Eur. Ct. H.R. (11 Sept 2007).

Wemhoff v Germany, App. no. 2122/64. Eur. Ct. H.R. (27 June 1968).

Yang Chun, Jian v Hungary, App. no. 58073/00. Eur. Ct. H.R. (3 Aug 2001).

Chapter 16
Prison Staff Under Stress: Causes, Consequences and Health Promotion Strategies

Heino Stöver

Abstract Stress among prison staff is widespread in all forms of custodial institutions. A variety of physical, emotional, and work-place related strains can cause stress and, if not properly relieved, can lead to various consequences such as burnout and other psycho-somatic disorders. Apart from stress caused by personal conflicts with prisoners or the experience of failure, the double-bind situation of reconciling punitive and rehabilitative tasks play a major role. Furthermore, organizational and administrative culture affects the health and wellbeing of prison staff and contributes to burnout. These 'administrative stressors' need to be identified and managed with health promotion activities. Health promotion working groups with detailed health-related and stress-reducing strategies need to be installed in every prison, and supported and acknowledged by all staff and the governors.

16.1 Introduction

According to many research studies, stress among prison staff is widespread in all forms of custodial institutions. However, staff at high security prisons and female staff are particularly affected. Threats of prisoner violence against staff members, actual violence, demands and attempts at manipulation by prisoners, and problems with colleagues and excessive demands by managers are all conditions reported to cause stress to prison staff in recent years. The situation is exacerbated by structural pressures on working conditions, which result in overcrowding, understaffing, extensive overtime, rotating shift work, low salaries, and the poor public image of employment in prisons.

Stress causes a number of reactions to change that requires a physical, mental or emotional adjustment or response, and can arise from any situation or thought or feeling that makes people feel frustrated, angry, nervous, or anxious. It is caused by an existing stress-causing factor or 'stressor' (Morrow 2011). Dealing with a serious

H. Stöver (✉)
Faculty 'Health and Social Work', Frankfurt University of Applied Sciences, Nibelungenplatz 1, 60318 Frankfurt, Germany
e-mail: hstoever@fb4.fra-uas.de

© Springer Science+Business Media Dordrecht 2017
B.S. Elger et al. (eds.), *Emerging Issues in Prison Health*,
DOI 10.1007/978-94-017-7558-8_16

illness or caring for people who are living in a total institution (Goffman 1961) can cause a great deal of stress.

When administered in small doses, stress can be healthy and productive, and can motivate ameliorating problems at work and dealing with complex issues. It is when stress becomes overpowering and out of control that it becomes dangerous and can lead to a phenomenon called 'burnout'. Lindquist and Whitehead (1986) define job burnout as 'A syndrome of emotional exhaustion and cynicism that occurs frequently among individuals who do people work of some kind.'

16.2 Consequences of Stress: Burnout

Prison staff face a variety of physical, emotional, and work-place related strains that can cause stress and can lead to various consequences such as burnout if not properly relieved. Stress also severely affects correctional workers' ability to perform their jobs and affects intricate parts of their social lives and complex relationships at home (Micieli 2013).

Bögemann (2007: 173) found out that

> an important factor for the development of a burnout syndrome is the fact that work with inmates often results in failures. Worthy of mention here are more and more complicated clients with an increasing readiness to resort to violence who also bring mental problems into the prison.

Experiences of stress and burnout contribute substantially to the high number of sick days among prison staff. Often this number is even higher than that of other professions, e.g. policemen, firemen, ambulance officers and other professions which are frequently confronted with extreme situations.

Stressful working conditions can massively affect those who work in a custodial setting. It is not rare for up to 20 % of the total prison staff to be off work sick at any time. The number of sick days results in a concentration of workload for other officers and thus is the focus of prisons' improvement of human resources management.

Prison officers experience phases of burn out which lead them to retire prematurely, and impair their family life. Referring to Cheek and Miller (1982), Cheeseman (2014, p.221) points out that Correctional officers "frequently reported letting out tensions at the wrong place" (at home), "tightening discipline at home and spending less time at home on their days off".

Cheek and Miller (1982) wrote that 'burned-out officers frequently lose interest in their jobs, become passive instead of active in carrying them out, and let things go. Thus harmful incidents may occur that could have been avoided if handled properly from the beginning.'

16.3   Causes of Stress

Apart from the causes mentioned above,[1] stress and subsequently burnout symptoms can also occur because of failed personnel management, lack of gratification and acknowledgement, and a feeling of a standstill in their career/job within the very hierarchical system of prison administration.

The special nature of correctional institutions coupled with the loss of control over discretion and decision-making causes stress. According to Higgins and Tewksbury (2006), correctional staff soon begin to realize that it is not the inmate population that is cause for concern so much as the stress of working in a bureaucratic organization with a quasi-military structure.

Morgan et al. (2002) confirmed these findings. They found that most stress came not from the inmate population, but from the lack of support from prison administrators and the lack of recognition for a job well done. Most officers feel that they are just one step up from the inmate population, as part of the correctional proletariat.

Garland's findings (Garland 2004) reported that correctional treatment staff who did not have administrative support and feared danger from the inmate population felt far more exhausted then those who did receive support. According to this study, '53 % of respondents reported job assignments and function' as causes of stress and burnout. This research opens the door for further investigations into how organizational and administrative culture affects the health and wellbeing of prison staff and contributes to burnout.

The findings of Schwarz and Stöver (2010: 153) support these results. According to a study on the health of prison staff conducted in a German prison, prison officers do not feel well acknowledged and supported in their daily routine by the management; they also feel uninformed and uninvolved in decision making. Furthermore, one third of interviewees reported bullying by colleagues, either of themselves or of others. Bögemann (2004) has also confirmed these findings, saying that the lack of interest in work can be explained by the atmosphere in the institution, including the lack of appreciation and solidarity, the hierarchy of the prison administration, the lack of cooperation and mistrust among colleagues.

'Administrative stressors' play a major role in the health of prison staff, in particular due to high level of inflexible bureaucracy, insufficient planning and coordination of competencies, unstructured organisation of processes and of units, insufficient transparency in administrative processes, inflexible hierarchies and static ways of processing decisions, concurrence among units, lack of cooperation and information flow, formalized systems of conferences without participatory and innovative elements, and the lack of corporate identity.

The various roles of a correctional officer can cause confusion and stress, especially when it comes to the relationship and impact of punitive tasks on the

---

[1] see Sect. 16.1.

one hand and rehabilitative orientation on the other. The role conflict of prison staff can be defined as the struggle of staff members to reconcile custodial responsibilities (which could include maintaining security through preventing escapes and inmate violence) with their treatment function (rehabilitation of offenders).

16.4 Coping Strategies

Prison staff have different abilities and coping strategies. Some officers have a good professional understanding and a strong internal locus of control, which afford them the ability to control their own stress and life events. At the other end of the spectrum are those who have an external locus of control that allows events and their environment (including the prison subculture) to control their ability to cope with stress (Robbins 2005). Anecdotally, cases are known where prison staff are even involved in criminal behaviour. According to Agnew and Cullen (2003: 143)

> The probability that persons will engage in criminal and deviant behaviour is increased and the probability of their conforming to the norms decreased when they differentially associate with others who commit criminal behaviour.

Tracy (2003:93) reported that

> burnout and stress are often treated as problems that correctional officers can and should deal with on their own. As such, employees are usually trained to identify personal stressors and address them using tactics such as biofeedback, meditation and relaxation techniques. And when employees are considered too stressed to do their work effectively, they are referred to employee assistance programs to work out their emotional difficulties behind the scenes. In other words, programs regularly focus on stress and burnout as an individual pathology.

All of these reported stressors can cause prison staff members to experience more health problems, have a shorter life span and on average die at an earlier age than the average worker (Lambert 2001). At the same time, these results make clear that there is a close connection between the work environment and job-related burnout.

Efforts to avoid and reduce occupational stress should start at the level of organisational development. Structural prevention efforts are needed and can be found in the strategic approach of health promotion activities for prison staff.

Health promotion programmes can successfully be introduced only once all personnel are addressed; this overcomes hierarchical barriers. Independent of status and rank, the necessity of health promotion needs to be understood by all staff. Sometimes an understanding of health measures can be reached easily, but sometimes there is resistance and mistrust, which can depend on the planned measure (e.g. tobacco smoking prevention). Prison staff members need to be persuaded of the positive outcomes for their own health. Ideally, there is a win-win-situation where the prison administration and the officers perceive advantages. Health promotion measures need to be adjusted towards the behaviour of prison staff and (working) conditions of the prison (physical environment, rules, time schedules for health promoting programmes etc.).

Health promotion activities need to be holistic, interdisciplinary and participatory. Health affects all staff members in their different rules and professions. Any new measures should aim to be regarded as regular status and not as special projects. They should be embedded into the health promoting processes of the institution.

As certain structures and processes, including 'administrative stressors', have been developed over a long period, it would be unrealistic to expect immediate changes. Thus effects (e.g. a reduced rate of sick days) might only be measurable after several years (see also Reno et al. 2010).

16.5 Health Promotion Working Group

First steps should include the foundation of a working group which consists of representatives of all units and professions. This working group should be installed as a planning and monitoring body, which is the motor of activities. The group should receive full support and be provided with the necessary competencies by the prison governor and full acceptance by the staff.

One of the first tasks of this group is an analysis of the status quo, comprising the following tasks: (i) analysis of the development of staff's sick days rate, (ii) analysis of workplace safety and work flow, (iii) assessment of workplace conditions, especially after threatening scenarios, (iv) interviews with personnel, (v) health quality working groups, (vi) diagnosis workshops/ focus groups, and (vii) health reporting,

After this process, which could last several months, concrete measures and programmes can be designed and planned. The following nine measures should be envisaged:

1. Active non-smoking measures.
2. Exercise at work/sports.
3. Conferences should be conducted in a lively way that invites participation, instead of using a directive style and culture.
4. Nutrition should be put high on the agenda.
5. Prevention of addiction should be taken seriously.
6. Analyse the physical environment and identify factors and structures which are barriers to health development.
7. Create a 'health day' which will take place once a year and which could be the starting point for health promotion activities.
8. Provide and organise a good climate in the institution.
9. The overall strategy and efforts should be directed towards prevention instead of curative measures.

The following indicators should guide the health promotion process. First, participation is important: how and to what extent are staff members involved in decision-making processes concerning their health? Second, integration plays a significant role: a high degree of awareness of health issues in all units and on all levels should be reached. Third, the approach should be as holistic as possible by combining behavioural and structural measures and ensuring a combination of risk reduction and support of healthy living. Fourth, effective project management should be achieved using systematic and embedded programmes and activities (needs analysis, setting of priorities, planning, conduct, monitoring of success (Bögemann 2010b)).

In addition to the proposed working groups in the institution, a state, region or nation should systematically and professionally support these institutions and working groups. This has been done in some countries by the responsible ministry. In one state in Germany the Ministry of Justice funded a health centre[2] which has the task of supporting all health-related efforts of working groups in custodial institutions.

The task of the central health centre is to deliver overarching support for health promotion activities of the prison in the state. The main five tasks are:

1. Health promotion: coping with stress, prevention of diseases, health counselling, general health education
2. Crisis intervention: crisis regulation, conflict management, self-help networks, crisis prevention, vocational training
3. Organisational development: counselling in communication, colleague counselling, creation of quality circles between institutions, organisation of supervision
4. Rehabilitation: cooperation with representatives of disabled persons, psychosocial counselling, dependence prevention
5. Scientific project support: initiation of projects, evaluation, interrogations of staff, health reports, cooperation with research projects (Bögemann 2010b).

Finally, all health policies and practice, either aimed at prisoners or prison staff have to keep gender aspects in mind. Prisons are dominated by men, and in most parts of the world the percentage of female prisoners does not exceed 5 % (see contribution about masculinity in prisons in this volume). But not only prisoners, but also prison officers are predominantly male, even in women's prisons. This leads to a twofold problem. First, the health behaviour of men is characterised by mostly avoiding preventive measures and care, which is supposed to be weak and non-male. Furthermore, Bögemann (2010b) reports that a substantial proportion of prison staff in Germany (40–70 %) are former soldiers. It can be expected that rituals of strength and male management of health topics are widespread, and that male prison staff have congruent conceptions of health and disease management, which results in traditional coping patterns.

---

[2]For more information see, http://www.reformzeit.niedersachsen.de/portal/live.php?navigation_id=3887&article_id=84852&_psmand=14. Accessed 6 Apr 2013.

References

Agnew, R., & Cullen, F. T. (2003). *Criminological theory, past to present.* Los Angeles: Roxbury Publishing Company.

Bögemann, H. (2004). Gesundheitsförderung in totalen Institutionen, am Beispiel einer geschlossenen Justizvollzugsanstalt. In H. Stöver & J. Jacob (Eds.), *Schriftenreihe 'Gesundheitsförderung im Justizvollzug, Band 10'.* Oldenburg, D: BIS-Verlag.

Bögemann, H. (2007). Promoting health and managing stress among prison employees. In L. Moller, H. Stöver, R. Jürgens, A. Gatherer, & H. Nikogosian (Eds.), *Health in prisons. A WHO guide to the essentials in prison health.* Copenhagen, D: WHO Europe. http://www.euro.who.int/__data/assets/pdf_file/0009/99018/E90174.pdf. Accessed 6 April 2013.

Bögemann, H. (2010a). Wer setzt Gesundheitsförderung im Gefängnis (eigentlich) um? In H. Bögemann, K. Keppler, & H. Stöver (Eds.), *Gesundheit im Gefängnis. Ansätze und Erfahrungen mit Gesundheitsförderung in totalen Institutionen.* Weinheim, D: Juventa.

Bögemann, H. (2010b). Gesundheitsförderung in meiner Anstalt – Von der Idee zur Tat – Das Gesundheitszentrum für den niedersächsischen Justizvollzug. In H. Bögemann, K. Keppler, & H. Stöver (Eds.), *Gesundheit im Gefängnis. Ansätze und Erfahrungen mit Gesundheitsförderung in totalen Institutionen.* Weinheim, D: Juventa.

Cheek, F. E., & Miller, M. (1982). *Prisoners of life: A study of occupational stress among state corrections officers.* Washington, DC: American Federation of State, County and Municipal Employees.

Cheeseman, K. (2014). Correctional staff and management. In A. G. Blackburn, S. K. Fowler, & J. M. Pollock (Eds.), *Prisons today and tomorrow* (3rd ed., pp. 203–232). Jones & Bartlett Learning.

Garland, B. (2004). The impact of administrative support on prison treatment staff burnout: An exploratory study. *The Prison Journal, 84,* 452–471.

Goffman, E. (1961). *Asylums: Essays on the social situation of mental patients and other inmates.* New York: Anchor Books.

Higgins, G. E., & Tewkbury, R. (2006). Prison staff and work stress: The role of organizational and emotional influences. *American Journal of Criminal Justice, 30,* 247–266.

Lambert, E. G. (2001). Absent correctional staff: A discussion of the issues and recommendations for future research. *American Journal of Criminal Justice, 25,* 279–292.

Lindquist, C. A., & Whitehead, J. T. (1986). Correctional officer job burnout: A path model. *Journal of Research in Crime and Delinquency, 23,* 23–42.

Micieli, J. (2013). *Stress and the effects of working in a high security prison.* https://www.ncjrs.gov/pdffiles1/224105.pdf. Accessed 6 April 2013.

Morgan, R. D., Pearson, C. A., & van Haveren, R. A. (2002). Correctional officer burnout. *Criminal Justice and Behaviour, 29,* 144–160.

Morrow, A. (2011). *Stress definition.* http://dying.about.com/od/glossary/g/stress.htm. Accessed 6 April 2013.

Reno, J., Marcus, D., Lou-Leary, M., & Samuels, J. E. (2010). Addressing correctional officer programs and strategies: Issues and practices in cooperation with the corrections Program Office U.S. Department of Justice, Office of Justice Programs. https://www.ncjrs.gov/pdffiles1/nij/183474.pdf. Accessed 6 April 2013.

Robbins, S. P. (2005). *Organizational behavior.* Upper Saddle River: Prentice Hall.

Schwarz, K., & Stöver, H. (2010). *Stress und Belastungen im geschlossenen Justizvollzug – Schriftenreihe Gesundheitsförderung im Justizvollzug, Band 19.* Oldenburg, D: BIS-Verlag.

Tracy, S. J. (2003). Correctional contradiction: A structural approach to addressing officer burnout. *Corrections Today, 65,* 90–95.